Cassell's Queer Companion

The Cassell Lesbian and Gay Studies list offers a broad-based platform to lesbian, gay and bisexual writers for the discussion of contemporary issues and for the promotion of new ideas and research.

COMMISSIONING:
Steve Cook
Roz Hopkins

CONSULTANTS:
Liz Gibbs
Keith Howes
Christina Ruse
Peter Tatchell

Cassell's Queer Companion

A Dictionary of Lesbian and Gay Life and Culture

William Stewart

Contributions by Emily Hamer
Illustrations by Frances Williams

CASSELL

Cassell
Wellington House
125 Strand
London
WC2R 0BB

387 Park Avenue South
New York
NY 10016-8810

First published 1995

Reprinted 1995

British Library Cataloguing-in-Publication Data
A catalogue record for this book is available from the British Library.

ISBN: 0-304-34303-X (hardback)
        0-304-34301-3 (paperback)

Cover Photograph by Robert Taylor
Design and typesetting by Ben Cracknell
Printed and bound in Great Britain by
Mackays of Chatham PLC, Chatham, Kent

Introduction

In 1994, twenty-five years after the explosive nights of the Stonewall Riot, when the drag queens first kicked their heels in the name of liberation, the daily lives of the majority of lesbians and gay men have changed so fundamentally that it is difficult to imagine life without the range of lesbian and gay social venues, businesses, welfare organizations and community institutions that now proliferate in cities worldwide. And yet, despite the fact that it is now possible for many of us, at least in Britain and America, to spend practically our entire lives in a queer milieu, the idea of a lesbian and gay 'community' remains as controversial as ever. Many argue that our differences far outweigh that which we have in common. There were times in preparing this book that I almost succumbed to this position, and wondered what we were all doing on the same pages. How for example do we reconcile those staples of the gay male scene – drag and public sex – with a lesbian-feminist analysis of male sexuality? I have not attempted to gloss over these tensions in the *Queer Companion*, and in fact believe that they give the book a greater strength. That a diversity of voices can all be given space in the same volume, sometimes arguing but never turning into an impossible Tower of Babel, is testament to the strength, not weakness, of our community.

I believe that the denial of lesbian and gay community stems in part from an overly rigid definition of what community is. No-one could dispute the great diversity of lesbian and gay lives; the experience of a white gay man on the London scene is worlds apart from other lesbians and gay men in the same city, let alone other nations. Yet, when I hear about the lives of others there is something that is resonant, in which I can recognize something of myself. This identification is not simply based on the common denominator of sexual desire. I freely admit that I spend far too much of my time desiring other men. But my gay identity does not switch off when the dark-eyed beauty I have been edging towards on the underground steps off the train. Nor are we bound only by the commonality of oppression at the hands of heterosoc, although the need to organize together is as relevant now, when so many of our rights are still withheld, as it was in June 1969 when the police swooped on that bar in New York City. My sense of recognition with other lesbians and gay men is based on the many creative and often humorous ways in which we build our lives as we want to live them, from the vibrant campery of 1990s political groups, to the institution of our own forms of family set-up, and the struggles of people with AIDS to have their dignity respected. We take and we subvert what is worth coopting from an otherwise drab mainstream, and increasingly we create our own artifacts – film, theatre, and literature – when we want to speak more directly of our own experience. It is this shared spirit of creativity and resistance that binds together the disparate subjects of the *Queer Companion* into what I believe we can talk about as 'lesbian and gay culture'. In this sense then, the tensions between different strands of lesbian and gay thinking need not belie the existence of community.

The idea of a lesbian and gay history is similarly problematic. Paradoxically, the painstaking work of lesbian and gay historians over the past few decades which has uncovered the existence of people who engaged in same-sex activities in all cultures at all times has also served to caution against assuming that lesbian and gay people, in the sense of people who define their social position to some extent through their choice of sexual partner, have also existed since the first life crawled out of the primordial soup. I believe that this caution is necessary from an academic standpoint to refine the ways in which we understand social ideas as having an important place in the individual's understanding of their own sexuality. And yet I have included historical material in the *Queer Companion* with impunity. In doing so I do not suggest that were we to sashay back in time and open a gay bar in Ancient Athens it would necessarily be full to bursting, nor that Queen Christina would necessarily be heading lesbian strength marches were she around today. I do however think that their lives can also serve as a point of recognition for lesbians and gay men of our time. To know that people throughout history have at least been enjoying the same sexual positions as us gives us succour to fight the abominations of a 'moral majority' which condemns us as unnatural, and to recognize that people have been abused, tortured, and killed for enjoying those sexual positions is a salutary reminder of why the fight is necessary. Thus, we are a people with a history, even if that history is not one of absolute continuity.

Within the *Queer Companion* are included entries on lesbian and gay politics, history, film, theatre, popular culture, style and slang.

Whilst America and the United Kingdom provide the bulk of material I have also included many entries from nations and cultures worldwide. Clearly, with such a scope the *Queer Companion* cannot hope to be exhaustive. There are many entries which could equally have been included, but which have been omitted. But all the entries that are included merit their place. In some way I hope to have at least sketched the most important landmarks of lesbian and gay experience. Perhaps future editions can have more of a claim to comprehensiveness.

In the frantic, nicotine-filled months during which I compiled the *Queer Companion*, I have received valuable suggestions from too many people to mention by name. My thanks go to you all. By far the largest contribution has been from Emily Hamer who, apart from writing many entries herself, has had the task of pointing out improvements that could be made on the whole work. Whilst her input has made this a much better and more balanced book, the responsibility for any flaws which remain still rests entirely with me.

William Stewart
LONDON, JUNE 1994

Note to the reader

The definite and indefinite articles at the beginning of entry headwords in English and other languages are ignored for filing purposes. Cross references to other entries are indicated by the use of small capital letters, e.g. GAY LIBERATION FRONT.

Adonis

À la Recherche du Temps Perdu
(Remembrance of Things Past) Long novel
in seven parts by the French writer Marcel
Proust (1871–1922), published between
1913 and 1927. The narrator 'Marcel' is
prompted to recall past events in order
to appreciate a meaning in them of which
he was not conscious at the time. The
novel introduces a kaleidoscopic cast, and
a wealth of different love relationships,
homo and hetero. In the fourth part *Sodome
et Gomorrhe*, Marcel discovers the homosexuality of the Baron de Charlus, who has
constructed a facade of heterosexuality
and who is represented somewhat stereotypically. The section also discusses the
way socially fashionable opinions change.
In addition, it also deals with the narrator's
suspicions of the lesbian tastes of his erst-
while lover Albertine. The novel played a
part in demystifying homosexuality in
Western literature, but Proust's happiness
with his own sexuality is uncertain.

Abba Swedish mega-pop-ensemble who
first shot to fame in 1974 when they
romped home to glory in the EUROVISION
song contest with their song Waterloo, an
everyday love story likened to Napoleon's
final capitulation, which remains to this
day the most stirring use of historical analogy in the pop canon. For a decade all eyes
were on the foursome not only as they
plundered a seemingly endless store of
pure pop classics, but also for fashion tips
since the two As could carry off a jumpsuit
like no others and displayed a devil-may-
care attitude towards the conventions of
eye-shadow application. Although the
group was fated to be rent apart as a result
of emotional problems (giving us wistful
classics such as 'Winner Takes It All' on
the way), they were subject to a timely
revival in the late 1980s.

abseiling Not an activity usually associated
with lesbian and gay protest. However,
when the protest against CLAUSE 28 of the

British Local Goverment Bill was at its height, the most impressive action was that of a group of lesbians who abseiled down from the gallery to the floor of the House of Lords during a key debate.

absinthe The essential drink of nineteenth-century homosexuals and aesthetes, it was a yellow/green liqueur distilled from wormwood (*Artemisia absinthium*) and flavoured with licorice and aniseed. The favoured drink of Oscar WILDE, who in complimenting the art of Aubrey BEARDS-LEY said, 'Absinthe is to all other drinks what Aubrey's drawings are to other pictures.' The drink is actually mildly toxic, and its sale is now illegal in most countries.

Absolutely Fabulous (Ab Fab) The British gay comedy cult of the 1990s, first produced in 1992 and with a second series in 1994. Starring Jennifer Saunders as Edina, the fashion-obsessed (names, darling, names), pretend PR-executive, and Joanna Lumley as Patsy the beehived beast that sponges off her, it depicts the kind of glamorous, pleasure-seeking life we all pretend we don't really want. Patsy, as a chain-smoking vamp, has become the ideal stuff for drag appearances on lesbian and gay Pride marches.

Abu Nuwas (*c.* 760–815) Persian poet who practised at the court of the Abbassid caliph of Baghdad, Harun al-Rashid (786–808). He surpassed his contemporaries to the point that he took on a legendary status and appeared as a character of folklore in the collection THE THOUSAND AND ONE NIGHTS. His works celebrated both the love of boys and the love of wine, a combination that didn't go down well among strict Muslims. Yet Abu Nuwas was unabashed, writing, 'If I'm thirsty I'll say: come on, be quick, some wine/And if I love a boy why keep silent about his name.'

AC–DC Dated British slang term for bisexual, but used mainly of closet cases who play straight in public, or of straights who toy with the scene.

Achilles In Greek myth the hero of the Trojan war and the King of the Myrmidons in Thessaly. A moody figure whose only vulnerability was his heel, Achilles argued with Agamemnon and threatened to withdraw from the war, but was persuaded against doing so, and sent his companion Patroclus into battle wearing his armour. Patroclus was killed by Hector, the son of the Trojan king. Achilles' grief at the death of his 'beloved companion' was so great that even the gods took pity. Although Homer makes no explicit implication of a sexual relationship between the two in the *Iliad*, that is no definite statement that it did not exist. Certainly, in later versions of the story, such as Aeschylus' lost play THE MYRMIDONS, Achilles' grief was taken as grief over a dead lover.

acid Slang name for LSD (lysergic acid dyethylamide), a hallucinogenic drug which is produced in the form of small squares of impregnated paper sometimes printed with small pictures after which certain of the tablets are named. Thus a Gorby had a small picture of the ex-leader of the Soviet Union and a joker a picture of the character from the *Batman* comic series. Acid was a common feature of the COUNTERCULTURAL scene of the 1960s and the gay scene of the 1970s, and has been described as one of the factors that allowed people to make and maintain the changes in lifestyle and personality that were attendant on the period.

ACT NOW (AIDS Coalition to Network, Organize and Win) After the founding of ACT UP in New York more than thirty groups sprang up in different cities around the United States. ACT NOW was the coalition that the groups formed to be able to work with one another and coordinate their actions.

ACT UP (AIDS Coalition to Unleash Power) Radical direct-action organization formed in March 1987 in New York to campaign around AIDS and HIV issues. Principal among its founders was the gay activist Larry KRAMER, who made an impassioned speech at New York's gay community centre calling for fellow activists to take to the streets. The group was felt by many people infected and affected by HIV to be necessary: after six years of the epidemic little progress had been made in the treatment of HIV itself, or of many of the opportunistic illnesses which affected people with AIDS, while many right-wingers were still denying the dignity and humanity of PWAs. Moreover, many of the AIDS SERVICE ORGANIZATIONS which had started from within communities at the beginning of the epidemic were becoming increasingly professionalized and dependent on official funding, thus making them less able to challenge the establishment management of the crisis. After the establishment of the New York chapter, groups formed nationwide to create the ACT NOW network. Their actions have included invading the perimeter of George Bush's summer home in Kennebunkport, besieging the Food and Drug Administration headquarters, and in 1989 invading New York's St Patrick's Cathedral to take issue with the AIDS phobia and homophobia of arch-conservative Cardinal John O'Connor. ACT UP organizations have also formed in Europe, although the wide provision of state health services in many European countries has given them less impetus than in America. ACT UP London was formed in 1989 and has taken up issues such as the representation of PWAs in the media, the provision of condoms in British prisons, and the availability of needle exchanges for intravenous drugs users. The CIVIL DISOBEDIENCE techniques employed by ACT UP groups revitalized lesbian and gay politics generally, and were influential in the creation of groups like QUEER NATION and OUTRAGE!

ACT UP, fight back, fight AIDS Slogan, used on posters and on demonstrations by chapters of the worldwide AIDS activist organization ACT UP.

acting The art of self-disguise. One of the central problems of the lesbian and gay movement is that for many lesbians and gay men the fact of their sexuality is not immediately obvious, and it often becomes easier to keep it that way rather than face constant problems. Thus many spend much time acting, or passing.

action = life Slogan, set on a pink triangle design, which has been used on materials produced by the American AIDS activist group ACT UP since 1987. It signalled that gay people needed to agitate vigorously to achieve the government interest and health care necessary to respond to the AIDS epidemic. *See* SILENCE = DEATH.

active/passive split The name given to the appearance in some societies of a characterization of male sexuality which is not defined by the gender of the sexual partner but rather by whether or not the male takes the active or passive role in intercourse. In such a system, as long as the male is penetrating (either the anus or the vagina), his masculine identity is unchanged. Should he be penetrated anally however, he crosses a boundary into an alternative form of sexual identity which is most similar to a homosexual identity. We can see antecedents of this notion in ancient Greek attitudes towards male sexuality, whereby it was considered a disgrace for an older man to be penetrated and he was open to accusations of effeminacy. This form of sexual categorization is most commonly associated with the countries bordering the Mediterranean (it is sometimes known as MEDITERRANEAN HOMOSEXUALITY), but it is actually found worldwide. Indeed in British and American societies the phenomenon of TRADE, whereby a straight-identified man is willing to be sucked or to fuck his partner but nothing else (*that's* queer), can be seen as part of the same idea.

activism The political belief that action on an individual or collective basis can effect political change. It does not deny that conventional institutional structures can be important factors of change, but encourages people to approach those structures directly, and failing that, to do whatever else might be necessary, be it demonstrations or direct action. Nor is activism confined to the radical end of political activity.

Any example of people taking on a voice in political processes that concern them is activism; it just seems that the activist soon becomes aware of the resilience of conventional beliefs and is pushed to ever more angry confrontation. Activism has an oddly symbiotic relation with the forces of repression, and grows where discrimination becomes more obvious. Thus the bloom of activism of the 1970s has found it more difficult to sustain itself with the granting of certain rights and with the growth of a stable scene in many towns and cities. See ACT UP; LESBIAN AND GAY MOVEMENT; OUTRAGE!

adhesiveness The quality that was used by the poet Walt WHITMAN to describe what he saw as the essence of the attraction between men, which was depicted by him in the Calamus section of his poetry collection LEAVES OF GRASS. He saw adhesiveness as a form of comradeship which could be pure and spiritually sustaining, and which could provide a bulwark against the spread of materialism. He contrasted it with the notion of 'amative love' which he saw as the bonding force between men and women. Whilst it is clear that Whitman himself enjoyed erotic attraction to other men, adhesiveness was a notion that could be read platonically, and Whitman was not eager to explain to what extent he wanted to present it as erotic. When quizzed about this by the British writer John Addington SYMONDS, Whitman defensively responded by claiming to have fathered a number of illegitimate children, none of which have ever been located. The term adhesiveness was borrowed from the popular nineteenth-century science of phrenology.

Adonis Male 'physique' mag, which was first distributed in 1951, and which used the work of agencies like the Athletic Model Guild. Since it would have been too difficult to publish an openly gay magazine, under the pretence of displaying the male physique so that young men could presumably learn to live healthily and look like that too, it showed photographs of built young things bare assed or in posing pouches. It was merged with another

'health' mag, *Body Beautiful* in 1958, and was published under the title of *Young Physique*, which became increasingly overtly gay.

adoption/fostering One of the central aims of the modern lesbian and gay movement has been to win the right to foster and adopt children, yet it remains one area on which many governments remain most intransigent. Thus, while lesbians and gay men are increasingly winning civil rights for themselves as people, heterosexual society still cannot grant that we be allowed a positive role in the upbringing of future generations. Even the most progressive countries of Europe – the Netherlands and Denmark – have not granted these rights under the law. In Denmark it was the one area that was not included under the 1989 partnership laws (*see* MARRIAGE), as a form of compromise with those that opposed the law. The arguments used against the granting of these rights range from the out-and-out homophobic – that we are likely to molest children in our care or 'turn them gay' – to 'liberal homophobia' arguments that in a prejudiced society it would be unfair on children who would be subject to insults and bullying about their home lives. the Albert Kennedy Trust is a British organization that specializes in placing lesbian or gay teenagers with lesbian or gay carers. It was named after a teenager who was in care in Manchester. Operating as a sex-worker, the boy ran away from his children's home, parents and boyfriend and killed himself. A number of carers in Manchester decided to set up the trust in his memory.

Advise and Consent 1962 film directed by Otto Preminger. Deals with an American senator who is being blackmailed and who is searching for the man with whom he has had a homosexual incident, and who has now become a hustler. Only remarkable because it depicts the first gay bar on the big screen. The bar is unconvincingly created with a seedy otherworldliness. So aghast is the senator by the sight of a world he entered, however briefly, that on returning to Washington, DC he slits his throat.

The Advocate Gay magazine, begun in 1967 by reporter Dick Michaels. Part of Michaels' motivation in founding the magazine was his experience in 1966 when he was arrested during a police raid on a gay bar in Los Angeles. The first issue, called *The Los Angeles Advocate*, had a print run of 500. Nowadays, tens of thousands are sold.

aestheticism Artistic philosophy which sought to advance the idea of a pure creative form which should only be measured for its artistic merits, rather than for its ethical standards. It thus became a way of justifying the use of lesbian or gay material for its artistic worth. The leading proponent of the British aesthetic taste was Oscar WILDE. When the *Scots Observer* newspaper had criticized his novella *The Picture of Dorian* GRAY by saying that 'if he can write for none but outlawed noblemen and perverted telegraph boys, the sooner he takes to tailoring (or some other decent trade) the better for his own reputation and the public morals', Wilde wrote, 'If a man sees the artistic beauty of a thing , he will probably care very little for its ethical import. If his temperament is more susceptible to ethical than to aesthetic influences, he will be blind to questions of style, temperament, and the like.'

affinity group Form of organization used by many lesbian and gay groups since the GAY LIBERATION FRONT. It can refer to two things. Within some broad-based organizations affinity groups can be set up as separate caucuses to work around issues of mutual interest, with guaranteed time to be able to present their opinions so that many voices, and not just those of bolshy men, can be heard. Affinity groups (or homerooms) are also used as part of CIVIL DISOBEDIENCE actions organized by groups like ACT UP or QUEER NATION as self-contained units whose members act together and take responsibility for each other's fate on the action.

African American Lesbian and Gay Alliance American organization, based in Atlanta and founded in 1989, which seeks to provide political representation for the lesbian and gay African-American community, and to forge bridges between gay and straight African Americans as well as between African Americans and other groups within the lesbian and gay community.

Against the Grain 1884 novel by French novelist Joris Karl Huysmans (1848–1907) which presents the embodiment of the DECADENT hero in its protagonist Des Esseintes. The subject of the novel is the search by the restive protagonist for unconventional experience and sensation to relieve the tedium of existence, sensation which he finds in painting, music and perfumes as well as love for circus acrobats and medieval Latin literature. Des Esseintes represented the same kind of transgressive, unmasculine traits as Oscar WILDE's Dorian GRAY.

Against the Law 1955 autobiography of Peter Wildeblood, a journalist who had been prosecuted in the notorious MONTAGU-WILDEBLOOD AFFAIR. A brave account of a man who had been imprisoned, who had had the carefully constructed boundaries between his gay life and his professional life shattered, and yet who had survived the ordeal with the confidence to squarely declare his gayness, 'I am no more ashamed of it than I would be of being colour-blind or of writing with my left hand.' The book served to debunk the hypocrisy and the political motivations of the legal treatment of homosexuality. In addition, the evidence that Wildeblood gave to the Wolfenden Committee had an impact on its final recommendations (*see* WOLFENDEN REPORT).

age of consent The legal age at which people are deemed to be responsible enough to assent to sex without the law swooping in and arresting the partner and the person themselves. In Europe most countries set the age somewhere in the early to mid-teens, and moreover have the same age for straight, lesbian and gay sex. In its infinite wisdom the British (and German) legal system has always maintained a discrimination between gay sex and straight/lesbian sex. Sex between gay males was illegal in England and Wales until 1967, when the SEXUAL OFFENCES ACT set the age at 21; later, Scotland and, even later still, Northern Ireland were brought within the remit of the Act. However, the age for straight sex has always been 16. In February 1994 there was a concerted attempt to reduce the age of consent for gay males to 16 through an amendment to the Criminal Justice Bill then going through Parliament, but the House of Commons compromised on 18. When campaigners on the candle-lit vigil outside Parliament heard that their esteemed legislators had refused the opportunity to equalize the two ages, the crowd erupted in anger. Lesbian sex has never been explicitly prohibited or legalized by Parliament, and there is no statutory age, but by default lesbian sex comes under the same conditions as straight sex. Some lesbians feel the need for a lesbian age to give them the legal visibility they do not now possess. Many more progressive campaigners feel that any age of consent is bound to be arbitrary as people mature at different ages, and that a democracy ought to be able to create legislation that can weed out coercive sex from perfectly consensual sex which at present would be declared under age. *Age of Consent* was the title of the 1984 album by the openly gay British music group BRONSKI BEAT.

ageism Tends to be more widespread in gay male communities than in lesbian ones. Partly this is a result of the belief that older people are a throwback to less enlightened times (rather than people who survived despite repression), and partly because of the worship of the body-beautiful, rather than body-saggy, which characterizes gay male communities. As gay American comic Tom Ammiano said, 'I'm now forty-three years old, which, in faggot years, translates to a hundred and two.' As a result, groups have been set up to provide support for older lesbians and gay men, such as Senior Action in a Gay Environment (SAGE) founded in 1977 in America. Ageism may also apply to a lack of concern for or interest in young people's rights.

aggressive When applied to women by (straight) men it functions as a code way of referring to at least a feminist and usually a lesbian. In these terms, any woman who defends her right to run her life as she wishes, or who disagrees with a man, or indeed who wants a successful career is seen to be committing an act of aggressive behaviour. The word is actually more usually applied to women than men since male forthrightness is to be expected and is not worth commenting on.

Agnodice (fourth century BC) The history of women who passed as men for the purpose of gaining access to male privileges is a long one. One of the first recorded cases is this Greek woman who disguised herself as a man to gain medical qualifications and who practised as a gynaecologist. She reportedly attracted the ire of her fellow medics with her popularity, and was accused of corrupting women. It was during this case that her biological gender was discovered.

agoraphilia Opposite of agoraphobia, it indicates a love of the market place. Queens seem bizarrely prone to this condition, often not happy unless carrying a clutch of hatboxes. *See* RETAIL THERAPY.

AID Acronym for artificial insemination by donor, the process by which a woman can choose to be impregnated by receiving injections of sperm from an unknown male donor. The term was commonly changed to donor insemination (DI) in the 1980s so that there was no confusion between it and AIDS. Since it is often difficult for lesbians who wish to become pregnant to receive officially sanctioned AID, they will frequently make private arrangements with a man, often gay, to receive his sperm.

AIDS (acquired immune-deficiency syndrome) Rather than a specific disease,

AIDS is a syndrome, or a set of different symptoms that may occur after progressive damage to the body's immune system thought to be caused by the HIV virus. Moreover, a definition of AIDS is increasingly hard to determine. One definition that has been used is if someone has a T-CELL count of fewer than two hundred. However, the precise relationship between the T-cell count and the onset of illness is not known, and it cannot be used as a prediction of illness or of the seriousness of illness. Another way is if a person develops one of a list of different illnesses. Yet this is also problematic since progress in treating opportunistic infections has meant that the list gives no indication of the seriousness of the condition. Many professionals now choose to talk of 'the latter stages of HIV infection' rather than AIDS. No one knows with any certainty where AIDS first developed. In all probability it had been with us for several decades before being identified as a separate condition. In the 1970s many drugs users suffered from what was known as 'junkie pneumonia', which many people now think was AIDS. The syndrome was first noted in June 1981 when the American Centers for Disease Control received reports of a number of unusual infections among gay men in San Francisco and New York, particularly KAPOSI'S SARCOMA and PNEUMOCYSTIS CARINII PNEUMONIA. The first chilling portent the gay community received of the epidemic that was about to strike was a report of these findings in the *New York Times* on 3 July 1981. It is this report which is referred to in the beginning of the film LONGTIME COMPANION. Although the syndrome, until July 1982 called GRID (gay related immune deficiency), continued to claim lives, it was not until 1983 that the HTLV-III virus was identified and proposed by some (such as Luc Motaignier of the French Pasteur Institute) as the probable cause of AIDS. It was only in 1984 that the virus (which began to be called HIV) was widely accepted as the cause of AIDS. Meanwhile, the compassionate religious fundamentalists and right wing appeared to take great glee in the illness. Jerry FAL-

WELL called it 'the judgement of God' in a sermon in June 1983, while US President Ronald REAGAN remained silent on the issue. In the absence of any government initiatives, people in the communities affected by AIDS organized themselves, and created AIDS SERVICE ORGANIZATIONS and education campaigns as well as fighting for the rights of those affected to be treated with dignity (*see* CAMPBELL, BOBBIE; PWA MOVEMENT). It was only after the death of Rock HUDSON in 1985 that it seemed that wider society sat up and took notice. Even then, gay communities did not receive the support they should have expected (*see* DE-GAYING OF AIDS), and it was left up to pressure groups such as ACT UP to remind governments of their responsibilities. In the early 1990s, although much success has been achieved in the treatment of some of the opportunistic illnesses associated with the syndrome and people who are diagnosed as being with AIDS are staying alive far longer, the world looks no closer to a vaccine or a drug for use against HIV itself. The only drugs that have showed any effectiveness against HIV are AZT and analogues such as DDI, but these are open to great controversy. It is hard to sum up the huge effect that the AIDS epidemic has had on gay communities worldwide. The 1980s were a time of immense grief as people found their whole social networks devastated, and had to care for the sick as well as cope with bereavement. It was also a time when we discovered that despite all the seeming progress of the lesbian and gay rights movement in persuading society of our basic humanity, governments did not put the same premium on gay lives as they did on the lives of what they termed the 'general public'. But it was also a time when the gay communities, including the large number of lesbians who were infected or who became involved in the struggle against AIDS, could be most proud of themselves. In spite of the bigotry we faced, in the main we demonstrated how to respond to a health crisis rationally and responsibly. We took up safer sex both for ourselves and our partners, we cared for the sick with compassion and gave them dignity. Instead of being over-whelmed with grief we revitalized our political movements, and we turned our bereavement into celebrations of life such as the AIDS QUILT. We will never forget, we should never forgive, but we will survive.

AIDS closet The difficulties faced by public figures who have received a diagnosis of HIV or AIDS in publicly declaring their ill-ness. Freddy Mercury had a knee problem, Rock HUDSON had anorexia, Liberace had lost a great deal of weight because of a diet of watermelons. All of them had AIDS, but none could admit it until the last moment. Liberace was outed posthumously by a coroner in Los Angeles. While everyone can understand the desire of PWAs to live without the glare of publicity about their illness, many AIDS activists feel that such secrecy does nothing to dispel the public denial and mythology about the syndrome.

AIDS Council of New South Wales Set up in mid-1983 and originally called the AIDS Action Committee. It coordinated the gay community's response in Australia to the onslaught of the AIDS epidemic. Its remit was subsequently broadened to take in other non-gay communities affected by HIV and AIDS.

AIDS – don't die of ignorance In 1986 the first large-scale British government cam-paign to educate people about the AIDS epidemic, used this slogan in its television adverts and literature. Rather than speak-ing frankly about HIV prevention, the tele-vision adverts employed the obscure imagery of craggy icebergs turning into a marble tombstone. And no, the govern-ment did not see fit at that stage to address anything specifically to the gay commu-nity, despite the fact that it was they who were clearly most at risk.

AIDS-related dementia Otherwise known as encephalopathy or ADC. The phrase is used as an umbrella term for a number of different symptoms, including memory loss, personality change and deterioration of intellectual or social skills, when these are thought to be directly related to HIV infection. Improved diagnosis seems to have decreased the incidence of such condi-tions. Many people with HIV and AIDS, due to anxiety and depression, often suffer minor mental difficulties, such as memory loss, but these are not the onset of dementia.

AIDS service organization An ASO is a non-governmental organization that works exclusively to provide services for people with HIV and AIDS. The term became common currency in the late 1980s, as a means of distinguishing such organizations from those which dealt with AIDS as part of a larger programme. Throughout the 1980s the pre-eminent ASOs were those which were originally set up by and within gay communities, although with the DE-GAYING OF AIDS they declared that their services were available to all. As a whole, such organizations have been called the AIDS service industry. Examples include in America GAY MEN'S HEALTH CRISIS, in the UK the TERRENCE HIGGINS TRUST, and in Australia the AIDS COUNCIL OF NEW SOUTH WALES.

AIDS test *See* HIV TEST.

AIDS Treatment News Biweekly American newspaper for PWAs and health profes-sionals which was founded in 1986. It car-ries news of any developments in the treatment of AIDS-related illnesses.

Ain't I a Woman Collective Describing itself as 'a collective of eight women func-tioning as a world wide conspiracy of Radical Lesbians', the 1970s US collective echoed the electrifying 1851 speech by Sojourner Truth, 'I could work as much, and eat as much as a man – when I could get it - and bear the lash as well. And ain't I a woman?'

air raid shelters Became wartime cottages in Sydney, Australia. A host of these small buildings were built in the city after Japan's entry into the Second World War in 1941, and many were located around parks and other traditional BEATS, or cruis-ing grounds. Since they could be sealed from the inside, they became a busy haunt for those seeking casual sex.

Akan Society in the African state of Ghana. Within this society women who had not married routinely engaged in lesbian affairs with other women, and occasionally carried on with the affair even after marriage. Group sex between women is also common, and Akan women reportedly acquired large beds to accommodate this.

Akhenaten Ancient Egyptian Pharaoh who reigned from 1379 to 1362 BC. He is sometimes known as the first individual in history for the way in which he challenged the polytheistic Egyptian religion and proclaimed one universal god, Aten the sun god. After the death of his wife Nefertiti (c. 1365 BC), Akhenaten took the prince Smenkhare, possibly his own nephew, as a co-ruler. Their relationship seems to have been one of dubious closeness. The young prince was known in the official hieroglyph seal as the 'beloved of Akhenaten', and some portraits show the two side by side with the Pharaoh stroking Smenkhare under the chin. The art of the period broke away from stylized Egyptian norms by emphasizing realism, and the statues of Akhenaten, unlike BUTCH old Ramses II, have a feminine quality with his curved hips and doleful expression casting a NELLY gaze over the millennia.

Aki no Yo no Nagamonogatari The best known of the Japanese CHIGO Monogatari story form. It dates from at least 1377. In it a priest agonizes over his inability to devote himself to his religious life, and he goes on a pilgrimage to pray for the inspiration necessary to reach enlightenment. On his way back he falls in love with a chigo. The chigo is kidnapped by goblins, which creates mayhem among groups of monks, resulting in destructive fighting. Finally, the chigo commits suicide, leading to the priest's ultimate salvation.

Albany Trust British organization initially set up in 1958 as the sister charity to the HOMOSEXUAL LAW REFORM SOCIETY. Antony Grey, one of the main protagonists in the Wolfenden reforms, was the secretary, and

then director, between 1962 and 1977. After the passage of the 1967 SEXUAL OFFENCES ACT the Trust took on more of a welfare role; it is still alive and kicking in the 1990s, and offers support and psychosexual counselling.

Albatross A 1970s American satirical magazine for lesbians.

Alec's Bar The fictional lesbian bar that is described in the Paris sections of Radclyffe HALL's novel THE WELL OF LONELINESS. Her vivid descriptions indicate that by the 1920s the Paris lesbian subculture was becoming more fixed. Hall also describes the sophisticated salons of Valerie Seymour, a thinly veiled representation of real-life Parisian hostess, Natalie BARNEY.

Alexander and Hephaestion One of the great love affairs of gay mythology. Alexander the Great (356–323 BC), King of Macedonia and conqueror of Asia Minor, Egypt and India, met and apparently fell in love with Hephaestion when both of them were studying under the Greek philosopher Aristotle. The two remained intriguingly close throughout Alexander's accession to the throne, his subjugation of the other Greek states, and his campaigns elsewhere. When Hephaestion died of a fever in 325 BC, Alexander allegedly had his body cremated on a monumental 200-foot pyre which contained wooden sculptures of ships, bulls, lions and wreaths. Thereafter Alexander's mental health began to deteriorate, and he died in Babylon after having been taken ill at a banquet. Whatever its historical veracity, the mythical love affair has made Alexander a staple in the long list of great historical gays that have been CLAIMed from history. He has also been celebrated in gay literature, most recently in the fictional works of English writer Mary Renault.

Alice B. Toklas Democratic Club Political group formed in the early 1970s as a unit for lesbian and gay support of the American Democratic Party, and to create the idea of a lesbian and gay voting block. The club was successful in getting candidates for national elections to make announcements in favour of lesbian and gay rights.

Alice blue gown American camp term for a police officer, popular in the 1950s and 1960s when gay men had to be vigilant at all times to avoid the long arm of the law. Alice blue was a pale blue named after Alice, the daughter of President Theodore Roosevelt. The term may have been derived from a poem by Joseph McCarthy, who wrote a song called 'Alice Blue Gown'. Policemen were also referred to as Betty (blue) badge and Lily law.

all they that love not tobacco and boyes are fooles. *See* MARLOWE, CHRISTOPHER.

ALOA *See* ASIAN LESBIANS OUTSIDE OF ASIA.

Alpine County Californian county in the Sierra Nevadas. In 1970 members of the Gay Liberation Front in San Francisco pointed out that it had fewer than 400 registered voters and that it would be possible for gays to move there en masse and take over the local government, thereby establishing a gay safe space. Although some people claim the whole episode was just a media stunt, nearly 500 people reportedly signed up to make the move. However, the residents of the county took pre-emptive action and froze all real-estate deals, as well as implementing a strict building code that doubled building costs. Wishful thinking aside, some gay men and lesbians did actually go on to establish small rural communities in America, such as in Golden, Oregon (1970); Elwha, on the Olympic Peninsula in the state of Washington (1973); in Wolf Creek, Oregon (1975); and a few years later (in the late 1970s), the Running Water and Short Mountain sanctuaries in North Carolina and Tennessee.

Alternate University A loft space in New York, on Fourteenth Street and Sixth Avenue, which in the 1960s served as a home for a number of radical groups. On 4 July 1969, in the aftermath of the STONEWALL RIOT, a group of lesbians and gay men evacuated a stormy meeting of the New York MATTACHINE SOCIETY, where they had been exhorted to educate the straight community 'with grace and good humour'. Feeling that Mattachine was letting down the energy of Stonewall, they relocated to the Alternate U, as it was known, and began meetings that would eventually turn into the GAY LIBERATION FRONT.

alternative medicine Given the seeming lack of any great biomedical progress in treating HIV itself, rather than the opportunistic illnesses with which it is associated, many people with HIV and AIDS have turned to forms of complementary medicine in an attempt to bolster their immune system. Particularly common forms of therapy include hypnotherapy, acupuncture, homeopathy, visualization therapy and herbal medicines. In fact, AIDS has been one of the main factors in popularizing such therapies in the West.

Alternative Miss World Annual alternative beauty contest invented by the gay artist Andrew Logan, in which everything weird and wonderful, grotesque or obscene was paraded down the catwalk in front of the gawping eyes of London's fashion glitterati and avant garde. It was featured in a 1980 film which followed the nail-biting twists and turns of the 1978 contest, at which a panel of judges including Lionel Bart, Joan Bakewell, Molly Parkin and Zandra Rhodes as well as the inimitable DIVINE presided over the impossible task of judging between such lovelies as Miss Wolverhampton Municipal Baths, Miss Windscale Nuclear Reactor and Miss Consumer Products. Social commentary on the idea of beauty, on British life, and a marvellous festival of campery and drag, it had it all.

Amarakaeri In this people of eastern Peru, it was reported that sex was almost exclusively homosexual among both women and men, except for heterosexual acts performed two or three times a year at ceremonial rites.

Amazon River The river was named by the Spanish colonialist Orellana who voyaged down it in 1541, and fought with the warrior women of the TAPUYA TRIBES.

L'Amazone Nickname by which early-twentieth-century Parisians knew the lesbian patron of the arts Natalie BARNEY.

amazonism Nineteenth-century sociologist Bachofen maintains that Amazonism is common to the origins of many societies, and uses this as the basis for his matriarchal theory of social origins. *See* MATRIARCHAL SCHOOL.

amazons Term for all-women warrior societies, taken from the Greek word meaning without breasts. The name refers to the myth that female warriors would remove one breast so as to draw a bow more easily, although this might just be a male myth to indicate the 'defeminizing' nature of women's power. Amazon societies are described in a number of historical and quasi-historical accounts. Scholars generally concur that the Libyan amazons, who inhabited north-west Africa, were the original group of amazon mythology, although there are numerous records of amazon societies throughout west and central Asia. In Greek prehistory, the Asiatic Scythian amazons are said to have laid siege to Athens and fought a four-month battle with Theseus for control of the city. Chic lesbian salon hostess Natalie BARNEY drew attention to the symbolic power of amazons for lesbians in her collection PENSEES D'UNE AMAZONE.

Amsterdam The Dutch city has become something of a Mecca for European lesbians and gays. This is partly because the Netherlands has an extremely progressive legal framework. Male homosexuality has been legal in some form since 1811, and the constitution includes the prohibition of discrimination on the grounds of sexuality. Marriage is not technically legal, but couples can register partnership contracts, although this does not allow them to adopt children. Amsterdam also has a very large and very visible lesbian and gay scene, and a number of sex shops and establishments that are quite an eye-opener for visitors from less upfront European countries. It is also the site of the Homo-monument, a pink triangle set in a canal in a park, which serves to commemorate the lesbian and gay victims of fascism, particularly the HOLOCAUST.

analingus Technical term for RIMMING.

Anamika Group for south Asian lesbians which formed in 1985 in the US. Its name is taken from the Sanskrit word anamika, meaning nameless, to address the lack of names in south Asian languages for relationships between two women.

Anandrynes Lesbian group in the late eighteenth century in Paris, the truth about which is difficult to establish from the exoticized and fictionalized accounts of the women's activity, which have been written with male titillation in mind. Given the amount of smoke, however, it is possible that there was at least a small fire. According to the accounts, the group was reported to have been founded by Madame Furiel, and to have met at her house. The membership supposedly consisted of high society women and actresses. New candidates to the group, or 'desirantes', would be appraised by Madame Furiel before being tutored in the arts of lesbian sex by another member. An initiation ceremony would take place in the 'temple of Venus', which was decorated with representations of the goddess Vesta. Another ritual involved the initiates tending the fire of Vesta in a room covered in phallic representations. Should the fire go out, the other women knew that the recruit had been distracted by the priapic display around her. The symbol of the club was a pair of turtle doves.

Ancient Greece Ancient Greece has served as a point of inspiration for lesbians and gay men throughout the centuries as a society known for its tolerant attitudes towards same-sex sexuality. However, the institutionalized form which homosexual relationships took was that of pederasty, namely an erotic attraction on the part of an older man (or woman, as the career of the poet SAPPHO seems to show) for an adolescent of the same gender. In male relations a young man was deemed unattractive as a beloved when he showed signs of physical maturity. The edifying nature of such relationships was often stressed, and it is possible that they were the remnants of ancient INITIATION rituals (*see* CRETE; SPARTA). Such pederastic relations often feature in Greek literature, drama and philosophy: later Greek opinion saw an erotic element in the relationships between ACHILLES and Patroclus in Homer's *Iliad*; Hesiod's *Shield of Heracles* portrays a pederastic relation between HERCULES and his page Iolaus; Sappho's poetry displays a lyric intensity in its description of her feeling towards the girls at her school which has been claimed as homoerotic despite the best attempts of nineteenth-century writers to misrepresent them as otherwise; the poet Anacreon of Teos described the love of boys in his vivid drinking songs; Pindar of Thebes dedicated his odes to young aristocratic boys; Aeschylus, Sophocles and Euripides all touched on homoerotic themes in their drama, as did Aristophanes through the use of sophisticated allusion; Plato provided some of the earliest philosophical justifications of homosexual relations in his SYMPOSIUM and although he later expressed negative opinions in *The Laws*, this was probably the result of disillusionment at the end of his life; Aristotle developed one of the earliest theories of homosexuality as congenital; Theocritus' Arcadian pastorals are informed by a homoerotic sentiment; finally the MOUSA PAIDIKI provides an entire anthology of poetry devoted to the love of boys. In addition to the many elements of homoeroticism in Greek mythology, ancient Greek civilization therefore provided numerous examples of the existence and acceptance of same-sex eroticism and, whilst we cannot see it as the same as homosexuality in the modern period, this wealth of cultural material has offered succour to generations of lesbians and gay men who were seeking to understand their sexual impulses, down to the modern period.

and that night I was happy The line most associated with a specifically homoerotic reading of the poetry collection LEAVES OF GRASS by Walt WHITMAN. In the CALAMUS section, he writes, 'For the friend I love lay sleeping by my side/In the stillness his face was inclined towards me...And his arm lay lightly over my breast/And that night I was happy.'

and that night they were not divided The earth-shattering line in Radclyffe HALL's novel THE WELL OF LONELINESS which came closest to mentioning sex between women. It was this intimation of sexual intimacy in conjunction with Hall's religious imagery – the protagonist Stephen GORDON is set up as a martyr being cruelly punished for a natural abnormality – that caused such a rumpus. References to homosexuality were acceptable, but it was going too far to suggest that lesbians and gay men could lead honourable and decent lives.

And the Band Played On 1987 docu-novel by gay author Randy Shilts, released in a film version in 1993. A mammoth undertaking, the work presented the history of the AIDS epidemic. It was most effective, and affecting, in its presentation of a scientific establishment which too often saw AIDS as an academic challenge, as a race to identify the cause to win gongs rather than as a human catastrophe, and of a government response to the deaths of thousands of 'undesirables' which at best displayed apathy and at worst passive collusion. The work was heavily criticized nonetheless for its posthumous persecution of PATIENT ZERO, a sort of AIDS 'typhoid Mary', and for its implications that AIDS was the price of sexual promiscuity in the 1970s, implications that many AIDS activists did not find particularly productive. It also implied that the disease had emanated from Africa, which reinforced a particular racist argument that the world was suffering from AIDS as a result of African promiscuity and lack of hygiene.

Anders als die Anderen (Different from the Others) 1919 German film directed by Richard Oswald and starring Konrad

Veidt, which dealt with a violinist who is blackmailed by the man who has seduced him. The film explicitly called for tolerance for what it termed the third sex. In the original film programme it said, 'Love for one's own sex can be just as pure and noble as love for the opposite sex...[The film] shows us how people with such tendencies are made to suffer for no reason.' The programme called for the end of PARAGRAPH 175. It was remade in 1927 as *Gesetze der Liebe* (The Laws of Love). All but one of the prints were destroyed by the Nazis, who also broke up performances of the film.

Andrew phenomenon Term used by feminist writers Liz Stanley and Sue Wild. It describes the phenomenon that however much gay men might claim to cherish and respect women when they are with them, the moment another man enters the room their attention is immediately distracted as they gauge whether or not he is worth cruising and, if so, whether or not he seems willing.

androgyne As a term for a hermaphrodite or eunuch its use has been recorded as early as the sixteenth century. It was later popularized as a term for homosexuals. Gay activist Harry HAY used the term androgynous minority to describe the lesbian and gay community.

androgyny The state of having both male and female characteristics. Can be used to refer to biological gender (hermaphroditism) or personal style.

androphilia A term for erotic attraction between two adult males which was used in the early twentieth century by German gay activist Magnus HIRSCHFIELD. He suggested it to differentiate relationships between adult men from other relationships which involved age differences, such as EPHEBOPHILIA and PAEDOPHILIA.

androphobia The fear and/or hatred of men. The word was developed within the feminist and lesbian-feminist movements to redress the imbalance caused by the lack of an opposite term for gynophobia. Like HETEROPHOBIA, some lesbian feminists would argue that there is nothing irrational about the concept, since it is men (in the form of the patriarchy) who are responsible for the enslavement of women.

Andros, Phil Nom de plume of the multi-talented Samuel M. Steward Ph.D. when he was writing the porn novels which have been considered superior by discerning consumers, providing descriptions of sex that were actually realistic. Steward led the kind of life we hope for. He left academic life to take up a career as a tattooist, performed SM sex (as a bottom) for researcher Alfred KINSEY, and wrote about Gertrude STEIN, and Alice B. TOKLAS, both as real people and fictional detectives.

Anecdotes of a Convent 1771 novel by Helen Williams in which a subplot tells of the ROMANTIC FRIENDSHIP between two young women in a nunnery. Louisa meets Fanny on the first day at the convent where they have both been sent for schooling, and the two become inseparable. Louisa delays her return home because she cannot bear to be parted, and when she does she faints at the mere mention of her beloved. Eventually, it is conveniently revealed that Fanny is really a man who has been brought up as a girl, and the two can marry. Interestingly, the relationship is viewed as unchanged even when it becomes heterosexual.

Angels of Light American radical drag troupe of the 1970s, which included some of the earlier members of the COCKETTES. They were more self-consciously political, and aimed their fabulous productions at issues such as class struggle and imperialism. Bringing in dance and costumes from India, China and Bali, they created spectacular visual effects.

anger The emotion which, according to liberals, we are not allowed to display. Expressing anger, we are told, marks us out as hysterical and irrational. Yet sometimes anger is the only rational and healthy response to a society which systematically discriminates against us. It is a sign that we are still both alive and defiant;

as Audre LORDE writes, 'My anger has meant pain to me but it has also meant survival, and before I give it up I'm going to be sure that there is something at least as powerful to replace it on the road to clarity.' Moreover, what evidence do we have to back up the liberal argument that calmness is a more effective political tool? It simply means that our oppressors can oppress us calmly. As Larry KRAMER has commented, 'I don't consider anger unhealthy or infantile...Being nice gets you nothing in this country [i.e. America] politically.' One of the great contributions of the different liberation movements has been to demonstrate that anger can be displayed without violence, that slogans can be hurled with all the force of years of pent-up frustration, but that does not necessarily have to mean a physically threatening posture. *See also* RAGE.

Angry Atthis 1969 song by lesbian feminist performer Maxine Feldman, which contributed to the growth in popularity of WOMEN'S MUSIC. The lyrics dealt with the singer's anger at not being free to hold her lover's hand. ATTHIS was a companion of the Greek poet SAPPHO, who was forced to leave her company.

anima muliebris virile corpore inclusa Latin phrase, meaning 'a female soul in a male body', which was the chosen explanation for homosexuality of many of the SEXOLOGISTS of the late nineteenth and early twentieth centuries.

anjaree In the Thai language, the word means 'one who has a different behaviour', and is used by Thai lesbians to refer to themselves since there is no specific word for lesbian. Anjaree was the name of the first lesbian group in Thailand.

Ann Arbor City in the American state of Michigan, which was the site of the first election of an openly queer person to an American public body. It happened in 1974 when Kathy Kozachenko was elected to the city council. In another first later that year, lesbian Elaine Noble was elected to the Massachusetts state legislature.

Anne, Queen (1655–1714) Queen of England from 1702, she was openly affectionate towards at least two women at Court: Sarah Jennings and Anne were childhood friends, and after Anne's marriage in 1683 Sarah, especially as Duchess of Marlborough, was to dominate Anne's household for 26 years; the two women exchanged frequent letters and notes as Mrs Morley (Anne) and Mrs Freeman (Sarah). Anne and her sister, Queen Mary, were never close and in 1693, after Mary had tried unsuccessfully to separate Anne and Sarah, Anne was accused of having a liaison with her. Queen Mary died the following year, and King William died in 1702. The Duchess of Marlborough sat with Anne in her coronation coach and was by her side at most State occasions. But in 1710 Anne finally broke with the Marlboroughs for political reasons, and Sarah's cousin Mrs Abigail Masham (formerly Lady Abigail Hill) became Anne's new favourite. Sarah quarrelled with Anne in public and remained angry and embittered.

Annual Reminder Picket that was held every year on 4 July, from 1965 to 1969, by organizations within the HOMOPHILE MOVEMENT in front of Independence Hall in the American city of Philadelphia. The first took place after the EAST COAST HOMOPHILE ORGANIZATIONS had held a series of pickets to protest against discrimination in federal employment, outside the Pentagon, the Civil Service Commission, the State Department and the White House in Washington, DC. The pickets were felt to be so successful, and exciting, that activist Craig Rodwell suggested that they hold one every year as an annual reminder that 'a group of Americans still don't have their basic rights to life, liberty and the pursuit of happiness'. The pickets were stage-managed to present as respectable an image as possible; everyone was to wear suits, and there were to be no overt displays of affection between men and women. The last was held after the STONEWALL RIOT when the younger and more radical lesbians and gays decided that such staid tactics were not suitable to the movement they wanted to build.

Another Country Play by Julian Mitchell, which deals with the experiences of a young gay man at an English public school. The young man, Guy Bennett, is marked as an outsider in the school because of his sexuality. He also understands that, since the other students will presumably become part of the British ruling class, he will be cast out from that as well. He thus decides to take revenge upon his school, class and country by the choice of espionage as a career. A film version was made in 1984 directed by Marek Kanievska and starring Rupert Everett.

Antinous (d. AD 122) Bithynian youth reportedly of peerless beauty who became the lover of the Roman Emperor Hadrian. The latter took him along on all his voyages. Antinous drowned in the Nile on a journey in Egypt. Historians speculating about the reasons for his death suggest that he committed suicide, either through weariness at the life of a courtesan or as a living sacrifice to avert disaster from the Emperor. In grief at the death of his beloved, Hadrian had him enrolled as one of the gods, founded the city of Antinöopolis in Egypt in his name, and renamed the youth's birthplace of Claudiopolis Antinöopolis as well. The youth's features also appeared on coins and on busts. This grief has put the affair among the great historical loves that form part of the corpus of lesbian and gay mythology. It was also subject to irreverent treatment by the British drag troup THE BLOOLIPS in 1992 where Antinous was presented as so beautiful that his bum lit up.

Aphrodite The Hellenistic goddess of love had developed from earlier female deities of the Syrian region such as Atargatis, the Babylonian Ishtar and the Phoenician Astarte. The ritual associated with the worship of these divinities was highly sexual and involved castration, transvestism and homosexual relations.

Aphrodite Urania *See* PLATO; URANIANISM.

Apollo The Greek god of flocks, healing, music and archery, was according to one tradition smitten by Admetus, King of Pherae in central Thessaly. Apollo was sentenced by Zeus to serve the King as a shepherd, but his service reportedly became devotion. Apollo helped Admetus to obtain a chariot drawn by a lion and a boar in order to be able to marry Alcestis, the daughter of Pelias, King of Iolcas, and also saved Admetus when Artemis threatened to destroy him because he had omitted to make sacrifices to the goddess. According to the Greek poet Callimachus (third century BC), 'We call upon Phoebus as shepherd also, ever since the day on the banks of the Amphrysus, when, burning with love for the young Admetus, he made himself guardian of the mares.' Apollo is also mentioned in the story of HYACINTHUS.

Apostles Also known as the Cambridge Conversazione Society. The most prestigious secret society at Cambridge University at the turn of the twentieth century. It included several queer luminaries who were to go on and form part of the BLOOMSBURY GROUP such as E.M. Forster (*see* MAURICE), Lytton Strachey and Maynard Keynes. In the Saturday night meetings of the society one member would give a reading, for which no subject was considered taboo. With the influence of Lytton Strachey the expression of homosexuality was according to Bertrand Russell 'for a time common'.

ARC (AIDS-related complex) A term for an AIDS-related illness which does not come under the list of illnesses prepared by the American Centers for Disease Control which result in a person with HIV being diagnosed as being with AIDS. However, as the list of opportunistic infections gets longer and AIDS becomes more difficult to define, most people have stopped using the term ARC, and instead talk of HIV-related disease.

Archibald Fountain Constructed in 1937 in Hyde Park in the Australian city of Sydney, it became and has remained a popular cruising ground. The large statues of nude men that adorn it must give it an extra frisson.

Ardhanari Literally meaning half-woman in Sanskrit. This is a form in which the Hindu deity Siva is represented with his right side male and left female, combining the male and female energies. Siva is the third deity of the main Hindu triad. S/he is portrayed as the destroying force, but also the restorer of that which has been destroyed. As a restorer s/he is represented as the phallus (*lingam*) alone or in combination with the vagina (*yoni*), which represents the SHAKTI, or female energy. In this form s/he is also known as Ardhanarishvara, or Pavangada.

Arena Three The magazine of the British MINORITIES RESEARCH GROUP, which was first published in 1964. It was the first publication in the UK produced by and for lesbians. It included short stories and poetry as well as advice and information. Through the magazine meetings were started, and it provided the first forum for British lesbians to come together. It finally closed in 1971, when some of its members went on to form the group SAPPHO.

Aristogiton *See* HARMODIUS AND ARISTOGITON.

armpits Bodily area which is an object for sexual fetish for some people. The practice of rubbing the dick in the armpit is known in gay male slang as playing the bagpipes.

Army of Lovers, or Revolt of the Perverts Rosa von Praunheim's second film, produced in 1978. It is an exploration of the extremes contained within the gay movement in America, told through a series of interviews intermixed with newsreel footage and photo stills, featuring gay parades and political gay theatre. It includes the timelessly inspiring piece of footage showing Anita BRYANT being hit in the face with a cream pie by a gay activist, which should be mandatory viewing for any queer preparing to come out.

Arnett, Chuck (1928–88) American dancer and choreographer, but best remembered for his painting, which documented the iconography of the burgeoning LEATHER scene in America from the 1950s onwards. His work appealed to, and painted the desires of, the leathermen who were forging masculine gay identities which, for better or worse, confronted stereotypes of effeminacy. Bikers, musclemen, athletes, construction workers and other soon-to-be-recognizable characters peopled his works, performing sex with all the force their broad shoulders could provide. Fittingly, a large mural of macho-looking things he had painted on the wall of the Tool Box leather bar in San Francisco appeared in an article in *Life* magazine in June 1964, entitled Homosexuality in America. The article presented the 'phenomenon' of macho homosexuality for the first time to a US public, and American queers who lived in isolation. It created quite an impact, and played a part in the gay exodus to San Francisco.

art for art's sake British name for the anti-utilitarian aesthetic theories which declared that any artistic work should be admired merely for its beauty as art and not for its moral or didactic qualities. The theory found expression in the works of nineteenth-century British poet Walter Pater and of the Pre-Raphaelite Brotherhood, and in the AESTHETICISM of Oscar Wilde, who in 1882 spent a year in America lecturing on the topic. Since lesbians and gay men have historically had a more than strained relationship with prevalent morality, gay writers and artists have tended to align themselves with aesthetic theories rather than moral ones, and it is conceivable that the twentieth-century accent that gay men in particular apply to style, such as in the CAMP sensibility, can be seen as part of this tradition.

Artemis *See* DIANA.

Article 121 The article of the Russian criminal code that was imposed in 1934 as part of Stalin's betrayal of the sexual liberalism of the RUSSIAN REVOLUTION. It made consensual sex between men punishable by up to five years in prison. The law was only repealed in June 1993 by President Boris Yeltsin. Although lesbian relations were not explicitly included in the law, lesbians in the Soviet Union were often incarcerated in mental institutions where they were liable to be forced to have therapies such as electric shocks or medication.

Artists' Ball Queer social event held once a year in the Trocadero Ballroom in George Street, Sydney, Australia. Eventually abandoned because of police harassment.

Arzner, Dorothy (1900–79) American film director, one of the very few women directors in American film history. Her best known films include *The Wild Party* (1929), *Working Girls* (1931), *Christopher Strong* (1933), featuring Katherine Hepburn, *Craig's Wife* (1936), and *The Bride Wore Red* (1937), which starred Joan Crawford.

As Is Play by William Hoffman, which was the first to deal with the subject of the AIDS epidemic. It opened at the Circle Repertory Theatre in New York in March 1985 and received three nominations for Tony Awards.

Ashton, Carol Fictional, Australian, lesbian detective who appears in the novels of Claire McNab and who lives and sleuths in Sydney. She features in *Fatal Reunion, Death Down Under* and her debut, *Lessons in Murder*, where she falls in love with her prime suspect.

Asian Lesbians Outside of Asia (ALOA) A British organization for lesbians of Asian descent which was set up in 1991 following a conference of Asian lesbians in Bangkok.

assimilationism Strand of lesbian and gay politics which seeks to emphasize the normalness of lesbians and gay men, and their common ground with straights. The hope is that, if lesbians and gay men behave in a way that is acceptable to society, they will eventually be allowed to operate within that society. Many other queers feel this approach is fundamentally misguided, as not only does it misunderstand the extent of societal homophobia, but it also does a disservice to the many members of the queer communities who do not want their lives dictated by a hostile society.

Moreover, since societal acceptance is also contingent on factors such as class, race and gender, it is no surprise that assimilationist creed is most often preached by white, middle-class men.

assinu Ancient Babylonian religious functionaries particularly associated with the goddess Ishtar, who danced, wore masks, played music and were apparently considered effeminate. Artistic representations show them carrying a spindle, which is symbolic of women's work. There is also some evidence that they were castrati. Specialists of Babylonian history believe that they were also engaged in RITUAL PROSTITUTION.

asylum Although in many countries it should theoretically be possible for a lesbian or gay man to claim asylum if the anti-gay laws of their own country put them at risk, such governmental magnanimity is not automatic. On the North American continent, the first time asylum was granted specifically on the grounds of one country's homophobic laws was in January 1992 when an Argentine gay man who had been raped and tortured by the Argentine federal police was granted refugee status in Canada. In the UK there is no official policy allowing this to take place, and the very few cases there have been have not been recognized as such.

At Saint Judas' American play dating from the last decade of the nineteenth century and written by the playwright Henry Fuller, it deals with the rather depressing story of a gay man who kills himself at the wedding of his ex-lover. It was however the first play on the American stage which deals overtly with issues gay.

Athletic Model Guild Los Angeles-based photographic organization which was formed by Bob Mizer in 1945. It became a leading producer of erotic photos of nude or partially nude men. Most of its output was printed in thinly disguised 'physique' magazines.

Atthis Greek woman who appears in the poetry of SAPPHO as a particular favourite.

One fragment of poetry recalls, 'It was you Atthis who said/"Sappho, if you will not get up/and let us look at you/I shall never love you again!"' It seems the two were parted, and remembering Atthis' departure and the fact that she has not had word from her, Sappho writes, 'And I honestly wish I were dead.' Atthis was celebrated in the 1969 song ANGRY ATTHIS.

Auction Block Area in Greenwich Village, New York near the Provincetown Playhouse, which by the early 1930s had become the centre of the queer subculture. A bustling cruising ground was pounded by gay men, and several bars catered to gay men and lesbians.

Auden, Wystan Hugh (1907–73) British-born poet who, like his schoolfriend and fellow student at Oxford University, Christopher ISHERWOOD, departed to America at the outbreak of the Second World War. Auden's most influential work, produced in the 1930s, was remarkable in seeking to incorporate the ideas of psychoanalysis and Marxism into the poetic art; he had sympathies with both, and believed that Marxism might relieve the world of its economic and social ills, while psychoanalysis would cure psychological problems. During the war he converted back to Anglicanism, and distanced himself from his earlier left-wing sympathies. Although Auden is considered one of the foremost of gay authors, he gave us little in the way of gay-themed work other than a series of (ungendered) love poems written to his longtime lover Chester Kallman, and the doggerel GOBBLE POEM.

Augustine, St (Aurelius Augustinus AD 354–430) Bishop of Hippo, early Christian Church father and philosopher, whose prolific works are fundamental to the doctrine of the Catholic Church. His writings on sin and grace, and his attacks on heresy, have been blamed for perpetuating the long tradition of the Western Church as suspicious of any expression of sexuality. But Augustine did not have the most holy of backgrounds. Born to a Christian mother and a pagan father, he had a long period of scepticism and indulgence, during which he is reported to have prayed, 'Lord, give me chastity...but not yet!', before being converted and baptized in AD 387. In gay male slang, to pull a St Augustine is to renounce the world of CRUISING and casual sex for a monogamous relationship. Also known as pulling a Mary Magdalene or taking the veil.

Aunt Nell Used by gay men in the UK in the mid-twentieth century and related to the gay slang system POLARI, the phrase was used to mean ears, or to hear. It could also be attached to the beginning of a sentence to warn the addressee to listen well.

auntie Slang term for an older gay man. Can be used negatively to imply some level of gossiping, tea-taking, prissiness. Can also be used self-referentially, with shades of agony aunt, to identify oneself as a caring non-sexual friend.

auparishtaka The title of a chapter in the Indian literary classic, KAMA SUTRA, which deals with oral sex. The text records that auparishtaka, or oral sex, is practised by male and female citizens who know each other well, male servants on their masters, and eunuchs with males. The *Kama Sutra* describes eight kinds of oral sex involving different kinds of pressure with the mouth, lips, tongue and hands.

Australian Lesbian Movement Lesbian political organization set up in the Australian city of Melbourne in January 1970. It was a branch of the American DAUGHTERS OF BILITIS organization.

auto-eroticism Masturbation, but also a humorous term for the kind of sexual experimentation that became possible with the advent of mass car ownership in the period after the Second World War. Cars were mobile bedrooms and gave those who were still living at home a space for sexual adventure. It enabled young queers from the suburbs the mobility to go and visit urban cruising grounds.

autumn colours Term used in gay CONTACT ADVERTS to advertise for a man who is eager, not to wear beiges, but to take part in WATERSPORTS and SCAT. It refers to the two colours associated with these practices in the HANKIE CODES and in contact adverts; YELLOW for watersports and BROWN for scat.

avenge Oscar Wilde Slogan used by the GAY LIBERATION FRONT in London in the early 1970s. It indicates the power Oscar WILDE has as an epitome of gay suffering at the hands of the establishment.

axe The double-headed axe as an emblem for woman-identification (*see* LABRYS) is symbolic, according to Mary Daly, of 'our own Wild wisdom and wit, which cut through the mazes of man-made mystification'.

Axgil, Axel and Axgil, Eigil Danish gay activists who founded the first gay organization in Denmark in 1948. On 26 May 1989 the Danish Parliament voted to legalize lesbian and gay marriages, and when the law took effect on 1 October of that year they were among the first gay couples to marry.

Azalea: A Magazine by Third World Lesbians American magazine set up in 1978 by black lesbians. Initially apolitical in editorial tone, the magazine became increasingly aware of the necessity of coalitions between black lesbians and their other black or lesbian sisters.

AZT Brand name of the drug azidothymidine which was the first drug passed for use in the treatment of people with HIV and AIDS by Western governments. It was first approved by the American government in March 1987, after tests had indicated that it may be useful in retarding the replication inside cells of the HIV virus. The drug was marketed by the pharmaceutical company Burroughs-Wellcome. When it initially became available a one-year prescription cost $10,000, a figure which created a storm of accusations that Wellcome was profiteering from the AIDS crisis. Recent trials of the drug have cast doubt on its effectiveness, and many people with HIV and AIDS have complained that it is actually detrimental to their health. *See also* CONCORDE TRIAL; GAYS AGAINST GENOCIDE.

Black leather Jacket

B and D *See* BONDAGE AND DISCIPLINE.

Babar (1483–1530) The founder of the Mughal dynasty in India. He is said to have been gay. In the *Tuzuk-i-Babri*, his collected writings, Babar wrote romantically about his affair with the boy Baburi at Andezan.

Baby Butch Term for a young BUTCH lesbian.

Bacchae In this tragedy, Euripides describes the Bacchae, a group of women who engaged in women-only ritual dancing on the wooded mountain-sides. In the play the god DIONYSUS leads Pentheus, the King of Thebes, on to the hillside where he is torn apart by the women, who then enter the city with his head on a stick. Go for it, sisters!

bachelor An unmarried man. When the word is prefixed with 'confirmed' it takes on specifically gay connotations because it implies that the man has some reason for never wanting to tie the knot with a member of the opposite sex. Thus, in the straight media, referring to a man as a confirmed bachelor often serves as a code way of pointing out his sexuality without having to mention the 'g' word. Gay men might use the term to refer to a man as a CLOSET CASE.

Bachelors for Wallace 1948 brainchild of Communist Party activist and MATTACHINE SOCIETY founder-to-be Harry HAY. It was to have been an organization for gay men, purportedly to work to promote the presidential candidacy of liberal candidate Henry Wallace, but also to work for the rights of what Hay called society's 'androgynous minority'. However, the plan never came to fruition for lack of support.

backgammon players Name given to homosexual men in Britain in the late eighteenth century. It probably derives, like its synonym 'gentleman of the back door', from the gay use of the back passage as a penetrable orifice.

backroom The darkened section of a gay male bar which is used for sex.

Bad Attitude Lesbian sex magazine first published in 1984, which was so called because women were traditionally not allowed to take control of their sexuality.

badges *See* BUTTONS.

Baghdad by the Bay Epithet applied to San Francisco by its early settlers in reference to the cosmopolitan nature of the city with its motley population of adventurers, bohemians and others who did not quite fit in elsewhere. The early gay subculture which grew up in the city also earned it another nickname from the less enlightened, 'Sodom by the sea'.

Bahuchara Mata Goddess of the HIJRA cult in northern India.

Baldwin, James (1924–87) Black American novelist and dramatist who lived most of his life in France, though his works tend to focus on America, exploring both black and gay 'themes'. His first novel, *Go Tell it on the Mountain*, drew on his upbringing in HARLEM, whilst his second, GIOVANNI'S ROOM, provided an honest description of a gay relationship. In *Another Country* Baldwin presented portrayals of a number of residents of New York, with a range of sexual orientations, all of whom are linked by their friendship with a black musician. With the rise of the black CIVIL RIGHTS MOVEMENT in America, Baldwin increasingly concentrated on black issues, though not always to great acclaim.

Bambi-sex Referring to the Disney film *Bambi*, with its wide-eyed and innocent deer hero. This term is generally used perjoratively by PRO-SEX LESBIANS to describe VANILLA SEX, i.e. lesbian sex which does not involve penetration, SADOMASOCHISM, BUTCH/FEMME pornography or SEX TOYS, but is more concerned with love and a fair division of orgasms.

bandana Used in the 1970s not only stuffed into pockets as part of the HANKIE CODES for signalling sexual preferences, but also worn round the neck for a bit of cowboy-macho chic. Despite their occasional co-option by straight society in the 1980s, bandanas have remained part of the basic gay wardrobe.

Bankhead, Tallulah (1903–68) Actress who starred in the films *Lifeboat* and *A Royal Scandal*. Fabulous gay icon with a sharpened wit who flaunted her affairs with both men and women (she described herself as ambisextrous), but who sometimes affected to be extremely bored with it all. 'Sex? I'm bored with sex. What is it, after all? If you go down on a woman, you get a crick in the neck. If you go down on a man, you get lockjaw. And fucking just gives me claustrophobia.' She died from pneumonia, her last words being, 'Codeine... Bourbon...'

Barbary Lane In San Francisco, it is known as the location for the house of Anna MADRIGAL in the TALES OF THE CITY series.

Barbette (1904–73) American FEMALE IMPERSONATOR who was born in Texas as Vander Clyde. Swinging from her stage trapeze, he was the star turn at the Casino de Paris in the French capital in the late 1920s. He was described by Jean Cocteau as 'an angel, a flower, a bird', and made a small appearance in Cocteau's film *Blood of a Poet* (1930) where he is glimpsed as a lady in a theatre box. Unlike many female impersonators, the fact that this was a man in DRAG was central to the act, and the theatricality of the gender roles was sent up when, at the end of every act, Barbette would remove his wig to gasps as he revealed his true gender. He was also reincarnated in the unlikely persona of Julie Andrews in Blake Edwards' gender-bending 1982 film *Victor/Victoria*. Barbette's career was cut short by an illness which stopped him performing his trapeze and tightrope stunts.

Barnes, Djuna (1892–1982) American novelist. Barnes moved to Paris from Greenwich Village in 1919, and she was intimate with the chic lesbian circle which included Natalie BARNEY, Janet Flanner and Dolly Wilde. They were subject to Barnes' affectionate satire in her privately printed *Ladies' Almanack*. In her other works Barnes has been criticized for displaying too much of a debt to the French aesthetic writers who portrayed lesbian love as an artificial and decadent passion (*see* EPATER LE BOURGEOIS). Her major work, *Nightwood* (1936), depicts love between women as tormenting and narcissistic: 'A woman is yourself, caught as you turn in panic; on her mouth you kiss your own.' Barnes returned to New York at the beginning of the Second World War, and settled back in Greenwich Village where she became something of a recluse. The poet e. e. cummings lived opposite her, and he would sometimes shout over, 'Are you still alive, Djuna?'

Barney, Natalie (1876–1972) Pullman car heiress who was the focus of chic lesbian life in Paris in the early twentieth century. She kept a distinguished salon which was frequented by Radclyffe HALL, novelist Djuna BARNES, and painter Romaine Brooks amongst others. Openly lesbian in her poetry, Barney also provided patronage for other lesbian and gay artists. Because of her uncompromising openness about her sexuality, she was known in Paris as 'L'Amazone'. She wrote a collection of thoughts about homosexuality entitled PENSEES D'UNE AMAZONE.

basir Male spirit mediums in Borneo who act as women in every way, including sexually. Thus they represent the local deity who is conceived of as androgynous, having both a male and female side. In addition, the position of spirit medium is changing from being a female role to being a male one, and men performing the role thus behave appropriately to the older, female, connotations of the position.

basket A man's crotch.

bathhouses Since Roman times, bathhouses have been popular meeting places for the homoerotically inclined, male or female. Their usually sex-segregated environments offer chances of sustaining lingering eyefuls of same-sex flesh quite legally, and they give the chance of check-ing out the merchandise down to the last mole. Roman epigrammatist Martial describes occasions of dick-watching in the baths. Nineteenth-century reports suggest that European vapour baths, found in all the major capitals, were the most popular place for both lesbians and gay men to encounter one another. In the sexual renaissance that was American gay culture in the 1970s, bathhouses occupied a place of almost religious significance, with cubicles and silent corridors full of greased-up and available men. Certain baths, such as the Everards in New York and the ones at Eighth and Howard in San Francisco, became legendary as a place of relief for men who 'had a case of the vapours'. With the advent of AIDS bathhouses came under particular attack, and many city authorities closed them down, often with the support of gay activists who denounced the bathhouse owners as profiting from the crisis which was afflicting the gay community. Few seemed to understand that if many men were having sex in the same place it was much easier to reach them with safer-sex education materials.

Battersea'd Infected with venereal disease. The word was popular in the eighteenth century, and referred to the fact that the London district of Battersea was a locale where a number of medicinal herbs were grown which might be used to treat the pox. It appears in some of the trial records that followed the purging of the MOLLY HOUSES.

Bayezid I (1347–1403) Ottoman Emperor who sent his soldiers to search the newly conquered lands for boys for his harem. Following his example, pederasty spread among soldiers, government officials, and the aristocracy generally.

BBWG *See* BRIXTON BLACK WOMEN'S GROUP.

BD Abbreviation of BULLDYKE.

BD Women's Blues 1920s blues song, sung by lesbian blues performer Bessie Jackson. The BD stood for bulldyke, and Jackson declared that women could do quite easily without men, 'Comin' a time, BD women, they ain't goin' to need no men.' The BD woman was a common figure in blues songs of the time.

bean queen (US sl.) Term of dubious political correctness for a non-Latino man who is attracted primarily to Latinos. Refers to the beans which figure highly in Hispanic cuisine. *See also* DINGE QUEEN; RICE QUEEN; SNOW QUEEN.

beat Slang term for cruising ground, used in both America and Australia.

beauty contests In the 1970s they were anathema to the radical feminist as well as the lesbian and gay movement, for peddling the restrictive idea of objectified womanhood in the most humiliating circumstances. The London GAY LIBERATION FRONT joined a protest against the Miss World ceremony outside the Albert Hall in 1970, which they called the Miss Used zap. Since then, the gay male community would appear to have forgotten its political objections to such objectifying ceremonies. Mr Gay UK competitions are held annually in gay clubs throughout Britain, and drag contests also mimic the beauty contest proceedings, although some such as the ALTERNATIVE MISS WORLD send up the genre.

beloved disciple New Testament figure most often associated with St JOHN THE EVANGELIST, he is also taken to be the nameless disciple whom 'Jesus loved' and who leant on his breast during the Last Supper. Scanty evidence perhaps, but it has been enough to spark off a longstanding rumour that the relationship between Christ and John was one of an erotic nature. This rumour is documented historically as having been repeated by both Christopher MARLOWE and JAMES I.

belt buckle On the American LEATHER scene of the 1950s, gay men were developing prototypical codes to communicate their sexual preferences to men they were cruising, which were to become far more elaborated with the HANKIE CODES of the 1970s. Belt buckles were a good first choice since

they could be pushed to the left or right to indicate who was a TOP and who a BOTTOM.

Benson The protagonist of Michael Carson's bestselling comic novels *Sucking Sherbet Lemons*, *Stripping Penguins Bare* and *Yanking Up the Yo-Yo*. The novels represent what *The Times* called a 'gay, Roman Catholic, Bildungsroman' (*see* COMING OUT NOVEL). They describe Benson's Catholic background, his life in a Catholic seminary, his dawning (and not guilt-free) acceptance of his sexuality, and his erotic adventures thereafter.

Bent Play by Martin Sherman, written in 1979 for the British lesbian and gay theatre company, GAY SWEATSHOP. It enjoyed huge worldwide success, indicating the thoroughgoing changes that were taking place on the English-speaking stage in terms of the acceptability of lesbian and gay subject matter. The play is notable for its treatment of gays during the HOLOCAUST, an often obscured subject. It depicts the gay life of Berlin in 1934, and the hellish existence which awaited gay men in concentration camps, such as Dachau, to which they were condemned. However, despite the tragedy, the play presents the love between its two protagonists, Max and Horst, as a spirit of resistance and a force that enables humanity to thrive in the face of degradation and death. In showing how the character of Max pretends to be straight to avoid getting the feared PINK TRIANGLE badge, the play also explores the attractions of closetedness. When he ultimately accepts the pink triangle it demonstrates the necessity of eschewing the closet for one's own integrity and self-respect. Thus the play bears relevance to lesbians and gay men of all ages.

Bentley, Gladys (1907–60) Lesbian transvestite Harlem entertainer of the HARLEM RENAISSANCE, who appeared in male evening dress, sometimes under the stage name of Bobby Minton. She appeared in the popular Harlem nightspot, the Clam House and at Barbara's Exclusive Club which she later opened. She also caused a storm by trying to marry a woman in the

American city of Atlanta. Sadly, after hormone treatments, she eventually 'became' heterosexual and distanced herself from her past.

berdache The word is most commonly associated with the particular insitution common to many traditional Native American tribes of individuals of both sexes who dressed in clothes that were considered appropriate to the opposite sex and who frequently engaged in sexual relations with people of their own biological gender. The word was actually derived from a Persian word referring to a male slave, and was imported into the European Romance languages as a term for a passive partner in anal sex between men. It was attributed to native-American TRANSVESTITES by French colonialists. The degree to which a person would appropriate the role of the opposite sex varied from case to case and tribe to tribe, but in the most complete cases the berdache would take up the occupations of the other gender and would take wives or husbands of their own sex. The most common reason for people to become berdaches was said to be because a goddess/god appeared to them in a dream instructing them to take up the role. For this reason, and also because of the special knowledge of both genders that berdaches possessed, they were often revered as above the ordinary, and many were called upon as healers or SHAMANS. They seem to have been accepted in a number of Native American tribes. Among the Sioux they were known as *winkta*, among the NAVAJO they were called *nadle*, and female berdaches in the MOHAVE tribes were known as *hwame*, whilst male ones were *hanos*. Among the KAMIA they were known as *warhami*. Many other tribes had specific names for their berdaches. With the tensions that were attendant on the destruction of their societies by colonialists, many tribes repudiated their traditions of gender swapping, and Native American communities have not always been the most tolerant places for lesbians and gay men. In the late twentieth century, however, groups such as GAY AMERICAN INDIAN have worked to re-examine the Native American tradition for lesbians and gay men, and American writers such as Paula Gunn Allen have brought attention to the fact that, far from being un-American, homosexuality is part of the heritage of the continent.

Berlin We have descriptions of lesbian and gay subcultures in the German city from the eighteenth and nineteenth centuries, and Xavier Mayne wrote in 1908 in THE INTERSEXES about assemblies and balls in German cities 'attended by the best element in female AESTHETIC life'. However, it was the period of the Weimar republic which firmly put the city in the annals of lesbian and gay folklore. During these years a burgeoning lesbian and gay social scene was complemented by the growth of a political movement, through the work of activist Magnus HIRSCHFIELD. The heady delights of the city of the time are demonstrated in Christopher Isherwood's Berlin stories, and by Russian film director Sergei Eisenstein, 'I was fascinated by Berlin...every kind of sexual deviation... this underworld of sexuality.' The period was drawn to an end by the rise of the Nazis, and the beginnings of the HOLOCAUST.

Bermondsey The London parliamentary constituency which gay activist Peter TATCHELL fought for the Labour Party in the by-election of February 1983. It became a by-word for the kind of homophobic vitriol of which the British press is capable. As a British-born but Australian-educated gay man with left-wing integrity (unlike many in the new-look Labour Party), he was the wet dream of tabloid bigotry. The nocturnal emissions of homophobia, xenophobia ('Red Aussie pouf') and commie-bashing from the press stained the news stands daily. And it didn't stop there. In what commentators described as the most violent by-election this century, Tatchell received thousands of hate letters and some thirty explicit death threats, while 'Tatchell is a communist pouf' was daubed in three-foot-high letters throughout the constituency. Ten thousand anonymous leaflets were distributed asking 'Which queen will you vote for?' as well as juxtaposing a picture of Tatchell with that of Elizabeth R, repository of all that is British (and straight). Throughout, Tatchell received no police protection. In this nadir of British democracy, it is not surprising that Tatchell lost, and the Liberals took the seat.

beso negro US Latino slang for rimming. In Spanish, it literally means a black kiss.

best friend *See* FRIEND.

Beth and Margaret They were the first 'lesbians' with leading parts in a British soap opera when their friendship developed into something more in 1993. Channel Four's *Brookside*, which depicts the mean and gritty life on a Liverpool housing estate, outraged the moral majority by showing a passionate kiss between the two young and pretty women at 8.30 p.m. – before the 'watershed' time of nine o'clock. The excitement of British lesbians at this innovative storyline was, as can be imagined, huge. Most debates have centred on whether Beth is more fanciable than Margaret, or indeed whether Chris, Beth's lecturer and ultimate seducer, is raunchier still.

Bethnal Rouge Early 1970s gay commune and bookshop which was located in offices in London's Bethnal Green district. Its members were part of London's GAY LIBERATION FRONT.

Better Angel 1933 novel by Forman Brown, writing under the nom de plume of Richard Meeker. It depicts the (successful) search by a young gay man for same-sex satisfaction. It was exceptional for its time in presenting a positive protagonist and a happy ending without the queer suicide which seemed almost obligatory for creative works with a lesbian or gay content.

better blatant than latent Gay rights slogan of the 1970s.

Bieris de Romans French Provençale female troubadour, or poet-musician, who lived in the thirteenth century. Her work is remarkable not just because she wrote love poetry to women, but because she did not feel constrained to adopt a male persona for her authorial voice.

Bifrost Name of a contemporary British group for bisexuals. It is taken from Scandinavian mythology, where it was the name of a rainbow bridge which linked Asgard (heaven) and Midgard (earth). It was said to be composed of precious stones which created the different colours. Thus the name serves as a metaphor for the role bisexuality has in linking heterosexuality and homosexuality, which are too often seen as discrete.

Bildungsroman *See* COMING OUT NOVEL.

Bilitis Fictional contemporary of the Greek poet SAPPHO, and imaginary author of the hoax anthology LES CHANSONS DE BILITIS.

binabae Vernacular term used in the Philippines to refer to males who do not conform in a variety of ways to gender stereotypes, through either dress, labour, or sexual object choice. Also known as bayot. *See* BINALAKI.

binalaki Tagalog term used in the Philippines, of recent coinage, used to refer to a wide range of identities for women who diverge from norms of gender behaviour, such as homosexuality, transvestism, hermaphroditism and lesbianism. The use of the term is similar to that of berdache in anthropological literature. Also known as lakin-on. Binalaki and lakin-on perform labour thought appropriate to men. The equivalent for males is BINABAE.

birkenstocks Particular kind of chunky moulded sandal that in the 1980s became the de rigueur footwear for American lesbians in particular, and gay men. Illustrative of the 'comfy shoe' paradigm of lesbian and gay footwear.

bisexuality Descriptive of a person who is erotically attracted to either biological gender. The concept of a person whose sexual identity is composed of such a dual attraction (rather than someone who gives in to the sin of sodomy) originated with the classificatory work of the nineteenth-century sexologists. Richard von KRAFFT-EBING and Havelock ELLIS talked of people with 'psychical (or psycho-sexual) hermaphroditism' who, according to Ellis, 'found sexual satisfaction with their own and the opposite sex'. Yet at this time the term that was used to refer to such people was HETEROSEXUAL. It wasn't until the late 1910s that the term 'bisexualist' or 'bisexual' appeared in the medical literature and began to be used as a standard term. In a society in which there was such a strong dualism between heterosexuality and homosexuality, it was difficult to conceive of bisexuality as a distinct identity. In talking of the POLYMORPHOUS PERVERSE, Sigmund FREUD seemed to imply that human sexuality started off in a state of original bisexuality, and Ellis flirted with the idea. But it wasn't until the reports of Alfred KINSEY were published that much credence was given to the idea that a large number of people might have had sexual experiences with members of both sexes. It would appear natural that bisexuals would be included in the programme of the lesbian and gay movement, and in some ways they represent the ideal of many lesbian and gay groups of a world without sexual classification, but this has not always been the case. Although there have been periods when there has been a fashion for bisexual experimentation (*see* LESBIAN CHIC), these have tended to be in bohemian circles, while lesbian and gay political groups have tended at best to ignore bisexuals and at worst to condemn them as politically incorrect. Those lesbians who came to lesbianism through the lesbian feminist movement considered themselves as having chosen lesbianism, rather than having uncovered the bisexual side of their sexuality, and bisexual women were criticized within lesbian feminism for only half-heartedly confronting patriarchy. Bisexual men fared little better among gay male communities, and those gay men who had been influenced by feminist thinking condemned them as 'another form of phallic imperialism – just another adventure in the quest for assistance in

masturbation' (John Stoltenberg) while others considered them as weak-kneed gays who didn't have the courage to admit their (homo)sexuality. As recently as the late 1980s, some lesbian and gay organizations (such as the lesbian and gay conference of the British National Union of Students) excluded bisexuals on the grounds that the possibility of being desired by a member of the opposite sex represented an invasion of the lesbian and gay 'safe space'. Meanwhile, although some people did call themselves bisexual in order to be more acceptable to straight society, for the majority of heterosexuals bisexuals were queer enough to be undesirable. It was only in the 1980s that bisexuals started to organize effectively by themselves. At the same time, many lesbians and gays were rethinking their attitude to bisexuality, with some QUEER theorists such as Peter TATCHELL arguing that (practically) universal bisexuality was the goal of the queer movement – that once the distortions of homophobia are abolished most people will be able to enjoy sexual relations with members of either gender. Meanwhile, some lesbians and gays have begun to extol the pleasures of sex with one another. While such experimentation is still relatively uncommon, there is the chance that the century-old, rigid, three-way categorization of homo-hetero-bi is beginning to break down.

bit a blow This slang term was used in the verb form in the MOLLY subculture of the eighteenth century to mean to succeed in pulling a trick. Another expression was to make a bargain, a seemingly self-explanatory metaphor where, according to Grose's *Classical Dictionary of the Vulgar Tongue*, the term actually derives from a popular, and not apparently intellectual, game known as selling a bargain. In the game one partner had to name their ass in answer to the question What?.

bitch (1) Used as a pejorative term by men for women who are perceived as being just a little too independent or quick-witted for them. Usually decried by feminists, though some have attempted to reclaim the word as a term for a woman who refuses to conform to society's expectation of her. According to Joreen's 1970 *Bitch Manifesto*, 'Bitches are good examples of how women can be strong enough to survive'. (2) Described by John SYMONDS as a term in use at Harrow School to 'indicate a boy who yielded his person to a lover'.

Black Cat Bar in San Francisco. In the 1940s it became the skipping ground for legendary gay activist Jose SARRIA, who began to cover for his boyfriend who worked there. On one occasion the pianist was tickling tunes from Bizet's *Carmen* on the ivories, and Sarria began to sing the arias as he served; he became an instant hit. But Sarria also took a pastoral interest in the clientele. He gave information on police entrapment campaigns in the parks where the men cruised. 'A blue fungus has hit the parks...it twinkles like a star,' he would announce, and he attempted to raise the men's spirits with the clarion calls of 'There's nothing wrong with being gay – the crime is getting caught' and 'United we stand, divided they catch us one by one.' He would end the evening by calling the men into a circle to sing 'God Save Us Nelly Queens', and then corral them outside to the jail across the road where queens who had been caught were imprisoned so that they could sing up and buck up those inside. Such activity didn't endear him to the police, and in 1949 the authorities attempted to close the Black Cat down because it was a place for 'persons of known homosexual tendencies' to meet. However, after a campaign by the bar's owners and clientele, the California Supreme Court ruled that these were not adequate grounds for denying a bar a licence. Yet this didn't end police harassment, and the city's bars had to set up a network to warn each other if plain-clothes officers were on the prowl. Nevertheless, by 1963 the endless harassment had proved too much for the bar owner, and he quit. A campaign to keep the bar open failed, and the bar closed the day after HALLOWE'EN 1963. Moving in for the kill, the police closed another five bars within a week of the end of the Black Cat.

black hankie On the queer scene, a black hankie is worn to indicate interest in leather/sadomasochism. Thus a black hankie worn on the left indicates a leather TOP, and on the right a BOTTOM. *See* HANKIE CODES.

Black HIV/AIDS Network British organization, founded in 1989, to provide home and community care services for black people living with HIV and AIDS, as well as support for carers, families and friends. It also runs a multilingual counselling service.

black leather jacket *See* LEATHER.

Black Lesbian Support Network The network was formed at the *We Are Here* conference of black feminists held in the UK in 1984. The conference was a public statement of the existence of black women as black feminists, and welcomed black lesbians. The network existed to provide advice and support for black women who were exploring their sexuality, as well as to collate information on black lesbians. It folded in 1986.

Black Lesbians and Gays against the Media (BLAGAMH) British organization that was set up in 1990 to monitor and challenge the representation of black lesbians and gays in the media. One of its most successful campaigns was against the homophobia in *The Voice*, Britain's leading black newspaper, especially after it had printed attacks on Justin Fashanu, a British black footballer who had come out as gay, and reports that American singer Whitney Houston was not a 'lesbo'. After a boycott, BLAGAMH was allowed a right-to-reply, and the paper agreed to enforce an equal opportunities policy regarding lesbians and gay men.

black triangle The black triangle badge was worn by some prisoners in concentration camps in Nazi Germany as a symbol of antisocial behaviour. Although lesbianism was not brought within the remit of PARA-GRAPH 175, a number of lesbians were apparently sent to the camps and were forced to wear this badge. The lesbian and gay movement has therefore taken up the black triangle as the counterpart of the PINK TRIANGLE worn by gay men. *See also* HOLOCAUST.

blackmailer's charter Nickname given to the LABOUCHERE AMENDMENT.

Black/Out Biannual American magazine for lesbians and gay men of colour, which carries the usual range of news, reviews and fiction. It was founded in 1986 and has a circulation of some 2,500 copies.

Blade American pornographer of the 1940s and 1950s, who produced erotic drawings as well as stories. In order to avoid any criminal investigations, he would seal his work in unmarked packages and deposit them either in gay bars or in lockers in bus stations. Locker keys would be passed from one consumer to the next to ensure security.

BLAGAMH *See* BLACK LESBIANS AND GAYS AGAINST THE MEDIA.

Blakk, Joan Jett The first official QUEER NATION candidate in Chicago's mayoral election of April 1991. A drag queen whose slogan, among others, was 'putting the camp into campaign', her main election strategy was to go on public shopping sprees in the boutiques of Chicago's well-heeled Gold Coast district.

BLK Los Angeles-based monthly magazine for black lesbians and gay men. Founded in 1988, it has a circulation of some 36,000 copies and carries news, features and art.

Blondel *See* RICHARD I.

Blood Money 1933 film directed by Rowland Brown and featuring Sandra Shaw as a partying blonde who enjoys wearing men's clothes. Although seen early on in the film waiting for her boyfriend, she is wearing full tuxedo and monocle at the time, and she later appears escorting another woman.

Bloolips British drag entertainment troupe, founded by the marvellous queen Bette Bourne in the early 1970s. Bette had been involved with the Notting Hill Street Theatre Group which was active within the London GAY LIBERATION FRONT, and the Bloolips style owed much to the RADICAL DRAG and the political theatre of that group.

Bloomsbury group Name given to the group of intellectuals, artists and writers who began to coalesce in London in 1904 around the Bloomsbury home of Clive and Vanessa Bell in Gordon Square, and of Virginia and Adrian Stephen in Fitzroy Square. The group included such figures as the writer Lytton Strachey who revolutionized the art of biography, Duncan Grant the artist, the economist Maynard Keynes, Leonard Woolf, Virginia Stephen (who subsequently married Woolf), and the Bells. It was known at the time for its championing of the progressive art movement of post-Impressionism, and of a freer intellectual, social and sexual expression which had been stymied by the re-imposition of Victorian puritanism after the WILDE TRIALS. The lifestyles of the members were similarly nonconformist, and they scandalized society by the free association between men and women, and by the dubiously close relationships between the men of the group. There were sexual relationships between Grant and Keynes as well as between Grant and Strachey. Lytton Strachey, who had long been aware of his gayness, had argued from his days in the Cambridge APOSTLES against the strictures of Victorian sexual morality, and wrote in somewhat exaggerated terms, 'The only hope of our ever getting a really beautiful and vigorous and charming civilization is to allow the world to fuck and bugger and abuse themselves in public and generally misbehave to their heart's content.' The group was first named the Bloomsbury group by the wife of Desmond MacCarthy, one of their number.

blow Verb, recorded as early as the 1930s, meaning to perform oral sex on a man – also called, more accurately, sucking someone off. Since the 1960s the term blow job has been used to refer to the act of fellatio. A number of derivatives come from blow job. A hum job is a blow job when the blower hums to create a stimulating vibration on the dick. An ice job is a blow job performed with ice or ice cream in the mouth.

Blue 1993 film by British filmmaker Derek JARMAN which served as a vehicle for him to express the many thoughts and feelings he experienced while living with AIDS. A moving account of a courageous journey, the film has no visuals other than an unchanging blue screen, so all attention is focused on his words.

blue discharge The kind of dishonourable discharge that lesbians and gay men received if they were found guilty of homosexual activity in the American armed forces. It was so called because of the blue piece of paper, stamped with a large H, on which the discharge was written.

blue ribbon *See* RED RIBBON.

blues The music form was derived from the songs of lament of black communities in the American south, from where it also got its name. But its presentation as music served to convey a black sense of style, strength and self-worth despite the best efforts of a racist society to destroy them. As the blues singer Alberta Hunter put it, 'We sing the blues because our hearts have been hurt, our souls have been destroyed. But when you sing the blues, let it be classy.' For this reason it has been appreciated by lesbian and gay audiences who are similarly trying to hold on to their self-worth in homophobic societies. In addition, the blues of the early twentieth century was often the musical hallmark of more accepting communities for both black and white lesbians and gays, such as in the HARLEM RENAISSANCE. Nonconforming sexualities often formed the lyrical content of the songs; for instance songs such as 'Sissy Man Blues', 'Fairy Blues', 'Two Old Maids In A Folding Bed', and BD WOMAN'S BLUES were an accepted part of the blues repertoire. Many of the black women performers of the early twentieth century, apart from maintaining their dignity in the face of a double oppression, also projected an androgynous gender image (*see for example* BENTLEY, GLADYS; RAINEY, MA).

blues parties House parties, with DJs, sound system and bar, which originate from the African-Caribbean heterosexual community, but which since the 1970s have become popular social events for British black lesbians, in response to the lack of other social venues for black lesbians.

bluestocking Usually contemptuous term for any woman who devotes her life to academic pursuits rather than upholding a traditionally restrictive feminine lifestyle. The name is derived from the group of men and women who met around 1750 at the home of English author Elizabeth Montagu and included a Benjamin Stillingfleet who always wore blue stockings. Many women have proudly reclaimed the label in recognition of a heritage of women who pioneered entry into traditional male domains.

Bluff New York lesbian slang of the 1950s and 1960s used to refer to KIKI women, who refused to adopt either the butch or femme role. A combination of BUTCH and FLUFF.

Boadicea (d. AD 62) British Queen of the Iceni tribe, located in latterday Norfolk, who led the biggest British revolt against the Roman invaders in the first century AD, after the death of her husband in AD 61. Her army razed the Roman settlements at St Albans, Colchester and London before she was finally defeated by Suetonius Paulinus. She torched the city of London, causing a huge conflagration. She reportedly swallowed poison rather than allow herself to be captured alive. Some lesbian historians have suggested that the historical etymology of the term BULLDYKE is in Boadicea's name. Whatever the historical validity of this claim, it indicates the symbolic power for lesbians of this warrior queen.

body of friends Term that Edward CARPEN-TER used to describe his vision of the kind of supportive network that lesbians and gays could form with one another. Compare with Harry HAY's CIRCLE OF LOVING COMPANIONS.

Body Positive British self-help organization founded in 1985 which provides support and welfare services for people who have been diagnosed as HIV-positive. There are various groups throughout the country. In contrast to America, British organizations concerned with HIV and AIDS have always tended to focus on the point of HIV diagnosis, rather than on the onset of symptoms associated with AIDS-related conditions.

Bom-Crioulo Brazilian novel, published in 1896 by the writer Adolfo Caminha. It told the story of an interracial gay affair. The book was one of the first published works to deal openly with gay relationships.

bomber jacket Fashion item with a physique built in! The bomber jacket gives anyone a bulky look despite a muscularity that might not exactly bring the sweaty air of the gym to mind. They have been on the scene since the CLONES worked on the military look in San Francisco of the mid-1970s and, despite their ups and downs and colour changes, they have been with us ever since.

bona From the British gay slang POLARI, meaning good or attractive.

Bona Dea Roman goddess worshipped solely by women. Historian Helen Diner writes of certain 'lesbian practices' at rites in her honour.

Bond movies Not suggesting that the talented Roger Moore became a gay pin-up, Sean Connery maybe, but Bond almost met his nemesis in the form of Colonel Rosa Klebb, the fabulous dyke spy played by Lotte Lenya in *From Russia with Love* (1963). Klebb almost finishes off our man after aiming a spike-tipped shoe at his crotch, when she is finished off herself by a young woman agent she had earlier tried to seduce. In *Goldfinger* (1964) Pussy Galore is a lesbian surrounded by an entourage of beautiful amazons. She is 'cured' by Bond. Very likely.

bondage and discipline Used to describe erotic play in which the submissive partner is tied up and disciplined. Related to SADOMASOCHISM, though often less intense.

Bonney, Anne (1697–?) The daughter of a wealthy lawyer, Bonney was a tomboy through her early years, and frequented the portside taverns in her hometown of Charleston in South Carolina, America. Having been disinherited by her father, she set fire to the family plantation and fled to the port of New Providence. Bonney eventually became the most notorious female pirate of the eighteenth century. On one occasion she and her accomplices are reported to have frightened a merchant ship into surrender merely by setting up a ghoulish tableau on their own ship. They covered the deck and sail with animal blood, and she stood on deck with an axe coated in blood. She sailed the seas with her accomplice Mary Read, known as Mark, whose mother had dressed her as a boy when young and given her her dead brother's name in order to ensure an inheritance. She took to the role with much gusto, and eventually found herself at sea as well. Reports suggest that the two were physically intimate, and through their exploits they remained inseparable, although both women were married several times. Despite being caught and convicted for piracy in 1720 the two escaped hanging by pleading pregnancy. Mary however died of an illness she caught whilst in jail, whilst Anne disappeared from historical records thereafter.

Book of the Planet Venus Collection of poetry by the Arab writer Ibn Da'ud who lived in Baghdad during the ninth century, and who developed the poetic content of 'odhritic love' named after a particular Arab tribe. The genre stressed a neoplatonist ideal of denial of sexual pleasure in order to feel desire for a beloved all the more strongly. This desire was equally likely to be expressed towards one's own gender. Ibn Da'ud wrote, 'To love you better I want to remain unsatiated.' Thus the concept lends itself to an almost mystically spiritual expression of feeling. The collection is sometimes known as the *Book of the Flower*.

Bookpeople 1970s American book distribution company which specialized in distributing the new women's books which were coming out of the feminist and lesbian feminist movements.

Boomerang Street Popular cruising ground of the early twentieth century in the Australian city of Sydney. It is situated near St Mary's Cathedral and legend has it that it was a popular haunt of gay clergy.

Bosie The nickname of Lord Alfred DOUGLAS.

Boston Lesbian Psychologies Collective Born out of the pioneering conference 'Lesbian Psychologies' attended by 500 women in 1984, the collective is dedicated to a feminist re-vision of the lesbian experience. It has produced the highly-respected anthology *Lesbian Psychologies – Explorations and Challenges* (1987) which addresses identity, relationships, therapies and community.

Boston marriage Name given on the east coast of America to household relationships where two women set up home together. These households started to appear in the mid-nineteenth century as women's education developed. It is estimated that roughly half of women graduates in this period never married. Marriage bars still existed in the vast majority of professions open to women, such as teaching so for women who wanted to use their education, marriage was not really an option. Moreover, for the first time it was possible for middle-class women to be economically independent of their families, and to be able to resist marriage. Boston marriages were seen as completely normal, providing companionship for women who had professional vocations, although they were not on a par with the

real (heterosexual) thing. The emotional commitment of these relationships was recognized, but the possibility of a sexual element was ignored. A famous but rather untypical portrait of a Boston marriage is contained in Henry James' THE BOSTONIANS.

The Bostonians Novel by Henry James (1843–1916), which described a BOSTON MARRIAGE between the Boston feminist Olive Chancellor and her pupil, the younger Verena Tarrant. We are told that the two 'love to be together; it seems as if one *couldn't* go out without the other.' The plot portrays the struggle between Olive and a man, her cousin Basil Ransom, for Verena's affections. While the anti-feminist Ransom wins, it is hinted that the heterosexual coupling will not be happy, and that Verena will not find the same fulfilment with him that she did under the influence of Olive's feminism. The novel was inspired by the story of James' sister Alice, who was reclusive and suffered from poor health. Alice eventually found an edifying relationship with a social activist, Katharine Loring, and her happiness delighted Henry and the rest of her family.

bottom Term for the passive partner in sex. It is most often used when talking about radical sexual activities such as SM, fisting, and bondage, and the bottom is the one who provides the body or orifice to be humiliated, restrained or fisted. Like TOPs, the role of bottom was taken very seriously within the SM scene of the 1950s, and there was little transference between the two roles. From the 1960s onwards there was an increased interest in the leather scene from those who were not necessarily very interested in heavy SM sex, and the rules of SM became diluted. In the 1950s bottoms were relatively scarce on the scene, but now the situation is reversed.

Boulton and Park affair Popular name given in nineteenth-century Britain to the arrest and trial of Ernest 'Stella' Boulton and Frederick 'Fanny' Park. Both were gay men who spent a large portion of their time in DRAG, which they wore while strolling around the streets of London. Indeed, on the day in April 1870 that they were arrested leaving a theatre, both were wearing satin frocks, Stella's low-cut in eye-catching crimson with white accessories while Fanny was sporting a more muted green. The police had taken an interest in the two for some time, mainly because Stella was the lover of Lord Arthur Clinton, son of the Duke of Newcastle and a Member of Parliament. Clinton was also arrested but died before the case came to trial. When their trial took place a year later, the two were acquitted of intent to commit a felony, namely buggery. This was because of the difficulty of demonstrating that the defendants actually engaged in anal sex, or intended to, despite stringent medical examinations. The acquittal demonstrated the difficulty of prosecuting gay offences under British law, and the reaction to it was partly responsible for the passing of the LABOUCHERE AMENDMENT fourteen years later.

bourgeois decadence The way in which communist regimes have characterized homosexuality. This means that, 'come the revolution', there will be no homosexuals. This is interesting for two reasons. First it links homosexuality with capitalism. Second, it is an example of how homosexuality has been constructed as 'foreign'; for the French, homosexuality is the *vice anglais*, while for the British it was seen as oriental and exotic – in working-class circles it was seen as posh, in upper-class circles it was seen as common, and so on.

Bowles, Sally Character in the Berlin stories of Christopher ISHERWOOD, a nightclub singer-cum-professional parasite. The film CABARET focused on the character of Sally, who was played by Liza Minnelli as a vulnerable torch singer with a protective shell of chutzpah and a cavalier facade towards life's sea of troubles.

bowling ball, to hold a A slang term for the sexual act between women in which one partner simultaneously stimulates the anus and clitoris of the other through

using her thumb and index finger. Also known as making SCISSORS of someone.

Boy George (real name George O'Dowd, 1961–) 1980s British pop phenomenon, who first shot to fame in 1982 when he and his band Culture Club topped the British charts with the single 'Do You Really Want To Hurt Me'. Culture Club rode high until George's conviction for drugs use in 1986. When he first appeared in the nation's living rooms on the television, he made a monumental impact, with impeccable SLAP and flowing effeminate clothing (though not feminine; he never wore full-length frocks, rather long shift affairs). He became the leading figure in 1980s gender-bending (*see* GENDER FUCK). The shock was, however, always in the way he looked, and not what he said. He was never upfront about his gay sexuality, and claimed to prefer a cup of tea to sex, although the nation never really swallowed the asexual/bisexual claims. George did not become self-consciously political until the late 1980s when he campaigned against CLAUSE 28. Nonetheless, he had a tremendous influence on many gay men who through him were able to play with the gender images they themselves projected.

A Boy's Own Story 1982 novel by gay author Edmund White. It is the coming-out novel par excellence, and has been handed to many parents whose child has just COME OUT to them. It is popular among gay men since it depicts that slow coming together of sexuality, emotional and intellectual life into an intelligible whole that has come to most of us at one time or other.

The Boys in the Band Play by Mart Crowley which opened off-Broadway in April 1968, and was adapted by Crowley as a film version in 1970. It deals with the tensions between a group of eight gay men and a straight (or is he?) former classmate as they gather for the birthday of one of their number. It functions as a link between pre- and post-GAY LIBERATION theatre, in that it portrays a gay community, rather than the tribulations of just one gay character. It also deals with the knotty problem of monogamy, as one character (Larry) challenges heterosexual paradigms of fidelity and talks of creating a relationship with 'respect for one another's freedom, with no need to lie or pretend'. However, in the main its characters are suffused with the guilt and self-hatred that results from the stuffy air of the closet. They spend much of the evening demolishing one another through cutting comments and sadistic party games, and all this self-torture makes it wear thin rather quickly. Despite this, it has remained popular with gay audiences due to its sharp dialogue.

Brandstetter, Dave Fictional Los Angeles insurance agent and sleuth (what a combination!) who has appeared in the detective novels *Fadeout, Nightwork* and *The Man Everybody Was Afraid Of* by writer Joseph Hanson. He has lived with several male lovers.

Breaking the Code Play by Hugh Whitemore first staged at the Haymarket theatre in London in 1986. It told the story of Alan Turing, one of the many gay victims of government homophobia and cold war hysteria. Turing (1912–54), a Cambridge-trained mathematician, broke two codes. During the Second World War he was employed by British intelligence services at Bletchley Park where he was instrumental in cracking Enigma, the German secret codes, which allowed British forces to gain in-depth knowledge of German plans, and helped bring the war to an end. Government showed little gratitude. When Turing reported his lover Arnold Murray to the police on suspicion of burglary, he let them know that they had been having a sexual relationship. As a result, he was prosecuted for gross indecency, and was forced either to accept a prison sentence or to undergo hormone therapy. He chose the hormones, and began to suffer disruption to his mental faculties as well as growing breasts. He committed suicide by eating a cyanide-coated apple, a form of death he apparently devised so his mother could believe

it had been an accident. The degree of complicity the British intelligence services had in his demise is a question of debate. At best his wartime contributions were classified, and could not be revealed in his defence in court. At worst the Government wanted him out of the way because of a cold war fear that he might reveal government secrets to his partners.

breeches-clad bawd In eighteenth-century England a bawd referred to a sex-worker and, by extension, any woman who did not take on the traditional female role. Thus a bawd who was breeches-clad and who was therefore wearing trousers could refer to either a male sex-worker or a PASSING WOMAN.

breeder As a word for heterosexual, it functions as an ironic commentary on the often declared argument that lesbian or gay sex is somehow unnatural because it does not lead to conception and implies that, while lesbians and gay men provide the world with wit and creativity, the production of children is the only really useful role of heterosexuality. The word has a long history in this meaning. It was used by some NEW WOMEN in the early twentieth century to refer to the role of wife and mother which they were expected to fulfil and which they were rejecting in favour of professional advancement. For example, in the novel SIND ES FRAUEN? one woman declares that women like her are willing to take on the label of INVERT as long as it gives them their 'own intellectual and physical freedom and also preserve for ourselves, who aren't breeders, our human rights'. By the 1980s the word was common currency among radical lesbian and gay activists who were critical of heterosexual institutions such as the FAMILY and who used the term, with a nod at the problems of global overpopulation, to indicate that QUEER people understand that there is more to life than procreation.

Briggs initiative Proposition which was put to the ballot in California in 1978 by State Congressman John Briggs. Also known as Proposition 6, it sought to exclude anyone who 'advocates, solicits, imposes, encourages, or promotes' homosexuality from teaching in the public school system. California lesbians and gay men set up the NEW ALLIANCE FOR GAY EQUALITY, and led a successful campaign which resulted in the proposition being comprehensively rejected. The campaign showed lesbian and gay communities the potential power of flexing the queer muscle.

Brinker, Beebo Recurrent protagonist of the series of five lesbian romance books by Ann Bannon published in the 1950s and 1960s: *Odd Girl Out; I Am a Woman; Women in the Shadows; Journey to a Woman;* and *Beebo Brinker.* The novels were phenomenally successful – *Odd Girl Out* was the second best-selling American paperback in 1957 – which is somewhat bemusing for a period in which lesbian and gay communities were more stringently policed than before. Not that their significance wasn't realized; according to Joan NESTLE, 'Buying an Ann Bannon book in the 1950s was tantamount to coming out yourself.' But lesbians bought them because they were one of the few easily accessible ways to gain an acknowledgement of their existence. Yet, since the STONEWALL RIOT, lesbian-feminist critics have tended to criticize them as gloomy and overly influenced by the patriarchal false consciousness of romance.

Brisbane The eastern Australian port, now capital of Queensland, was founded in 1822 as a penal colony. Its inhabitants were composed almost entirely of those who had been convicted of practising the 'sins of the cities of the plain'. Must have been quite a place. The capital of New South Wales, SYDNEY, was also famous for its gomorrhan goings-on.

British Sexological Society *See* BRITISH SOCIETY FOR THE STUDY OF SEX PSYCHOLOGY.

British Society for the Study of Sex Psychology British organization founded in 1914, to provide education and disseminate scientific 'knowledge' about sex and sexuality. Its remit was described as 'to organize understanding in the lay mind on a larger scale, to make people more recep-

tive to scientific proof, and more conscious of their social responsibility'. Its first president was Edward CARPENTER. Although disrupted in its early work by the outbreak of the First World War, in the 1920s the society began to hold monthly talks, and published them in pamphlet form. It changed its name to the British Sexological Society. Although the influence of its work was largely limited to intellectual circles, for the period until it folded in the mid-1930s it was the only British organization concerned with the issue.

Brixton Black Women's Group (BBWG) Founded in 1973, it met in London at the Brixton Black Women's Centre which existed to provide advice, space and support for black women. It drew black women in from both the WOMEN'S LIBERATION MOVEMENT and the black liberation movement who wanted to find a space where the issues of feminism and black liberation could be combined. Many of the founding members were lesbians, although they found the issue of sexuality was not a high priority. The Centre was closed in 1986. The BBWG was prominent in the creation of the ORGANIZATION OF WOMEN OF AFRICAN AND ASIAN DESCENT.

Brixton Faeries British community group which evolved out of the south London GAY LIBERATION FRONT and which produced political theatre, such as a radical gay interpretation of the scandal which had overtaken Jeremy Thorpe, the leader of the British Liberal Party from 1967 to 1972, entitled *Minehead Revisited.*

Bronski Beat The first big-time and openly gay pop group in the UK, composed of Jimi SOMERVILLE, Larry Steinbeck and Steve Bronski. They released their album *Age of Consent* in 1984 which was adorned with the PINK TRIANGLE on the front and the various AGES OF CONSENT of European countries on the back. It was quite an eye-opener for some (it was for me, since I realized I was legal just about everywhere apart from my own nation). Their hits, all sung in a sometime scrotum-tightening falsetto by Somerville, further banged home some elements of the gay experience. 'Smalltown Boy' (and its accompanying video) dealt with provincial narrow-mindedness and QUEERBASHING. It reminded the (gay) listener that 'the answers you seek will never be found at home'. An encounter between the bashee and another man on a train in the video seems to hold out the hope that things are likely to be far better in the city. 'Tell Me Why?' was a statement of gay incomprehension at HOMOPHOBIA, and their version of 'It Ain't Necessarily So' was particularly timely in the decade when compassionate ministers were declaring that AIDS was God's punishment. After leaving the group, Somerville went on to more success in his new coupling, 'The Communards'.

Brooks, Romaine Goddard (1874–1970) American artist who settled in Paris and became one of the central figures in the circle of expatriate lesbian artists and writers that lived in the city at the beginning of the twentieth century, including Gertrude STEIN, Alice B. TOKLAS, Djuna BARNES and Natalie BARNEY, with whom she had a relationship that lasted some fifty years. Eschewing the modernist movements, Brooks is best remembered for her contribution to portrait painting, including one of Una Troubridge, the lover of Radclyffe HALL, which projected an androgynous quality.

brown In the gay male HANKIE CODE and in CONTACT ADVERTS, brown refers to the practice of SCAT.

Brown, Rita Mae (1944–) American lesbian activist and writer, Rita Mae has had a finger in most of the many pies of the US lesbian movement. In the late 1960s she became a member of the STUDENT HOMOPHILE LEAGUE chapter at New York University, but finding it too male dominated she left for the NATIONAL ORGANIZATION FOR WOMEN. Not that she found acceptance there, either. Whenever she brought up the subject of lesbianism, she was met with a strained silence, and little support from women who considered lesbianism the LAVENDER MENACE. Although

she was editor of the national newsletter, tensions with other officers led to her being relieved of her duties, but this was not without her putting out a final issue blasting the leadership for its sexist, racist and class-biased attitudes. She briefly joined the REDSTOCKINGS, but again left because of its unwillingness to take on lesbian issues: 'I became the token lesbian once more'. After the STONEWALL RIOT, Rita Mae became active in the GAY LIBERATION FRONT, working within it to ensure representation for lesbians and, among the lesbians in the group, to raise consciousness of their oppression as women. She was also a member of the Washington-based FURIES collective. Rita Mae is equally well-known for her writing, RUBYFRUIT JUNGLE (1973) being one of the classics of lesbian literature. She has published six other novels, and has worked on television and film screenplays, co-writing *The Long Hot Summer* in 1987. In 1982 she moved back to Virginia.

The Brown Family US slang of the 1940s meaning the gay subculture and community. The origins are uncertain, but might refer to the practice of anal sex.

Bryant, Anita (1940–) Virulent American homophobe. Singer and orange juice promoter, she took it upon her pious shoulders to save the American nation from the threat of perversion. She founded the Save Our Children Campaign, and led a campaign in 1977 to repeal a gay rights ordinance in Dade County, Florida, which gave lesbians and gay men protection in employment and housing. She sparked off a massive coming together among lesbians and gay men to fight her, and a queer boycott of orange juice was maintained until her contract was cancelled with orange juice producers. Unfortunately, the ordinance was repealed in June 1977. Bryant was very much public enemy number one for lesbians and gay men in the 1970s, and has been subject to much vitriol. Entertainer Robin Tyler declared, 'Anita, you are to Christianity what paint-by-numbers is to art.' Chicago columnist Mike Royko wondered, 'If God dislikes gays so much, how come he picked Michelangelo, a known homosexual, to paint the Sistine Chapel ceiling while assigning Anita to go on TV and push orange juice?' Gore Vidal commented on her prowess at singing, 'The only people that might shoot Anita are music lovers.' She has also been subjected to attack of a more active nature (*see* ARMY OF LOVERS).

Bryher The pen-name by which the English novelist Annie Winifred Ellerman (1894–1983) is best known. Her works dealt with subject matter ranging from ancient Greece and Rome to the battle of Hastings and the seventeenth century in England. Bryher is also known for her relationship with the poet Hilda DOOLITTLE, and her front marriage to the British poet and publisher Robert McAlmon, who published some of Doolittle's work.

Buddies 1985 film directed by Arthur J. Bressan, which tells the story of a gay man who is dying from HIV-related infections, and how his BUDDY, provided for him by the local gay centre, copes with his illness and death. The sick man has spent most of his life engaged in political activity for the gay movement, and at first he doesn't like his otherwise apolitical GUPPY buddy. However, the relationship that the two develop demonstrates the way in which disparate elements of the gay community come together as a result of the AIDS epidemic.

buddy A person who voluntarily gives their time to befriend a person living with HIV or AIDS. Most AIDS SERVICE ORGANIZATIONS run buddying schemes whereby PWAs are assigned a volunteer who regularly visits them to chat, do the shopping, clean the home or do anything else. This is the form which most volunteer work for AIDS takes. It was especially crucial in the early years of the AIDS epidemic when societal hysteria about the syndrome meant that PWAs often found themselves rejected by friends and family (a scenario which is still all too common).

buddy films Heterosexual genre of film that usually depicts close friendships between straight men as a means of exploring homoaffectionality. The genre tends to make women expendable, except that *Thelma and Louise* might be seen as a female version of the oeuvre. Although queerness was virulently denied, any queen in the audience knew exactly what was going on. Take *Butch Cassidy and the Sundance Kid* for starters.

las buenas amigas Spanish for good friends, and used in American Latino communities as a euphemism for lesbian relationships. Also the name of a New York Latina lesbian group.

buffet flats Flats where sex circuses were exhibited for a paying audience in HARLEM in the 1920s. Often, these sex shows would be for a queer clientele.

buggers can't be choosers Perhaps apocryphal, but usually attributed to Sir Maurice Bowra (1898–1971), after he had decided to get married, and had chosen a girl, when a friend remonstrated that he 'couldn't marry anyone as plain as that'.

Buggers' Charter Slang reference to the 1957 WOLFENDEN REPORT.

buggery Anal sex between men. The term derives from the name of the country Bulgaria, and refers to the heresy and sexual impropriety which the rest of the Christian world associated with the Eastern Orthodox Church which was practised there. The English word is a version of the French term *bougre*.

built Slang term describing someone with a gym-toned and impressive musculature.

bulldicker American lesbian slang for a lesbian whose clitoris is of such a magnitude that she can actually use it to fuck another woman. Derived from BULLDYKE plus dick, meaning penis.

bulldyke or **bulldike** A lesbian, usually a BUTCH one. The term is often used pejoratively against women who are, or are perceived to be, lesbian, but it is also used by lesbians themselves, especially to describe a woman who is quite open about her sexuality and who won't brook any opposition. It is probably derived from DYKE but with an added 'bull', for emphasis, although some writers have argued that it might derive from the name of the British warrior queen BOADICEA. The term appeared as early as 1921 in some medical literature about women who described themselves as 'bull-diking', which indicates it was probably in use much earlier than this. It is defined as 'lesbian' in the glossary to Carl Van Vechten's *Nigger Heaven* (1926), and Bessie Jackson sang *BD Women's Blues* in 1935. Bulldiking was also used in the early twentieth century as a verb meaning to have lesbian sex. An alternative form is bulldagger, which lesbian writer Judy Grahn finds an empowering term. She writes that it 'strongly suggests "castrating woman", something Lesbians are often accused of being merely by our existence'. *See also* DIESEL DYKE.

Bulow vs. Brand 1907 libel case in Germany, which formed part of the series of scandals and trials that was later known as the EULENBERG AFFAIR. *See* DER EIGENE.

bumper to bumper Slang term for lesbian sex. Stems from an unimaginative view of lesbian sex as merely a question of rubbing genitals.

but, darling, what difference does it make as long as you look fabulous? Reply given by the transvestite queen Holly Woodlawn to the pigeonholing question of talk show host Geraldo Rivera in 1976, 'What are you? Are you a woman trapped in a man's body? Are you a heterosexual? Are you a homosexual? A transvestite? A transsexual? What is the answer to the question?' Rather a crystallization of a certain CAMP gay sensibility.

butch (1) Specific type of lesbian identity which involves a rejection of conventional femininity and an adoption of 'masculine' attributes: trousers; beer; tattoos; short hair; boots; muscles; possessiveness; chivalry; initiating relationships and sex; and so on. This identity is linked to a specific bar culture which is urban and working class. Butches were extremely recognizable both to other lesbians and to

straights and, as recognizable lesbians, butches suffered physical and verbal assaults, police harassment and discrimination in jobs and housing. For a woman to dress in 'male' clothes was actually illegal in many American states, and butches would be taken off the streets and stripped to see if they were wearing the requisite items of women's underclothing. SODOMY in the United States, and of course homosexuality, were defined as an illness until 1973 so lesbianism had a higher and more risky profile in that country than in the UK, and butches were the focus of this anti-lesbian hostility. There is a continuity between butches and PASSING WOMEN. Passing women were, however, trying simply to do a man's job or to travel unmolested. Butches, on the other hand, had a specific erotic identity, usually referred to in conjunction with the FEMME identity, which is a more 'feminine' lesbian identity, and the BUTCH/FEMME relationship. A powerful and positive account is in Leslie Feinberg's novel *Stone Butch Blues* (1993). *See* STONE BUTCH. (2) Adjective, meaning a lesbian who looks masculine or hard. This usage does not necessarily imply that one has taken up a specific butch identity. (3) Gay male term referring to explicit masculinity. In the 1970s gay men reacted to the effeminate stereotype of homosexuality en masse, and the butch CLONE look predominated.

Butch and Marge American lesbian slang for the butch and femme roles within a lesbian relationship.

butch bottom/femme top With the new exploration of gender roles in the 1980s, new roles within lesbian relationships emerged. The butch bottom refers to a woman who dressed and acted in a butch style but who took the submissive role within sexual role playing, while the femme top referred to a femme woman who was dominant.

butch button When gay men are talking over the phone and are trying not to sound effeminate, they are said to have pushed the butch button.

butch drag The first generations of female college graduates from the new women's institutions and newly coeducational colleges in nineteenth-century America often faced great prejudice on entering professional life. As a result, many of them felt pressure to dress in as butch a manner as possible to deflect attention from their gender. Thus suits, shirts and ties, proto-power dressing, became de rigueur for many professional women.

butch/femme Until the 1970s BUTCH and FEMME identities and relationships were a staple of the Anglo-American scene. some accounts of the working-class bar scene of the 1950s describe the conventions as very restrictive: butch lesbians were expected only to form relationships with femme lesbians, and lesbians were expected to identify with one role or the other, with those that didn't conform sometimes being referred to derisively as KIKI. Others assert that the roles were far more free and that not only were women free to switch from one to another, but also they were not expected to conform. However, as gender has become less rigid in its demands, the easy recognizability of butches has been lost, and even straight girls are not as feminine as twenty years ago. Butch/femme was harshly attacked by feminists in the 1970s as a self-oppressive attempt to heterosexualize lesbianism and the pernicious legacy of the SEXOLOGISTS' 'explanation' of lesbianism. These charges are repudiated by lesbians such as Joan NESTLE, who argue that the butch–femme relationship and identities are not an attempt to replicate heterosexuality but a uniquely lesbian way of negotiating the relationship between desire, gender, sexuality and sex. Since the late 1980s, butch–femme has had a revival as a result both of the PRO-SEX LESBIAN lobby's wish to re-eroticize lesbianism and because of the interest in academia in 'gender as performance'; if all manifestations of gender are always performative, butch–femme ceases to be peculiarly artificial.

butch shift The process that took place in the gay male communities in the 1970s when gay men started to adopt the BUTCH CLONE or UNIFORM look.

butt plug Artificial phallus for anal sex; like a dildo but firmer and with a tapered end to ease insertion. And, glory, glory, some lesbians have fun with butt plugs too.

butterfly In various countries the butterfly is sometimes used as a slang analogy for the coloured flightiness which is assumed to be characteristic of (effeminate) gay men. In Spanish, for example, mariposa is used as a term for a (passive) gay male. The GAY LIBERATION FRONT in the early 1970s also used the butterfly as a symbol for the lesbian and gay movement, probably with the implication that the butterfly comes out of its poky little cocoon into marvellous colourful flight.

buttons (1) Buttons or badges pinned to clothing not only have become a way of getting across a gay rights message without having to open your mouth (see SLOGANS), but are also a good way of communicating your sexuality to others in order to facilitate the job of cruising. (2) Buttons on jeans serve as a fairly limited way of communicating your intentions to a potential sexual partner. According to various conventions, you can leave either the top, middle or bottom button open. It all means the same thing – that you are looking for sex. But they could have guessed that by the hungry look in your eyes.

C

Calamity Jane

Cabaret 1972 film version based on part of Christopher Isherwood's Berlin stories. In the film Brian (Michael York), who is an English teacher in 1930s Berlin, represses his homosexuality for most of the film for a relationship with Sally Bowles (Liza Minnelli). Finally he does relent and sleeps with a German baron, but Sally cancels her marriage to him for fear that he might slip again. Through all of this Nazism is seen taking hold. Although based on his own stories, Isherwood himself was critical of the portrayal of gay sexuality in the film. However, Minnelli does get to sing a couple of marvellous torch song numbers.

Cadmus, Paul (1904–) American artist who gained notoriety when in 1934 his painting *The Fleet's In!* which depicted a group of sailors on shore leave carousing with a group of women (and one fairly swish-looking man), was exhibited at the Corcoran Gallery in Washington. All firm thighs in tight trousers and skirts (though fairly disappointing crotches on the sailors), the painting caused a furore when one retired admiral took umbrage at this slur on the spotless reputation of the navy. The picture was removed, though not without protest, and Cadmus' career was assured. Cadmus is also known for his male nudes, and he has always been open about his sexuality.

Caesar, Gaius Julius (100 or 102–44 BC) According to rumour, the Roman general and statesman was no stranger to erotic experiences with members of his own sex. As a young man he went east on a diplomatic mission to Bithynia where he fell under the spell of King Nicomedes' charms, an experience which was the source of much humour for Roman gossips. Bibulus, Caesar's colleague in the consulship, describes him in an edict as 'the Queen of Bithynia... who once wanted to sleep with a monarch, but now wants to be one'.

Cafe Cino The first OFF-OFF BROADWAY the-atre, which was opened in a coffee shop in 1958, and which regularly produced plays with gay themes. It provided one of the first places where gay playwrights could express themselves freely.

La Cage aux Folles Film version of a French stage play which was produced in 1978, directed by Edouard Molinaro. It deals with a gay couple, Renato and Albin, who run a St Tropez drag club, where Albin is top of the bill. When Renato's son announces his engagement, the couple pretend to be straight for the deeply con-servative family of his fiancée. Since he is congenitally incapable of acting butch, Albin plays the part of the mother. With its showtime glitz and safe homosexual couple, the film was a great hit with audiences.

Caged 1950 film directed by John Cromwell which was one of the more memorable of the genre of women's prison films. It tells the story of a young woman (played by Eleanor Parker) who is corrupted while doing time in jail together with a lecherous vice queen Elvira (Lee Patrick) and a sadis-tic matron (Hope Emerson).

Cagney and Lacey American television series, started in 1981, about two tough New York women police officers who always get the upper hand over the boys in the precinct, which has become something of a dyke cult, Cagney's numerous het trysts and Lacey's cloying marriage to 'Harv' notwithstanding. The series origi-nally starred Meg Foster as Cagney, but she was dropped for being too 'strident' (most unlike an undercover detective) and for portraying a relationship with Lacey in which some pervy readers saw dyke undertones. Sharon Gless took over, but she was just as much of a hit with the girls.

calamite Term for gay man, a merging of the words CATAMITE and the name of the plant CALAMUS. It was developed by the British poet Algernon Swinburne as a pejo-rative word to describe John Addington SYMONDS.

Calamity Jane (*c.* 1852–1903) Wild West heroine, a miner, trapper and hunter who usually wore male clothing. She was a fast draw on her gun, especially with men who impugned her sex. Immortalized in the 1953 film starring Doris Day as 'Calam', dressed in buckskins and singing the showstopping *Secret Love*.

Calamus The Greek myth records that Calamus and Carpus were lovers. Calamus was changed into the reed that now bears his name when he was grieving after his lover drowned. As a result, the Calamus plant has been historically associ-ated with homosexuality. Calamus is also the name of the section of Walt WHITMAN's poetry collection LEAVES OF GRASS which deals most overtly with what he called ADHESIVENESS between men.

Califia, Pat American lesbian activist who has been effective in explaining and popu-larizing RADICAL SEX within the lesbian community. She edited *The Lesbian SM Safety Manual*, which was a treasure trove of information for LEATHER DYKES. It included information on STDs, on keeping SM sex safe, both emotionally and physi-cally, and on communication within SM relationships. Califia also collected some of her best short erotic fiction in her best-sell-ing collection *Macho Sluts*. The volume breaks through the handcuffs of many sexual taboos in its exploration of such sce-narios as incestuous relations and child sex, as well as various SADOMASOCHISTIC scenes. Califia is always very critical of what she perceives as an anti-permissive strand of lesbian feminist thinking. As she wrote in the introduction to *The Leading Edge: An Anthology of Lesbian Sexual Fiction* (1987), 'Could it be that the real fear of those who want to use sexual repression to fuel the Women's Movement is that we might actually make so much progress that (gasp!) we would not go to meetings at all?'

California American state. The name was taken from the 1510 romantic novel by Garcirodriguez de Montalvo, *Sergas de Esplandian* (Deeds of Esplandian) which was based on Columbus' report of his journey to the New World. Montalvo wrote of Califia, Queen of the AMAZONS, who inhabited a territory called California which was 'very close to the earthly paradise, inhabited by Black women without a single man amongst them.'

Caligula (AD 12–41) Roman Emperor famed for his cruelty. He was also an early drag queen. Whilst emperor, Caligula would occasionally go out dressed up as Venus, the Goddess of Love. He forbade anyone from looking at him from above, in case they should see his chest hair, which might spoil the general effect.

Callas, Maria *See* LA DIVINA.

calvins In gay male communities the underwear made by the Calvin Klein company, both briefs and shorts. They became particularly fashionable after the company had used the American singer 'Marky' Mark Wahlberg in its adverts. However, after an incident on the British television programme *The Word* in which the singer refused to condemn the homophobia of Jamaican ragga artist Shabba Ranks, there was a move to boycott the brand, until the company dropped Wahlberg.

Cambacérès, Jean-Jacques Régis de (1753–1824) Duke of Parma who was consul of France under the 1799 constitution, and from 1804 was arch-chancellor of the French Empire. His *Projet de Code Civil* formed the basis of the CODE NAPOLÉON, and was responsible for the legality of homosexuality under that code, and therefore throughout the Empire. He was popularly believed to be gay himself, and he was nicknamed 'Tante Urlurette'. The triumvirate of Napoleon, Cambacérès and the politician Charles-François Lebrun was labelled 'hic, haec, hoc', which was Latin for 'this one' in the masculine, feminine and neuter genders respectively.

Camille CAMP NAME given to any gay man who is wallowing in self-pity, especially after the end of a relationship. It is derived from the heroine of the 1848 novel and 1852 play, *La Dame aux Camélias* by Alexandre Dumas. Camille leaves her lover Armand at the pressure of his family and goes heartbroken to Paris. She is consumptive, dying and full of despair by the time she and Armand are reunited. The drama was used as the basis of Verdi's opera *La Traviata*, and OPERA QUEENS will use the name of the opera's heroine, Violetta, as an alternative to Camille for the same effect. To pull a Camille meant to overdramatize unpleasant incidents. *See also* DRAMA QUEEN.

camp (1) Many writers have entered into explanations of camp with the best of intentions and yet have emerged with treatises so po-faced that you wonder if they themselves could be camp even if you put them in a tangerine jumpsuit and sent them off to represent Iceland in EUROVISION. Camp is often defined as the gay 'sensibility', which is broad-ranging enough to convey the fact that camp can be found anywhere: art, film, conversations, shoes, practically anything can be held as camp – but what makes it so? Undoubtedly, it has something to do with the ability to separate, or at least see the disjunctions, between surface and content. And who are better qualified with this ability than gay people who have usually spent a large portion of their lives projecting one surface while being something different: we who are past mistresses at reading between the lines in books, films and the words of others to find queer traces in which to recognize ourselves or discern the sexuality of others, who are acutely conscious of our lives as one big performance? Thus, when we declare our undying devotion to celebs who are little more than the glamorous outpourings of the PR department (yes, that's you Ms. Ciccone, but you knew that anyway), or when the British queer rights group OUT-RAGE! follows up the shameful and tragic failure of the British parliament to equalize the gay male AGE OF CONSENT with that of heterosexuals with an action that involved requesting the Queen of Denmark to invade, complete with versions of the Danish national anthem, it's our cosmic retaliation to make others do the wondering. It is here that we can see some roots of camp in the traditions of ART FOR ART'S SAKE and AESTHETICISM with their divorce of ethical value from the artistic merit of any creative work. Camp adds the other side of the equation, by admitting the possibility of treating something with undeniable political or moral import with an entirely unserious demeanour; even a QUEERBASHING story can become the tale of outrage at how one's tights managed to get laddered. But it's not quite as simple as making the serious flip, and vice versa. Have you ever noticed that the moment you hold something up as 'really camp' it suddenly becomes 'really naff'? There's the rub; camp can only be seen out of the corner of the eye. We all know that Eurovision is crap, but to be camp you can never admit it. Oh no, you have to draw up your own scoring sheet, spend the next week insulting anyone Irish, and writing letters of consolation to Sonia, Frances, Michael or even Mary Hopkin (you won't be forgotten). And gay people seem to be best at keeping up this pretence. Which is why, if you meet two men pulling each other's hair over the relative merits of LA DIVINA and LA STUPENDA your eyes go immediately for the crotch. But is camp a solely gay phenomenon? A sticky wicket, that one. In the 1990s it is fashionable to declare that only lesbians and gay men can wield camp, while any straight attempt is doomed to be an also-ran such as kitsch or pop. A tempting argument, but one that leads to the tautology that (nearly) anything gay is camp and vice versa. It is nonetheless undeniable that gay people are relatively more able to spend the energy to turn the blackness of existence into the *taxi-de-Londres* of being, and perhaps we should just leave it at that. (2) Camp or kamp was Australian slang of the early twentieth century which was used similarly to the word gay nowadays, either referring to gay men themselves, or used as an adjective to describe things within the gay world.

camp as a row of tents A rather obvious metaphor for a rather sophisticated sensibility, although in the style of camp it can be extended grotesquely until we get to the point of talking of things which are as camp as a scout jamboree.

CAMP Inc. *See* CAMPAIGN AGAINST MORAL PERSECUTION INC.

Camp Ink Newsletter of the Australian gay rights organization, CAMP INC. First produced in November 1970, it gave queer people a voice since nearly all mainstream newspapers were conservative in their editorial line.

camp names The use of women's names for gay men is one of some historical standing (*see* MOLLY HOUSES). A large amount of the mental creativity of gay men on the scene in the 1970s was expended on making up camp women's names for one another to refer archly to particular attributes. Cruella was a queen who was either extremely bitchy, or one so attractive as to break the hearts of every man he met. Flagella enjoyed whipping during sex. Greta (after GARBO) was a gay man who enjoyed his own company, socially and sexually. Helen Twelvetoes or Salome was one who enjoyed dancing. Karma Miranda was a queer hippie. Madge was frumpy (compare Dame Edna Everage's dowdy assistant Madge). Prunella Paranoid needs no explaining. Nora Naugahide was dressed from head to toe in leather, and Tokyo Rose (after the Japanese propagandist of the Second World War) was a Japanese gay man. A PISS-ELEGANT queen might be titled the dowager, or duchess. In addition a rebuke might be prefaced by the name Dorothy, and one's Jane was the feminine side which might involuntarily manifest itself in an effeminate scream or mannerism. *See also* CAMILLE.

camp parties Australian slang for large private gay parties that would have been held in Sydney and other cities between the two world wars.

Campaign Monthly gay magazine, the first in Australia, which began publishing in

1975 in Sydney. Available in newsagents throughout the country, it kept queers in touch who were not regulars on Sydney's fast-burgeoning gay scene.

Campaign Against Moral Persecution Inc. (CAMP Inc.) Organization set up by Chris Poll and John Ware in July 1970 in Sydney, Australia to campaign on gay rights issues, which convened its first public meeting in February 1971. The title referred to the Australian slang usage of the term camp to refer to queer people themselves. Along with the AUSTRALIAN LESBIAN MOVEMENT, CAMP Inc. was the earliest gay rights organization in the country which sought to publicly challenge attitudes rather than just lobby for law reform. As such, and with its emphasis on coming out as a loco-motive for change, it marked the growth of a gay identity politics movement which Australia had not really experienced previously. Several branches of the organization were set up in different Australian cities.

Campaign for Homosexual Equality (CHE) British group for lesbian and gay rights. Originally called the Committee for Homosexual Equality, it evolved out of the NORTH-WESTERN HOMOSEXUAL REFORM COMMITTEE. In 1971 it changed the 'Committee' to 'Campaign', presumably as a nod to the new radicalism which had penetrated the movement. In the early 1970s the organization didn't really live up to the spirit of the times, and had a fractious relationship with the GAY LIBERATION FRONT, which it saw as too extreme.This all changed after a CHE conference in 1974 which marked a new commitment by the group to more militant forms of activity, and witnessed a greater cohesion between the different elements that made up the CHE and the GLF.

Campbell, Bobbie (1952–84) One of America's first AIDS activists and vocal PWAs. He described himself as the 'AIDS poster boy' because he was so active in raising awareness for people with the condition. Bobbie died of AIDS-related illnesses on August 15 1984, in San Francisco, at the age of thirty-two.

camping Unrelated to the dominant meaning of CAMP, camping is used in South Africa to refer to cruising.

CAMPus CAMP Branches of the Australian Gay Rights organization CAMP INC. which were set up in Sydney University and the University of New South Wales. Over 1972 and 1973 these organizations became GAY LIBERATION FRONTS.

Cantici di Fidenzio Sixteenth-century collection of Italian poetry written by Camillo Scroffa and satirically describing a teacher who is infatuated with a beautiful student.

Cantonese Groin Plant, shaped like a phallus. It had the marvellous property when soaked in hot water of expanding and hardening. For this reason it was often used in China as a DILDO.

capitalism Capitalism has a very different meaning for lesbians and for gay men. Capitalist enterprises have given gay men a large number of institutions (newspapers, travel companies, clubs, bars and so on). However, capitalism has had a much smaller effect on lesbians. On average, lesbian incomes are lower than those of gay men, as more generally women's are lower than men's under capitalism. The fabled PINK POUND/DOLLAR is largely a gay male thing, as are the goods and services it provides. Historically however, capitalism, despite the fact that it is built on a family-based division of labour, has had an important role in the development of lesbian and gay communities, particularly in the growth of urban centres where lesbian and gay subcultures could thrive.

Capri The island became famous as a resort for homosexuals, especially after it was popularized in the writings of George Norman Douglas (1868–1952), the English writer who adopted it as his home and who lived a life of hedonism there. It was also the site of the elaborate home of Friedrich Alfred Krupp (1854–1902), heir to his father's German steel industry, who reportedly entertained attractive Italian youths there.

The Captive See LA PRISONNIÈRE.

Cara a Cara Los Angeles AIDS service organization which serves the Hispanic population. The name means face to face.

Caravaggio, Michelangelo Merisi da
(1571–1610) Italian painter who challenged
the mannerist conventions of painting of
the day by introducing a ground-breaking
realism in his works. The peasant types
which he painted from models drawn
from the streets were denounced as not
suitable for biblical and religious scenes.
He also painted a number of ambiguous-
appearing men (for example in *The
Musicians*) which appeal to a gay viewing.
In 1986 British film director Derek JARMAN
portrayed the painter in a visually stunning film that echoed Caravaggio's own
use of light and shade, and emphasized
the painter's homoerotic affair with one of
his models.

Carlini, Benedetta (1590–?) A nun born in
the mountains of Tuscany who had a
sexual relationship with another nun. Her
sexuality was discovered however, and
she was sentenced to spend the last thirty-
five years of her life in prison.

Carpenter, Edward (1844–1929) English
social activist, socialist, advocate of
women's emancipation, vegetarian and
inspiration to many. In his publications
such as *Love's Coming of Age* (1896), *Iolaus:
An Anthology of Friendship* (1902), THE
INTERMEDIATE SEX (1908), INTERMEDIATE
TYPES AMONG PRIMITIVE FOLK (1914), and his
memoirs *My Days and Dreams* (1916), he
developed his ideas that intermediate
types 'might possibly fulfil a positive and
useful function' in human society.
Towards the end, Carpenter's life was
itself utopian. He was sexually repressed
until he read the works of American poet
Walt WHITMAN, in which he 'met with the
treatment of sex which accorded with [his]
own sentiments'. Thereafter his social
activism and his passionate espousal of
democracy led him to be regarded by some
as England's own Whitman. His socialism
was based upon his own ethical system,
and had elements of anarchism and spirituality (he had taken holy orders earlier in

life). He believed that society was becoming fixated on consumption and was
becoming disjointed. It was only among
the manual labourers of towns such as
Sheffield that any wholeness was, he
believed, to be found. In 1883 he bought
MILLTHORPE, a house outside Sheffield
where he lived for much of his life
amongst these people, presenting the
socialist cause there and on lectures elsewhere. Sex was also central to his philosophy, and he felt that unless the individual
appreciated the body the rest of life was
likely to be dislocated. He wrote, 'Sex still
goes first, and hands, eyes, mouth, brain,
follow: from the midst of belly and thighs,
radiate the knowledge of self, religion and
immortality'. To Carpenter the pleasures
of the body were of importance in themselves, and he was one of the first to argue
against 'the arbitrary notion that the function of love is limited to childbearing'. He
also questioned societal notions of gender,
and believed that gender roles had been
exaggerated and that androgyny was a
more natural and desirable state. This led
him to support the movement for the
emancipation of women. He placed a great
deal of importance on feminism, and once
remarked that he believed that 'the women
will save us'. In 1891 he met his partner
George Merrill on a train, and the latter
soon moved into Millthorpe, where the
two of them lived until Merrill died in
1927. Their happy life together was as
much an inspiration to other gay men of
the time as that of THE LADIES OF LLAN-
GOLLEN was to women of theirs. His influence has been rather mixed. Although
important as a propagandist for the socialist cause, even during his lifetime some
within the Independent Labour Party felt
that his openness about his sexuality was a
liability, and after his death his contribution to socialism tended to be under-
played. For the gay movement he was and
is a prophet. He was a natural candidate
for the post of first president of the BRITISH
SOCIETY FOR THE STUDY OF SEX PSYCHOLOGY,
and his writings provided succour for
other gay people. For example, his work
Love's Coming of Age led to the establish-

ment of an Italian group for the discussion of sexual matters whilst his personal friendship with E. M. Forster had an influence on the ideas of the BLOOMSBURY GROUP. Even as late as the 1970s and 1980s gay men within the RADICAL FAIRY movements seized upon his descriptions of the spiritual power of androgyny, and of gay people, in their attempt to find a gay spirituality.

Carrington, Stephen Character in the American soap opera *Dynasty*, played by Al Corley between 1981 and 1983, and Jack Coleman thereafter. The son of Blake and Alexis Carrington, Stephen was a sensitive man who was relatively unlucky in love; two of his love objects died whilst one simply faded away.

Carwash 1976 comedy film. Unremarkable apart from the memorable character of Lindy, a loud and militant transvestite played by Antonio Fargas. When the black Abdullah suggests that Lindy is an example of white corruption and emasculation of the black community, Fargas enunciates archly the immortal line, 'Honey, I'm more man than you'll ever *be* and more woman than you'll ever *get*'.

Casement Diaries Diaries of the British public servant Sir Roger Casement (1864–1916), which included explicit incidents of his gay sexual activities, and described the men he slept with and the size of their dicks. After trying to get German aid for the Irish rebellion of 1916 against the English, Casement was accused of treason and was sentenced to be hanged. Many considered the charges to have been embroidered somewhat, and there were many calls for clemency from the international community. In order to quell this criticism, the British government released sections of Casement's diaries. The ploy succeeded and Casement was hanged in August 1916.

Castlehaven affair The trial and execution of Mervyn Touchet, Lord Audley and Earl of Castlehaven, for sodomy, and for abetting the rape of Touchet's wife, was one of the most notorious prosecutions under

HENRY VIII'S BUGGERY ACT, and was referred to in subsequent homosexual scandals for two centuries afterwards. The trial, which began in April 1631, showed Touchet to have been a vile husband: on the night of his marriage to his second wife he forced her to study the dicks of each of his manservants, and he later held her arms while one of them raped her. Yet his trial was important for two reasons. First, it demonstrated how the aristocracy could construct the space for their own pleasures. Touchet had offered employment, and his bed, to a number of lusty Irish lads whom he had assembled in order to create his own fantasy homoerotic world. It was when he was having sex with one, Lawrence Fitz-Patrick, that he was detected, and this led to the prosecution. Secondly his trial set an important precedent, since the evidence of the men with whom he had had sex was declared to be admissible despite the fact that they were part of the same 'offence'. This led the way to numerous prosecutions of homosexuals thereafter. Touchet was executed on 14 May 1631. Two of his servants were also hanged shortly afterwards.

Castro San Francisco street which in the late 1960s and early 1970s became the centre of the city's gay life. The street had been part of a traditionally blue-collar neighbourhood, but from the 1950s the area declined as workers moved out to where the new factories were, and others decided to move to the suburbs. House prices fell, and the area was ripe for a takeover. It began in the late 1960s with the opening of the first gay bar, and by 1973, when Harvey MILK opened his camera shop there, more than half the new residents were gay.

casual sex Temporary sexual encounters. Casual sex is usually seen as a physical affair only, and is contrasted with sex which involves emotional interaction. Within the traditions of feminism it has usually been defined as a male preoccupation which ensnares women to the satisfaction of the male libido and which objectifies and dehumanizes one's partner, while heterosexuals who can only see us as sexual machines construct it as a homosexual phenomenon. Many lesbians and gay men have rejected these negative connotations of casual sex and have described it as a healthy way of relieving sexual desires, which need not be devoid of emotional contact; as American sex researcher Ralph Bolton says, 'It is in the après sex milieu of a casual sexual encounter when people often open up and speak honestly and profoundly about their lives, sharing thoughts with a partner that may never be voiced in any other context.'

cat Australian slang for a man that likes to have sex with other men.

Catacombs San Francisco private SM club. It opened in 1975 and quickly became a famous venue for FISTFUCKING parties. Fisters from all over the world made the pilgrimage to attend parties in its LEATHERSPACE. In time, it took on a role as community centre for the local SM and fisting population. Designed with minimum fuss to 'help the butthole open up, relax and feel good', it had a room for limbering up, with inner rooms for serious sex festooned with leather slings. The venue opened later to women and mixed gender groups. Going through three incarnations it finally closed in 1984, largely as a result of the growing AIDS hysteria.

catamite Term for a boy who is kept by an older man for sexual purposes. It derives from the Roman name Catamitus, the Roman version of the Greek GANYMEDE, the cupbearer to the god Jupiter (Greek Zeus). It was a standard term for homosexuality in the nineteenth century.

catcher American slang term derived from the sport of baseball, referring to the receptive partner in anal intercourse. *See* PITCHER.

caterwaul Eighteenth-century British slang term for cruising which derives from the image of a cat on heat and desirous of a sexual partner.

Cather, Willa (1873–1947) One of the most highly rated of twentieth-century American novelists. Cather was born in Virginia, and as a child and young woman she identified as a man, William Jr, cross-dressing and cropping her hair, to the consternation of those around her. However, by the time she left college, she had adopted a more feminine form of dress, though she remained on the butch side of ladylike. She is best known for her novel *My Antonia*, where the hero, Jim Burden, is her alter ego. Cather lived an emotional life in which her primary emotional relationships were with women, including Louise Pound, Isabelle McClung and Edith Lewis, with whom she lived for forty years. Cather is variously claimed as a lesbian or as a ROMANTIC FRIEND; the fact that she destroyed many of her personal papers before her death does imply that she herself believed that there was some impropriety in her emotional affairs, a belief more consistent with lesbianism.

Catholic priests Despite the historical and intransigent homophobia of the Catholic Church, its priests are held by the popular imagination to contain among themselves huge numbers of gay men, and there are more lesbian Catholic nuns than you could swing an incense burner at as well. This became particularly the case after many heterosexuals left the priesthood in the 1960s and 1970s in order to marry. This is probably why the Church is slow when it comes to expelling homosexual clergy, since if it conducted a thorough inquisition it would be left with a severely depleted payroll, and its hypocrisy would be laid bare.

cats The archetypal lesbian pet, probably because they are more intelligent than the nasty yappy dogs that seem to have been associated with gay men. According to San Francisco lesbian comedian Suzie Burger, you can tell a lesbian at work by the fact that where colleagues will have photos of their families on their desks, she'll have a picture of her mog.

Cavafy, Constantine P. (1863–1933) Greek poet, who was born and spent most of his life in the Egyptian city of Alexandria and who was reportedly no stranger to its male sex-workers, relying on the family servants to keep any knowledge of his nocturnal escapades from his mother. Although Cavafy's output was small, his works have become part of the canon of gay poetry not simply because of the individualistic simple style in which they were written, but also for the world of Alexandrian gay street life that he captured in such poems as 'In the Street' (1916) and 'Two Young Men, Twenty-three to Twenty-four Years Old' (1927).

cavalier In women's colleges in nineteenth-century America all-women dances were frequently held. An older student would take along a younger student, and the former's expected behaviour was known as 'playing the cavalier'. The older student would send flowers to her partner, call for her, take her to dinner and return her home at the end of the evening. These rituals and the dances were taken extremely seriously, and many tears were shed in pursuit of the desired partner.

CD4-cells Alternative name for T-CELLS.

Le Cercle *See* DIE KRIES.

CFEHAF *See* COMMITTEE TO FIGHT EXCLUSION OF HOMOSEXUALS IN THE ARMED FORCES.

Chaeronea, Battle of Great battle of 338 BC when the Macedonian cavalry, under Philip (and his son Alexander the Great), decimated the Athenian forces, including the SACRED BAND OF THEBES. According to the Greek writer Plutarch (*c.* AD 46–120), when Philip learned that the men he had destroyed were the renowned group of lovers, he burst into tears and declared, 'Perish miserably they who think that these men did or suffered aught disgraceful.' A huge statue of a lion marks the grave of the men. It was restored in 1902. *See also* ALEXANDER AND HEPHAESTION.

chalking the pavements An activist tactic with a long history. In the SUFFRAGE movement in the early twentieth century in the UK and America, women would chalk the time and place of a suffrage meeting or action to advertise it to other women. In the late twentieth century, women chalk the outline of a human body on the pavement to mark the spot where a woman has been raped, while AIDS activists do the same to remind people of the number of AIDS-related deaths that have occurred.

chana con chana The Brazilian word *chana* translates literally as cunt in English, but according to Brazilian feminists it has more significance than a description of the female genitals (as if that wasn't significant enough), but has a phonetic similarity to the Brazilian words for chance and flame. *Chana con Chana* (Cunt to Cunt) was the name of a Brazilian lesbian magazine founded in 1982.

Les Chansons de Bilitis Collection of erotic poetry published in 1894, with many poems having a lesbian theme. It was claimed to have been written by a contemporary of the lesbian poet SAPPHO. The French Pierre Louÿs claimed to have translated it into French from the original Greek. However, despite hoodwinking many of its readers, Louÿs was later unmasked as actually having written the collection himself. The American lesbian group DAUGHTERS OF BILITIS took its name from the hoax book.

chapel Since the days of the MOLLY HOUSES lesbians and gays have referred to bedrooms, or indeed any other place they have sex, as the chapel. The usage indicates the fact that in the absence of legal recognition of our partnerships we have to invent our own ways of making our relationships meaningful, and sex is, of course, one of those ways.

The Charioteer Novel by English writer Mary Renault which was one of the few positive portrayals of male homosexuality appearing in the grim years of the 1950s. Set in England during the Second World War, it dealt with a soldier's journey to accept his own sexuality, and the competition on his affections of his pure love for a young conscientious objector and his erotic feeling for a self-assured naval officer.

Charles, RuPaul Andre Black American drag queen whose pop career took right off in 1993 and 1994. It not only gave him enough dollars to keep in furs for a lifetime, but also made him probably the best known male face in slap and big wig either side of the Atlantic. Sufficiently establishment to be invited to present the British record industry awards ceremony in 1994 along with singer Elton John, RuPaul has managed to take all the mean talk out of his drag, leaving him superbly glamorous but not that sassy, and thus more in the tradition of BOY GEORGE, though he does the whole drag, and is quite upfront about his sexuality.

Charlus, Baron Palamède (Mémé) de Important aristocratic character in Marcel Proust's A LA RECHERCHE DU TEMPS PERDU. The Baron was a closet homosexual who tried to cultivate the image of a virile heterosexual.

CHE *See* CAMPAIGN FOR HOMOSEXUAL EQUALITY.

checked shirt De rigueur on the CLONE scene of the 1970s. Worn over T-shirts or tied round the waist, they have survived into the 1990s. Reeking of macho chic, they bestow the lumberjack look on boys who haven't been nearer to a tree than while cruising in the park.

Cherry Grove Area near New York in the resort of FIRE ISLAND which was a chic summer vacation destination for moneyed lesbians in the 1950s. It remained popular until, horrors, unsophisticated butch and femme dykes started coming along. Like the rest of Fire Island, the area was also popular with gay men.

chick In American prison slang of the 1970s a chick was a passive partner in anal sex. *See* PUNK.

chicken A gay teenager, or a young gay man in his early twenties. A chicken hawk is an older gay man who is attracted to and pursues the younger breed.

chigo Medieval Japanese term referring to boys between the ages of about seven and fourteen who resided in temples as if they were at boarding school. A second meaning of chigo evolved which was that of youths involved in gay relationships with priests. A literary genre of chigo monogatari emerged which were fictionalized accounts of these affairs. Same-sex relationships seem to have been common in medieval Japan, and secondary characters in chigo monogatari actively support such liaisons of the principals. The archetype of the genre is the AKI NO YO NO NAGAMONOGATARI.

The Children's Hour Stage play by Lillian Hellman, later made into a 1962 film version released in the UK as *The Loudest Whisper*. It was based on the true story of two Scottish schoolteachers, Marianne Woods and Jane Pirie, who were accused of lesbian activity. In the film version the character of Martha Dobie (Shirley Maclaine) suddenly realizes her own lesbianism as a result of the accusation, 'I'm guilty', she cries. Since the Hollywood dictates of the time demanded the demise of lesbians and gay men, this insight costs her her life, the first of a series of suicides of lesbian and gay characters. However, in the original Scottish case the two women brought a successful legal action against the woman who had spread the rumours of their sexuality, largely because the judge could not believe that two women could do such a thing. Although their careers were destroyed, they maintained their relationship.

Christina (1626–89) Queen of Sweden. She succeeded to the Swedish throne in 1632. Many believed Christina to be a hermaphrodite. She enjoyed dressing in male garb, and was reportedly in love with Countess Ebba Sparre. She elected to abdicate in 1654 in favour of her cousin when she was put under pressure to marry and bear an heir to the throne. After her abdication, she went under the name of 'Count Dohna' in her travels through Europe. Embracing Catholicism when she was in Brussels, she reportedly entered Rome on horseback, dressed in the costume of an amazon. *See also* QUEEN CHRISTINA.

Christopher Street American monthly magazine for lesbians and gay men which was founded in 1976, and features the usual range of articles. It has a circulation of around 4,000. The name derives from the street on which the Stonewall Inn was situated. In its early days it attempted to tempt advertisers with the lure of the PINK POUND, by declaring, 'What people do in the privacy of their homes is their business – big business.'

Christopher Street Street in New York's Greenwich Village which became legendary as home to the Stonewall Inn, centre of the 1969 STONEWALL RIOT. The group that formed to organize the anniversary parade for the riots, the first PRIDEmarch, called itself the Christopher Street Liberation Day Committee. It was set up by the East Regional Conference of Homophile Organizations in November 1969.

Chrysippus In Greek mythology the son of Pelops (*see* POSEIDON). According to one Greek tradition, pederastic relations were brought into Greece when Laius, the legendary King of Thebes (and father of Oedipus), abducted Chrysippus in his chariot after staying at his father's house and becoming enamoured of the youth. Another version relates that the youth, like GANYMEDE, was actually abducted by Zeus.

chubby (sl.) An overweight or merely generously built man, often used affectionately rather than maliciously. A chubby chaser is thus someone who is erotically attracted to his stout brothers.

church The lesbian and gay universe, particularly used in black lesbian and gay slang. Thus 'She goes to my church' would mean 'She is also a lesbian'. The word connotes the strong links of support that exist among lesbian and gay communities. *See also* RELIGION.

Chutzpah Contemporary gay Jewish social group in the Australian city of Sydney.

cigarettes They became a sign of effeminacy and male homosexuality in the UK at the turn of the twentieth century because they were associated with the aesthetic movement and, in particular, Oscar WILDE who said, 'They are everything you could wish for in a vice as they always leave you unsatisfied.' Some people have argued that the word FAGGOT derives from the British slang term 'fag', for cigarette.

cinema Like the library, the cinema has been one of the places where lesbian and gay people have begun to recognize and accept their sexuality. The dark movie theatre, in which the audience is atomized and relates only to what is on the screen, allows you to identify with whoever you want in the film, unlike watching the television with parents when constant awareness of their presence prohibits true relaxation. There is many a gay man who realized that it was actually the heroine into whose shoes he wished to step, because of her opposite man as well as because of her glamour. Perhaps this goes some way to explaining the cults of cinema diva ICONs. Throughout the twentieth century, the cinema has also offered the chance of escapism, of worlds more glamorous and happy than the daily round of homophobia and queerbashing.

Circle of Loving Companions Six months after helping to found the South California GAY LIBERATION FRONT, the activist Harry HAY and his partner John Burnside moved to an Indian community in New Mexico. The couple opened their house as a lesbian and gay space, and named it the Circle of Loving Companions. For some time it was listed as the only open gay venue in the state.

cities of the plain The term for the two biblical cities of SODOM AND GOMORRAH, in the Vale of Siddim, which were supposedly destroyed because of the homosexuality of their inhabitants. The 'sins of the cities of the plain' has served as a euphemism for homosexual love.

The City and the Pillar 1948 novel by Gore Vidal, which was the first American novel with a gay theme to receive widespread public attention. It began with two high school students who have sex on a camping trip. One of the boys, Jim Willard, is obsessed with the experience, and when he remeets Bob years later he tries to seduce him. When his advances are refused he rapes him. In the early editions of the novel, however, Vidal was pressured by his publishers to include the tragic ending which had become almost mandatory for queer books, and Jim actually murders Bob. The original ending was restored in the 1965 edition. The gay subject matter of the work received such attention that Vidal later referred to the work as the invention of homosexuality.

city of friends The utopian idea of community described by Walt WHITMAN in LEAVES OF GRASS, built on the ennobling foundations of ADHESIVENESS; 'I dream'd in a dream I saw a city invincible to the attacks of the whole of the rest of the earth,/I dream'd that was the new city of Friends.'

civil disobedience Usually, but not always, non-violent. Civil disobedience is a radical form of direct action which involves the selected breaking of laws to make a political protest. The laws broken can be directly relevant to the political movement concerned. For example, a traditional lesbian and gay action is a kiss-in where lesbian and gay couples will snog one another in public places to challenge indecency legislation which theoretically could render such lewd displays illegal. Or, the law broken can be secondary to make the political point that we do not acknowledge the legitimacy of a state and its legislation if that legislation is used to infringe our rights. For example, the British group OUTRAGE! has twice held marches in defiance of laws which prohibit demonstrations within a mile of Parliament while it is sitting, or lesbians and gay men might withhold taxes from the state which oppresses them. Civil disobedience within the modern lesbian and gay movement takes its inspiration from a number of sources, from the Chartists, through the SUFFRAGISTS, to the huge and courageous freedom marches led by Martin Luther King which were so successful a technique for the black CIVIL RIGHTS MOVEMENT.

civil rights Term that originated in the black civil rights movement in America. Described by Alice Walker as a term 'totally lacking in colour' which 'could never adequately express black people's revolutionary goals', it refers to a social contract under which any citizen of a country should be able to expect the same opportunity and treatment. It is often used interchangeably with the term HUMAN RIGHTS, but the two are not entirely synonymous. The term civil rights is often used by lesbians and gay men to emphasize the second-class citizenship to which they are subject.

civil rights movement The American movement of the 1950s and 1960s which fought for racial equality was tremendously influential and inspirational for those who later went on to work within the country's gay liberation movement in the 1970s. Not only did it show that myths about a particular minority group could be unmasked as precisely that – the ideological construction of a particularly powerful class – but it also demonstrated the importance of mass protest in achieving such ends. The many lesbians and gays who participated in the movement later took this expertise to their work for lesbian and gay rights in the 1970s.

claiming One of the traditional ways lesbians and gay men have sought to demonstrate the worth of their sexuality has been to document the wealth of great historical figures who have also shared their same-sex desires. Often this has meant going against the smokescreen sent up by heterosexual historians who have tried to remove all trace of queerness in order to 'protect' (misrepresent) their subject (*see* ERASURE). This practice of claiming homosexuals back from heterosexual mythology has a long historical pedigree. In his defence of his affections for George Villiers, JAMES I referred to the relationship between Christ and ST JOHN THE EVANGELIST, while in one of the most notorious cases of entrapment by the SOCIETIES FOR THE REFORMATION OF MANNERS, that of Captain Edward Rigby in 1698, Rigby was reported to have said to

William Minton, who had been paid to act as bait, 'It's no more than was done in our Fore fathers' time…the French King did it, and the Czar of Muscovy made Alexander, a Carpenter, a Prince for that purpose.' When Rigby talked about 'our Fore fathers', he probably meant the people of ANCIENT GREECE and ROME, who have for centuries provided inspiration that a better world had existed for lesbians and gay men. It is not coincidental that two of the most common words for a woman who loves women, 'lesbian' and 'sapphist' refer to the Greek poet SAPPHO. Sappho was herself claimed by lesbians, who asserted that her poetry represented an erotic interest in women, as opposed to the arguments of (male) historians who chose to concentrate on stories of Sappho's unrequited love for Phaon.

Claire of the Moon 1993 film directed by Nicole Conn and starring Trisha Todd as Claire and Karen Trumbo as Noel. It was billed as a second DESERT HEARTS, but although enjoyably Hollywoodized it is not on a par with this film. For one thing, it does not have a 'look, no hands' sex scene…

Clause 25 This clause of the Criminal Justice Bill, which became Section 31 of the 1991 Criminal Justice Act, empowered judges to impose more stringent penalties on a number of 'crimes' contained in the British statute book to police the sexual behaviour of gay men. In reality, these crimes were consensual acts, including soliciting by a man, procuring of homosexual acts (in any way helping two men to have sex together even if they are both above the legal age of consent), and indecency between men, which included any expression of gay affection outside the home.

Clause 28 In a shameful episode in British history, the Tory government proposed a clause in the 1988 Local Government Bill which sought to prohibit local authorities from using public funds to 'promote' homosexuality, either directly themselves or through financing other groups. Initial

parliamentary apathy, including the tacit support of the Labour Party for the measure at first, was eventually galvanized into a huge campaign, as the slogan went, to 'stop the clause', which involved large demonstrations throughout the country. Most memorably a group of lesbians managed to smuggle abseiling equipment into the visitors' gallery of the House of Lords, and gaily dropped in on the proceedings as they were discussing the measure. Some of the same women also broke into the studios of the BBC six o'clock news in May of that year and disrupted the live broadcast. Despite the protests, the bill was passed, and the clause became Section 28 of the Local Government Act. The wording of the measure was deliberately vague so as to cast its net more widely, and its most insidious effect has been that of self-censorship, not only of homo-friendly arts events but also of balanced discussion of lesbian and gay issues in schools run by local authorities. The wording was also adopted by the virulent American homophobe Jesse HELMS, in his amendment to the federal budget legislation for AIDS funding. It is however an ill wind that blows no good, and not only were many lesbians and gays instantly radicalized by the protests against the bill, but seasoned campaigners remarked that the period saw the biggest mobilization of lesbian and gay activity since the heady days of gay liberation in the 1970s.

clean In the language of contact adverts, refers to a circumcised man.

clenched fist The symbol of the black CIVIL RIGHTS MOVEMENT in America, it was taken on by the feminist movement, and often combined with the VENUS SYMBOL as an emblem of female power and will to win the struggle against patriarchy.

Cleveland Street scandal An affair unearthed in 1889 when a Georgian house in Cleveland Street, London was discovered by police to be a a busy male brothel. The police investigation revealed that the clientele of the house included some illustrious names such as Lord Arthur

Somerset, a close friend of the Prince of Wales, and Prince Albert Victor, the eldest son of the Prince of Wales and heir apparent to the throne. Although Somerset had to flee the country to France, the government and the Royal Family managed to contain the scandal.

clone Most prevalent social type within gay communities until the advent of AIDS in the early 1980s. They symbolized a post-STONEWALL RIOT liberated gay male identity which could explore new forms of male gender roles. The clone look was screamingly butch and emphasized the workman look. At the same time, it was obviously gay. Clones wore work boots, flannel shirts and button-up levis, which were as tight as possible to emphasize the ass and crotch. The dick was always in evidence, usually crammed into improbable formations to make it look bigger. A gym-toned NAUTILUS body, short hair and lots of facial hair were also considered necessary.

close companion The term is now mainly used in obituaries by straight newspapers to mark homosexual relationships, being synonymous with longtime companion. It has also been used self-referentially by lesbians and gay men to refer to their lovers. Historically, if 'close companion' is used it suggests either homosexuality or a ROMANTIC FRIENDSHIP.

closet The metaphorical space occupied by those who are aware of their same-sex impulses, but who are unwilling to declare them to anyone else. Thus 'to be in the closet' is to live one's life ostensibly as a heterosexual, and to be 'out of the closet' is to acknowledge one's sexuality. This does not mean that someone in the closet does not enjoy same-sex activities, more that they are unwilling to be open about them. In reality several closets exist, since people can be open to lesser or greater extents. Some are open to family and colleagues, others just to friends on the SCENE. There are also closets imposed by various forms of more unorthodox sex (*see* LEATHER CLOSET). A closet case (male/female) or closet queen (male) is someone who is in the closet. *See also* COME OUT.

closet rights The rights of individuals to be in the closet about their sexuality. Proponents of closet rights argue that sexuality is an essentially private realm, and the extent to which people are open about it is an individual issue. Others argue that it is the responsibility of lesbians and gay men to add their voices to the movement for human rights, i.e. that if you're not part of the solution, you're part of the problem. *See* OUTING.

CMV *See* CYTOMEGALOVIRUS.

coalition politics The alliance between different political groups with broadly similar aims in order to exert a greater political leverage. Often, but not always, coalition groups are composed of different movements of identity or class-based politics which tend to work with mainstream politicians on the left of the political spectrum, such as the RAINBOW COALITION in the United States. Such coalitions are often highly problematic, however, since no two groups have the same agenda, and specific identity has to be subsumed to some extent. This is particularly true of extreme-left organizations which often conceive of class as being of greatest importance whereas issues of race, sexism or homophobia are seen as being derived from class relations and, hence, secondary. Within the lesbian and gay movement arguments about the worth of coalitions have existed since the GAY ACTIVISTS ALLIANCE split from the GAY LIBERATION FRONT because of the latter's support for other political struggles. Indeed the idea of a lesbian and gay movement is a coalition in itself, and lesbians have often found it impossible to work with gay men because they feel that gays are unwilling to give due thought to the specific problems faced by lesbians as a result of sexism.

COC *See* CULTUUR EN ONTSPANNINGS-CENTRUM.

cock (1) As a word to refer to the penis, cock has been recorded as far back as the sixteenth century. Its etymology is probably from the word cock used to mean a small pipe. (2) Cock can also be used as a general term for sex. Men go out CRUISING to look for cock.

cock ring Ring or loop, made usually of metal or leather, which is fixed around the base of the cock and balls, or just the cock. It increases the ferocity and endurance of an erection. Also known as a napkin ring.

Cockettes Camp, drag street entertainment troupe of the late 1960s and early 1970s in San Francisco, which launched drag queen SYLVESTER into stardom. Their productions were described by gay poet Allen Ginsberg as 'transvestite-glitter-fairie-theatric-masques'. While the Cockettes were just having a good time themselves, their work was described as subversively outrageous by political gays. They gave their last performance in 1972.

Cocteau, Jean (1889–1963) French dramatist, author, filmmaker, actor and artist, he is one of the most important and versatile figures of the twentieth-century arts. Cocteau was usually surrounded by an entourage of gay artists, and had open relationships with some of them, including the novelist Raymond Radiguet, whose death shattered him, and the actor Jean Marais. His vast outpouring of creative works are not in the main 'gay-themed', though among other projects he produced an adaptation of Oscar WILDE's *The Picture of Dorian GRAY* and drawings for Jean GENET's novel QUERELLE OF BREST, while his 1930 film *The Blood of a Poet* contained homoerotic elements.

Code Napoléon Penal code prepared under the direction of Napoleon (1800–04). The code was enforced throughout the French empire, and also became the model for the legal code of many other European countries. Included in it was the legalization of homosexuality. It formed the basis of modern French law, although subsequent anti-gay clauses were inserted and then repealed.

codpiece A pouch worn by men to cover, and simultaneously draw attention to their genitals, popular in the sixteenth century. They started as a flap to make pissing easier, but soon evolved into an elaborate status symbol. They were sometimes jewel encrusted, and often padded to the point of suggesting a priapic erection. By the late sixteenth century, they began to be eschewed as undignified.

Colette Sidonie Colette Goudeket, (1873–1954) French novelist whose works deal in the main with the trials and tribulations of love, and its sometimes ironic passage. In such works as *The Pure and the Impure*, she rebelled against the image created by DECADENT writers that lesbianism was little more than an exotic but ultimately bitter sensuality, and argued that it represented a far more meaningful emotional bond. Married three times, Colette had a number of affairs with women.

The Collar of the Dove Collection of poetry by the Arab writer Ibn Hazm who lived in Andalusia in the eleventh century. The anthology set out the panoply of manifestations of love, and figuring highly was the love of boys. All the stages of desire were described, from the perfection of the beloved on first meeting to the sorrows of parting.

collar-and-tie Abbreviation to denote male clothing, especially when used by cross-dressing women. In 'Prove It On Me Blues' (1928), Ma RAINEY, sang 'It's true I wear a collar and tie.'

Color Purple, The Alice Walker's 1982 novel (winner of the 1983 Pulitzer Prize for Fiction) that describes a powerful and positive relationship between Celie and Shug Avery. It is unforgiveable that Steven Spielberg chose to erase any explicit lesbian liaison when he filmed the novel in 1985. But Whoopi Goldberg fooled none of us with her look at Shug as they sat on the bed...

come As a verb, to reach orgasm. As a noun, it means semen (usually spelled cum). The verb has had sexual connotations since the sixteenth century, when the phrase 'to come in unto' could be used to describe sexual intercourse. In the nineteenth century, come was used to refer to the process of butter forming when being churned, a usage easily extended to sexual metaphor. The alternative spelling of cum probably originated in the twentieth century to differentiate from the more common usage of come.

come back for coffee Monumentally transparent euphemism for sex. Thus, when a guy wants to take another home after a night on the town, he can ask him back for a coffee without actually having to mention sex. Since both parties know exactly what is on offer, and it doesn't usually come in a jar, one wonders why they bother with the pretence.

Come, Let Us Bugger Finely Song reported to have been sung by the clientele of one of the MOLLY HOUSES which was subject to police action in 1725/6. One of the police who had infiltrated the house mentioned it in his evidence, but the lyrics have unfortunately not been preserved. While singing the song, the men performed their own lewd country dancing. Another song which contemporary accounts mention begins with the stanza, 'Let the Fops of the Town upbraid/Us, for an unnatural Trade,/We value not man nor Maid;/But among our own selves we'll be free.'

come out Abbreviation for the phrase to 'come out of the CLOSET', which is used by lesbians and gay men to describe the process involved in coming to be open about one's lesbian or gay sexuality. Best conceived of as a process rather than a single act, coming out involves a number of stages, including the acknowledgement of that sexuality to oneself, the first experience of sex with a member of the same gender, telling family, friends and colleagues, and incorporating a recognition of homosexuality into other areas of life, such as taking part in the lesbian or gay SCENE. These stages need occur in no particular order, nor over any prescribed time-scale.

As an example, an individual can come out and be celibate, or can take part on the gay scene with friends without telling parents or children. Different pressures will come to play to determine when each step might be taken. For example, black lesbians and gays remark that it is often more difficult for them to come out, since they are more reliant on their families within societies which still exhibit great degrees of racism, and they cannot take the risk that their families might turn their backs on them. Nor indeed can the process ever be said to have fully ended. There are always new acquaintances to tell, and even the most seasoned lesbians and gays can suddenly find themselves being very coy about themselves or a partner when they had thought that there was no one on earth who didn't know. Most lesbians and gays will, however, pick out one or two instances, such as telling the first person, telling parents, or the first time they had sex when everything suddenly seemed to make sense, which they regard as the significant rites of passage on their path to becoming a self-accepting guilt-free queer. They will often trade them as coming out stories among themselves as a way of bonding and demonstrating shared experience. The notion is of such significance to lesbians and gays that they employ it for other metaphorical purposes. For example, gay historians talk about the STONEWALL RIOT as the 'coming out' of the lesbian and gay movement, in spatial and metaphorical terms, since it involved gay life spilling out from the confines of a bar to demonstrate out on the streets. Transvestites, or lesbians and gay men who enjoy more radical forms of sexual expression, such as SADOMASOCHISM, also refer to coming out about these practices. An individual who has come out is described as 'out'.

Come Out! The newsletter of the New York section of the GAY LIBERATION FRONT. In its first issue in late 1969, it declared that 'we are going to transform the society at large through the open realization of our own consciousness'.

Come Together The newsletter of the London GAY LIBERATION FRONT and produced by its media workshop. The name was not only representative of the collectivist aspirations of the GLF, but also included a sexual innuendo and a conscious reference to the John Lennon song of the same name. The first issue appeared in November 1970, and the newsletter lasted for sixteen issues until it folded in 1973. With the intention of not refusing any articles written by members of the GLF, *Come Together* served as a written think-in, and documents the changes in political thinking that occurred in the early 1970s, particularly the realization on the part of many of the women that they should organize separately from the men.

coming out novel One of the popular forms of lesbian and gay literature, the coming out novel echoes the experience of most lesbians and gay men in describing the realization of one central character of their sexuality and their coming to terms with it. It provides a point of identification for people who have been through the process, and a much needed boost for those that are going through it, as well as giving space for a few juicy adolescent sex scenes. A BOY'S OWN STORY and RUBYFRUIT JUNGLE are two examples of the genre and, while much criticized, THE WELL OF LONELINESS performed the same purpose for a time. It has often been noted that coming out novels have historical precedents in the Bildungsroman genre of literature which was first associated with Goethe, and which was a standard form in German literature, where the central feature is the description of the development of one central character, particularly through the youth and a journey from the provinces to self-discovery in the metropolis – a route also common with lesbians and gay men. The Japanese watakushi shosetsu is also related, and *Confessions of a Mask* by Yukio MISHIMA is as an example of the Japanese form of the genre.

coming out story One's own personal experience(s) of COMING OUT.

Committee to Fight Exclusion of Homosexuals in the Armed Forces (CFEHAF) Organization founded in 1966 by leaders of the American HOMOPHILE MOVEMENT. While the committee might be seen as having supported the American war in Vietnam, it was not seeking only to have homosexuals admitted to the military forces. It also acted as a clearing house, giving information and support to young homosexuals – as well as straights who did not want to serve – to avoid the draft. In May 1966 the committee held a nationwide protest, with some 500 protesters in San Francisco alone.

community Within the social sciences, a 'community' is described as a concentration of those who identify themselves in one way, and organize themselves into primary groups. The notion also involves a spatial concentration of residence and of community institutions, learned norms, institutional completeness, collective action and a sense of shared history. Thus gay communities, particularly in urban areas, fit any definition of communities even on these strict criteria.

Community Research Initiative American organization founded in New York in 1987 by a coalition of people with AIDS. It aims to provide community-based study for drugs which promise to be effective for the treatment of AIDS and AIDS-related illnesses.

a company of amazons Name given by the writer Katherine Anne Porter to the women who graduated from America's colleges in the nineteenth and early twentieth centuries, who rejected the conventional female roles of their society, and who struck their own professional path, 'usurping' male privilege.

Compound Q A Chinese herbal medicine, formally known as trichosanthin, which in the late 1980s began to raise hopes as a possible treatment for HIV and AIDS. It was licensed in America in 1989 as a research drug for investigation in human trials, which effectively restricted who was allowed to take it.

compulsory heterosexuality A concept originally developed by lesbian feminists to refer to the complex and multifaceted ways in which women have been steered towards heterosexuality. For lesbian feminists, women have been literally forced into compulsory heterosexuality where their role is to service men sexually, physically (via housework and childcare), and emotionally. Historically it can be argued that the impossibility of women supporting themselves economically made autonomous lesbian lifestyles almost impossible and heterosexual marriage almost a necessity. Moreover, owing to the suppression of the history and of images of lesbians and women who lived without men, and owing to verbal and physical attacks on these women, heterosexuality has been presented as the only option. The concept of compulsory heterosexuality has been important in lesbian feminist theory, particularly in analysing the workings of patriarchy. Since the mid-1980s, the term compulsory heterosexuality has been used more by gay men and lesbians to describe the automatic assumption that everyone is, and will continue to be, heterosexual – specifically, the way that images in the media and experiences in housing, jobs and healthcare assume that everyone is heterosexual.

computer sex Sexual avenue that emerged as a possibility in the 1980s with the development of information technology systems that enabled people to write sexually explicit notes to each other via computer billboards.

comradeship Seen as a bonding between men, the idea of comradeship was idealized by writers of the late nineteenth and early twentieth centuries as a pure form of affection. Particularly associated with the idea is Walt WHITMAN, who describes his collection LEAVES OF GRASS as an attempt to 'celebrate the needs of comrades'.

Concorde trial A large-scale clinical trial of the effects of the drug AZT on the course of HIV, run by the British Medical Research Council, the full results of which were published in April 1994. It showed that there was no clear advantage to taking AZT early in HIV infection, rather than taking it when symptoms develop. Early AZT was seen to have only minor benefits for the T-CELL count, and on lesser illnesses, over a short period. Many people took the results of this survey as an indication that AZT itself does not work, although the trial itself offered no support for this position.

Conditions A feminist journal, founded in New York in 1976, with an emphasis on new writing by lesbians; it concentrated on issues of race and class in lesbian action.

condom Latex device for covering the dick during intercourse to prevent venereal disease and also, for straights, conception. The birth of condom-like devices is shrouded in historical mystery. Some maintain they were developed at the time of the Roman empire, others during the sixteenth century in Italy by the anatomist Gabriel Fallopius in order to retard the spread of syphilis. Another theory is that an English physician, Dr Conton, developed them as a contraceptive device for the royal court of Charles II. Throughout history, various materials, including silk, linen, tortoise shells and leather, have been used to make them. The sheep intestine was the favoured material until the rubbery species was created in 1844 with the advent of vulcanized rubber. In the 1980s the condom came into its own as a means for preventing transmission of the HIV virus during anal or oral sex. The reliance on condoms to prevent HIV ushered in what some have called the era of LATEX LOVE.

congenital inversion Explanation for male and female homosexuality developed by the late-nineteenth-century SEXOLOGISTS, principally Karl Heinrich ULRICHS, Richard von KRAFFT-EBING and Havelock ELLIS. Previously, homosexuality had been characterized as a moral failing from which anyone could suffer; it now became a congenital abnormality. The effects of this theory were profound and contradictory.

It changed the nature of what constituted homosexuality, making it a psychosexual condition which was beyond individual choice, instead of a wilfully chosen evil and immoral act. The abnormality in question was that of a mismatch between physiological gender and emotional gender: gay men were female souls trapped in male bodies; lesbians were male souls trapped in women's bodies. Thus homosexuality was a condition of the congenital inversion of the normal match between emotional sex and physical sex. Those who took on the congenital invert label were freed from the expectation of heterosexual marriage and, further, were provided with an argument against the moral approbation concerning their sexuality since they could argue that they were unable to do anything about it. Moreover, it gave lesbians and gay men the opportunity to organize around their naturally-occurring abnormality, to develop homosexual identities and hence homosexual communities. In general, while the work of the sexologists is seen as positive in respect to gay men, there is greater debate over its effects on lesbians. It has been argued that the sexologists actually gave women space to be sexual by giving them a masculine, i.e. sexually-desiring, inverted self. Conversely, it has been argued that the theory of congenital inversion sought to deny an autonomous sexually-desiring self for women, by routing all sexual desire through the male side of the invert. Notwithstanding the strategic importance of the theory of congenital inversion in the early part of the twentieth century, it has had clearly negative effects. First, because the theory of congenital inversion offered symmetrical explanations for male and female homosexuality, it actually highlighted lesbianism as a condition which was just as serious as male homosexuality. It made it more likely that women would be stigmatized as 'lesbians'. Second, the explanation of congenital inversion required the creation of a stereotype of the congenitally inverted man and woman. The stereotype of a congenital lesbian that was developed was that of the mannish woman, of the congenital male homosexual that of an effeminate man. These stereotypes remain the dominant images of lesbians and gay men in the straight world. Third, homosexuals were not completely exonerated from evilness by the sexologists, because the sexologists believed that what attracted the invert was the 'normal' type of both sexes, and that the invert would seek to corrupt these 'healthy' men and women and transform them into pseudohomosexuals. Thus although the invert could not be blamed for the perversity of his or her desires, that person must be restricted or restrained to prevent the corruption of the normal. This belief that anyone can be 'turned' may well be true. However, it has constantly been used as a way of restricting lesbian and gay rights by those who believe that homosexuality is basically a bad thing. There are many within the lesbian and gay community who argue for lesbian and gay rights on the grounds that our sexuality is genetically determined and beyond our control.

Conradin *See* SANTA MARIA DEL CARMINE.

consciousness raising groups Common event within liberation politics, which involves a group of people talking together about their experiences of oppression within society. Such groups were a particular feature of the feminist movement in the 1970s, where women could discuss sexual politics in relation to their own personal experience of patriarchy.

consenting adult Around the time of the WOLFENDEN REPORT and the SEXUAL OFFENCES ACT, the term consenting adult was so frequently used to describe the people who might want to take part in homosexual activities that it became a slang term for a gay man himself.

contact adverts The use of personal adverts by homosexuals seeking others who share their sexuality apparently dates from the beginning of the twentieth century, when lesbians and gay men in France and Germany placed adverts in the classified sections of mainstream newspapers calling for partners. In the 1960s the liberalism that was offered by the underground newspapers of the counterculture allowed such adverts to become more explicitly gay. Many lesbians and gay men who were not part of such communities meanwhile continued to place discreet adverts in 'respectable' publications, although they were often drawn to ones that had an apparently large gay readership (*see for example* FILMS AND FILMING). After gay liberation, with the growth of community newspapers scanning the personals has become a lesbian and gay sport, on a par with LIPSYNCHING. Gay male adverts in particular have become extremely explicit, with their own complex series of abbreviations (*see for example* FF; GDLK; JO; LIAHO; LVS; SM; WS). *See also* HANKIE CODES.

convent *See* MONASTICISM.

Copenhagen The Danish capital city became associated with TRANSSEXUALISM in the early 1950s, when Christine (née George) Jorgensen (1926–89) returned from there to the United States to great media attention as the century's most renowned post-operative male to female transsexual. She went on to make numerous appearances on American TV to try and explain the phenomenon to the public. Consequently, GENDER REASSIGNMENT SURGERY became known in American gay slang as 'going Copenhagen'. More recently, Denmark has become famous for the marked liberalism of its laws regarding homosexuality, and particularly on lesbian and gay partnerships (*see* MARRIAGE).

coprolalia Technical term for the use of sexually stimulating language during sex. Also known as talking dirty, or providing a soundtrack.

coprophilia Technical term for SCAT.

cornholer American slang for a gay man who engages in anal sex. It originated in rural America, where dried corncobs were apparently used for anal cleanliness. The verb to cornhole therefore means to be the active partner in anal sex.

Corydon In the second *Eclogue* of the Roman poet Virgil (Publius Vergilius Maro, 70–19 BC) Corydon is the shepherd who is lovesick for the boy Alexis. Corydon is a native of Arcadia, a place that has become mythically associated with simple and open living not only by the literati, but by gay men as well. It seems likely that Virgil himself was not a stranger to devotion to other men. A poem, which was written as a youth when leaving Rome, mentions his 'chiefest love', one Sextus Sabinus. Virgil's nickname of 'Parthenias' (The Virgin), indicates that he may well have been a little wallflower and held back from actually consummating that love. Although the *Eclogues* all deal with sentiment between men and youths, it is Corydon who has stuck in the gay imagination. This was as a result of the essay by French writer André Gide, begun in 1907 but not published until 1924, which discusses the place of homosexuality in society. Taking the form of a dialogue, the essay argued that homosexual desire was an 'important and not contemptible' part of human experience.

cottage British gay slang for a public toilet where men go to cruise for sex (*see also* TEAROOM). The word was part of the British gay slang POLARI. Cottages are so named because most British toilets are set in small buildings in parks or squares, and have a decidedly Hansel and Gretel feel about them. To go cruising for sex in a toilet is known as cottaging. The practice is the focus of some controversy. Not only are those who go cottaging liable to arrest, but many women feel that it is part of the aggressiveness of male sexuality to engage in public sex, and conventional wisdom on cottaging is that it is only done by sad homosexuals who are usually married and who are deeply closeted. Thus they are unable to visit a more salubrious sexual arena and have to settle for sordid sex in such environs. However, there are a substantial number of perfectly well-adjusted gay men who choose to go cottaging as an alternative to the ritual of cruising and posing in bars. They argue that if one is looking merely for a casual sexual contact they might as well go here, where everyone seems to be interested in sex, as any-where else. Moreover, many positively enjoy the frisson of danger, and the smell of urine and the meditative dripping of taps can become addictive. Yet gay ASSIMI-LATIONISTS who seek to clean up our image deny these arguments and prefer to peddle the conventional wisdom. After all, if cot-taging is bad and only CLOSET cases cot-tage, then gay liberation will end cottaging. For this reason it is very difficult for a gay man to be open about his cottag-ing practices – he is held within a cottage closet. Cottaging has made a limited breakthrough into the media. It is usually dealt with in the form of voyeuristic docu-mentary. However, the film TAXI ZUM KLO incorporates a scene in which a teacher takes a taxi from the hospital for sex in a toilet, and sits marking essays while wait-ing for action. The film PRICK UP YOUR EARS shows the cottaging scenes about which Joe ORTON was very candid in his diaries.

Council on Religion and the Homosexual Consultative body set up between the San Francisco lesbian and gay rights groups, the MATTACHINE SOCIETY and the DAUGHTERS OF BILITIS, and some more liberal Protestant ministers within the city in order to begin to change the position of organized reli-gions on homosexuality. In order to raise funds, a New Year's Ball was held in 1965 at which the police employed extremely intimidating tactics such as floodlighting the entrance and photographing everyone coming in. Many of the ministers who attended were so shocked by the treatment they saw meted out that they came to sup-port fully the lesbian and gay rights cause, and sparked off debates within Protestant churches about queer sexuality. The pub-licity surrounding the incident also led to the setting up of a police liaison to the gay community.

counterculture A culture with beliefs and value systems which are at odds with those of the dominant society. The word is particularly associated with the HIPPIE movement of the 1960s when a great many young people in Europe and America began to question the lifestyles expected of them, developing alternative political views which included an accent on non-violence and the environment, as well as the doctrine of free love, and a freer atti-tude to personal dress, which tended to a more unisex style. The movement had a large impact on the expression of lesbian and gay politics in the early 1970s. While the movement undoubtedly enabled many men to question the basis of the social role of men, it has been heavily criticized from within the later women's movement as doing nothing for the position of women; they were expected to play a nurturing 'earth mother' role which differed little from dominant ideas of motherhood, and were also required to be sexually available without being sexually in control.

cow In the works of lesbian poet Gertrude STEIN, such as *Lifting Belly*, *A Sonatina Followed by Another*, DIDN'T NELLY AND LILLY LOVE YOU and *As a Wife Has a Cow: A Love Story* a code is employed to refer to inti-mate sexual details between women. In this code the word cow is used to mean orgasm.

Coward, Sir Noël (1899–1973) English actor, composer and playwright, who is an epit-ome of the stereotype of the gay 'theatrical type'. Coward first achieved attention on the stage as a boy in a 1911 production of *The Goldfish* by Lila Field. His polished plays create a world of the leisured, mon-eyed and pleasure-seeking classes that was somewhat at odds with the hard times in which they were produced. His works did not however add significantly to the canon of gay-themed works, although *Design for Living* (1933) contains a depiction of an unconventional ménage à trois, whilst one of his last works, A SONG AT TWILIGHT, has an exploration of closetedness.

Cowardly Lion One of Dorothy's compan-ions in the 1939 camp film classic THE WIZARD OF OZ, the lion joined her in his own search for courage. He struck a chord with gay audiences when he sang, 'It's sad believe me missy, when you're born to be a sissy...'

crabs To have crabs is to play host to an infestation of crab lice, the nasty little parasite that takes over the pubic hair, chest hair and even, horrors, the facial hair, and which won't sit still. In the fast-moving world of gay casual sex, crabs are presented between men faster than you can snap a claw. Slang terms for the unpleasant experience include crotch crickets, love bugs, social dandruff and even, when you get to know them well enough, the family. Gay men will often keep a vat of Quellada on hand, just in case.

cream Slang term for sperm. The verb to cream therefore means to come. On meeting a particularly horny man, gay men will often claim to have creamed (in) their jeans.

Crete Among the aristocracy of archaic Crete homosexual relations were used as part of the initiation process, in a way which was similar to the institutionalized homosexuality of SPARTA. In fact, many Greeks believed that pederastic practices had originated in Crete. A young man would announce his intention to abduct a boy, and would go ahead if he received approval from both families. He would usually take the boy to a country house where he would hold feasts for his friends, and the two would engage in sexual relations. The boy would remain with his lover (*philetor*) for some two months, and on his return would be presented with a suit of armour and a bull to sacrifice to Zeus. The ritual shares in common with initiation rites in other areas the fact of removing the boy from his family for a temporary period. The story of Zeus and GANYMEDE has been read as as a symbolic representation of this ritual.

Crisco Popular brand of lubricant which was used widely in the 1970s for anal sex and FISTING. It declined in popularity with the advent of AIDS since it was oil based and so weakened the rubber of condoms.

Crisp, Quentin (1909–) British writer, actor and propagandist of life in America. The man who described himself as one of the 'stately homos' of England is something of an enigma to post-liberation gays who equate being out with being proud with being militant, and vice versa. Crisp, who was plastering on the slap when the WOLFENDEN REPORT was still a tree, spent the early twentieth century as 'not merely a self-confessed homosexual, but a self-evident one'. He was reviled within the nascent gay subculture because his flamboyance was too homo for safety, and he risked violence daily on his solo crusade to bring swish to the streets of London. Even after the television showing of THE NAKED CIVIL SERVANT in 1975, he was still the subject of criticism in the gay press from 'normal' gays who felt that he rocked their hetero-friendly canoe a little too much. And yet he obstinately refuses to be a hero for post-liberation politicos. He is critical of the effect on Joe Het of the activism of ACT UP and QUEER NATION, and he has not put himself into the fight against AIDS. He even described disco music as 'a high price to pay for one's sexual preference'. Perhaps it is best to see Crisp as obscuring any easy division between closet and radical. If not self-consciously political, his has been a life lived in honesty, and with the belief that style and integrity could eventually win through; as he said, 'Those who once inhabited the suburbs of human contempt find that without changing their address they eventually live in the metropolis.' In the 1990s Crisp has made a few film and TV appearances: as the most stately Queen Elizabeth I in Sally Potter's version of Virginia Woolf's ORLANDO (1992); in the party scenes in PHILADELPHIA (1993); and on Britain's Channel Four on Christmas Day delivering the *Alternative Queen's Speech* in which he eulogized the New York lifestyle and disparaged British coldness.

cross-dressing For women, the act of cross-dressing has often been connected with attempts to transcend the position into which they have historically been forced. During and before the nineteenth century, history records numerous cases of women who dressed entirely as men (*see* PASSING WOMEN) in order to enjoy male privileges of employment and freedom. The nineteenth century saw certain examples of women publicly and partially cross-dressing. At first these were associated primarily with the growth of the feminist movement, as with the French writer George Sand or the American medical practitioner Mary Walker. As the century progressed and the writers on sex associated male characteristics with the female INVERT, any male dress began to be associated with lesbianism.

crowd The clientele of a particular queer bar or club. The people you see every time you go to a place, but never talk to.

Crown and Woolpack Pub in Islington, London, which held women-only dances in the 1970s.

crucifix In a statement that demonstrated her ongoing struggle with the deep-seated effects of her Catholic upbringing, the redoubtable MADONNA declared, 'Crucifixes are sexy because there's a naked man on them.'

cruise To be on the hunt for a sex partner. Cruising can go on anywhere, and with gay men it usually does, in bars, on trains and in cruising grounds, or the parks, toilets and other public places where gay men meet for sex. Gay men have cruising down to a fine art, and are always ready should somebody cute come along, at however inconvenient an hour.

Cruising Widely-panned film released in 1980 and starring Al Pacino as a straight cop who goes into the New York gay SM community to track a serial killer. Since queerness is contagious, he eventually ends up confused about his own sexual identity. Occasioned criticism from gay activists who disliked the fact that it centred on SM, giving us all a bad name, from moral majority types who disliked the SM focus for different reasons, and from film critics who simply thought it was a dreadful film, which didn't explore anything in a particularly interesting way. Funnily, it bombed.

cruising codes Before the days of red NECKTIES, suede SHOES and elaborated HANKIE CODES gay men had already developed sophisticated ways of making contact with one another when on the hunt for sex. One record of 1781 describes how eighteenth-century MOLLIES might tip the wink to one another: 'If one of them sits upon a bench he pats the back of his hands; if you follow them, they put a white handkerchief through the skirt of their coat, and wave it to and fro; but if they are met by you, their thumbs are stuck in the armpits of their waistcoats, and they play their fingers upon their breasts.'

crush Name given, usually within a college environment, to an infatuation. The use of this term has been recorded since the late nineteenth century in American women's colleges.

crush hour That magical moment, the twitching hour, when the clientele of a gay bar or club realize that it is pushing closing time and they have yet to score for the night. Palms sweat, dancing becomes more frenetically exhibitionist, and standards evaporate as anything with a pulse is accepted. While not always the stroke of midnight, a few pumpkins are usually in evidence. Men pulled at this time are affectionately referred to as DESPERATION NUMBERS.

crypto Cryptococcus, an infection in people with AIDS which usually causes meningitis with fevers, headaches and neck-stiffness.

Cullen, Countee (1903–46) Black American poet who was associated with the HARLEM RENAISSANCE. He became known as Harlem's poet laureate with the publication of *Copper Sun* and *The Ballad of the Brown Girl*. A disastrous marriage to Yolanda DuBois, the daughter of black scholar W.E.B. DuBois followed, and he eventually eloped with his best man, Harold Jackman. His writings included black themes, but topics such as lynching were not always consonant with his lyrical style.

cultural feminism The pejorative description of a strand of lesbian feminist thought, which, it is claimed, is more concerned with the reclaiming and sanctifying of traditional womanliness than with the challenge of sexism, misogyny and homophobia in the real world. To ascribe essential and transcendental qualities to men and women is one of the hallmarks of cultural feminism, for instance that women are peace-loving and nurturing while men are aggressive and focused on material success. The lesbian politics that cultural feminism produces leaves little space for lesbian SM, lesbian meateaters, lesbian soldiers or lesbian lotharios, all of whom are believed to have been brainwashed by patriarchy. It should be noted that lesbian feminists deny that their interest is a conservative and spiritual cultural feminism, and suggest that the model of cultural feminism has been set up by PRO-SEX LESBIANS in order to discredit lesbian feminists.

Cultuur en Ontspannings-Centrum (COC) Dutch gay organization founded in 1946 and held to be the oldest lesbian and gay organization that still exists. In the 1960s, with a membership of some 4,000, COC was the largest such society in the world.

cum *See* COME.

cum shot The obligatory part of a gay male porn film, where even if one guy is fucking another, he takes his dick out and comes over his ass, back or stomach. Many viewers have taken this to be a porn reaction to HIV, but the custom predated safer sex and has always been a means of showing torrents of virile cum.

cunt Slang term for the vagina. Derived from the Latin *cunnus* meaning vulva.

cunt art Lesbian feminist art form which became popular in the 1970s, and sought to draw on the female anatomy as an artistic resource. Lesbians have also claimed the work of American artist Georgia O'Keeffe, whose luxuriant paintings of flowers have a seductive erotic potency.

cuntry Alternative form for the word country, indicating the centrality of women's relations with one another in creating the social make-up of a state. Using the word cunt as a root, it also humorously uses women's bodies as the centre of social relations.

custody Married women who come out as lesbian often face the prospect of losing their children; arguments that their lesbianism makes them unsuitable as a parent often play a large part in court proceedings. However, since the late 1970s an increasing number of lesbians have won their custody cases. In a landmark case in America in 1979, the Michigan Supreme Court reversed a lower court ruling which had denied Margaret Miller custody of her daughter, saying that her sexuality was immaterial to the case. Nevertheless, it is still difficult to set legal precedent in this area, since court rulings need not be explicit about the importance of a mother's lesbianism in denying custody.

cut Adjective for a circumcised dick, the opposite being UNCUT. Men seem prepared to go to war in defence of their foreskin, or lack of. Cut men smugly announce that their way is more healthy, since reports suggest that having a foreskin can leave one more open to certain forms of cancer and that cuts to the foreskin during sex can lead to greater vulnerability to HIV transmission. Further, they claim, it is more hygienic and olfactorily pleasing, since foreskins can harbour nasty COCK CHEESE. Uncut men counterargue that the foreskin preserves the sensitivity of their jewel, and looks nicer, and if washed properly doesn't need to smell at all. Apart from religious traditions that require circumcision within Judaism (*see* KOSHER), the practice is more common in America, for health reasons. Slang terms for a cut dick include a clipped cock and a low neckline.

cut sleeve (duanxiu) The 'passion of the cut sleeve' was a classical Chinese euphemism for male homosexual affection. It derives from a popular story which describes how the Emperor Ai of the Western Han dynasty (6 BC to AD 1) fell asleep during the day with his male favourite and lover,

Dong Xian, lying across the sleeve of his robes. When the Emperor needed to get up, he did not want to wake his lover, and instead he cut the sleeve of his robe off. According to the RECORDS OF THE CUT SLEEVE, the episode was so admired by the Emperor's courtiers that they also removed one sleeve from their tunics. Moreover, men of subsequent ages used the term cut sleeve to describe their homosexual feelings, thus locating themselves within an ancient and illustrious tradition which had at one time been entirely integrated into Chinese life.

Records of the Cut Sleeve Anthology, editor unknown, of short vignettes dealing with same-sex eroticism, which was collected during the Ming dynasty in China (1368–1644). *See also* CUT SLEEVE.

cutting The activity of cutting the body, with knives, razors or needles, may be practised as a part of SADOMASOCHISTIC sex, though it is less common than PIERCING or TATTOOING. SM theorists, who seek to link their sex with the rituals of other cultures, point to the anthropological literature on scarification as part of the ceremony of reaching adulthood which is common in parts of Africa, among Australian aboriginals, and on many South Pacific islands. Thus, for them, cutting represents part of the ceremony of reaching majority as a serious SM player and of entry to the masculine cult which for many SM exemplifies. *See also* TATTOOING.

cytomegalovirus (CMV) A generalized infection which is often contracted by people with AIDS. It can be present in the eye (retinitis), gullet (oesophagitis) or intestines (colitis). Retinitis results in deteriorating eyesight in those who are affected. CMV has been linked to African KAPOSI'S SARCOMA.

D

Drag

daddle Verb meaning to have lesbian sex in a face-to-face position.

daddy American prison and working-class lesbian slang of the 1930s which described the BUTCH partner in a lesbian butch/femme relationship.

Dahomean Amazons Dahomey was an African state which became Benin in 1975. The Dahomean army included a battalion of women described as its shock troops. The battalion comprised units of musketeers, archers and razor women who carried sharp knives especially designed to decapitate enemy chieftains.

Dahoum The name given by English soldier and folk hero T. E. Lawrence (Lawrence of Arabia, 1888–1935) to Salim Ahmed, the Arab boy whom he kept as his companion, and to whom he dedicated *The Seven Pillars of Wisdom*. The emotional, if not the sexual links, between Lawrence and two Arab boys are explored in David Lean's 1962 film *Lawrence of Arabia*, where their deaths play a part in understanding the sometimes enigmatic decisions that are the hallmarks of Lawrence's career.

daisy chain Slang term from the 1950s for occasions when more than two men engage in anal sex simultaneously, with the man or men in the middle both fucking and being fucked. To get all the rhythms synchronized takes quite a feat of stage management. Also known as a chain gang, or a floral arrangement. The man in the middle of a three-man daisy chain is known in US slang as lucky Pierre or a chicken on a spit.

Dallas, Jodie Gay character in the spoof TV series *Soap*, who was played by comedian Billy Crystal. Jodie was originally billed to be effeminate and to enjoy dressing in his mother's clothes. However, BUTCH gays protested and Jodie eventually appeared as a more masculine character. By the second series Jodie became bisexual, and fathered a son.

Damon and Pythias Couple in ancient Greek legend. Pythias was condemned to death by the tyrant Dionysus, but was freed temporarily to go home and organize his affairs. Damon stayed under arrest in his place to make sure that he returned. When Pythias did in fact come back, Dionysus was so affected by their devotion to one another that he released them. Speculation exists as to how close they really were.

dandyism The concept of the dandy was developed around the turn of the nineteenth century. It was most associated initially with the character of George Bryan 'Beau' Brummell (1778–1840), who was a 'close friend' of the Prince Regent and who was famed for his immaculate dress and impeccable manners. The dandy style thus became one of perfecting external appearances, with the implication that the surface was more important that anything that lay beneath. The style can be seen as an embodiment in terms of personal behaviour and dress of the artistic theories of AESTHETICISM and ART FOR ART'S SAKE. It was very much a style of the nobility and, since the nobility was regarded as less than masculine, it was seen as an effeminate concentration on the women's domain of sartorial fineries. Since in the nineteenth century ideas of gender and of sexuality were so often conflated, the effeminate was by extension homosexual, the dandy had connotations of homosexuality, and the homosexual was represented as a dandy. However, the category was also one that was understandable to gay men themselves because they had customarily only been able to imply their sexuality through dress, mannerism and oblique reference, rather than through direct statement. The word dandy served as an acceptable way of intimating homosexuality even during the twentieth century. In THE WIZARD OF OZ the 'sissy' COWARDLY LION sings of himself as 'a dandy-lion'.

Danebury or the Power of Friendship A 1777 poem written by an anonymous 'lady' which deals with the passionate relationship between two women during the battles between the Saxons and Danes. One woman, Elfrida, is injured by a poisoned arrow, but she is saved by Emma, who sucks the poison into her own body. Emma is eventually cured, and the two live happily ever after.

dangle queen Male exhibitionist, who likes to let it all hang out for others to see. A common feature of COTTAGES. *See* QUEEN.

Daughters of Bilitis First lesbian organization in America, founded in 1955 in San Francisco by Del Martin and Phyllis Lyon. Other chapters were later formed in other cities. The first East Coast chapter was established in New York in 1958, with lesbian activist Barbara Gittings as president. Initially created as a social group, the organization soon found it impossible to avoid working to demand lesbian rights. The name of the group was taken from the hoax poetry anthology LES CHANSONS DE BILITIS. The group published its own magazine, THE LADDER.

David Michelangelo's famous eighteen-foot marble sculpture, crafted in 1504. Known as 'Il gigante', the sculpture was erected in the porch of the Palazzo Vecchio in Florence. Palpably erotic, the statue has at various times been fitted with a fig leaf to cover its dignity, and pictures of it, as often the only available representation of a nude man, have been used by gay men as a prototypical wank mag.

David and Jonathan The David and Jonathan story is, along with ALEXANDER AND HEPHAESTION, at the top of the hit parade of mythical gay relationships that appear in the writings and speech of gay people. In the Bible's Book of Samuel it was after he had slain the Philistine champion Goliath that David, described as 'goodly to look at', met and seemingly attracted the ardour of Jonathan, the son of King Saul, who 'loved him as his own soul'. Saul became increasingly worried about David's influence, and eventually David was forced to leave the court. The two lovers had one final meeting, where 'they kissed one another and wept one with another' (1 Sam. 20:41). When David ultimately heard the news that Jonathan had been killed in battle with the Philistines, he declared, 'I am distressed for thee, my brother Jonathan: very pleasant hast thou been to me: thy love to me was wonderful, passing the love of women' (2 Samuel. 1:26). After the deaths of Jonathan and Saul, David went on to become the second king of Israel. The story has become a standard point of reference for other lesbian and gay relationships. The British poet Anna Seward (THE SWAN OF LICHFIELD) referred to it in her description of THE LADIES OF LLANGOLLEN, while friends of black poet Countee Cullen referred to him and his close 'friend' and best man, Harold Jackman, as David and Jonathan as well.

Davis, Bette (Ruth Elizabeth Davis, 1908–89) Member of the A-list of gay male ICONs, and staple part of the act of every DRAG QUEEN in the galaxy, with her easily recognizable and easily caricaturable mannerisms, arched eyebrows and cigarette permanently held aloft. But her career full of chunky roles stopped her becoming a caricature of herself. She is most often recalled for her fading Broadway queen in *All about Eve* (1950), since goddess playing goddess provides a double dose of gay iconography. Her line from the 1949 production *Beyond the Forest*, 'What a dump!', has also entered the standard repertoire of gay repartee.

a day to blow or get blown From the poem 'The Platonic Blow', written in 1948 by W. H. Auden, and which sometimes appears in unauthorized versions as 'The Gobble Poem'. The two opening lines refer to a spring day as an occasion for a lay, with the air smelling like a locker room, 'a day to blow or get blown'. It was Auden who, in singing the joys of Arab youths in Morocco, wrote, 'Here's to women for they have such lovely kiddies.'

a day without human rights is like a day without sunshine Gay rights slogan subverted from the orange juice commercial which was fronted by American arch-homophobe Anita BRYANT.

DDI (didanosine) Drug that is sometimes used to treat people with HIV and AIDS who are unable to tolerate the side-effects of AZT. It is part of a line of drugs related to AZT which are being developed, and was the second drug that was licensed by America's Food And Drug Administration to be used for people with AIDS. DDI also causes side-effects in some people, although ones different to AZT, such as diarrhoea, pancreatitis and pains, pins and needles and numbness in the feet. DDC is another such analogue.

de-gaying AIDS The process that took place amongst AIDS educators and some parts of the media from the mid-1980s to challenge public conceptions of the epidemic. They sought to emphasize that sexually transmitted HIV was a potential health threat to all sectors of the population and not, as it had been conceived before, just to gay men. Thus, a flurry of education materials appeared that stressed the possibility of HIV transmitted through heterosexual intercourse. Somewhat paradoxically, the effort took off in 1985 as a result of the panic which ensued from the high-profile death of film star Rock HUDSON, when a complacent America had been shown that one of the icons of its masculine ideal was actually a masquerading queer. Gay activists colluded in the process, in the hope that it would lessen the discrimination and abuse that was being levelled at the whole gay community as a result of the epidemic. Thus gay AIDS organizations began to stress that they were there for anyone affected by AIDS, not just gay men. *See* RE-GAYING AIDS.

Death in Venice Novella by Thomas Mann. It deals with the infatuation felt by the disillusioned and middle-aged writer Gustave von Aschenbach for the young Tadzio whilst on holiday in Venice. Adapted for the screen in 1971 by Luchino Visconti. In the film version, Aschenbach becomes a composer. The film occasioned criticism for being too homoerotic.

debutante A gay man who is on his first visit to a gay bar or club, a gay virgin who is about to embark on his first taste of the forbidden fruit of gay sex, or a man who is stepping out for the first time in a frock and heels.

decadents Literary term narrowly applied to the French symbolist poets such as Stéphane Mallarmé (1842–98) and the turbulent couple, Arthur Rimbaud (1854–91) and Paul Verlaine (1844–96), who had a relationship which ended in Brussels with a prison sentence for Verlaine and bullet wounds for Rimbaud. The term is also more broadly applied to the mainly French writers of the post-Romantic period who with their call of EPATER LE BOURGEOIS deliberately chose subject matter which they knew would affront middle-class sensibilities, including same-sex eroticism, and who were similarly sensational in their social behaviour. In their attempts to emphasize form rather than ethical content of artistic works, they were related to the ART FOR ART'S SAKE movement of British AESTHETICISM, which included Oscar WILDE.

Declaration of Sentiments and Resolutions Document based on the American Declaration of Independence which was passed in 1848 by the American Women's Rights Convention. It was one of the first signs of a growing feminist movement.

Declaration of the Rights of Women and Citizens 1791 feminist document by the French dramatist Olympe de Gouges. The work was inspired by the aims of the French Revolution, and its title was a reference to the Declaration of the Rights of Man which set forth the principles of the revolution and was passed by the French Constituent Assembly in 1789. De Gouges was however acutely critical of the way in which women had been treated under the Revolution. The declaration marked the beginning of the feminist movement in France.

deedee Hindi word for sister. It is used in camp talk by south Asian queens to refer to one another.

deep-throating Oral sex with a bloke during which you go down on the whole length of his dick. Often associated with mouth fucking, when instead of the person sucking providing the movement it is the one being sucked who jams his dick in and out, as he would with any, or nearly any, other orifice.

Deephaven 1877 novel by the American writer Sarah Orne Jewett (1849–1909). The book portrays an exquisite ROMANTIC FRIENDSHIP between two young New England women. The two toy with the idea of setting up home together, like THE LADIES OF LLANGOLLEN, though they are in the end unable to renounce their Boston activities. The novelist was herself active in the feminist movement, and railed against the detrimental effects of marriage on women. She had a series of romantic friendships when young, and lived in a BOSTON MARRIAGE with Annie Fields. The two spent much of three decades together, parting every now and then so that they could concentrate more fully on their work.

Delafield, Kate Fictional lesbian detective created by the queen of lesbian crime, Katherine V. Forrest. She appears in the novels *Amateur City, Murder at the Nightwood Bar, The Beverly Malibu* and *Murder by Tradition*.

Demeter The story of Demeter and Persephone is one in which many lesbian writers have found a lesbian reading. According to Greek legend, Persephone ('the maid') was collecting flowers when she reached for the NARCISSUS, a flower that is associated with homosexuality, and was abducted into the underworld. Her mother, Demeter the earth mother, with the aid of the crone goddess HECATE went off to search for her, withholding the fruits of the earth for the duration of her travels. When she was found, Persephone embraced Hecate and became her companion. American lesbian writer Judy Grahn argues that there are strong bonds of attraction not only between Persephone and Hecate, but also with her mother as well. Moreover, Grahn reports that some historians believe that the rites associated with the worship of the two goddesses involved lesbian sex.

dental dam A small square of latex, which can be placed over the vagina or anus to ensure that cunnilingus or rimming are safe from any threat of HIV transmission. They are of fairly unprepossessing appearance and taste, and many have claimed that they might as well be going down on a shopping bag.

Denver Principles *See* PWA.

A Description of Millennium Hall Title of a novel by the English author Sarah Scott which was originally published in 1762 and which quickly went through four editions. It tells the story of two ROMANTIC FRIENDS, Louisa Mancel and Miss Melvyn, who find a perfect relationship with one another whilst at boarding school. They vow to stay together after they finish at school, but this vow is temporarily confounded when Miss Melvyn marries and her husband forbids her to see Louisa. Fortunately, the husband dies, allowing the two women to be together, and with some financial means. Together with two other romantic friends they set up home, where they devote themselves to good works such as training women for employment, and providing a welcome for the old and infirm. The novel is mirrored by the author's life. Although Scott was married, she divorced, and the settlement included an income which allowed her to set up home with her romantic friend, Barbara Montagu. The novel is perhaps the archetype of the romantic friendship genre.

Desert Hearts 1985 film directed by Donna Deitch based on Jane Rule's 1963 novel of self-discovery, and emergent lesbian identity, *Desert of the Heart*. It tells the story of a staid college lecturer (played by Helen Shaver) who goes to Nevada to collect her divorce and, whilst on a ranch there, falls in love with the openly lesbian daughter of the ranch-owner (Patrica Charbonneau). An inspiring if fairy-tale love story, steamily erotic, the film caught the hearts and minds of lesbian audiences, though it never really broke into the mainstream, unlike later movies which steered clear of overt lesbian love, such as THELMA AND LOUISE.

Design for Living 1933 play by Noël Coward (1899–1973) which presented an ambiguous ménage à trois between two men and a female interior decorator, who tries to share her life with the two and to marry a third. It was advertised as a play about 'three people who love each other very much', and was one of the first plays to mention the love-word to explain the relationship between two men. As one explains, 'I love you. You love me. You love Otto. I love Otto. Otto loves you. Otto loves me.' Whilst a 1979 television version showed the men showering together, the sexual nature of their relationship is only hinted at.

desperation number Slang term for the kind of pick-up you make when a bar or club is about to close and you haven't yet scored. It is at this time that people's standards begin to plummet, and you often end up with something that you wouldn't look at twice normally.

deviance (1) Descriptive term used from the 1920s to label all sexual and gender behaviour and identity which is not missionary-position heterosexuality. (2) Sexual deviation was theorized from the 1950s in an Anglo-American sociological analysis which focuses on those who deviate from societal rules and norms. Deviance analysis assumes that breaking a social rule, and suffering the penalties which go with this, is the same kind of act whatever the rule that is broken. Thus the term lumps together flashers, rapists, paedophiles, gay men, lesbians, sadomasochists, drag queens, transsexuals and all other prohibited sex and gender behaviour, without asking why people have broken social rules or why and how those particular social rules developed in the first place. Thus it not only refuses to see the differences between different forms of 'deviance', but also undermines any political thrust of any of these identities. This notwithstanding, QUEER activists and PRO-SEX dykes have tended to use the label of deviant self-referentially. Yet, while 'Sexual deviant – OK!' might be a good slogan for a T-shirt, the group of sexual deviants picked out by deviance analysis is so diverse that such analysis seems about as useful as analysis of society by brand of toothpaste.

diamonds are a girl's best friend Title of a 1949 song with music by Jule Styne and lyrics by Leo Robin.

Diana Ancient Roman goddess who was identified with the Greek goddess Artemis. As Diana, she was associated with hunting and with fertility. Hence she was the object of devotion by many women. As Artemis, she is associated with virginity, and was said to have demanded the chastity from her attendants that she practised herself. It is not surprising then that many women who lived without compromising themselves by marriage chose to identify with this active and (heterosexually) chaste goddess. For example, European WITCHcraft has been seen by some historians as the vestiges of a Diana cult. She also appears as an icon for NEW WOMEN in the title of the novel DIANA VICTRIX.

Diana: A Strange Autobiography An autobiographical novel by Diana Frederics, published in 1939, which presented a positive view of lesbianism uncharacteristic of literature of the period. As a schoolgirl, Diana falls in love with a schoolmate. She is alarmed at this, but her brother introduces her to the works of Havelock ELLIS and Sigmund FREUD. By the end of the novel she lives happily with another woman. The novel asserted that only women with character and intelligence would acknowledge their lesbianism and express it. It is explicit about lesbian sex, and offers a spirited defence of casual sex between women, saying that, since lesbian relationships are not recognized, there is no need for lesbians to consider the restrictions society places on heterosexual relationships.

Diana Victrix Novel by Florence Converse published in 1897, which describes the emotional bonds between two women, Enid and Sylvia. Both reject the drudgery of marriage for their ROMANTIC FRIENDSHIP, and the freedom it gives them to pursue professional accomplishments. It is this nurturing and understanding relationship that allows them to contravene the marital conventions of Victorian society, and allows the goddess DIANA of the title's inference to reign supreme. The physical intimacy between the two is also described. They sleep together and whisper 'very many things very softly in the dark'. By contrast, their acquaintance Rosa has internalized the Victorian female role to the extent that success for her rests on landing an impressive marital catch.

dick (1) Slang term for penis. It is probably derived from the English word dirk, which meant a small sword, itself derived from the term dorke, which meant an animal's horns. Alternatively, in the sixteenth century dick was used to mean a fellow, and was therefore applied to the little fellow down there in the nineteenth century. (2) Used by gay men to refer to sex itself, as in 'I'm going to get some dick tonight'.

Dickinson, Emily (1830–86) American poet, whose terse works belong in a tradition of American poetry that also includes Walt WHITMAN. Dickinson's emotional life remains shrouded in a great deal of mystery. However, what is certain is that most of her most intense relationships were with women, particularly Sue Gilbert and Kate Scott Anthon. Many of her letters to women are written with a passion which cannot be ascribed simply to the flowery language of convention. Unfortunately, only a small proportion of her correspondence has survived. To what extent these relationships were 'lesbian' is more controversial, and depends, of course, on the definition of lesbianism (i.e. whether it necessarily means genital sexuality) that is used. Dickinson's poetic voice is usually one of the lover pursuing her beloved and seeking security in a relationship. Such affections are not always returned.

Didn't Nelly and Lilly Love You 1922 poetic rendition by Gertrude STEIN which describes her 'proposal' to her lover Alice B. TOKLAS. Although Stein uses the masculine gender throughout to refer to herself (and the feminine for Alice), the subterfuge is easily penetrated. The title derives from the fact that Gertrude was buoyed in her confidence about the proposal because she knew that Alice had had close relationships with Eleanor Joseph (Nelly) and Lily Anna Hanson (Lilly) and thus would not be perturbed by any protestations of affection. The poem goes on to describe the two women setting up home together in Paris, as well as their sexual relationship (employing the word COW to mean orgasm as Stein does elsewhere). A lesbian romance with a happy ever after, quite remarkable for early-twentieth-century literature.

diesel dyke A particularly BUTCH lesbian, the sort with a skinhead, big leathers and massive DOC MARTENS. *See also* DYKE.

Dietrich, Marlene (1904–92) The apparition-like screen queen, who became an overnight sensation in the vampish image of Lola in *The Blue Angel*, vies with GARLAND for the position of gay ICON supreme. As mysterious as GARBO, but with an arched eyebrow that spelt sexual awareness and control as well as scepticism about the protestations of love that she received. When she sang 'See what the boys in the backroom will have' in *Destry Rides Again* (1939), she showed herself as a woman who knew what was what, and the connotations for a gay audience were obvious. Her butch performances in MOROCCO and *Blonde Venus*, where she donned male clothing and made sexual advances towards other women (however playful) have entered lesbian cinematic iconography. This appealing androgyny was something she carried into her real life; she was one of the first women to wear trousers in public, and in her performances of the 1950s she put on tails and sang love songs without switching pronouns to heterosexualize the lyrics.

Dignity Organization for gay Catholics, formed in Los Angeles in 1969. Oddly enough, that centre of world progressiveness and tolerance, the Vatican, has not welcomed its queer members with open arms.

dildos Artificial phalluses. Dildos have been with us since the dawn of time. The ancient Egyptians used them, as did the Greeks, who fashioned them from wood or leather. The Chinese made them from glass, lacquered wood and ivory, and even created a device to spurt warm fluids from the dildo into the orifice in which it was inserted. With the advent of rubber, dildos have been able to look much more like dicks, or even certain famous dicks. One popular brand is fashioned from a cast of the cock of popular porn star Jeff STRYKER.

dilly boys In British twentieth-century gay slang, dilly boys are RENT-BOYS, or male sex-workers. They are so named because of the notoriety of Piccadilly Circus in London as a place to pick them up.

dinge queen Particularly nasty term for a white gay man who is erotically attracted solely or primarily to black men. *See* QUEEN.

DINK Acronym for double income no kids, a term coined in New York in the 1980s as part of a hilarious set of neologisms to describe new social-class formations. Some (middle-class and usually male) gay couples used the term to describe their household set-up, and the fact that the minute likelihood of either of them having children meant that those incomes were not likely to drain away on nappies and toys. *See also* GUPPY, LUPPY.

dionian or **dioning** In the terminology of URANIANISM, a heterosexual.

Dionysus Fittingly, the Greek god of wine, drama and fun was often depicted as both beautiful and either homosexual or bisexual. According to a record of Clement of Alexandria, there is a story of Dionysus travelling to Hades. Not knowing the way, he asks directions of a certain Prosymnus, who only reveals the information on the promise from the god that he will allow himself to be fucked on his return. When Dionysus does return, he finds that Prosymnus has died, and in lieu fashions a dildo, which he sits on. This apparently led to the linking of Dionysus with the phallus. Dionysus is known as Bacchus in Roman mythology.

direct action Political tactics in which you take your grievance directly to confront the people responsible for it, or for perpetuating it. Direct action is usually regarded as the antithetical style to LOBBYING, but the two are not necessarily exclusive. In fact, as British lesbian and gay campaigning stalwart Peter TATCHELL declared, when lobbying concentrates on persuading legislators and opinion-makers through 'respectable' means, and direct action is calculated to demonstrate the strength and size of community feeling, the two 'reinforce each other to create a more effective campaign'. Often, but not always, entailing CIVIL DISOBEDIENCE, direct action techniques involve ZAPS and demonstrations, and see the communities who suffer from discriminatory legislation or prejudice as the most important agents in forcing change. Direct action has been with us since Spartacus led his slave rebellion against Rome in 73 BC, but the most effective modern examples are those of the SUFFRAGISTS and the black CIVIL RIGHTS MOVEMENT. Although members of the earlier HOMOPHILE MOVEMENT did employ direct action techniques such as picketing, it only became a staple on the lesbian and gay political scene with groups such as the GAY LIBERATION FRONT and GAY ACTIVISTS ALLIANCE in the 1970s. Even today with groups such as OUTRAGE! and ACT UP the tactics remain controversial with some accusing them of being counterproductive.

dish In American gay argot, dish as a noun can refer to the latest piece of topical gossip about a particular victim. In the verb construction dish-the-dirt, it means to discuss titbits of gossip, maybe cackling at another's difficulties over a cup of scandal soup (or tea). In the UK, dish is more likely to be heard to mean an attractive man.

dishonourable discharge The kind of wank one has alone and at home, so I've heard, after going out to find a pick-up but having failed to even pull a DESPERATION NUMBER.

La Divina The name by which the opera diva Maria Callas (1923–77) is known to her fiercely devoted clique of fans. Callas won instant recognition after she appeared in *La Gioconda* in Verona in 1947, and went on to sing all the main roles, until her last stage performance as *Tosca* at Covent Garden in 1965. She had many of the qualities that make a gay ICON of the first order. The dramatic passion of her stage style was complemented by the sufferings of her life, giving her an added aura for her gay audience. The break-up of her marriage to the Italian industrialist Giovanni Meneghini and her subsequent relationship and rejection by Greek shipping magnate Aristotle Onassis were all featured heavily in the press. Like GARBO, she died a virtual recluse in Paris in 1977. *See also* LA STUPENDA.

Divine (Glenn Milstead, 1945–88) Some say, the most beautiful woman in the world. Transvestite star of the underground films of cult director John Waters, he appeared in Waters' *Pink Flamingoes* and *Female Trouble*, as well as more overground films such as *Lust in the Dust* (1985) and *Trouble in Mind* (1985). Divine also made a brief career as a pop chanteuse. The larger than life character died just as the success of his final collaboration with Waters, *Hairspray* (1988), made him look as if he was about to break into the big time.

dizzy Adjective applied to any excitable, confused, disorganized or merely vapid gay man, usually in the form dizzy queen. An alternative form is a giddy queen.

Doc Martens (DMs) Tradename for a British brand of heavy-duty, thick-soled boots or shoes. They were originally worn by workmen, but became part of the skinhead look in the late 1960s. In the 1970s they were picked up by gay men as part of the BUTCH look on the British scene to accompany leather and denim jackets and tight jeans, and have stayed with us ever since. In the 1990s they are worn with KILTS, making a chunky pair of calves look delicious. They are now an essential part of the butch lesbian wardrobe.

Dog Day Afternoon 1975 film by Sidney Lumet which was based on the real-life story of John Wojtowicz. On 22 August 1972 Wojtowicz was arrested whilst attempting to hold up a Chase Manhattan bank branch and to steal $29,000. His companion in the crime was shot. Wojtowicz later explained that he needed the money to pay for a sex-change operation for his gay lover. The movie version featured Dustin Hoffman in the leading role.

dogs According to Larry KRAMER in *Faggots*, dogs are 'faggot children'. Pre-liberation it was rat-like Pekinese or groomed poodles which were the big closet-opener; as Michael observes in THE BOYS IN THE BAND, 'If one is of the male gender, a poodle is the insignia of one's deviation.' In the BUTCH old 1990s of course we're just as likely to have a rottweiler to stand guard over the Dusty Springfield collection. The grape-vine has it that gay men are the dog-owners, while lesbians have cats; it's probably more true to say that the world is divided into dog- and cat-owners depending on whether you want an independent minded ingrate who only appears to demand feeding, or a slobbery fool who can fetch sticks, but can't tell the kind of company in which it is appropriate to mount your leg. At least neither a cat nor a dog goes through adolescence.

dolly dimples Australian slang for lesbians.

dom Slang term used within BONDAGE and SM communities. It is an abbreviation of dominant, and refers to the TOP in an SM scene.

dominatrix A female TOP in bondage or SM sex.

Donovan, Casey (1943–87) Gay porn actor, who stepped into the porn public eye in 1971 when he starred in the popular film *The Boys in the Sand*, directed by Wakefield Poole. The film was a box office hit in America, which made Donovan a gay sex symbol. Donovan later tried to break into mainstream acting, and although he never made it in film, he continued to be active in the theatre, producing a version of *The Ritz* on Broadway in 1983. He died of AIDS related illnesses in 1987.

don't ask – demand 1970s lesbian and gay rights slogan which argued against the case that lesbians and gays saw as being presented by many within the HOMOPHILE MOVEMENT, that the way to attain such rights is through presenting a respectable front to heterosexual society and requesting its magnanimity.

Doolittle, Hilda (1886–1961) American poet who was associated with the Anglo-American imagist movement in poetry, which broke with poetic convention through its use of controlled free verse and its demand on the accurate and uncluttered depiction of the individual image. In 1913 H.D. (the name she wrote under) married the English imagist Richard Aldington, but her most intense relationship was with Annie Winifred Ellerman, the English historical novelist who is better known under her pen-name of BRYHER. Bryher was impressed with H.D.'s 1916 work *Sea Garden* and when she sought out Doolittle the two began a relationship which lasted until H.D.'s death. The two women travelled together to Greece and Egypt, trips which influenced the subject matter of Doolittle's verse.

double oppression The experience recorded by many lesbian and gay members of other minority groups in Western countries. They find themselves subject to prejudice within mainstream society, including lesbian and gay communities, and subject to homophobia within their other minority community.

douche Like the MANICURE, the douche is a usual prerequisite to a FISTING scene. It refers to the practice of taking a lengthy enema to clean thoroughly the rectum and colon before embarking on sex. Valuable for aesthetic reasons, to make fisting more stomachable, it was also useful from a health point of view since fecal matter can serve to transmit some diseases. In camp gay slang of the 1970s, a douche was also a routine bath or shower.

Douglas, Lord Alfred Bruce (1870–1945) English poet, son of the 8th Marquess of Queensberry. Nicknamed 'Bosie', he is best known in gay history for his relationship with Oscar WILDE, to which his father objected, thus precipitating the WILDE TRIALS. Wilde said that he 'understands me and my art, and loves both. I hope never to be separated from him.' It was Douglas who wrote the poem 'Two Loves', which gave the world the phrase, THE LOVE THAT DARE NOT SPEAK ITS NAME. Ironically, his sexual relationship with Wilde was short-lived, and it was Douglas who often used to procure Wilde's sexual partners. During the trials he went to France to avoid being called as a witness. Unfortunately, eleven years after Wilde's death Douglas became a convert to Catholicism and repudiated their relationship, to the point that at a libel trial in 1918 he described Wilde as 'the greatest force for evil that has appeared in Europe during the last 350 years'.

Down on Pennsylvania Avenue Blues song recorded by singer Bertha Idaho in 1929 which described a queer bar in Baltimore. The song was one of the first signs of the creation of a visible queer sub-culture in America.

drag Most commonly, the clothes of the opposite gender when worn for theatrical effect – also known as a fairy gown. Wearing drag differs from transvestism in that the transvestite is generally attempting to pass as the opposite sex, whereas the DRAG QUEEN or DRAG KING is self-consciously and obviously mimicking the opposite gender, usually for a particular social occasion. The word is derived from nineteenth-century British slang for the heavy petticoats worn by male actors who were playing in female roles. The drag act

or female impersonator is such a fixture on the gay scene that individual drag queens can take on something of the status of celebrity within particular communities, a homegrown and homedecorated diva (*see* LYPSINKA; CHARLES, RUPAUL; SAVAGE, LILY). It has also made the odd appearance in film: Michel Serrault as Albin in LA CAGE AUX FOLLES; Jack Lemmon and Tony Curtis in *Some Like It Hot*, Julie Andrews pretending to be a man pretending to be a woman in *Victor/Victoria*, Craig Russell in OUTRAGEOUS!, and most foolishly, Dustin Hoffman in *Tootsie*. Perhaps the most eye-moisteningly touching portrayal of a drag queen is Harvey Fierstein's Arnold Beckoff in TORCH SONG TRILOGY. The practice is no stranger to controversy however. Lesbian feminists since the 1960s have condemned it as an insulting parody of women as bitchy man-hungry stereotypes, which does nothing to explore the conventions of dress which women are expected to wear by men and even colludes with such dress codes by presenting drag queens always in teetering heels and constrictive corsetry. Related terms include a drag ball, a large gathering of drag queens and kings; drag face, when a man adorns his face with SLAP but otherwise wears male clothing as opposed to full drag which is the complete works (with accessories); and a drag race, a frenzied competition to reach the best bargains in a clothing sale. Radical drag was practised by some men within gay liberation groups of the 1970s, and involved wearing some items of female clothing but still remaining identifiably male underneath so as to draw attention to the arbitrariness of gender roles (*see* GENDER FUCK). Often they would wear heavy little tweedy numbers so as not to be accused of parodying stereotyped images of women's dress. To drag up (or frock up) is to dress up in drag. More recently, theorists have described as drag the surface nature of any of the images which we project for the benefit of others, whether that is in terms of gender or even profession or hobby. Thus straight men who want to appear as unimpeachably straight through their dress and mannerisms are also accused of wearing some form of drag. As RuPaul says, 'You're born naked, and the rest is drag.'

The Drag 1927 play by Mae WEST. Not particularly memorable for its plot, which depicts a closeted married homosexual in love with a straight man who is in turn in love with the closet's wife. It diagnoses homosexuality as a problem in that it can be concealed successfully, and so heterosexual women are left vulnerable to deception and exploitation. It was however memorable in being one of the first plays on Broadway to openly deal with gay themes, which aroused the ire of religious groups such as the Society for the Prevention of Vice, and it was prosecuted. It also used a fair amount of the gay slang which West was aware of from her own circle of acquaintances from the gay theatre.

drag king A woman who dresses up in male clothes for a particular occasion. Since the turn of the twentieth century women have routinely worn many items of 'male' clothing. Thus the traditional male drag for women is black tie and tuxedo, as modelled by many of the blues singers during the HARLEM RENAISSANCE of the 1920s (*see* BENTLEY, GLADYS; RAINEY, MA), or even Britain's own lesbian author Radclyffe HALL in the pictures that were shown during the trial for obscenity of her novel THE WELL OF LONELINESS. In American lesbian slang of the 1960s dragging up was also known as masquerading, or macking it.

drag queen Any man in a frock, though the term is usually reserved for FEMALE IMPERSONATORS, who dress to perform. There are as many types of drag queen as there are shades of eye shadow. Some go for the bitchy full-frontal assault (take the Australian horror Dame Edna Everage, who owes more perhaps to pantomime than sexual politics, and who perhaps most deserves to draw down the ire of the feminists, *see* DRAG), others are grotesquely and marvellously outrageous (DIVINE), while others beguile with the vulnerability of the torch song (Virginia Hamm in TORCH

SONG TRILOGY). Some do their own vocals (even to the music of Verdi and Puccini, *see* LA GRAN SCENA), whilst others employ that other art form, LIPSYNCHING (*see* LYPSINKA). Most at some point in their careers attempt the odd impression of a gay ICON. Many ASSIMILATIONIST gay men have had great difficulty in coming to terms with any public acknowledgement of any gay capacity for effeminacy, and have criticized the practice of drag by ordinary gay men as creating a 'bad impression'. Given this, it is somewhat surprising that drag shows have always been such a big fixture on the gay scene. Some theorists argue that the drag queen represents a sort of scapegoat for male anxieties about being perceived as effeminate, and gay men can laugh while distancing themselves from them. However, the role of scapegoat has never been easy, and the drag queen is far more likely to be abused, verbally and physically, than anyone STRAIGHT-ACTING. Thus it is unsurprising that they were among the first to be politicized in the gay community, and were such a high profile part of the STONEWALL RIOT.

drama queen Any gay man who is given to great theatrical displays in the conduct of his social and emotional life. Unlike the self-destruct queen, the drama queen is usually producing his tragic soliloquies for effect and, however much his mascara might run at the memory of a broken relationship, when the attention ends, so will his histrionics. *See also* CAMILLE.

Drill Hall, The This popular venue in central North London prides itself on giving space to lesbian and gay theatre and cabaret. It has created stars of so many gay troupes and troupers. A midwinter must has been the hilarious lesbian pantomime – *Robiana Hood* and *The Snow Queen* were favourites – that promote all the right family values in children of lesbian and gay parents, and of straight parents too.

drop a hairpin To give out clues about your homosexuality, especially when trying to make a pick-up with someone whose sexuality you do not know. Thus a few clues are injected, which if the listener picks up on indicate that the person is open to proposition. The hairpin, as a quintessentially female implement has attained a symbolic status among camp gay male circles as a signifier of gay culture. *See also* THE HAIRPIN DROP HEARD ROUND THE WORLD; PINNING UP YOUR BOBBY PINS.

The Duchess Title given to the gay activist Harry HAY who exhibited great stage presence when he worked as an actor in America during the great depression of the 1930s. It was through his relationship with another actor and leftist, Will Greer, that Hay was introduced to the Communist Party, an experience which informed his gay politics and the organizing strategies of the MATTACHINE SOCIETY which he helped found.

Duffy, Maureen Author of *That's how it was* (1962), an autobiographical wartime tale of working-class life and lesbian love; Duffy is acclaimed as Britain's first lesbian novelist to come out.

Dust Track on a Road Title for the autobiography of Zora Neale Hurston (1891–60), the lesbian writer who was active in the period of the HARLEM RENAISSANCE. Hurston, who dressed in male clothes for much of her life, was also a lesbian, and her autobiography tells of her relationship with a woman known as 'Big Sweet'.

dyke As a term for a lesbian, the word probably derives from the verb to dike, recorded as early as 1851 in America, meaning to dress formally for social occasions, particularly for men. The term bulldyker, recorded in black American slang of the 1920s, therefore refers to a woman in male dress. Originally a term of abuse, the word dyke was reclaimed by lesbians in the 1970s and used as a positive term to describe themselves. Subsequently, it became a common self-referential term.

dyke + fag = queer Popular slogan of the 1990s. *See* QUEER.

dyke spotting What lesbians do when waiting for a bus, walking down the street, sitting on the tube or visiting long-lost relatives. Most dykes believe that they can spot those that bat on the same team through invisible lesbian antennae. Successful dyke spotting usually produces a smile, a wink, a free drink and, if you are really lucky, a new girlfriend.

dykes and tykes The component of lesbian and gay PRIDE marches which includes lesbians and their children. Dykes and tykes is also the name of an American organization which provides support to lesbians with children.

Dyke's Delight American lesbian compilation published in 1993 by Knockabout Comics, featuring work by America's top dyke cartoonists, including Kate Charlesworth, Lucy Byatt, Grizelda Grizzlingham, Roberta Gregory, Jennifer Camper, Angela Martin and Annie Lawson. It features characters such as 'Bitchy Butch – the World's Angriest Dyke', the 'Big Girls', and 'Auntie Studs'.

Dykes, Disabilities and Stuff Quarterly American magazine for lesbians and feminists with disabilities which carries news, features, letters to the editor, reviews, fiction, poetry and drawings.

dykes on bikes Fabulous LEATHERWOMEN contingent on PRIDE marches worldwide, usually at the head of the parade.

Dykes to Watch Out For Alison Bechdel's fantastic and long-running cartoon describing the life and times of Mo, a neurotic and depressed lesbian working in a radical bookshop. Between Mo and her friends dealing with pregnancy, childbirth, mixed-race relationships, love, sex, cats, demos, pizza and the washing-up, the cartoon manages to strike a chord with every urban, Western, broke and depressed lesbian who reads it. Hours of fun are obtained from arguing about who you, your friends and your worst enemies most resemble: Mo, Harriet, Lois, Ginger, Sparrow, Clarice or Toni. The cartoon calendar is the perfect Christmas present.

dyketactics The political tactics employed by radical lesbian groups

E

Edward II

earring The wearing of a single earring by men is the sort of effeminate act that has marked them out as gay for much of the twentieth century. Gay men turned this to their advantage by using earrings to covertly signal to other men their sexual orientation for the purposes of cruising. On the bar scene of the 1950s and 1960s earrings were worn, like KEYS, BELT BUCKLES and HANKIE CODES, on the left ear to indicate that the wearer preferred the active role in sex, and on the right to mean the passive. These messages were slightly confused when in the 1960s men within the COUNTERCULTURE also began to wear earrings. In the UK straight-identified 'lads' also started to wear a single earring as a fashion item in the 1980s. The confusion was sorted out by the tacit understanding that an earring on the right meant gay, and on the left straight, although confusion over the sides led some men into unforeseen scrapes.

Easbourne This town on Britain's south coast became the country's biggest lesbian mecca for one week in June every year during the Ladies' Tennis Tournament. Bands of spectacular bodies in shocking pink shell suits ogled Martina on the practise courts through a haze of their own cigarette smoke. It is the original home of what promoters of the game call the 'Martina factor'. The Tournament died when Martina retired in 1994.

East Coast Homophile Organizations (ECHO) Alliance of different American lesbian and gay groups which was formed after the demise of the MATTACHINE SOCIETY as a national organization, thereby leaving local chapters to go their own way. ECHO comprised four organizations: the New York DAUGHTERS OF BILITIS and the former Mattachine chapters of New York, Washington and Philadelphia (which was now called the Janus Society). Established in January 1963, it was the most active of the various regional groupings that formed the NORTH AMERICAN CONFERENCE OF HOMOPHILE ORGANIZATIONS.

ECHO *See* EAST COAST HOMOPHILE ORGANIZATIONS.

ecstasy MDMA and related drugs Adam (MDA) and Eve (MDEA) – or known simply as e. Recreational drug which is found in powder, capsule, tablet or crystal form and which provides a stimulant and hallucinogenic effect, thus allowing us disco dollies to manage to keep up with today's rhythms and to stay up all night; no mean feat. It has recently become the focus of some health scares centred around ecstasy which had been cut with other substances.

EDGE *See* EDUCATION IN A DISABLED GAY ENVIRONMENT.

educated spinster With the growth of women's educational establishments in the US and Britain in the nineteenth century, a new class of educated women emerged who were able to support themselves economically. Since they were excited about the new opportunities available professionally, and wanting to explore relationships with the kindred spirits of other educated women, many college graduates elected to eschew marriage. The educated spinster was a feared entity for straight society, but a new opportunity for the women, who could now run their lives with a greater degree of autonomy.

Education in a Disabled Gay Environment (EDGE) New York-based organization, founded in 1986, which aims to provide support for lesbians and gays with all forms of disability, including people with sensory disabilities, amputations and cerebral palsy.

Edward II (1284–1327) King of England. This Plantagenet King has entered gay folklore for his relationship with Piers Gaveston, who had become his companion when the two were teenagers. Edward's father, Edward I, had Gaveston banished in 1307, but died shortly thereafter. Edward reinstated him, and left him as guardian of the kingdom in 1308 when he left for France to marry Isabella, the daughter of Philip IV. Angered at Gaveston's influence the English nobles demanded his banishment, and twice he was forced to leave the country. Eventually, the nobles rose and, capturing Gaveston, had him executed in 1312. Edward found new favourites in Hugh le Despenser and his son, but was eventually defeated by an alliance between his wife and many disaffected nobles. He was murdered in Berkeley Castle in 1327, apparently by means of a red-hot poker inserted into his rectum, a punishment for his 'sins' that did not mark his body. The tale was dramatized in 1593 by gay playwright Christopher MARLOWE, whose rendition of the story left little ambiguity as to the relationship between the two men, 'Embrace me, Gaveston, as I do thee.' He also placed much of Isabella's motivations in her fury at being spurned for another man, 'For never doted Jove on GANYMEDE/So much as he on cursed Gaveston.' Marlowe's play was in turn subject to adaptation in 1991 by queer filmmaker Derek JARMAN, who showed the nobles' opposition to Gaveston as being motivated by homophobia, and thus cast Edward's relationship as a blow for gay liberation. This link was made (too?) explicit by the incorporation of a full demonstration by members of the direct-action group OUTRAGE! In 1991 a radio version of the story written by Colin Haydn Evans drew on oral history sources to present the idea that Gaveston was a follower of pre-Christian religion, and his persecution represented the suppression of paganism by the Christian Church.

Der Eigene: Ein Blatt für Mannliche Kultur (The Exceptional: A Magazine for Male Culture) Claimed by some to be the first homosexual periodical in the world, it was founded in Germany in 1896 by the gay activist, Adolf Brand. The periodical was troubled by obscenity charges, but perhaps the biggest case was in 1907 during the series of scandals and trials that made up the EULENBERG AFFAIR, when Brand was charged with libel for distributing a pamphlet in which he alleged that the Imperial Chancellor, Bernhard, Prince von Bulow, had been having an affair with his secretary and had been blackmailed as a result of his sexuality. Further, the pamphlet stated that, being gay, the Chancellor had a duty to use his influence to push for the repeal of the anti-gay PARAGRAPH 175 of German law. One of the earliest cases of OUTING. During his trial for libel, Brand argued that, since he had a positive view of homosexuality, he was not intending to insult Bulow, but wished to speed the repeal of Paragraph 175. He was found guilty and sentenced to eighteen months. The magazine carried on however until 1931.

Elegies for Angels, Punks and Raging Queens 1992 musical drama by Bill Russell which was inspired by the true life stories of thirty-three of the names on the AIDS QUILT. The characters, who all tell their own stories range from a drag queen to a drugs user, a clergyman and an old woman. It showed a tiny part of the various compelling, dignified and often uplifting stories of those we have lost to the epidemic.

ELISA (enzyme-linked immunosorbent assay) The technique most commonly used to determine the presence or otherwise of antibodies in an HIV TEST. It was placed on the commercial market in March 1985. It is not a test that has incontrovertible diagnostic value, but indicates whether a particular process has gone on in the blood of the subject.

Elizabeth was King, now James is Queen Witticism that was often heard in London on the accession of James I of England (James VI of Scotland) in 1603. It played upon the fact that Elizabeth I was forceful in her leadership, and James was known to be gay.

Ellis, Edith (1856–1916) Lesbian, who was also the wife of nineteenth-century sex researcher Havelock ELLIS. Her marriage was more a companionate affair, and Edith had numerous affairs with women while with Havelock. Havelock's pioneering STUDIES IN THE PSYCHOLOGY OF SEX was to

some extent written in an effort to understand Edith's sexuality, and she was the subject for one of the case studies included in the book. Unfortunately, Havelock's attitude to lesbians was not as informed as that towards gay men, and he tended to view them as suffering from GENDER DYSPHORIA. Plagued increasingly by emotional problems in the last part of her life, Edith eventually died in a diabetic coma.

Ellis, Henry Havelock (1859–1939) English writer on sex. Trained initially in medicine, he became one of the leading figures in turn-of-the-century Britain who argued for progressive attitudes towards sex in general and homosexuality in particular. Starting from the basis that homosexuality had existed everywhere, and was accepted in many other cultures, he developed the term INVERSION to refer to homosexuality without connotations of disease. In the 1897 work SEXUAL INVERSION he argued that the large numbers of homosexuals of great talent refuted the idea that they suffered from degeneration. Any disorders associated with an inverted sexuality were likely to be caused instead by societal attitudes which, he asserted, created an argument for law reform. In his chapter *Sexual Inversion in Women*, however, Ellis was less progressive despite his marriage to his lesbian wife Edith (*see* ELLIS, EDITH). While he asserted that lesbianism, along with male homosexuality, was not necessarily pathological or morbid, his case studies concentrate on examples of lesbians who commit murder or suicide. In addition, despite the fact that he questioned the link between effeminacy and male homosexuality, in the case of women he persistently obfuscated gender and sexuality by equating lesbianism with 'mannishness' or transvestism. Nor was he particularly supportive of the feminist movement, which he claimed was likely to lead to an increase in women's neuroses. Ellis distinguished, like many other sexologists, between 'true' lesbianism and such relationships as the crushes of women in schools. His arguments for law reform extended only as far as true, congenital, inversion.

encephalin *See* ENDORPHIN.

endorphin Opiate-like chemical which is naturally released in the brain at times of physical exertion or pain which produces an effect similar to morphine, mitigating pain and creating euphoria. Thus an endorphin high is the pleasurable sensation produced by endorphins, recognized by athletes after strenuous activity or SM practitioners after a heavy scene. Some masochists refer to themselves as endorphin junkies. Other naturally secreted chemicals with similar effects are known as encephalins.

enema Process for cleaning out the bowels used before medical operations. It involves injecting luke warm water into the colon and rectum. Unsurprisingly, it has been adopted by some queers as a sexual practice in itself. In addition, an enema, or DOUCHE, was de rigueur for those who were about to engage in FIST-FUCKING.

England has always been disinclined to accept human nature From E.M. Forster's novel MAURICE, spoken by the doctor when Maurice confesses to him about his sexuality.

English Aristophanes Nickname given to Samuel Foote (1720–77), English playwright and satirist known for his cutting wit and sometimes libellous stage productions. In a prefiguration of the Oscar WILDE affair well over a hundred years later, Foote was the architect of his own downfall through his untimely satire on the Duchess of Kingston in his 1775 play *The Trip to Calais*. The Duchess was on trial for bigamy at the time, and Foote's allusions to her bigamy in public led her secretary to produce his own satirical pamphlet *Sodom and Onan*, which was clearly aimed at Foote and which presented him as a stereotypical homosexual. In the pamphlet Foote is likened to other notorious men of the time who had been accused of sodomy. The Duchess subsequently launched legal proceedings against Foote for sodomy, getting some of his former servants to testify about his improper conduct on their persons. Though he was acquitted, the affair broke Foote's spirit, and he died on his way to France in October 1777. His reputation was so besmirched that his position as a leading luminary on the British theatrical scene of the eighteenth century has all but been forgotten.

Entertaining Mr Sloane Comedy by Joe Orton, first produced in 1964. It explores the competition between a brother and sister for the charms of Sloane, a young man who revels in his position as a bisexual object of attraction. The two siblings eventually agree to share the young man, as a 'punishment' for the murder of their father, about which they are little concerned. Camp and witty, the play became a gay favourite, and its guilt-free anti-hero was indicative of a changing ability of the British stage to handle gay themes without the overtones of disease hitherto conventional.

d'Eon de Beaumont, Charles (1728–1810) Known as the 'Chevalier d'Eon'. French diplomat of the eighteenth century, who dressed as a woman even whilst on diplomatic business. Havelock ELLIS used his name to describe the practice of transvestism, which he dubbed eonism, although this term never became popular.

eonism Transvestism. *See* EON DE BEAUMONT CHARLES D'.

épater le bourgeois Slogan of French writers from the 1830s, such as Théophile Gautier (1811–72, author of MADEMOISELLE DE MAUPIN), Honoré de Balzac (1799–1850) and Charles Baudelaire (1821–67) who deliberately employed subject matter which they knew would challenge the values of the bourgeoisie. Thus they depicted images of exotic sex between women in their poetry and prose, as well as female transvestism. Their portrayal of lesbianism probably said more about their relationship with what was actually their own class, and with the moral proscriptions of the Catholic Church, than the life which French lesbians actually lived.

However, their works did have a substantial effect on French public opinion. Coinciding with the work of sexologists who wrote about homosexual sexuality, they gradually led to a greater societal knowledge of the possibilities of sexual relations between women. The by-product of this in the short term was the growth of anti-feminism and of suspicion of romantic friendships between women. However, in the long term such pressures helped build the foundations for a twentieth-century lesbian identity.

ephebophilia Term for erotic attraction to adolescent male youths. The word is used to draw a distinction between other forms of homoerotic attraction such as PAEDOPHILIA and ANDROPHILIA. It derives from the Greek *ephebos*, which described a young man about to enter into full citizenship. The term was used by the German gay activist Magnus HIRSCHFIELD.

The Epistle of Barnabas Historian John Boswell cites this first-century text as responsible for creating a link between various animals and homosexuality, associations which still had currency in the middle ages. The Epistle described various proscriptions supposedly laid down by Moses. Among these was eating the flesh of the hare since, as the hare develops a new anus annually, the meat would make one a pederast. The hyena was also taboo, since it changes gender every year. Finally, the weasel was said to conceive through its mouth, and was therefore guilty of immoral oral acts. So no weasel steaks either.

Epstein–Barr Virus The virus which causes glandular fever, or mononucleosis as it is more commonly known in America. It is also responsible for the condition ORAL HAIRY LEUCOPLAKIA, which is commonly found in people with AIDS.

erastes In ancient Greece the name of the older partner in a pederastic relationship. On CRETE they were known as *philetor* (lover), in SPARTA as *eisphelos* (inspirer).

erasure The process of removing the presence of lesbians and gay men from the history books. This can take an active or passive form. Examples of active erasure are the changing of the pronouns of Michelangelo's sonnets so they are addressed to a female beloved, or the actions of the niece of nineteenth-century American poet Emily Dickinson in removing any passages from her letters to her ROMANTIC FRIEND, Sue Gilbert, which seemed too emotionally expressive to protect her from accusations of lesbianism from a twentieth-century audience. Lesbians and gay men have often colluded in this process themselves for fear of damage to their career or reputation. Willa Cather, the American writer, wrote her most autobiographical characters as men, and destroyed letters and diaries that gave evidence of her forty-year relationship with Edith Lewis. Passive erasure is when, in the absence of detailed knowledge of the sex lives of historical figures, they are assumed to be heterosexual, until students of LESBIAN AND GAY STUDIES can CLAIM them back. It is also the failure of social historians to bother exploring the ways in which people expressed their homosexual desires in the past. Other groups complain of erasure even within lesbian and gay communities. Thus black gay men and black and white lesbians complain that the predominant depiction of white gay men even within gay publications does not acknowledge that they are also part of the community.

eromenos In ancient Greece the younger partner in a pederastic relationship. In CRETE they were named *aîtes* (hearer) and in SPARTA *parastatheis* (standers by).

Eros: On the Love of Men German two-volume anthology of references to homosexuality throughout history including manuscripts from Greece, Rome and Persia. It also pressed for the repeal of laws which criminalized homosexuality, one of the first books to do so. It was published by Heinrich Hossli, a Swiss milliner.

eroticizing safer sex In the early days of the AIDS epidemic, not only did the sexual behaviours that we were being told were safe contrast with the huge experimentation of the 1970s, but also the kind of educational materials produced by official agencies read with all the heat of a computer manual. Since few of these materials were specifically addressed to gay men, we produced much of the early material on our own, and a different emphasis – on the erotic potential of safer sex – was obvious from the first. In books such as HOW TO HAVE SEX IN AN EPIDEMIC pious injunctions to cut down on the number of partners were removed, and the focus instead was on enjoying safer sex rather than doing it out of fear. In the mid-1980s workshops on eroticizing safer sex became a common feature of the gay male scene, where men could get together and discuss safer sex in a way that was sexually exciting.

erotophobia The fear of sex and sexuality. Although institutions of government and particularly the Church have long looked askance at the expression of sexuality, the term only really gained currency in the 1980s when the reactions of these institutions infuriated AIDS educators. It was reasonably argued that to prevent the spread of a virus that could be transmitted through sexual intercourse widespread sexual education was important, and sexual education that also included gay sex, since it was gay men who were most at risk. Sex education campaigns were, however, frequently restricted because governments were not willing to put their names to something which they irrationally feared would encourage people to greater sexual expressiveness. Like people didn't know what oral sex is! As late as 1994 the Tory government in the UK censored a picture of a petrol pump on a safer-sex poster because of its sexual implications.

essentialists Those who, within academic discourse on lesbian and gay history, assert that sexual categories are not historically specific, and that lesbians and gays with exclusive erotic attraction to members of their own biological gender have always existed.

Eton crop Short hairstyle, which became popular for British women in the 1920s and 1930s. Although its widespread popularity made the style acceptable, it also became a sign for lesbians to recognize one another, especially since the crop was an essential part of the butch image of Radclyffe HALL, who had become the public face of lesbianism in the UK. Its name derives from the name of the British public school.

eucharist The Christian sacrament during which grown men kneel down in the belief that they are consuming the body of JESUS has always been open to an irreverent gay reading. There is, however, historical evidence which indicates that the practice may have developed from certain Gnostic sects who, believing that the mind can remain pure while the body is doing what it wants, incorporated sexual acts, including homosexual ones, into their ceremonies. Such practices were suppressed by the forerunners of the orthodox church, but were perhaps transformed into the non-sexual eucharist.

Eulenberg affair The much-reported sexual scandal which titillated the readers of German newspapers from 1906 to 1909, and which involved the close adviser to Kaiser Wilhelm, Philipp, Prince zu Eulenberg-Hertefeld, as well as other public and military figures. Essentially a saga of political manoeuvring, it began when the right-wing editor of *Die Zukunft* newspaper publicly alleged that the moderate and anti-Imperialist Eulenberg was homosexual in an attempt to diminish his influence within German politics. Rumours even circulated about possible trysts between Eulenberg and the Kaiser himself. The security scandal motif appeared, with allegations that State information was going to France via Eulenberg's gay coterie. At the various libel trials that ensued, Dr Magnus HIRSCHFIELD was called as an expert witness on homosexuality. The scandal rocked German politics and Eulenberg was ruined, and the loss of his influence, as well as an anti-modern backlash that developed as a result of the affair, can be seen to have contributed towards the German entry into the First World War and the abdication of the Kaiser. What's more, the affair created strong anti-gay repercussions that hindered the campaign to repeal PARAGRAPH 175 of the criminal law, although it did create widespread knowledge and acknowledgement of gay sexuality as well as popularizing the term homosexuality as a neutral one. *See* DER EIGENE.

eunuch Name given to a wide group of men who do not conform to the male stereotype. The Indian literary classic, the KAMA SUTRA refers to two kinds of eunuchs in India. The first are those who imitate the dress, speech, gestures, tenderness, timidity, simplicity, softness and bashfulness of women. They derive their imaginative pleasure and their economic livelihood from AUPARISHTAKA, or oral sex, on men. The second group are those who behave as males, but who lead the lives of shampooers and practise oral sex with the males they shampoo. *See also* HIJRA.

Eurovision The name, for the cognoscenti, of the Eurovision Song Contest, the annual parade of Europe's finest musical, and sartorial, talent competing in a nail-biting battle for the accolade of Europe's best song. Begun in 1956, the contest provides an annual platform for the sneers of serious (straight) music critics who seem unable to enter into the spirit – unlike its legions of gay fans. And why? For starters, the list of former competitors reads like a camp wet dream: Abba; Brotherhood of Man; New Seekers; Nana Mouskouri; Olivia Newton-John; Sonia; Bucks Fizz; all of them have sat backstage at some point anxiously awaiting the results of the jury. What's more, the contest combines the two gay favourites of glamour and passion. Even the dowdiest Polish entry can be guaranteed to sport a frock to die for, while the feverish scoring can provoke the most mild-mannered to scream at their television at the Greeks and Cypriots who hope that we haven't noticed them voting top marks to one another yet again. A truly gay evening in.

every man's wife and every woman's husband One of the several descriptions applied to Julius Caesar, this one is attributed to Curio the Elder. It alludes to the reports of Caesar's sexual liaisons with men. *See also* QUEEN OF BITHYNIA.

every other inch a gentleman Description reportedly applied to Oscar WILDE by Viscount Castlerosse, a journalist.

Examination of the Herald Drawing by the late-nineteenth-century artist Aubrey Beardsley. It showed a messenger boy with a vast erect dick which comes up to his shoulders. The drawing was produced for an edition of Aristophanes' comedy *Lysistrata*, and occasioned considerable criticism when it was first seen.

eye sex Lingering erotic looks that one person might give other people in a lesbian or gay bar while they are cruising them. Involves mentally undressing them to ascertain whether or not they are the chosen one.

Femme

face-fucking Oral sex. *See* DEEP-THROATING.

Faderman, Lilian (1940–) Professor of English at California State University and author of two classic lesbian historical studies: *Surpassing the Love of Men* (1981) is the award-winning comprehensive study of passionate friendships from the sixteenth century until now using much previously unpublished source material; *Odd Girls and Twilight Lovers* (1991) is the definitive history of the evolution of lesbian life in the United States from the turn of the century. Faderman also wrote *Scotch Verdict* , a recreation of the trial in Scotland on which THE CHILDREN'S HOUR was based.

fag hag Slang term for a heterosexual woman who spends the majority of her time with gay men. Used pejoratively, the term can indicate the misogyny that exists within gay male communities, and the mistrust of women's motives in wanting to socialize with gay men. However, the phenomenon can show the understanding that can exist between gay men and straight women.

fag power! dyke power! queer nation! Slogan which became an old favourite on QUEER NATION demonstrations.

Fag Rag Annual American magazine for gay men which was founded in 1970.

faggot Slang term for a gay man. Originally pejorative, the word has been adopted by gay men to describe themselves. The derivation of this use of the term is unclear. It may derive from the English public school practice of 'fagging' whereby older pupils would oblige younger pupils to perform services for them including, it is reported, sexual services. Alternatively, it is suggested somewhat fancifully that the practice of burning sodomites at the stake using bundles of sticks, or faggots, to ignite the blaze gave rise to the term. The British slang use of fag to refer to cigarettes, which in the early twentieth century were considered an effeminate alternative to manly cigars, is another possible etymology. Finally, faggot as a pejorative term for women has been recorded as far back as the sixteenth century, and the association between pejorative terms for women and for gay men is a longstanding one. *See* FRUIT; GAY.

faggots' finishing school Gay male slang for PRISON.

fairy or **faerie** Slang term for a gay man, with overtones of effeminacy. Like the terms FAGGOT and DYKE, fairy has been adopted by some gay men to describe themselves. In America the RADICAL FAIRY movement has politicized the word in its rejection of the conventional male role.

Falwell, Jerry (1933–) Right-wing American preacher who led the MORAL MAJORITY. Falwell made numerous vicious and cruel attacks on lesbian and gay people, but reached new depths when the AIDS epidemic began. He called it 'the judgement of God', an opinion for which he was attacked by gay activists and humane Christians alike.

family The family, as the building block for heterosexual society, is probably on its last legs in the late twentieth century, although this doesn't stop right-wing politicians from resurrecting its memory in their efforts to restore 'proper' social values. Unsurprisingly then, the heterosexual majority are very protective of its boundaries, labelling any lesbian or gay attempt at bringing up children a 'pretend' affair. Lesbians and gay men often have strained relationships with their biological family, and describe the support networks within the lesbian and gay communities as a surrogate family.

The Family Way 1966 film in which consternation is engendered when a shy young bridegroom (Hywel Bennett) does not consummate his marriage in his father's home. When his father objects that his son 'can't prove his manhood', and suggests he might be 'queer', his wife replies, 'And suppose he were? Is it something to get at the lad for?' While the two never really doubt their son's heterosexuality, it was the first film speech in which a parent moots the possibility that a queer child might not be cast out.

FDA Protest Massive protest organized by AIDS and gay activists in Washington DC in October 1988 to protest against the fact that the Food and Drugs Administration (FDA), which has the responsibility of certifying drugs for use by people with HIV and AIDS, was not allowing the release of experimental drugs. Over a thousand people participated in the demonstration, and more than 150 activists were arrested.

feast of fools The early founders of the MATTACHINE SOCIETY, such as Harry HAY, had wanted to explore ancient (European) folklore and festivals to examine the way in which lesbian and gay people could fit into the long historical traditions of social and sexual heterodoxy. One of the festivals they wanted to bring back was the feast of fools, a long period preceding the spring equinox during which rituals were performed in which people of different social levels would trade places with one another. They felt that it could help overcome the tendency towards hierarchy of their organization. However, when the society split in 1953, such efforts were swept away in the interest of lobbying for law reform, and it was only with the RADICAL FAIRY movement that examinations of gay folklore began again. *See also* MARDI GRAS.

feasting with panthers Phrase employed by gay writer, martyr and wit Oscar WILDE, to describe his sexual encounters, predominantly with young working class men. Wilde was always mindful that a discovery of his sexual tastes could deliver him, as it did, to disgrace and prison. Thus the men with whom he had sex had an incredible power over him, they were the panthers who could maul his liberty and reputation. Yet he described this danger as giving the sex an added frisson, an exquisite fear.

feel-good politics The kind of politics that concentrates on the individual reaction to their oppression, rather than on confronting the oppressors themselves in any meaningful way. It is generally used as a critical term by activists who see it as an exercise in therapy, rather than a serious attempt to challenge the conditions of oppression, and is employed to describe anything from CONSCIOUSNESS-RAISING GROUPS, through to meetings which are all discussion and no decision, to demonstrations which function well as a way of exorcizing individual anger but stand little chance of actually changing anything. However, many other lesbian and gay activists argue that since oppressive systems are aimed at killing the individual will to challenge, the fostering of a spirit of resistance, in whatever way it is expressed, is politically significant. In particular, within lesbian feminism it has been argued that the act of women understanding the mechanism of patriarchy on their lives is a challenge to patriarchy (*see* PERSONAL IS POLITICAL).

felch Sexual practice which involves sucking out the cum one has just ejaculated into the ass of a partner, and returning it to their mouth with a kiss. Even some faggots find this a bit much to stomach. Moreover, since it involves fucking without a condom, it is a risky activity from the point of view of HIV transmission.

Felipa 1876 story by Constance Fenumore Woolson, which is remarkable as practically the only example of writing dealing with lesbian passion in nineteenth-century American literature. In it Felipa, a twelve-year-old girl from Florida, falls in love with a woman, and then the woman's fiancé. Distressed when the couple are due to leave, she attempts to stab the man to death. Her grandfather seems aware of the implications, and when the narrator attempts to say that Felipa loved both equally, he replies, 'The stronger [love] thrust the knife.' The story shows an awareness of the writings of the sexologists of the time.

Female Dialect The slang that was developed in the eighteenth-century London subculture of the MOLLY HOUSES. In what seems to have been an age-old hobby of gay men, much effort was devoted to the development of CAMP NAMES. The titles Miss, Madam and sometimes (as today) Auntie were popular, while Molly, Mary and Margaret were the most common forenames chosen. Some names were a reference to the occupation of the molly who bore them: Dip-Candle Mary was a double entendre name for a candle-maker; Orange Mary was an orange vendor; Old Fish Hannah a fishmonger. Others were chosen for a particular characteristic of the molly concerned: we can only imagine what Susan Guzzle liked to sip on, but she probably deprived Thumbs and Waist Jenny of her proper sustenance. Others displayed the gay preoccupation with royalty and aristocracy: Princess Seraphina was a butcher and Queen Irons a blacksmith.

female ejaculation It and the G-spot are much mythologized. There is a sad lack of medical evidence on the subject. However, the accumulated dyke lore is this: about four centimetres into the vagina, on the opposite side from the clitoris, is the G-spot which has a more sponge-like texture (utheral sponge) than the surrounding vaginal walls. Stimulation in the area of the G-spot produces a gush of liquid ('like a fire hydrant', as Susie Bright says) which takes both of you by surprise, and cannot be mistaken for the general wetness of good sex. This liquid is clear and watery, and for the ejaculator it feels not unlike peeing (which it is definitely not). Ejaculators say that ejaculating is a by-product of good sex, but that it is not in itself orgasmic. Many lesbians have never experienced female ejaculation, but it has a symbolic importance in that it is a sign of how lesbians can do everything the boys can do – and many of them better.

feminism is the theory, lesbianism is the practice Aphorism which has been attributed to the radical feminist Ti-Grace Atkinson. It featured heavily in lesbian and radical feminist circles of the early

1970s as a slogan to indicate the theoretical and practical contiguity between the two. It was especially opportune at a time when the feminist movement had been equivocal about the support that it should give to lesbian issues (*see* LAVENDER MENACE). In fact, the words came from a paper which Atkinson delivered to the New York chapter of the DAUGHTERS OF BILITIS in which she questioned the link, 'Feminism is a theory...but lesbianism is a practice.' She did later change this position.

Feminists against Censorship A group set up in Britain in the mid-1980s to campaign against the belief that all feminists want to outlaw pornography or sexually explicit material. They have mainly argued against the Campaign against Pornography's 'Off the Shelf' campaign, which aims to get porn taken off the shelves of newsagents. British debates against pornography have involved lesbians working on both sides; both FAC and CAP have high lesbian involvement.

feminology Alternative term, coined by the Danish librarian Nynne Koch, for WOMEN'S STUDIES.

femme (1) The counterpart of the BUTCH lesbian in the American and British lesbian bar culture of BUTCH/FEMME in the 1950s and 1960s. The femme would play the 'feminine' role, and would not be allowed to either make advances on a butch woman, or be active in a sexual sense. Required dress for a femme lesbian was inch-thick make-up, teetering heels, and skirts or Capris. (2) Australian slang for the drag queens who would entertain the troops during the Second World War. They were a common part of wartime entertainment companies, and gave a good number of queens a legitimate reason to throw on a frock in the name of patriotism.

femme-bot Femme robot. 1970s lesbian slang term for a femme woman who didn't think for herself.

femme top *See* BUTCH BOTTOM.

Femø Small Danish island where an international women's camp used to be held in the 1970s.

Festival of Light zap Demonstration against the anti-permissive Christian organization which is fondly remembered by those involved as one of the highlights of 1970s radical political activity. It took place at London's Westminster Central Hall in 1971, and demonstrators included the GAY LIBERATION FRONT, the radical *OZ* magazine and radical feminist groups, as well as a couple of NUNS. Protesters threw stink bombs and showered the crowd with pornographic magazines, before being ejected.

FF (1) Abbreviation used within CONTACT adverts for fone freak, or a gay person who enjoys PHONE SEX. (2) Abbreviation for FLAMING FAGGOT. (3) Slang term for effeminate, derived from the middle letters and from the colloquial term 'effie'. With its many uses the double-F has become a common title for gay magazines and clubs.

fiction of the gynaeceum Genre of fiction which deals with relationships between the women in the sex-segregated environment of the girls' school. Unsurprisingly, since they deal solely or predominantly with women, such novels have profound lesbian connotations. Examples of the genre include COLETTE's *Claudine at School* (1900), and Dorothy Bussy's *Olivia* (1949). It remains a useful tool for other lesbian writers; thus Iona McGregor's LESBIAN THRILLER *Death wore a Diadem* (1989) is set in the Scottish Institute for the Education of the Daughters of Gentlefolk in Edinburgh.

Michael Field Collaborative nom de plume for the joint works of Katharine Harris Bradley (1846–1914) and Edith Emma Cooper (1862–1913). The two were related to each other, Katharine being Edith's aunt, and they studied together at University College. They were both confirmed feminists and rejected the traditional role allotted to women within their society. In *Underneath the Bow* (1893) they declared, 'My love and I took hands and swore/against the world, to be/ Poets and lovers evermore.' They compared their own collaborative work style with the individual works of their contemporaries, the Brownings, and declared that theirs was the closer union. Edith died from cancer in December 1913, and while nursing her, Katharine developed the disease herself and died little more than half a year after her beloved.

Fierstein, Harvey (1954–) American actor and playwright who is best known for the stage musical of LA CAGE AUX FOLLES and his three-play set entitled TORCH SONG TRILOGY, for both of which he received Tony awards. In the film version of *Torch Song Trilogy*, he himself played the drag queen Virginia Hamm, belting out Cole Porter's 'Love for Sale' in the voice of pure gravel which gives him such presence in one memorable club scene, and creating his own version of the Jewish mother to his adoptive son. In addition, he wrote and acted in the television drama *Tidy Endings* (1984) in which he played a gay man in conflict with his deceased lover's wife; he appeared as a gentle gay man on FIRE ISLAND who tries to help locate Greta Garbo in Sidney Lumet's film *Garbo Talks* (1984); and he can be heard in voice only as the gay secretary in THE SIMPSONS.

fighting for our lives The name given to a candle-lit march by PWAs in San Francisco in 1983. It was one of the first protests staged by people who were actually affected by AIDS, and gained nationwide media coverage.

Films and Filming British magazine begun in 1954, devoted to film but which quickly became a closet gay magazine. It printed pin-up photos of half-clothed male film stars, and ran adverts for the kinds of fashion shops that were frequented by a largely gay clientele. Its small ads section became increasingly gay, and by the 1960s had become explicit as a place for gay contact ads.

Findlayson, Don Gay character in the Australian soap *No. 96*. He was a handsome and popular lawyer who survived blackmail attempts and broken relationships.

finger As a verb, it means to manually stimulate the clitoris, or to shove a finger (or more, though at some point it becomes FISTING) into the anus or vagina. Also known as finger-fucking.

finger-fucking Fingers are long and flexible sex toys for lesbians who enjoy penetration.

fingernails They have had an obvious significance for lesbians since time immemorial. Jagged or long fingernails can cause pain to a lover's clitoris and vagina, and for either men or women fisting necessitates short fingernails. Safe sex has also placed an emphasis on short fingernails to avoid the HIV risk of breaking the skin. Specific groups of lesbians have had particular codes about fingernail length with certain fingers, presumably the fucking fingers, being lesbianized while the rest of the nails remain long. Fingernail length is usually one of the factors considered when DYKE-SPOTTING.

finocchio Italian slang for male homosexual, with overtones of effeminacy. The Italian word is actually the name of the fennel plant.

Fire Island Coastal resort situated on a spit of sand near New York, which has a long history of lesbian and gay tourism. It included various lesbian and gay communities, such as CHERRY GROVE, a resort area which dated back to the 1920s, and the Pines, a newer community for those who disliked the 'plebeian' atmosphere of Cherry Grove. In the 1970s the island became the particular stamping ground of the gay party set, and the chic thing to do was to rent a house for the summer with a group of friends. The discos, drinks parties, pool parties and cruising grounds typified for many the heady pleasure-making of the decade.

The Firehouse An old fire station in the SoHo area of New York which became the home of the GAY ACTIVISTS ALLIANCE at the beginning of 1971. The Firehouse served as the centre for gay political activity in the city, as well as hosting popular weekly dances.

First World War While the First World War did not have the importance of the second for the growth of lesbian and gay subcultures, it was significant for the growth of the feminist movement in the UK and America. In both those countries women realized the weight their contribution to the war effort could give to their call for suffrage. In 1917, the National American Women's Suffrage Association pledged its support to the war, and in the following year all adult American women were given the vote. In the UK women over the age of thirty were given suffrage. The war also saw the breakdown of what had been rigorously maintained divisions between occupations considered suitable for men and women, with women driving ambulances and buses, using heavy equipment and working in arms factories. Attempts to reclassify these occupations as male after the war could not be entirely successful, and women found themselves with greater opportunity to earn an independent wage, with huge implications for their ability to live in lesbian relationships.

fish Gay male slang for women. It derives from the male idea of the smell of the female genitalia, and should not be encouraged. A fish queen is gay male slang for a heterosexual man.

fish queens 1950s queer slang for straight men who would go along to lesbian bars in the hope of finding someone on whom they could perform cunnilingus.

fistfuck Often abbreviated to just fisting. Fisting is when one partner inserts the whole hand, sometimes up to the elbow, into the anus or vagina of the other. During the early years of the AIDS epidemic, fisting was condemned by many educators as unsafe. In actual fact, since the hand is impervious to HIV unless cut, it is a reasonably safe practice, and certainly so if a latex glove is worn. The condemnation probably said more about the educators' disapproval of fisting as an act,

rather than its health implications. Fisting hit the headlines in the UK in late 1993 when gay comedian Julian Clary made a joke about fisting a former British Chancellor of the Exchequer at the British Comedy Awards Ceremony. The ensuing press furore was an eye-opener for many straights who had no idea what fisting was. Also known as 'handballing' or 'shaking hands with the baby'.

flagellation To incorporate whipping, either with a proper leather whip or with a stand-in such as a belt or piece of rope, into sex. Standard part of the repertoire of people interested in SADOMASOCHISM or BONDAGE AND DISCIPLINE. A fladge fiend or whippersnapper is a lesbian or gay man who is especially fond of whipping, and SM relationships are sometimes referred to as fladge parties.

flaming An adjective, common in 1960s and 1970s American gay slang to describe a gay man so effeminate he couldn't hide his sexuality with a tarpaulin. Usually prefixed to the word faggot to create pleasing alliteration.

flats In eighteenth-century England, lesbianism was known as the game of flat(t)s. It was derived from the term for playing cards, and alludes to the (male) belief that lesbian sex could be accomplished only by rubbing together the (flat) pudenda of female lovers. In the nineteenth century this VANILLA lesbian sex act was sometimes referred to as a flatfuck.

Les Fleurs du Mal Volume of poetry by French symbolist poet Charles Baudelaire published in 1857. Three of the poems, including one entitled 'Lesbos', touched on lesbian themes. None tried to portray an accurate picture of love between women, however, but presented lesbian sex as part of the voyeuristic panorama of exotic immorality with which Baudelaire sought to EPATER LE BOURGEOIS. 'Lesbos' even presents sex between women as a form of titillation for a male onlooker. Nonetheless, the collection was influential, especially after a trial for obscenity publicized it, in disseminating to the French public a knowledge of the possibility of lesbian practice.

flipped Adjective to describe a BUTCH lesbian of the 1950s/60s who allowed a FEMME woman to take any kind of active role, against convention. Thus a STONE BUTCH who allowed her partner to be sexually aggressive with her, or a butch who was approached by a femme in a bar, was said to have been flipped. To a real stone butch, being flipped is a matter of some shame.

A Florida Enchantment Play by Archibald Gunter which was first produced in New York at the Park Theatre in 1896, and was adapted as a film version in 1914. It depicts a young heiress, Lillian, from northern USA who visits her aunt in Florida. While there she discovers a chest containing seeds which if swallowed will reverse the gender of the taker. She swallows one and awakes the following day sporting a thick black moustache which she immediately shaves off. Pretending to be a woman but possessed of male drives, she scandalously courts other women in her aunt's conservative southern hometown. Whilst, tediously, Lillian awakes to find that it was all a dream and that the sexes are restored to their 'natural' order, the film included gender/sexuality playing which was resonant for lesbian and gay audiences of the time. When the film was first shown, cinema attendants reportedly kept cold water to revive those who felt faint at the sight of two women kissing one another.

fluff American lesbian slang for a FEMME lesbian.

Folsom Street The heartland of the San Francisco leather scene. Since the mid-1960s, when three leather bars opened there, it has anchored the leather community and economy, which continued to evolve and expand throughout the 1970s. The onset of the AIDS epidemic dampened the leather spirit for most of the 1980s.

fone frk Abbreviation used in the parlance of gay CONTACT ADVERTS, to refer to a man who is a phone freak, that is, someone who enjoys talking dirty over the telephone while jacking off. With the spread of the AIDS epidemic in the 1980s such communal and safe activities became increasingly popular.

The Fool of Fonthill (1760–1844) Nickname given to the fabulously wealthy English writer William Beckford. He was involved in one of Britain's first public gay scandals after a visitor to his home had caught him in bed with the young William Courtenay, whose aunt he had taken as his mistress to be near the boy. He went to Switzerland, where he began his writing. Partial to the Gothic in both his writing and in architecture, when he returned to England after ten years, he attempted to construct a huge Gothic cathedral on his estate at Fonthill Abbey. The cathedral collapsed under its own weight.

fop's alley Dated English name for the central aisle in a theatre, down which theatregoers will promenade to reach their seats. The term indicates the long association that the THEATRE has had with those who do not quite fit the masculine ideal.

The Forever War 1975 sci-fi novel by American Joe Haldeman (1943–). It presented the scenario that by 2023, the world's population would have grown to the extent that same-sex sexuality was encouraged. Later, the entire population would be lesbian or gay.

Forrest, Katherine V. (1939–) America's most popular lesbian novelist with eleven published titles; creator of the lesbian detective KATE DELAFIELD, editor of lesbian novels for Naiad publishers, and twice winner of the LAMBDA LITERARY AWARD. Forrest's novels range from the great sex and passion of *Curious Wine* (1983) and the sci-fi *Daughters of a Coral Dawn* (1984), to LESBIAN THRILLERS such as *Murder at the Nightwood Bar* (1987) that combine murder with issues such as abuse or sexual discrimination, and the modern political chronicle *Flashpoint* (1994).

four h's The shorthand way in which the groups that were initially most affected by the AIDS epidemic were described. The four were: homosexuals; haemophiliacs; Haitians; and heroine users.

Frankie Goes To Hollywood British rock group of the early 1980s who presented a raunchy sexuality which contrasted with the sexless gender-bending of BOY GEORGE and the overt politicking of BRONSKI BEAT. Although only two members of the band, Holly Johnson and Paul Rutherford, were gay, their message was not diluted. Their 1983 single 'Relax', which contained tips on achieving sexual satisfaction, became a succès de scandale when it was banned by the BBC station Radio One. The video which accompanied the single was replete with SM imagery. Johnson went on to a successful solo career after the band split, and was admired when in 1993 he went public about his HIV-positive status.

freedom rings Series of small metal rings, in the colours of the RAINBOW FLAG, worn on a chain round the neck. Freedom rings have become as reliable a way as the PINK TRIANGLE used to be of communicating your sexuality to others.

The Freewoman British feminist journal of the early twentieth century. The early FEMINIST MOVEMENT was not, in general, eager to align itself with the promotion of the rights of lesbians, and this journal was the only feminist organ to even discuss issues of same-sex eroticism. In 1912 column space was devoted to the debates then current around the 'causes' of homosexuality, and Edward CARPENTER contributed an article which discussed the phenomenon of ancient Greek sexuality. The relation of lesbianism to the women's movement and its implications for women taking control of their sexuality was not, however, made explicit.

French The French race have clearly got a reputation for being hot-blooded lovers, as they give their name to more than one erotic act. French kissing is deep kissing with tongues, while French sex is American gay slang for oral sex between men. Thus, in gay contact ad language, 'Fr act' refers to the partner whose dick is sucked, while 'Fr pas' is the partner who sucks. Finally, a French Embassy is American gay slang for any building where it is easy to find sex, such as the gym, the YMCA or, heaven forbid, the public toilets just about anywhere.

Freud, Sigmund (1856–1939) Austrian founder of psychoanalysis, the 'Copernicus of the mind'. His works on human sexual progression have been perhaps the most influential of any writings about sex, and have insinuated themselves into all manner of sexual discourse, popular and academic. To oversimplify grossly, he believed that the impulse for homosexual eroticism was among the morass of sexual urges, the POLYMORPHOUS PERVERSE, that all humans are born with and that during the socialization process those urges are usefully repressed. Thus lesbians and gay men, due to some form of trauma which arrests their development, represent a stunted form of sexuality. He did not believe, however, that it is a sickness, nor a 'condition' that could be treated and changed. Despite his 'liberalism', he was not able to control the way in which his successors would use his theories. Thus later psychoanalysts focused on the idea of 'arrested development', and advocated treatment to spur that development. Not only did they cause immeasurable harm to the lives of countless lesbian and gay individuals by forcing them through aversion therapy, and in extreme cases electro-convulsive therapy and hormone treatment, but the general idea of homosexuality as a sickness is one that pervades the twentieth century. More positive discourses have come out of Freud however. Those who chose to focus on his theory that the unsocialized mind was home to all forms of 'undesirable' sexual impulse believed that many neuroses were therefore caused by blocking these 'latent' sexual urges. Thus it was held to be dangerous to stop anyone from gratifying themselves in whatever way they chose. Such popular theories were fashionable among progressive communities in the 1920s, especially in bohemian areas such as New York's

Greenwich Village. Even in the late twentieth century some within the lesbian and gay rights movement have argued that if at root everyone's sexuality is undifferentiated, then heterosexuality is a socially constructed phenomenon and can have no claim to any inherent normality, much less any moral superiority. Freud was also important for having created widespread discussions about sex that were led by doctors, and not by intransigent Church leaders. It could be argued that it was essential for sexuality to be talked about widely, and for the subject to be secularized, for both the feminist and lesbian and gay movements to have made any progress. *See* MEDICALIZATION OF HOMOSEXUALITY.

Die Freundin German magazine published in the late 1920s and early 1930s which discussed lesbian issues.

Fried Green Tomatoes at the Whistle Stop Café This 1987 novel by Fannie Flagg remained uncherished until it was used to make a hugely successful movie in 1991. If there is ever doubt about the relationship between Idgie and Ruth, it is resolved when Idgie receives the Old Testament reference to the biblical RUTH, a perfect example of an 'insider reference' for lesbians in the audience. The film made the novel a bestseller.

FRIEND (Fellowship for the Relief of the Isolated and Emotionally in Need and Distress) British counselling organization that was set up by the CAMPAIGN FOR HOMOSEXUAL EQUALITY in 1971, originally called Task Force. With local government funding FRIEND was able to offer support for lesbians and gay men who were coming to terms with their sexuality. Many FRIENDs were set up in different towns nationwide.

friend or **best friend** How many lovers over the years have had their importance understated by being described as a 'friend' to those whose reaction to queerness was feared to be somewhat less than progressive?

friend of Dorothy As a code term for a gay man, there is some debate as to its lineage.

Some swear that it actually refers to the American one-woman one-liner factory, Dorothy PARKER, whose snappy put-downs have turned her into a gay icon. More plausibly, and more obviously, it refers to the homespun heroine in THE WIZARD OF OZ, whose friends included the sissy COWARDLY LION. It became popular in the 1950s as the tragic Judy GARLAND gathered her moist-eyed gay following through her vulnerable stage performances, and was revived in the 1970s after her star and that of gay liberation collided when the STONEWALL RIOT was sparked on the night of her funeral. The term could be used by gay men to draw attention obliquely to their own sexuality, and was useful when cruising, when men could use the innocuous question 'Are you a friend of Dorothy?' to sound out the sexuality of their prey.

Friendship and Freedom The newspaper of America's earliest gay rights organization, the Chicago SOCIETY FOR HUMAN RIGHTS. It was also probably America's earliest gay rights magazine.

frig A useful sexual term. In nineteenth-century British erotic literature it usually referred to masturbation. In US slang it refers to sex between women, either involving body rubbing, or one partner rubbing the genitals of the other with her hand. The word is recorded as early as the fifteenth century in Britain, with the sense of to wriggle, and is probably related to the Old English *frigan*, meaning to love.

frightening the horses Phrase used to indicate the potentially shocking power of lesbian or gay behaviour in public. It was coined by the British actress Mrs Patrick Campbell (Beatrice Stella Turner), who issued the following decree at the time of the Oscar WILDE scandal, 'It doesn't matter what you do in the bedroom as long as you don't do it in the street and frighten the horses.' Many lesbians and gay men now use the phrase when they deliberately intend to upset straight TOURISTS.

frog queen US slang for a man erotically attracted to French or French-Canadian men. Can also be used to refer to French men themselves. *See also* BEAN QUEEN; DINGE QUEEN; RICE QUEEN; SNOW QUEEN.

The Frogs Play by the ancient Greek master of comedies, Aristophanes, written *c.* 405 BC, which deals with DIONYSUS' descent into Hades to bring back Euripides. It transpires that there is a special place reserved in the underworld for men who cheated male sex-workers of their pay. The play indicated the extent of male sex-work in ancient Athens, where male brothels were common and a tax was even imposed on the proceeds.

front marriage Also known as a marriage of convenience. Marriage between a lesbian and a gay man, or between a queer person and a knowing straight. Queer people take part in such dissimulation in order to deflect any speculation about their sexuality. Such marriages were common in the early twentieth century when the social costs of being out were too much for some, especially women who were often unable to be economically independent. Today, front marriages can help those of us with immigration problems.

frottage Sex where a man's dick does not penetrate the ass, but is rubbed between thighs, in the armpits or against his partner's chest. *See* INTRAFEMORAL SEX; PRINCETON RUB.

fruit North American slang for a gay man, less common in the UK. Like the word GAY, this usage of the term evolved from a previous meaning of a 'loose' woman, and then in the early twentieth century became an epithet for an effeminate gay man.

fruit fly An equally dubious alternative to FAG HAG, which has been with us since it was used by American gay communities in the 1970s. It plays on the word FRUIT as a noun for a gay man.

Fruits of the Earth 1897 work by French writer André GIDE, originally published in French as *Les Nourritures Terrestres*. It consists of a poetic paean to the joys of seeking new experience, and contains injunctions on a fictional youth, Nathanaël, to cast off the restraints of convention. The work was strongly influenced by Gide's growing acceptance of his homosexuality.

fuck bar Australian slang for backroom bars where gay men could cruise and have sex on the premises. Such establishments would usually have a cruising room in which men could pose and make contact with sexual partners, and a pitch-black backroom where the sex would take place. Popular in the 1970s, such bars declined with the advent of AIDS.

fuck buddy Term used by both lesbians and gay men to describe a friend with whom they occasionally have sex, without all the binds of emotional responsibility that sometimes spring unwantedly from the sex act. Such a friend is the sort of person you can ring if you want a fuck, knowing that it ends when it comes. While some would accuse us of effacing our emotions in the interest of our libidos, it seems that we are about the only species who have been able to combine sex and friendship without tears. The term has been around for some time; Cole Porter (1891–1964) used it to describe his relationship with the actor Monty Woolley, whom he had met at Yale University.

furies The furies – snake-haired women of Greek mythology who had sprung from the blood of Uranus and who lived in the underworld emerging only to pursue those who were guilty of heinous offences – have often been co-opted within the feminist and lesbian-feminist movements as symbolic of the power of women's anger at their subordination. In effect, this represents an ironic reworking of Greek myth, since the Greek furies were primarily associated with avenging patricide, yet latter-day furies are committed to ending patriarchy. *The Furies: Lesbian-Feminist Monthly* was an American lesbian-feminist magazine that started publication in 1972. Its first issue explained the choice of name as stemming from rage at the injustice of patriarchal systems: 'We are angry because we have been suppressed by male supremacy. We have been fucked over all our lives by a system which is based on the domination of men over women.'

The Further Perils of Laurel and Hardy A 1968 compilation film which featured Stan Laurel in very natural-looking drag. Laurel typically related to Hardy in a very feminine sense. Their relationship was elaborated interestingly in the film *Their First Mistake* in which the duo opt for a nuclear family set-up, with a baby who sleeps between them.

G

Glamour dyke

GAA *See* GAY ACTIVISTS ALLIANCE.

gadar From gay and radar. The intuitive force that allows gay men to recognize one another, or leads them to places where they can find sex even when they are in a strange place. It can also be used for the heightened awareness, when in public, of the dangers of QUEERBASHING. Also known as a gay man's cosmetic intuition.

GAG *See* GAYS AGAINST GENOCIDE.

gail The slang that is used by gay men in the South African city of Cape Town. The name is an abbreviation of gay language. Gail is used to talk without straight eavesdroppers being able to understand. It relies heavily on the use of women's names to refer to things. For example, Hilda means ugly, Jessie means jealous, Laura means love, Nancy means nothing, Patsy means party, Sally is a suck, Stella means to steal, and Wendy means white (racially).

gamahuching Term which became popular at the end of the nineteenth century, especially in pornographic literature, which could refer to both fellatio and cunnilingus. It was derived from the french verb *gamahucher*.

Ganymede (1) In Greek mythology Ganymede was a youth who, because of his extraordinary beauty was abducted by the god Zeus to serve as his cup-bearer. In Homer's *Iliad* Ganymede is described as the 'loveliest born of the race of mortals'. And from the sixth century BC onwards the story took on an explicitly sexual tone in literature when Theognis of MEGARA declared that 'the love of boys has been a pleasant thing ever since Ganymede was loved by Zeus'. Ovid, the Roman poet, describes how 'the King of the Gods once burned with love for Phrygian Ganymede', and tells how Zeus abducted the boy while disguised as an eagle. The story entered Roman folklore, and the

Roman version of Ganymede's name, Catamitus, spawned a word for a passive homosexual that lasted until the early twentieth century. The myth formed a staple part of art and poetry in the Italian Renaissance, and in English drama (*see* EDWARD II). (2) From the myth of Ganymede, the name has been used as a term for a gay man.

Garbo, Greta (Greta Lovisa Gustafsson, 1905–90) The enigmatic movie goddess became an immediate figure of fascination and legend from the time she started work in America in 1925 and through her major successes of the 1930s, such as *Anna Christie* (1930), QUEEN CHRISTINA (1933), *Anna Karenina* (1935), CAMILLE (1937) and *Ninotchka* (1939). Her reclusive life after her 1941 'retirement', bearing out the line usually associated with her from *Grand Hotel* (1932) that 'I want to be alone', served only to increase the fascination. Garbo had something for everyone. Her fragile beauty, glamour and enigma have made her the perfect candidate for status as gay male ICON, whilst in *Queen Christina* she presented an androgyny that was far more suggestive of the lesbian monarch than the producers of this heterosexualized version perhaps intended. Meanwhile, her characters were regularly punished for their moral transgressions.

Garland, Judy (Frances Gumm, 1922–69) American actress, singer and exemplar par excellence of the gay ICON. From her attempted suicide in 1950 she was the best example of the explanation of gay iconography that says it is the tragic figure with which gay audiences empathize. And no one could be more tragic than a puffy Garland at her dipso worst, looking like she'd been roughed up. Yet hers was also a story of incredible resilience; that she made so many come-backs when the chips were down must have been part of the attraction for gay audiences who were similarly in need of tremendous reserves of inner strength to function within a homophobic society. As the drag queen says in the GAY SWEATSHOP production of *As Time Goes By*, 'I loved her because no

matter how they put her down she survived.' Her rendition of OVER THE RAINBOW in THE WIZARD OF OZ demonstrated the quality that was needed to find that inner strength, the power to fantasize a place where work-a-day tribulations were nonexistent. Garland at times exhibited the androgynous quality that we can also appreciate in GARBO and DIETRICH. When she donned a tuxedo and fishnets to sing 'Get Happy' in *Summer Stock/If You Feel Like Singing* (1950) or when she performed 'In-Between' declaring 'I'm just a circle in a square', she demonstrated that she did not entirely fit in either. Garland was such a gay institution by the time of her death that many New York gay bars were draped in black as a sign of respect. But of course, it was the ensuing events that have most linked her with the gay movement, when the STONEWALL RIOT broke out on the day of her funeral.

GASA *See* GAY ASSOCIATION OF SOUTH AFRICA.

the Gates Name by which British lesbians referred to the GATEWAYS CLUB.

Gateways Club For much of the postwar period, the most famous lesbian club in London. Situated in the London district of Chelsea, the Gateways was originally opened in the 1930s and became established as a meeting place for bohemians and the artistic community. After the Second World War its clientele became increasingly gay, and mainly lesbian. This process was mirrored by the story of the proprietor Gina, who initially ran the bar with her husband and then with her lesbian lover Smithy. 'The Gates' served its last pint in 1985. The bar achieved its fifteen minutes of fame when it was featured in the 1968 film THE KILLING OF SISTER GEORGE, with some of its clientele serving as 'real' lesbian extras.

gay The word has been through a variety of primary meanings. Originally meaning cheerful, by the seventeenth century it had come to be used to describe straight male philanderers. Its meaning had been extended by the nineteenth century to refer to women who were seen as sexually available, and finally both male and female sex-workers. It was probably in the early twentieth century that it was adopted by both lesbians and gay men to refer to themselves. It served two purposes, not only as an alternative to the rather clinical 'homosexual', but also, since this usage of the word was not widely known, it could be used as a discreet way of drawing attention to one's own sexuality, and finding out about the sexuality of others. As a term for lesbians to refer to themselves, examples can be found from as early as 1922 in the writings of Gertrude STEIN. After the 1970s it became the standard word for homosexuals, even among heterosexuals. In 1987 the *New York Times* even began to use it (only adjectivally) in its reports. However, in the same period it declined as a word for lesbians to describe themselves because lesbian feminists saw it as referring primarily to gay men. With the growth of the gay liberation movement, a distinction was drawn between 'homosexual' and 'gay', the former being used to refer simply to sexual orientation, whereas the latter was used to indicate a man who has elected to become part of a gay community – involving the process of coming out and of acknowledging his sexuality as informing his identity to a significant degree.

Gay Activists Alliance (GAA) American lesbian and gay rights group, founded in New York in December 1969 by former members of the newly formed GAY LIBERATION FRONT who were unhappy with the fact that the GLF also campaigned on other non-gay liberation issues and with the anarchic style of GLF meetings. The GAA fitted somewhere in between the GLF and the older pre-STONEWALL RIOT groups. Like the GLF, it emphasized pride in lesbian and gay subcultural differences, and was also committed to direct action tactics. The group carried out a number of ZAPs: on the mayor of New York, John Lindsay; on the county clerk's office to demand lesbian and gay marriage rights; on *Harper's* magazine for expressing anti-gay views; and general protests and petitions in favour of

civil rights legislation. Unlike the GLF, it was not trying to overhaul heterosexual society, but it was attempting to gain access for lesbians and gays within society on equal terms. The group wanted an end to harassment and entrapment, equal access to employment and housing, and the abolition of sodomy laws. Chapters of GAA were set up in other American cities, and soon it eclipsed the GLF as the main force in lesbian and gay activism.

Gay American Indian (GAI) Organization for lesbian and gay Native Americans which was created in San Francisco in 1975 by Barbra Cameron, a Lakota Sioux, and Randy Burns, a Northern Paiute. Growing from a small social organization to a national grouping, GAI sought to re-examine the roles of lesbian and gay people within Native American societies, and to further their position within contemporary Native American and mainstream American society.

Gay and Lesbian Alliance Against Defamation (GLAAD) An American organization founded in 1985 in New York, with several other chapters throughout the country. Its specific aim is to monitor the presentation of lesbians and gays in the American media, and to campaign for positive representation. It meets with media folk to show them examples of balanced and biased reporting, particularly that kind of reporting which involves giving a platform to anti-gay extremists and presents them as responsible spokespersons, in the belief that this somehow makes a story 'fair'. It also protests against homophobic public figures, and campaigns against the forces which seek to censor the works of lesbian and gay artists. One memorable little success was to get the Empire State Building lit up in lavender for the duration of Gay Pride Week in 1990.

gay antennae The intuitive ability possessed by lesbians and gay men to pick up references to their sexuality, even where they don't explicitly exist. Slight discrepancies with pronouns, the lack of gendered pronouns when others are talking about their relationships, or the use of words such as PARTNER or SIGNIFICANT OTHER often start off the alarm that we are dealing with someone of the same sexuality. Cultural references, the knowledge of lesbian and gay authors, the casual hint about some of the bars that people go to also serve the same purpose.

gay apostolic succession Or the 'cosmic daisy chain' of sexual relationships between certain of this, and last, century's greatest gay figures. Walt WHITMAN, it seems, slept with Edward CARPENTER, who slept with Gavin Arthur, grandson of American President Chester Arthur, who slept with Neal Cassady, who slept with Allen Ginsberg. The chain has been proudly declared by Gavin Arthur, who worked with both Alfred KINSEY and Magnus HIRSCHFIELD on their researches into gay sexuality.

Gay Association of South Africa (GASA) The most prominent gay organization in South Africa, which was founded in 1982 by a group of predominantly white men. An affiliated organization for black men, called the Saturday Group, was founded in 1984.

Gay Bob A marketing first. A 1970s gay doll, created by Out of the Closets Inc., Gay Bob came along with jeans, plaid shirt, boots and earring. He was also 'anatomically correct', and came in his own closet presentation pack.

Gay Cable Network Lesbian and gay cable television service which was founded in New York in 1982. It produced a variety of programmes, including game shows (*Be My Guest*), political programmes (*Pride and Prejudice*), and news (*The 10% Show*) which was syndicated to several American cities.

gay days In the summers of 1971 and 1972 gay days were held by the London GAY LIBERATION FRONT in London parks. They were both a social and a political event, since they were aimed at creating a greater visibility for the lesbian and gay communities.

Gay Games Lesbian and gay athletics tournament which is held every four years. The first competition took place in August and September 1982 at the Kezar stadium in San Francisco. Two dozen countries were represented by around 1,300 lesbian and gay athletes who participated in some seventeen sports. The games were organized by former member of the US Olympic decathlon team Dr Tom Waddell, and were originally to be called the Gay Olympics. However, a law suit brought by the US Olympic Committee forbade Waddell from using the name Olympics in the title. The decision sparked a lesbian and gay boycott of the Visa company which sponsored the US Olympic Committee, with hundreds of queers destroying their cards. The games have been held every four years since, and some 15,000 athletes were scheduled to participate in the fourth event in New York in 1994, which actually surpassed the number in the 'real' Olympics in 1992.

gay gaze The term is used in various ways: the particular look a man has when he is out cruising for a sexual partner; or the inexplicable way in which you can tell the other gay men when you are cruising in a place which is not openly gay; the look that lesbians and gays share amongst one another when they have both heard or seen something which they both understand as typifying the obtuseness of heterosexuals, usually while they are deciding who is going to explain that you can't say things like that. The term is also used in film criticism to describe the particular point of view of a lesbian or gay audience, especially when they are managing to find the gay subtext in a work that is ostensibly 'not about gays'.

gay girl As a self-referential term for lesbians, gay girl was common from the 1940s, and was used by Lisa Ben in the magazine VICE VERSA. In the CONTACT ADVERTS of the 1970s it carried the implication that the woman using it was non-political and not part of the lesbian or lesbian-feminist movements. The term had a revival in the 1980s, since when it has been used to imply trendy women who are active on the lesbian social scene.

gay is good Slogan which became popular among lesbian and gay activists in the mid-1960s. It borrowed from the 'Black is beautiful' slogan used by black civil rights activists and indicated a new upfront feel to queer politics which contrasted with the assimilationism of the 1950s. The slogan was adopted by the North American Conference of Homophile Organizations in 1966.

Gay Liberation Front (GLF) Radical lesbian and gay organization that was set up in New York, and other American cities, in the immediate aftermath of the STONEWALL RIOT in 1969. Many younger lesbians and gay men wanted to turn the energy released by Stonewall into militant activity, but realized this would not be possible within the more conservative organizations such as the MATTACHINE SOCIETY. They began to hold discussions at New York's ALTERNATE UNIVERSITY, which eventually became the GLF, the name chosen to express solidarity with liberation struggles in Algeria and Vietnam. Two British men, Aubrey Walter and Bob Mellors, who encountered the organization while travelling in America transported the idea back to London, and the first British meeting was held in the London School of Economics in October 1970. Although the organization had to shift its base from the LSE to Covent Garden and then to Notting Hill, by 1971 some 400 or 500 people were coming to meetings. In addition, other gay liberation groups formed throughout the UK, and smaller London groups were created to focus activity. The GLF was often labelled leftist, because its politics went beyond the attempt to prove the 'respectability' of lesbians and gay men so as to allow them to integrate into mainstream society that was characteristic of the HOMOPHILE MOVEMENT, and because a number of GLF members expressed support for many other liberation struggles. This was particularly true of the New York group, and divisions led to the foundation of the GAY ACTIVISTS ALLIANCE. The GLF

espoused a radical critique of society and gender, and of the possibilities for lesbian and gay communities to transform society. It aimed itself as much at lesbian and gay self-oppression and liberal 'tolerance' as at overt discrimination and persecution. While men were always far better represented than women, there were genuine attempts to incorporate an analysis of sexism into its actions, which led some of the men to use radical DRAG as a way of highlighting the stupidity of socially created gender roles. Tensions between men and women persisted however, and in both London and New York lesbians felt the need to organize separately. The organization also placed prime importance on lesbians and gay men COMING OUT and coming together to gain strength in numbers (the magazine of the London GLF was entitled COME TOGETHER, while that of new York was COME OUT!). It was not however separatist, and did not want to create a lesbian or gay GHETTO. Organizations were non-hierarchical with no officials, arranged around AFFINITY GROUPS, and meetings attempted to find consensus through discussion that was open to anybody. Such soul-searching was bound to uncover tensions between different members, and by the mid-1970s the majority of GLF groups in the UK and America had become all but defunct.

Gay Liberation Front Manifesto 1971 document produced by the London GAY LIBERATION FRONT which outlined some of its analysis of the political situation for lesbians and gay men, and which set out the aims of the organization and the route to liberation. It represented an attempt to create a theory of homosexual oppression within the feminist theories of society. It demonstrated the growth of pride which had taken place within the community: 'At this moment in time, the freest and most equal relationships are most likely to be between homosexuals.'

Gay Male SM Activists (GMSMA) American organization founded in New York in 1980 after one of its founders, Brian O'Dell, had placed an advert in the

Boston gay *Community News* for the setting up of a discussion group for SM practitioners. Like the LESBIAN SEX MAFIA which was founded at about the same time, GMSMA marked a new stage in the life of the SM communities in America. It was the first exclusively gay organization for leather men that was founded as an open group, rather than drawing its membership through personal referrals. As such, it indicated that gay SM was coming out of the LEATHER CLOSET and was beginning to politicize its demand to be respected as a natural part of the lesbian and gay movement. This was reflected in the name of the group, which evoked the old Gay Activists Alliance. It was also partly set up in reaction to a gay scene that comprised a lot of men who were interested in wearing leather but were not into SM sex, and it aimed to give men advice about SM technique. It was hugely successful, and drew upwards of a hundred men to its meetings within a year.

Gay Men Fighting AIDS (GMFA) British organization set up to work within the gay community to prevent HIV and AIDS, in recognition of the fact that the majority of official funding and support was not going to the community which was still most heavily affected by the syndrome. The group has run many EROTICIZING SAFER SEX workshops throughout the UK, which are called 'Days of Sex'.

Gay Men's Health Crisis American AIDS service organization. It was founded in January 1982 in New York by Edmund White, Larry KRAMER, Dr Lawrence Mass, Nathan Fain, Paul Popham and Paul Rapoport, all of whom had seen friends die of AIDS-related illnesses. In April it held its first fundraising which brought in $30,000. It rapidly became America's largest AIDS service organization, providing a variety of legal, counselling and welfare services.

Gay News British gay newspaper which was produced fortnightly from its founding in June 1972. It was first created by a collective which included members of the GAY LIBERATION FRONT and the CAMPAIGN FOR HOMOSEXUAL EQUALITY, but soon came under the editorship of Denis Lemon. It was designed to appeal to the 'whole' gay community, and carried the usual features and reviews, as well as series such as 'Hets of the Month' which featured public figures whose heterosexuality was not quite unimpeachable. In 1974 it was dragged into the courts when an attempt was made to have a cover photo of two men kissing judged obscene (it wasn't), and again in 1977 when it was successfully prosecuted for blasphemy (*see* LEMON CASE).

gay science Described by Edmund White in *States of Desire* as 'that obligatory existentialism forced on people who must invent themselves...Once one discovers one is gay one must choose everything, from how to walk, dress and talk to where to live, with whom and on what terms.' It represents the lesbian and gay understanding that there is nothing which is objectively NORMAL or NATURAL, but that everything is mainly composed of pretence and surface; a strategy of survival, it allows us to realize that we can be anything we want for a short time, or within the sanctuary of the lesbian or gay bar, and that is enough to keep living. CAMP humour is a product of gay science which asserts that we can decide what is and what is not important. Gay science can also refer to the esoterica about gay ICONS with which lesbians and gay men are required to be au fait in order to be able to take part in polite society.

Gay Sweatshop British theatre group founded in 1974, with the help of the Inter-Action community arts trust. Although Inter-Action provided much support, most of the initial backbreaking work to create the company was voluntary, hence the name Sweatshop. Initially, it was a group of gay men who came together in order to produce plays by gay authors which put their lives and experience literally centre stage. Many of the founding members had been active within the GAY LIBERATION FRONT, and this was their attempt to bring those politics into the world of professional theatre. Their first series of plays was called HOMOSEXUAL ACTS. It was not until 1976 that the company produced work for and by lesbians, producing Jill Posener's *Any Woman Can*. The company has toured around the UK and has performed in schools where its work helps to create positive images for gay schoolchildren. Yet the group has not always been welcome; it has been subject to demonstrations by religious fundamentalists, and in 1983 the Devon education authorities banned it from performing for fear of the effect there might be on children. The work of the company has given early support to a number of people who were to go on to great things, including Drew Griffiths and Martin Sherman.

Gay Times The auntie of British gay publishing. *Gay Times* was resurrected from the ashes of the soft-porn *Him Monthly* in 1984, and hired several staff members who had worked for GAY NEWS. It has been with us through thick and thin every month since then. Most view it with the sort of affection they would a comfy old DM, hardly new but reliable, some think it has one sling-back in the grave and the life-support machine ought to be switched off. It has been through several revamps, most recently in April 1994 in response to a (b)rash of young pretenders attempting to steal the fashion-conscious market. *Gay Times* often carries excellent features, reviews, photos of apparently the same clientele in different venues around the UK, and trusty favourites like 'Mediawatch', which presents us with the homophobic offal offered up by the straight press in the preceding month.

A gay Vietnam vet. 'When I was in the military they gave me a medal for killing two men – and a discharge for loving one.' Inscription on the gravestone of American Air Force sergeant and gay activist Leonard MATLOVICH, who is buried in the Congressional Cemetery in Washington DC. Matlovich stepped into the public eye in 1975 when he appeared on the cover of the American *Time* magazine, after he had commenced a legal battle to challenge the US military policy of automatic dismissal of lesbian and gay armed service personnel. Matlovich joined the ranks of those we have lost to AIDS in 1988.

gay window Term used by gay activist Harry HAY to describe the special perspective on life that is shared by lesbians and gay men.

Gays against Genocide (GAG) British group founded in 1993 to protest against what it saw as the dangerous prescription of the drug AZT for people with AIDS and HIV. Later, it also went by the name of Concern over Concorde (*see* CONCORDE TRIAL). While some of its aims might have been reasonable – to question the reliance of communities affected by AIDS on 'knowledge' about treatment on a scientific establishment that is too heavily bound up in the commercial interests of pharmaceutical companies – its tactics are not, involving, as they do, personal intimidation and even death threats.

Gay's the Word Bookshop and information centre located in the Bloomsbury district of London which developed out of the GAY LIBERATION FRONT anti-psychiatry group, Icebreakers. Gay's the Word is still London's only lesbian and gay bookshop, although there is Silver Moon on the Charing Cross Road which is Europe's largest women's (and lesbian) bookshop.

GDLK Abbreviation which forms part of the standard lexicon from which gay CONTACT ADVERTS are compiled, meaning either goodlooking, or godlike, depending on the arrogance of the user. Since absolutely everyone describes themselves as good-looking, the term loses some of its impact. One touching alternative for those who could not describe themselves as good-looking without fearing the fires of hell is 'told goodlooking', but that gives the game away immediately.

gemblakan Javanese institution in which an older man will indicate his wealth and social standing by showering a male favourite with gifts. The young man would live with his sugar daddy for a number of years, after his parents had been paid in gifts.

Gemeinschaft der Eigenen (Community of the Exceptional) Gay organization founded in Berlin in Germany in 1903 by the gay activist Adolf Brand (1874–1945), who also produced the journal DER EIGENE.

gender blend As a verb, to emphasize an androgynous sexuality through dress and hairstyle. Also known as gender-bending.

gender dysphoria The technical term that is used to describe TRANSSEXUALISM, or the feeling of being the 'wrong' gender. The concept is very similar to the nineteenth-century 'explanation' of homosexuality found in the notion of CONGENITAL INVERSION.

gender fuck Practice which emerged from the sexual politics of radical lesbian and gay groups such as the GAY LIBERATION FRONT of the 1970s, which involved self-consciously mixing the clothing of both genders as a way of drawing attention to the artificiality of gender roles as they are expressed through appearance. It was usually practised by gay men who were seeking a way of discarding the power that was given to them merely by virtue of being and appearing male, whether or not they wanted it. It differed from CROSS-DRESSING and DRAG because gender-fucking men did not seek to create the illusion of womanliness (however parodied), but retained something (such as visible chest hair under a frock) which marked them out as unquestionably (biologically) male. It also differed slightly from the unisex fashions of the hippie movement because it was aimed more at making a political statement to affront conventional ideas of gender. Gender fuck reappeared in a different guise in the 1980s as gender-bending. However, the most famous proponent of gender bending, BOY GEORGE, was less anxious to make a political statement through his dress, and in fact made himself as acceptable as possible by presenting an almost asexual public image.

gender gap The disparity between the expectations and achievemnents of men and women. All other things being equal, men have higher expectations of what they will achieve and subsequently do attain more success and status than women in their peer groups; it follows that men achieve more purely because they are men. A gender gap exists in the lesbian and gay community just as in any other social institution, with gay men on average earning more than lesbians.

gender reassignment surgery Medical euphemism for the sex change operation. The operation is preceded by a period of hormone taking, which for male to female operations will cause the reorganization of body fat and the growth of breasts. Body hair may also be removed through a process of electrolysis, usually requiring upwards of 200 sessions for a full body job. Genital surgery then takes place, with the penis being removed and testes taken from the scrotum. A vagina is constructed, either through using the scrotal sac, or by using the skin of the penis. For female to male operations a penis can be constructed from body tissues taken from the thigh but this will lack sensitivity.

Genet, Jean (1910–86) French dramatist, novelist and essayist. He spent much of his early life drifting through and earning his daily bread through sex-work, crime, drug-dealing and begging. He served a number of jail sentences and was only saved from a life sentence by the intervention of artists such as Jean COCTEAU and Jean-Paul Sartre, who had admired the writings he had produced whilst in jail. While Genet's plays do not really emphasize homosexuality as a theme, his novels, including *Our Lady of the Flowers* (1944), the autobiographical *Thief's Journal* (1949), and the work that launched a thousand fantasies, *Querelle of Brest* (1953) often deal with an underworld in which gay relations are commonplace. Genet displays great affection for the residents of this demimonde, and contends that moral labels are subject to question in a hypocritical society. Genet also scripted and directed the

1950 film *Un Chant d'Amour*, which depicted the erotic currents between men in prison.

gentleman of the back door Slang term for gay man which is recorded in the 1785 *Classical Dictionary of the Vulgar Tongue* edited by Captain Francis Grose.

Gerber, Henry (1892–1972) One of the earliest American gay rights activists. In the early 1920s Gerber served in the American army of occupation in Germany, where he witnessed at first hand the growing German gay rights movement. On returning to Chicago Gerber founded the SOCIETY FOR HUMAN RIGHTS, the first recorded gay rights group in the United States, through which he sought to educate the public about gay issues and to campaign for the repeal of legal barriers to gay sex. Gerber carried on his work after the demise of the organization, publishing defences of gay sexuality and planning a bigger and better gay rights organization. He joined the MATTACHINE SOCIETY when it was founded, but never really became prominent.

gerontophilia Technical term for sexual interest in older people.

ghetto In sociological literature, an urban neighbourhood housing a dense concentration of institutions and residents of any particular minority. The ghetto allows its inhabitants to spend the majority of their lives within one community since it provides the majority of the services necessary for life. The ghetto also functions as a symbolic and political space. Although lesbian and gay communities might not be entirely self-contained geographically, it is becoming increasingly possible to restrict many meaningful emotional and financial transactions to lesbian or gay community institutions. One aim of the lesbian feminist movement was to create women's spaces, institutions and enterprises and, though less politically motivated gay men have been doing the same with the growth of businesses owned and run by gays. In this sense the ghetto offers a space in which lesbian and gay people can live apart from an oppressive heterosexual world. Thus the politics of the ghetto is a term that is used (generally critically) to describe the importance placed by some lesbians and gay men on building up community self-reliance, rather than in aiming all energy at attacking homophobia or patriarchy. The issue is controversial within lesbian and gay political groups. Some people argue that only a self-reliant community can achieve the strength to mount an attack on society, and that a ghetto is challenging in itself since both homophobia and patriarchy work most insidiously on the level of the individual. However, other activists warn that while it may improve the quality of life of some lesbian and gay people, it is too inward-looking and directs political attention away from the real oppressor – heterosexual society – upon which they are bound to be dependent at some point.

Gide, André (1869–1951) French writer and editor. He was brought up in an austere Protestant household and, though he rebelled against the stringencies of revealed religion, the search for identity that was a main theme in his works was often handled with the use of religious idiom. In 1891 he met Oscar WILDE and the encouragement which Wilde gave him freed him of inhibition regarding his homosexuality, a freedom represented in his 1897 work FRUITS OF THE EARTH. In the early twentieth century he became an important figure in French intellectual circles, with his written attacks on French colonialism in Africa, his attraction and disillusionment with Communism and the Soviet system and, of course, his public affirmation of his sexuality. The EULENBERG AFFAIR in Germany had prompted the dialogues published under the title CORYDON, which argued that homosexuality was a natural part of the human psyche, and that sexual pleasure was a separate thing to reproduction. The response to *Corydon* spurred him to publish his memoirs, IF IT DIE. Gide was important for creating public discussion about homosexuality, for arguing its naturalness against the orthodoxies of the SEXOLOGISTS, and for using his own personal experience in his writings.

Giles Hot-Sea Baths Baths at Coogee beach, near Sydney in Australia, popular in the early twentieth century. With indoor and outdoor facilities, as well as a tidal pool and access to secluded rocky outcrops, the baths provided ample opportunity for sexual encounters, and were famous for the amount of cruising that went on there.

The Epic of Gilgamesh Mesopotamian blockbuster that was written in the Akkadian language between 1800 and 1600 BC, which remained popular throughout the Middle East for well over a thousand years. It tells the story of Gilgamesh, King of Uruk who, legend has it, was the fifth ruler after the flood, and who was probably a historical personage. Although wise, Gilgamesh is not initially a popular ruler, since all young men have to keep leaving their families to fight in his campaigns. The people pray for help, and the goddess Aruru creates Enkidu, the equal of Gilgamesh, who has to divert him from his energetic military escapades. The two become sworn friends and travel together to slay the monster Humbaba. However, when Gilgamesh refuses to marry the goddess Ishtar, in anger she gets the god Anu to send a great bull to destroy him. When the two friends kill the bull, the gods decide that they have gone too far, and send an illness to Enkidu which kills him. Gilgamesh cannot believe that his friend has died until his body begins to decompose. Distraught with grief, he leaves the city and wanders in the wilderness, and eventually travels to the land of death to find out the secrets of mortality. Because of the close relationship between the two heroes, and Gilgamesh's refusal to marry the goddess, the epic has become something of a classic of gay prehistory.

gin Quintessential gay male drink. Newspaper reports of the 1930s commented on the preference for gin in queer bars of the time.

ginger Abbreviation of ginger beer, British rhyming slang for queer.

ginseng Plant root, originally used in China where it is made into a tonic tea. Became popular outside that country since it was considered to have aphrodisiac properties. Recently, it has been used as a complementary therapy by people living with HIV to help build up their immune system.

Giovanni's Room 1956 novel by James Baldwin (1924–87) about the ill-fated relationship between American jock and Italian waiter which eventually leads to Giovanni's execution for murder. The book served as a metaphor for the destructive relationships between whites and blacks in America. It was also understood as a commentary on the unhealthy effect of the CLOSET, and the title even became a slang term for that nasty little cupboard.

girl guides All-women organizations, begun in 1910 by General Baden-Powell and his sister Agnes Baden-Powell. In America they began in 1921 and were known as Girl Scout groups. They are made up mainly of teenagers who often, to promote the pure life, go off together to camps in the wilderness. No prizes for guessing what goes on in a lot of those tents.

girlcott A women's boycott. Beginning in the 1970s, women within the feminist movement would embargo sexist institutions and commercial establishments to get them to change their policies.

gism Slang for cum. Also written jissom or jism. Its etymology is unknown.

give head To give someone a blow job.

GLAAD *See* GAY AND LESBIAN ALLIANCE AGAINST DEFAMATION.

Glad To Be Gay 1977 song by Tom Robinson, which while ostensibly an anthem for Gay Pride was a sophisticated description of the worst features of homophobia in British society – within the police force and the tabloid press – and ended with an admonition of gay apathy in the face of it all. The song's chorus (few dizzy queens could remember the whole of it) was often used as a chant on demonstrations throughout the 1980s. Robinson, who had been active in the GAY LIBERATION MOVEMENT in the 1970s and had worked with the LONDON LESBIAN AND GAY SWITCHBOARD and the GAY SWEATSHOP theatre company, disappointed many of his gay fans by settling down with a female lover and becoming a father. But he refused to be drawn on the issue. 'All these kinds of labels...are really pointless and restricting.'

glamour dyke (aka designer dyke) 1980s phenomenon on the lesbian social scene. Within the 1970s lesbian feminist movement the orthodoxies of political correctness tended to proscribe the fripperies and patriarchal implications of women's fashion. In the 1980s lesbians seemed more free to explore variations of the female role through dress and cosmetics.

GLF *See* GAY LIBERATION FRONT.

von Gloeden, Baron Wilhelm (1856–1931) German photographer who moved permanently to Sicily where he ran an interesting byline persuading local young men to strip and pose nude for his camera.

glory hole Slang term for a hole that is carved or drilled in the partition between cubicles in public toilets. Can be used to take a look at the person in the next cubicle, and the dick can be put through it for an informal blow job or fuck. A suck factory is a slang term for a public toilet with a large number of glory holes.

Gluck The name taken by Hannah Gluckstein (1896–1978), the extremely successful British Jewish painter. Gluck's family were very rich; they owned the Lyons Coffee House chain. Gluck wore men's clothes and loved women for her entire adult life. Her most famous painting is *Medallion*, a portrait of herself and her lover Nesta Obermer in noble profile which is used on the cover of the Virago edition of THE WELL OF LONELINESS. Gluck's lovers also included Constance Spry, the flower arranger and hostess, and Edith Shackleton Heald, the journalist with whom she lived for nearly forty years.

Gluck spent the later years of her life waging a battle to restore the quality of artists' materials.

GMFA *See* GAY MEN FIGHTING AIDS.

go down on someone To perform oral sex on someone.

Go Fish 1994 film by American lesbian filmmakers Rose Troche and Guinevere Turner. It tells the story of a group of girlfriends who conspire to fix up one of their number, Max (Turner herself), with the seemingly unsuitable Ely (V.S. Brodie). The film depicts the sassiest of American lesbian life, along with a sexual openness which scatters sexual imagery throughout the whole film as well as in the big love scene, which immediately became notorious for the fact that Ely appears to give Max a fist. A comedy of great vitality.

Go Guys Early gay magazine, first produced in early 1963. Included erotic photographs, although dick shots were still forbidden at the time. Also included homoerotic photostories, with suggestive commentary, explicit cartoons, features, and bits on gay history and art.

The Gobble Poem *See* A DAY TO BLOW OR GET BLOWN.

Goblin Market Poem by the English poet Christina Rossetti (1830–94) which has been described as a poetic representation of the joys of cunnilingus. It describes how two sisters are tempted to eat some forbidden fruit by deformed male goblins. The particular fruits mentioned, cherries and figs, bear no small symbolic resemblance to the vagina. Only one sister gives in to the temptation and tucks in, whereupon she loses control: 'She sucked their fruit globes fair or red...until her tongue was sore.' Now, what does that sound like?

God of Vengeance Play by Sholom Asch, produced on Broadway in 1923, having first been seen all over Europe. It relates the story of the owner of a brothel, who was anxious that his daughter should not become involved with any of the clients. Instead she becomes attached to a female sex-worker. The lesbian theme led to the prosecution for obscenity of the director, producer and cast.

God Save Us Nelly Queens The rousing song, sung to the tune of the British national anthem, which legendary entertainer Jose SARRIA instructed the patrons of the BLACK CAT bar in San Francisco to sing in order to affirm their solidarity in the face of police harassment.

God, was I drunk last night Identified in the play BOYS IN THE BAND as the most common tactic a 'straight' man will use after a same-sex indiscretion. The syndrome, in which he professes to have lost all memory, allows him and his partner of the time never to have to talk about it or face up to it.

goddess A female deity. Twentieth-century feminists, particularly new age feminists, have often scoured the accounts of ancient mythologies for examples of strong goddesses with which to construct their own feminist mythologies. Goddesses particularly associated with this practice are DIANA (Artemis), VESTA, Venus (APHRODITE), Athena, Persephone, DEMETER, and KALI. Sometimes these deities have been rolled into one composite goddess to represent the entirety of women's spiritual power.

godemiche Nineteenth-century term for a DILDO, an artificial object shaped like a phallus, to use for penetration either of the anus or vagina.

The Golden Girls American comedy soap opera produced between 1985 and 1992, about three older women sharing an apartment in Florida along with the even older, but by no means gaga, mother of one of them. The barbed wit the women employ, together with the camaraderie, as they end up eating cheesecake in the kitchen late at night, have made the show a cult classic among gay men. This is despite the fact that there have been relatively few lesbian and gay characters – Dorothy's 'widowed' friend and Blanche's brother being two notable but short-lived exceptions.

Golden Orchid associations Women's organizations in nineteenth-century China, associated with the 'marriage resistance movement' centred in Guangzhou. Membership was exclusively female, and lesbian relationships were a common part. The women could perform certain rites of 'marriage' with one another, where one partner was designated 'husband'. Sexual practices such as genital rubbing called 'grinding bean curd' and the use of dildoes, have been described. The couple could adopt female children and these children would adopt the property of their 'parents'. This freedom was probably due to their economic independence which resulted from the expansion of the (traditionally female) silk industry. The women themselves would explain by saying that they were fated to be together but reincarnation had created them of the same gender in this incarnation.

golden screw Anal sex where the fucker also pisses into the anus of the fuckee. Since it involves fucking without a condom, it is a very risky activity from the point of view of HIV transmission.

golden shower A jet of urine, when it is used as part of erotic play. Thus golden showers refers to the practice of WATER-SPORTS. Often used within gay CONTACT ADVERTS to express a preference for the full-bladdered man.

Gomorrah *See* SODOM AND GOMORRAH.

The Good Play by Chester Erskine which enjoyed only a short run on Broadway in 1938. The young protagonist, Howard, finds his attraction to the local choirmaster requited, but disclosed to his family when he tells his doctor about the relationship. The play was uncharacteristic of portrayals of gay love at the time as it eschews a traditional tragic ending. What is more, Howard refuses to feel the usual guilt and shame at his love, and asserts that such a relationship is not inherently sordid, an assertion rather too progressive for the American stage of the time.

good goddess A new age feminist expletive, associated with the lesbian author Anna Livia.

The Good Gray Poet Nickname for American poet Walt WHITMAN which was derived from a defence of his LEAVES OF GRASS in 1866 by William D. O'Connor, following an attack which had declared the book to be 'immoral'.

goose Verb meaning to penetrate a man anally, which was popular in the nineteenth century. A soldier comments in THE SINS OF THE CITIES OF THE PLAIN, 'As soon as (or before) I had learned the goose step I had learned to be goosed.'

Gordon, Stephen The butch protagonist in Radclyffe HALL's novel THE WELL OF LONELINESS, who became the most famous/notorious lesbian in fiction, just as her author became the most recognizable lesbian in public life for much of the early twentieth century. Her body, broad-shouldered and athletic, was the hallmark of her difference. As writer Blanche Wiesen Cook said, 'Most of us lesbians in the 1950s grew up knowing nothing about lesbianism except Stephen Gordon's swagger.' Described as a man in a woman's body, Stephen Gordon has been decried by many lesbians as a capitulation to the theories of the nineteenth-century SEXOLOGISTS, whilst others have argued that she represented a crucial point of identification for many lesbians since she symbolized the stigma that public acknowledgement of lesbianism has always entailed.

Gorgidas Greek military commander who formed the SACRED BAND OF THEBES in 378 BC. He established the battalion in order to unite couples who had hitherto been scattered throughout the Theban army.

gossip This principal lesbian and gay pastime was originally derived from the Old English *god-sib*, meaning a god-relative. It gradually evolved to refer to a woman's best friend, and eventually came to mean the kind of talk that best friends engage in.

government-inspected meat Gay slang term of the 1970s for a gay man within the armed services. It is a play on the initials GI which were presumed to stand for government inspected and to be stamped on any items produced for the armed forces. Erroneously as it happens, since they actually stood for government issue, but we needn't let that spoil a good joke.

La Gran Scena Opera Company American drag opera company, which was formed in New York in 1980 by cabaret performer Ira Siff (whose diva persona is the fabulous but enduringly modest Madame Vera Galupe-Borzkh). The company produces its own drag parodies of the most famous of the OPERA QUEEN's repertoire, but always with a respect for the piece, and with the occasional barb at the pretensions of real-life opera divas.

Dorian Gray The eponymous character of Oscar WILDE's 1890 novel, *The Picture of Dorian Gray*, whose portrait aged and showed the physical toll of his amoralities, while his physique remained as fresh-faced as ever. An aesthete, Dorian embodied a series of qualities at odds with those valued in Victorian manhood. He was delicate, artistic, and adored perfumes, jewellery and embroidery. The significance of these qualities was not lost on the novel's audience.

The Great Geysers of California Probably a very edifying work, but of little interest in this context, other than that its author Laura De Force Gordon (1838–?) was a lesbian. She buried a copy of the book in a time capsule, which was unearthed 100 years later in 1979. On the flyleaf she had written, 'If this little book should see the light of day after 100 years' entombment, I should like the readers to know that the author was a lover of her own sex and devoted the best years of her life in striving for the political equality...of women.' Gordon was a forceful woman, and had brought a case to the California Supreme Court to win the right to enrol at law college.

The Great Mirror of Male Love Japanese anthology of short stories dating from 1687. The stories deal with amorous episodes between samurai and their pages, and kabuki actors and their patrons.

Greater London Council London's administrative body, which replaced the London County Council in 1963. It became renowned (and reviled in some quarters) for its support of community initiatives for lesbians and gay men, as well as for London's black communities. It was abolished by the Conservative government in 1986 in a move which spelt funding difficulties for many of these initiatives.

greek In American gay slang the word can be used as a verb to mean to engage in anal sex. It can also be used adjectivally so that in contact ad-speak 'Gr act' means the penetrating partner in anal sex, while 'Gr pas' refers to the one who is fucked.

Greek love Because of the associations of the civilization of ANCIENT GREECE with accepted and institutionalized homosexual relations, the term Greek love has historically served as a code term for homosexual affection, especially in the nineteenth century. Thus, when Edward CARPENTER described Walt WHITMAN as 'the most Greek in spirit' of all contemporary writers, he was referring to the homoerotic implications of the American poet's work.

green Though not as commonly associated with homosexuality as the colour LAVENDER, green does have its queer connections. For Oscar WILDE it was associated with decadence, both artistic and moral. In his essay *Pen, Pencil and Poison* (1889) Wilde discussed the forger Thomas Wainewright, and wrote that he had 'that curious love of green, which in individuals is always the sign of a subtle artistic temperament, and in nations is said to denote a laxity, if not a decadence of morals'. American lesbian writer Judy Grahn remembers that while at school in the 1950s there was a children's custom that maintained that if you wore green clothes on a Thursday it showed that you were 'queer'. She writes that the origins of this custom might be found in the pagan FAIRY culture of medieval Europe, a culture in which green was a special colour, for camouflage and to express links with the natural world. She also quotes the historian of WITCHcraft, Jeffery Burton Russell, who stated that French witches, who she sees as inheritors of the fairy mantle, would congregate on a Thursday.

green carnation The verdigris carnation, a sort of greeny-blue colour, was one of the hallmarks of Oscar WILDE's attire at the opening nights of his plays. He had written about his association of the colour green with decadence, and thus it was natural for him to pick on the green carnation when he was composing a small in-joke for the opening night of *Lady Windermere's Fan*. One of the characters in the play, Cecil Graham (played by Ben Webster), was to wear one, as were several of Wilde's friends in the audience in addition to the playwright himself. The ruse appealed to Wilde's sense of secret signs, which though they meant nothing would keep others guessing. In 1894 Robert Hitchens published the book *The Green Carnation* which parodied Wilde's relationship with Lord Alfred DOUGLAS. Although it was written out of fascination with Wilde, it did nothing to quell the disquiet growing about Wilde's sexuality, and raised the ire of Lord Alfred Douglas' father, the Marquess of Queensberry.

Greenwich Village Neighbourhood of New York which in the early twentieth century was already becoming a bohemian community of artists who prided themselves on their nonconformism. While the tolerance of heterosexuals in the community was limited, the village was more comfortable for lesbians and gays than other areas, and in the 1920s a queer subculture was becoming visible. It has remained a centre of lesbian and gay life, and it was here that the STONEWALL RIOT, the folkloric beginning of the modern lesbian and gay movement, took place.

GRID (gay related immune deficiency) The first name given to the syndrome now called AIDS, which was first identified in 1981 when a number of American gay men began to suffer inexplicable breakdowns in their immune system. The term was criticized by gay activists as blatantly prejudiced, especially when it became clear that non-gay communities were beginning to suffer from the same syndrome. It began to be ditched for the term AIDS from late 1982.

Grier, Barbara (1933–) Best known as a lesbian publisher (Naiad) and activist; editor of *The Lesbian in literature: a bibliography* (1981), a goldmine of about 7,000 American and British titles, each given a rating for lesbian interest. Grier has written under several pseudonyms.

Guards From the eighteenth century the Guards were associated with prostitution (*see* SEX-WORK) in both Britain and Germany. Around the time of the EULENBERG AFFAIR many people were publicly worried about the extent of prostitution among the armed forces, a phenomenon which seemed to strike at the heart of German manhood.

gunsel Slang term for passive partner in anal sex. Originated around 1915 as part of prison/vagrant slang, and was especially used to refer to an inexperienced young male companion. A corruption of the German and Yiddish word gansel or gosling, meaning young goose. In the film *The Maltese Falcon* the character of Joel Cairo is dismissively called a gunsel by Bogart. By the 1930s the term had evolved to mean a gangster.

guppy A gay yuppy, or young upwardly mobile professional. Term coined in America in the 1980s to describe the career-minded gay men who were eager to put their hands on an ever larger (pay) packet. Gay male designers, executives and media types have littered the urban gay scene from the 1980s. *See also* DINK; LUPPY.

gymnasium From the Greek meaning to exercise naked, the gymnasium was the centre for the education of adolescent boys in ANCIENT GREECE. Since their education was generally in the physical arts and was usually conducted naked, it comes as little surprise that the gymnasium functioned as the main locus for homosexual relations. Which provides a link with today, when the gymnasium is the haunt of the MUSCLE MARY, and the showers provide more than post-iron-pumping hygiene.

gynander Term for a butch lesbian, which was fairly common around the beginning of the twentieth century. It was constructed from a fusion of the Greek terms for female and male.

H

Hankie codes

H.D. The initials with which the American poet Hilda DOOLITTLE signed her works. The use of initials had been suggested by American writer Ezra Pound.

Hadrian *See* ANTINOUS.

Hair This swinging full-frontal musical was one of the greatest shows in theatrical history; *Hair* opened on Broadway in 1968 and was easily the most controversial musical of the decade with explicit references to bodies and all manner of sex, including the blockbuster song 'Sodomy'. More than 4 million Americans enjoyed it during its first two years on stage, and the show was equally successful in London. A limp film version came out in 1979, and a staged revival in London in 1993 was a total flop.

the hairpin drop heard round the world Description of the STONEWALL RIOT published in the MATTACHINE SOCIETY newsletter.

Hall, John (Marguerite) Radclyffe (1886–1943) is still one of the world's most famous lesbians as a result of writing the notorious, best-selling and groundbreaking THE WELL OF LONELINESS (1928). Brought up by her mother and grandmother, Radclyffe Hall inherited a considerable sum on her father's death in 1898. Until meeting the married Mable Batten (Ladye) in 1907, she travelled extensively in Europe and America and formed a number of close relationships with women. At this time she saw her metier as lyric poetry, publishing *'Twixt Earth and Stars* (1907) and *A Sheaf of Verses* (1908). As a result of his wife's relationship with Hall, George Batten, the Secretary to the Viceroy of India, moved out of the family home and Hall moved in. The relationship between Radclyffe and Mabel probably did not come as a great surprise to the elderly Batten, as his wife's fondness for female company was already well-known. Hall continued writing, with *Poems of the*

Past and Present being published in 1910. In 1915 Hall met Una Troubridge (1887–1963) a sculptor and the wife of Rear-Admiral Troubridge. An unpleasant situation quickly developed as the now elderly and ill Mabel and the young and beautiful Una fought for Hall's affections. The death of Mabel partially resolved the situation, although for the rest of her life Hall felt guilty about her infidelity with Una, and communicated her remorse to Mabel via mediums and psychics. Una and Radclyffe established an enjoyable and glamorous life, and largely moved in lesbian circles which included Teddy Gerard, the British actress, and Tallulah Bankhead, the American sex goddess. Hall started to write novels *The Forge*, *The Unlit Lamp* (1924) and *Adam's Breed* (1926). These won considerable acclaim, winning the Femina Vie Heureuse and the James Tait Black Memorial prizes. *The Unlit Lamp* is a novel of love between women, and Hall started to receive fan letters from lesbians from the date of its publication. Although Hall realized that *The Well of Loneliness* was the first explicit attempt to claim that inverts had a moral worth, and that homosexuality and lesbianism were natural and therefore part of a pattern ordained by God, she was stunned by the fury that its publication caused. In the *Sunday Express* James Douglas wrote 'I would rather give a healthy boy or a healthy girl a phial of prussic acid than this book.' The book was, of course, subsequently banned as obscene. Both contemporary and current responses to *The Well* are mixed, mainly as a result of the butch/femme identities ascribed to the characters Stephen GORDON and Mary. Hall was deeply influenced by the sexologists' explanations of homosexuality which made these connections between mannishness and lesbianism; she believed that she was an invert with a man's soul in a woman's body. The very facts of Hall's life – her theft of two men's wives, and her adoption of masculine dress (smoking jacket, ETON CROP and monocle) – exacerbated the media outrage: how dare such a perverted woman hold up her head and speak publicly!

Undoubtedly, the fact that Hall took the most stigmatized stereotype of lesbianism and *still* made a claim for the moral high ground was a major factor in the book's vilification. Her line was very much, 'We're here, we're queer, deal with it.' Hall has also been criticized for being conservative, Catholic, right-wing, wealthy, and for not being a feminist. However, the relevance of these points to an evaluation of *The Well* is debatable. They do not change the fact that the novel was a brave and committed attempt to make straight society accept that lesbians and gay men had rights and deserved more than they were, and are, getting. Hall published nothing after *The Well*, and she was increasingly racked by ill health, although she did have a tempestuous affair with Evguenia Souline, a woman employed by Hall and Una as a nurse. Una managed to hang on to Radclyffe throughout an undoubtedly difficult few years, and was with her at the time of her death from cancer.

Hallowe'en In America the gay festival par excellence. Huge costume parades and drag balls are held in the gay areas of cities, and the whole community turns out to revel in the party atmosphere. The festival on 31 October was the last day of the year in the old Celtic calendar, and was co-opted by the Christians as the eve of All Hallows, or All Saints. Lesbian writer Judy Grahn chooses to trace the lesbian and gay involvement with the festival back to its Celtic tradition, when witches and warlocks were at large and when the safest way to travel abroad was by impersonating a spirit. Thus dressing-up was common. It was a time when the usually discrete worlds of spirits and mortals were believed to merge, and thus is a suitable festival for the one evening when gay communities spill out from their ghettos to decorate other areas of towns. Whatever the validity of these theories, Hallowe'en has always been a time of year when the gay communities experienced greater freedoms. Even in the 1940s and 1950s when police harassment of gay bars was at its height, Hallowe'en was the one fairy-tale evening when the drag queens could come out with impunity. In San Francisco the chief of police would traditionally escort queen and activist Jose SARRIA downtown, declaring, 'This is your night – you run it.'

Hamilton, Mary (1721–?) English PASSING WOMAN. She was seduced by a female neighbour, Miss Johnson, at the age of fourteen, and took to lesbian life with great gusto. Hamilton worked as a teacher in Dublin where she married a widow, only to flee when her sex was discovered. In Devon the same thing happened when she pretended to be a doctor and eloped with one of her patients. She arrived in Somerset where she married eighteen-year-old Mary Price. When the truth came out that she was a woman she was arrested and prosecuted under the Vagrancy Act. At the trial there was produced an exhibit of 'vile, wicked and scandalous a nature' which had been found in her trunk. Presumably this was a dildo, which had enabled her to deceive so many women about her gender. Found guilty, Hamilton was publicly whipped and imprisoned for six months.

Hampstead Heath Large green area of leafy north London known simply to its PARK QUEEN clientele as 'the heath'. It is London's premier resort for outdoor recreation of an erotic variety, and ramblers can be spotted at most hours inspecting the wildlife. In the democracy that is gay casual sex, areas have become designated for particular sexual acts, and many's the time a heath virgin has been disarmed by the nocturnal wailing and smacking noises emanating from the SM copse. The heath has been no stranger to controversy, in 1968 the newspaper *The People* ran a shocking expose of 'at least one hundred men' cavorting in the bushes. Must have been quite a night. An uneasy truce seems to have been established with the local constabulary however.

Hampton Court William III (1650–1702), King of England, elected to lead a private life, and spent most of his time outside London at Hampton Court Palace, where his bedchamber was decorated with scenes of the myth of Zeus' abduction of GANYMEDE. Unlike the myth itself, the Trojan shepherd in these scenes was portrayed as long past his adolescence, reflecting William's own inclination towards the more mature male.

Hampton-Giddes The ghastly prissy queen couple from Hades in Armistead Maupin's TALES OF THE CITY series. Horribly closeted, the Hampton-Giddes view any sexual openness, and most of the gay scene, as just terribly vulgar. They divide all gay men into A-gays and B-gays, depending on criteria of culture and wealth. If you're a B-gay then you're off the dinner party list. The Hampton-Giddes have become a term in gay folklore for the viciously uptight with ideas above their station.

hankie codes Method of advertising sexual tastes in public used by gay men since the sexual heyday of the 1970s in order to facilitate cruising. Since men know exactly what they are letting themselves in for, it means that there is no risk of going home with the wrong merchandise. It consists of a series of different coloured hankies representing different activities or attributes. They are worn in the different trouser pockets with a hankie on the left meaning I do it to you (or I am that type) and on the right meaning you do it to me (or I want that type). Predictably, gay communities were too dizzy to actually get together and agree on one series of meanings, so there are variations used, but the generally agreed meanings go thus: navy blue for fucking; yellow for WATERSPORTS (left piss on you, right piss on me); red for FISTING; black for SADOMASOCHISM (on left master, on right slave); beige for RIMMING; light blue for cocksucking; brown for SCAT; robin's egg for SIXTY-NINE (side immaterial); mustard for big cock (left I have one, right I want one); green for HUSTLER (left I am one, right I'll pay); gold for threesomes (left couple looking for single, right the reverse); apricot for CHUBBY (left chub, right chaser); olive for military role-play (left military top, right military bottom); magenta for armpit sucking; lavender for

DRAG (though where does the drag queen put the chiffon? In her tiara, perhaps); fuchsia for spanking; coral for toe-sucking; purple for PIERCING; russet for cowboy role play; and, finally, orange for anything (left I'll do anything, right I don't want anything). In addition, in the 1980s the black-and-white checked SAFE-SEX HANKIE was developed. The colours are also used in contact adverts to indicate the kind of respondent desired.

hard fucking Anal sex which involves vigorously ramming the dick up another man's ass, often while slapping his butt at the same time to add a degree more titillation. Common component of the sex in porn films, and on the butch gay scene of the 1970s.

Hardwick vs. Bowers American legal case in which the US Supreme Court upheld the right of the state of Georgia to have its anti-sodomy laws. The case began when, on 3 August 1982, Atlanta police raided the home of Michael Hardwick with a warrant to arrest him for non-payment of a ticket which he had in fact already paid. They found him in flagrante with another man, and instead arrested him for that. The case was taken to the Supreme Court in an attempt to strike down Georgia's laws as an infringement of constitutional rights to privacy. However, on 30 June 1986 the Supreme Court ruled in favour of Georgia. The case sparked off a huge campaign from lesbian and gay activists. On 13 October 1987 some people were arrested in a non-violent action on the steps of the Supreme court to protest against the decision.

hare Animal which had an association with homosexuality in the middle ages. *See* THE EPISTLE OF BARNABUS.

Harlem In the 1920s the bars and cabarets as well as the sex circuses and marijuana parties of Harlem offered lesbians and gays social opportunities and a safer space alongside black communities, the social position of which queer people were beginning to realize was comparable to their own. Undoubtedly there was an element of social imperialism in the way white people viewed black communities as exciting and exotic, but gays and lesbians, both black and white, could find more tolerance here than within the mainstream culture. On occasion, black lesbians in BUTCH/FEMME relationships would marry each other, and apply for a legal marriage licence either by making one of their names masculine, or by getting a male acquaintance to stand in for one of the women.

Harlem renaissance The name given not just to the thriving black social and musical culture of 1920s HARLEM but also to the outpouring of writings from black authors of the time, a large number of whom were also lesbian, gay or bisexual. Bisexual and lesbian entertainers who were popular on the Harlem scene included Ma RAINEY, Bessie SMITH and Gladys BENTLEY as well as 'Moms' Mabley. Celebrated writers included Countee CULLEN and Langston HUGHES, as well as (Richard) Bruce Nugent, whose short story 'Smoke, Lilies and Jade' (1926) is regarded as possibly the first published exploration of black homosexuality, and Wallace Thurman, who gave an ironic depiction of the Harlem renaissance in his 1932 novel *Infants of the Spring*. The white writer Carl Van Vechten was the mouthpiece for the white people who (through often dubious motives) were attracted to the freer atmosphere of Harlem of the time.

Harley-Davidson Type of motorbike which was one of the necessary trappings on the leather and SM fraternity of America in the 1950s.

Harmodius and Aristogiton Two lovers who, in Greek history, were credited with the preservation of Athenian democracy by challenging the rule of the tyrant Hippias in 514 BC. According to the historian Thucydides (c. 460–c. 395 BC), the young Harmodius refused the attentions of Hipparchus, the brother of Hippias. Fearing retaliation, the two lovers secretly planned to overthrow the rulers, and murdered Hipparchus. Though the two died in the attempt, Hippias ruled only three more years over the Athenians, and the two were celebrated for their stand against tyranny.

harpy In classical mythology, a fantastic winged creature with the torso and head of a woman who appears in the writings of Homer and later writers. Harpies were reputed to be of frightening appearance, looking half-starved and were associated with storms. The term has also been used historically by men to describe any woman who refuses to be subordinate, with the implication that such a refusal to take on the feminine role renders them grotesque and unhuman. The harpy has thus been conscripted by the feminist movement as a symbol of female power, as part of a tradition of HAGS and wise women who have refused to lie down. Some women are happy to be nightmarish, as long as it is men who suffer the nightmares. Gay men also use the word to allude to any ageing or bitchy DRAG QUEEN, or one whose make-up is so grotesquely applied as to disturb sleep.

Harvey 1944 play by Mary Chase which told the recognizable story of Elward P. Daud, an older unmarried man who lives with his sister and who causes embarrassment to his family by bringing his close male 'friend' to social events and introducing him to everyone. The oddity is that the friend is a person-sized, invisible male rabbit. The two are only welcome at the bar where they met. The play was hardly the most sophisticated usage of the allegoric form.

hasbean A woman who has renounced her lesbian identity. The word is often used of women who were active in the lesbian feminist movement in the 1970s as POLITICAL LESBIANS but who have since given up political activity and have returned to heterosexual relations.

Hay, Henry (Harry) (1912–) As an inspirational gay activist, theorist and co-founder of the MATTACHINE SOCIETY in the early 1950s in America, Hay is often referred to as the founder of modern gay liberation.

He had a long history of activism. When young he was a member of Industrial Workers of the World, and in the 1930s he was involved in a Los Angeles agitprop theatre group. He also taught the history of people's music. A member of the Communist Party, he brought his experience of working within radical political groups to his work within the lesbian and gay movement. In the 1960s he and his partner, John Burnside, worked within the movements to oppose the war in Vietnam, and to fight for the rights of Native Americans. In the 1970s he worked within the GAY LIBERATION FRONT in Los Angeles and then became active in the RADICAL FAIRY movement. His work for gay liberation has always been more radical than simply to ask for law reform, and he has always argued that gay people are a minority inherently different from heterosexuals who bear the potential for developing entirely different social structures. *See also* CIRCLE OF LOVING COMPANIONS; FEAST OF FOOLS.

he never sucked *my* cock Line from the sharp-witted actress Tallulah BANKHEAD, which was reportedly (and possibly apocryphally) issued when asked if a friend of hers was gay. Another version recounts that she was at a party when the heartthrob actor, Montgomery Clift (1920–66) arrived in a drunken haze and passed out on the floor, at which another partygoer remarked that it was a pity he was a cocksucker.

he'll have his hair cut reg'lar now Remark reportedly made by a female sex-worker outside the courthouse in which Oscar WILDE had just been convicted. Sometimes uttered by gay men as a commiseration to another man who has, for example, been apprehended by the police while out cottaging.

The Heart in Exile Novel by Rodney Garland in which a gay psychiatrist investigates the suicide of his ex-lover, and in the process expounds upon the discrimination that thwarted the lives of British gay people in the 1950s. It also provides documentation of the subculture of bars and clubs which was available to gay men of the time.

heart values The cohesive force described by women who chose to live in ROMANTIC FRIENDSHIPS or BOSTON MARRIAGES in nineteenth-century America, which they contrasted with the 'muscle values' emphasized by male pursuits. The term indicates the spiritual sustenance which women found in their relationships with one another, against the backdrop of a society in which they were denied the privilege that men claimed. It also demonstrates the dichotomy that was drawn by many women as well as men at the time between the 'rationality' of masculinity and the 'emotionality' of women.

heavy tit work Strenuously sucking, biting and pulling the nipples.

Hecate The ancient Greek goddess of the underworld. Like many of the ancient goddesses, she has been employed by women as a symbol of female power to use in their fight against patriarchy. Hecate is one of the deities most associated with the new age GODDESS worship of the late twentieth century.

Heliogabalus (AD 205–222) Roman Emperor, also known as Elagabalus, who reportedly enjoyed dressing in sumptuous clothes and tried to locate a surgeon who could perform a sex change operation on him. He is also reported to have addressed an assembled crowd of Roman sex workers while dressed in drag. The subject of his lecture was an evaluation of different sexual positions. Unfortunately, Heliogabalus was eventually assassinated and his body dumped in the sewers.

Hellfire Club Chicago-based SM club, founded in 1971. It was one of the first organizations for those interested in SADO-MASOCHISM which formed part of the sexual renaissance of the 1970s. The club also runs a weekend SM camp called the Inferno, which has been held annually since 1976. Although entrance to the Inferno is by invitation only, demand for

places is so high that in 1990 a second annual session was instated.

Helms amendment An amendment to the American federal law on funding for AIDS/HIV education that was passed through the Senate in October 1987, proposed by the arch-homophobe Republican senator for North Carolina, Jesse Helms. It prohibited federal dollars being spent on any education initiative that 'promotes homosexuality', an objective that Helms had been trying to accomplish for some years. The amendment stopped a great deal of essential work within gay communities to increase knowledge of SAFER SEX. In response to the amendment, gay communities announced a boycott of Marlboro cigarettes, since the company that produced them, Philip Morris, contributed funds to Helms' election campaign. It was no coincidence that the Thatcher administration in the UK used precisely the same phraseology for CLAUSE 28 which appeared at about the same time.

hemaneh Transvestite members of the Cheyenne tribes of Native Americans, who would be part of war parties. Their role was to charge the enemy first, and alone, protected only by the magic power which their same-sex sexuality gave them. The Cheyenne believed this would frighten their enemy, and get them to waste their weapons. Doesn't sound like much of a job.

Henry III (1551–89) King of France, and probably a transvestite. Quite the campiest thing to come out of the sixteenth century, Henry founded a flamboyant court in Paris and surrounded himself with a collection of male favourites whom he called his mignons. However, he tended to vacillate between periods of dissolute excess and sometimes fanatical periods of religious zealotry. Possibly an early self-destruct queen.

Henry VIII's Buggery Law Law enacted in Britain in 1533 during the reign of Henry VIII. This was the first time homosexuality was brought within the remit of the civil law, rather than that of the Church. It decreed a death sentence for the 'detestable and abominable Vice' committed with man or beast. The last execution in Britain for homosexual acts took place in 1836, although capital punishment remained on the statute books until 1861.

Hephaestion *See* ALEXANDER AND HEPHAESTION.

Hercules Speculation has romantically linked the mythological Greek hero with a number of men, although Plutarch writes that it is difficult to record the lovers of Hercules 'because of their number'. In his *Idylls*, the Greek poet Theocritus (early third century BC) writes that Hercules loved 'charming Hylas, whose hair hung down in curls'. Meanwhile, Plutarch describes that 'it is related...that Iolaus [the master charioteer and athlete] who shared the labours of Hercules and fought by his side was beloved of him'. Plutarch also records that the tomb of Iolaus was a site for male lovers to swear their loyalty to him and pledge their devotion to one another. Edward CARPENTER called his collection of records of homosexual love, *Iolaus: An Anthology of Friendship*.

herstory Alternative word for history which had wide currency within the feminist movement of the 1970s, and is still widely used. It replaces the implied male pronoun 'his' with the female. In it is an implicit critique of the academic discipline of history as glorifying male values of war and power, and dealing only with events concerning men. It also indicates the possibility of a woman-centred analysis.

het or **hettie** Gay slang reference for heterosexual, usually used in exasperation at some particular act of stupidity or narrow-mindedness. The shorter form has the added advantage, being only one syllable, of being utterable with a note of perfect disdain.

hetero- Prefix which can be attached to words to indicate a specific reference to heterosexual norms and to heterosexual society.

heterocentrism Term developed within the lesbian and gay liberation movement of the 1970s to describe a concept similar to HETEROSEXISM. While heterocentrism does not deny the fact that lesbians and gays exist, it is the automatic assumption that people are heterosexual unless they forcefully state otherwise. Thus to assume that any public figure who happens to be married is heterosexual without considering the possibility that they may be living in a FRONT MARRIAGE, or at least be bisexual, is a heterocentric position. It is also obviously demonstrated in the assumption that any historical figure of note who was not involved in a messy trial for 'indecency' was heterosexual, until the painstaking work of lesbian and gay historians to CLAIM them as homosexual succeeds. In such circumstances, the homophobia of the heterocentric position is often made manifest, since people will often go to great pains to 'protect' historical figures from such 'slurs'.

heterodoxy Club of middle-class women in 1920s GREENWICH VILLAGE that aimed to bring together women of all sexualities in a spirit of nonconformism. The club was pledged against constrictive rules, and lesbian couples within the group were supported by the other women.

heterofeminists Term coined by Adrienne RICH to describe heterosexual women involved in the feminist movement. In the radical days of the 1970s, though less nowadays, heterofeminists were accused by lesbian-feminists of sleeping (literally) with the enemy, and of taking women's energy to give to men.

heterogressive Term, a fusion of hetero and regressive, which describes an unthinking acceptance of the standards and mores of heterosexual society. It developed within the radical lesbian and gay movements of the 1980s and 1990s, and is used by those who believe that the lesbian and gay communities hold the potential for more progressive social forms. Thus those who believe that monogamy (*see* MONOTONY) is a heterosexual construction, and that casual sex offers a more suitable way for some people to structure their emotional lives, will criticize the assertions of the more ASSIMILATIONIST lesbians and gays that 'we are just as capable of long-term relationships as anyone else' as heterogressive. Lesbian and gay groups which are also seeking to work without the hierarchies of other organizations will also term any attempt to create office-holders as heterogressive. The term is often put to humorous effect to imply that anything wrong in the world, for example Bri-Nylon, or the colour beige, is the result of a heterogressive society.

heterophobia The fear and hatred of heterosexuality and heterosexuals. A perfect opposite of HOMOPHOBIA, other than that heterophobia is entirely rational given what they put us through, in terms of both their grasp of the institutions of society and the horrifying parade of man-made fibres that marks their dress sense. Fortunately, with the growth of the gay scene in Europe, America and Australia, there are whole swathes of urban areas where lesbians and gays can go about their business without a whiff of Bri-Nylon. The term heterophobia is also employed seriously by those activists within the more radical lesbian and gay political groups, from the early MATTACHINE SOCIETY, the GAY LIBERATION FRONT to the modern FEMINIST and QUEER movements, who set their sights not just on law reform and the integration of queers into extant institutions, but on a complete overhaul of societal mores. They critique the heterosexual-built institutions of FAMILY, church, employment and State as oppressive for those who wish to construct their own lifestyles, and seek to build alternative institutions which would allow greater personal freedom.

heterosexism Term for prejudice against lesbians and gay men that is analogous to the terms racism and sexism. Its relation to the concept of HOMOPHOBIA is similar to the relation between sexism and misogyny; that is, the relation is simply a question of degree. Both heterosexism and homophobia form part of the same continuum of anti-gay feeling, and are built upon the belief that heterosexuality is somehow inherently normal and superior. Heterosexism can sometimes be careless or unthinking, but homophobia never can. Heterosexism is usually expressed in the form of the automatic assumption that everyone is straight unless they clearly mark themselves out otherwise, and in the exclusion of any acknowledgement of lesbians and gays as a fundamental part of society. Thus to produce forms which only offer boxes to describe oneself as single, married or divorced is heterosexist. Whilst it might not be as violently expressed as homophobia, it creates the conditions where homophobia is likely to be found. Thus, one could say that a heterosexist society fosters homophobic individuals. The term, which developed in the late twentieth century, is important as it demonstrated that lesbians and gays had developed the pride to assert that their voices formed a natural part of society, and an exclusion of them was an ideological position.

heterosexual Someone who actually enjoys sexual relations with members of the opposite sex. The creation of the category of heterosexual as a distinct social grouping actually followed that of homosexual; until the 'other', the 'invert', was invented, it was assumed that everybody shared the same basic sexuality, and the question of whether one engaged in homosexual relations was more a question of the ability to withstand the temptation of sin. The term heterosexual first began to appear in the medical literature about sexuality in the 1890s, but until the twentieth century it actually referred to someone who enjoyed sexual relations with members of both sexes. Even today the term is not used enough. It is not pointed out, for example, that 'society' is in fact heterosexual society, that films are heterosexual films, that shops and services are heterosexual shops and services. Meanwhile, any film which includes the most fleeting lesbian or gay character is a film 'about gays/lesbians' (and usually indicates a queer takeover of

Hollywood). While, of course, no hetero-sexuals have questioned what made them that way (that kind of questioning is done only with 'undesirable' conditions), some lesbian and gay theorists, particularly within the feminist movement of the 1980s (for example, Juliet Mitchell in *Psychoanalysis and Feminism* (1986)), have returned to Sigmund FREUD to create their own psychoanalytical theories of what makes heterosexuality. Returning to the idea of the POLYMORPHOUS PERVERSE, theo-rists have argued that it is the process of socialization which has created the hetero-sexual condition. A seductive idea, it implies that there is nothing NATURAL about heterosexuality at all. Terms for het-erosexuals include: BREEDER, HET (or hettie), 'them' and 'officer', but the concept is usu-ally communicated by a rolling of the eyes skywards and a groan.

heterosexuality, causes of At the lunchtime series of plays by the GAY SWEAT-SHOP theatre company called HOMOSEXUAL ACTS, a large poster by the writer of one of the plays, Alan Wakeman, entitled 'Causes of Heterosexuality' appeared in the foyer. It announced that heterosexuals were 'obsessed with the gratification of their curious desires', and discussed what it is that makes heterosexuals like that, sug-gesting it was due to hormonal imbalance, economic conditioning, fear of death, cul-tural deprivation, pathology, social condi-tioning, childhood trauma or parental problems.

heterosoc Heterosexual society, and the institutions it has spawned. With the sinis-ter undertones of Orwell's *1984*, the word implies the coercive methods that society uses to force people into heterosexuality and to suppress those that refuse.

hettie *See* HET.

Hibiscus (George Harris, d. 1982) Gay entertainer, who founded the 'radical DRAG' troupes, the Cockettes and Angels of Light. Hibiscus died in May 1982, the first celebrity of many to die as a result of AIDS.

hic, haec, hoc *See* CAMBACÉRÈS, JEAN-JACQUES RÉGIS DE.

Highbury Fields demonstration The first public demonstration of the London GAY LIBERATION FRONT, which took place in November 1971. After Louis Eakes, the leader of the Young Liberals, had been arrested for soliciting there, the GLF led a torchlit procession across the fields in soli-darity, shouting slogans and holding a kiss-in for the benefit of the press that had assembled.

hijras Name given to a group of transsexu-als, most prevalent in northern India, who dress and live as women and sometimes undergo castration. Indians believe that they derive special powers from their knowledge of both genders, and their tra-ditional way of earning a living is in ritual acts such as blessing newborn babies, dancing at weddings or collecting alms. Many Hijras, however, earn money through prostitution. Hijras are devotees of the goddess Bahuchara Mata, and it is in accordance with their worship of her that the emasculation operation is carried out; and those men who do not undergo the operation are looked down on by other members of the cult. Siva is also sometimes worshipped. According to folklore, hijras recruit members by carrying off children who are hermaphroditic, but given the status of homosexuality in India, many gay men enter the hijra community, which allows them a chance of sexual expression. The hijras are organized into a set of seven houses (jemadh), located in Bombay, each of which has a guru or leader who is responsible for the initiation ceremony during which the disciple (chela) takes a new female name and is presented with gifts and a sacred drum (dhol). Hijras live in houses of as many as forty people, and refer to other hijras using female kinship terms. The word hijra is also sometimes used as a term for gay men in India.

Hikane: The Capable Womon Quarterly American magazine for disabled lesbian feminists and their friends which was founded in 1989. It is also recorded on cassette for women with sight disabilities.

Hillbrow The Johannesburg equivalent of Greenwich Village. A previously white bohemian area which is now racially mixed. Johannesburg lesbians and gays are drawn to the area, since, like other trendy places, it is more accepting of diversity.

hippie movement The rise of the hippie movement in the 1960s, with its creed of unisex style, challenging authority and free love, gave some people the freedom to experiment with gay sex. It also served to make queer sexuality seem less outré within society. *See* COUNTERCULTURE.

Hirschfield, Magnus (1868–1935) German gay rights activist and sexologist, Hirschfield began his career as a general medical practitioner, but was spurred to devote his work to the scientific research of homosexuality by the WILDE TRIALS and by the suicide of a patient who was about to be married. In 1897 he founded the SCIENTIFIC-HUMANITARIAN COMMITTEE and in 1899 the JAHRBUCH FÜR SEXUELLE ZWIS-CHENSTUFEN. In 1913 he spoke at the Fourteenth International Medical Conference in London, where he displayed photographs of homosexuals and caused a minor sensation. One of the first gay activists, Hirschfield and his work are often seen as the beginning of any organized gay political movement. However, he was a follower of the sexologists with their arguments of CONGENITAL INVERSION, and the widespread attention his work gained for these theories has not only been blamed for perpetuating the flaws within them, but it could be argued that it reinforced the arguments of the Nazis that homosexuality was a degeneration.

historic lesbian Term that is used within the LESBIAN FEMINIST movement to describe a woman who believes in the essential nature of her sexuality, as opposed to a POLITICAL LESBIAN or NOUVELLE LESBIAN, both of whom have tended to come to lesbianism through their politics. It is particularly used of older women whose lesbianism was defined before the growth of the feminist and lesbian movements.

HIV (human immunodeficiency virus) The virus that is believed by most experts to be the cause of AIDS. First isolated in 1983, HIV exists in many body fluids but only in blood, semen and vaginal fluid in sufficient quantity to be able to infect another person, and then only if it enters the blood stream of that other person. Thus it can only be transmitted in a small number of ways: through anal or vaginal intercourse or fellatio without the protection of a condom; through transfusions of infected blood or blood products (though this means of transmission has been virtually eliminated in developed countries and is becoming rarer in developing countries); through the reuse of needles or syringes (most particularly associated with intravenous drugs-users); and from mother to baby. When it has entered the bloodstream, HIV primarily infects cells of the immune system and especially the T4-CELLS. When it has reproduced itself in sufficient numbers (the process of seroconversion), the antibodies produced by the body are also sufficient to register on an HIV TEST. A positive test for antibodies is taken as an indication that a person has been exposed to HIV. However, HIV-positive status does not indicate that AIDS will soon follow. The incubation period between transmission of HIV and developing AIDS is on average 8–12 years, and some people have been infected for upwards of 12 years without becoming ill. Some scientists and journalists have questioned whether HIV is in fact the cause of AIDS at all, and suggest that lifestyle factors may be at root. However, they are very much in the minority, and few people give their views much credence.

HIV test Commonly and erroneously referred to as an AIDS test, since the test can determine only whether or not a person has been infected with HIV and does not say anything about whether he or she has any of the opportunistic illnesses associated with an AIDS diagnosis, or the likelihood of developing such illnesses. In fact, it is not even an HIV test but a test for the antibodies which are produced by the body's immune system on exposure to the HIV virus. An HIV-positive status indicates that HIV has entered the bloodstream and that antibodies are present. However, the main testing techniques, ELISA and western blot, are not entirely foolproof, and throw up some false positives as well as false negatives. Since it takes the body some six weeks or more to develop antibodies on exposure to HIV, if a test is taken in that time a negative result may be obtained even though the person is infected. In some cases people have also not developed antibodies in sufficient numbers to register on the test and a false negative may be obtained. Rarely, a false positive may be obtained if the test picks up antibodies for another condition which produces similar antibodies.

hockey team The fraternity of gay men. When talking about another man, a camp way of asking if he is also gay would be to ask if he is also in the hockey team.

Hollywood uterus 1970s American gay slang for the anus. Alludes to the large number of closeted gay men who work within the Hollywood film industry, and also the large gay population of the Los Angeles municipality of WEST HOLLYWOOD.

Holocaust One of the peoples that was singled out by the Nazis for genocide is often forgotten by those who write about the Holocaust, maybe because those people – gay men and lesbians – are still not entirely welcomed in society. Berlin in the 1920s had become a fabled centre of lesbian and gay life and, with the campaigning work of Magnus HIRSCHFIELD, it seemed a safe future was assured. Within weeks of the Nazi Party coming to power in January 1933, however, all that changed, and an ordinance was issued banning all organizations which offered support to homosexuals. More and more gay men were prosecuted under PARAGRAPH 175, and in May 1933 the INSTITUTE OF SEXOLOGY was ransacked by the Hitler Youth, its huge library being burnt in the street. In the

same year the first concentration camps were established. The wave of repression continued unabated and in 1934, after the NIGHT OF THE LONG KNIVES, a special unit was set up within the SS with the aim of clamping down on homosexuality. In 1935 the terms of Paragraph 175 were extended and a law was passed under which homosexuals, along with drugs users, schizophrenics and the disabled were subject to 'compulsory sterilization' which often simply involved castration. Between 1936 and 1940 Himmler, the head of the SS, made several declarations that 'the homosexuals must be entirely eliminated', and in 1942 the punishment for homosexuality was extended to death. Throughout this time the vast majority of men who were convicted under Paragraph 175, and there were nearly 25,000 between 1937 and 1939 alone, were sent to concentration camps after they had finished their sentence. Their lives there were a hell on earth. Gay men wore the PINK TRIANGLE badge, and personal accounts indicate that the men with the pink triangle were the special focus of attack by both guards and other inmates. If they weren't killed through gruelling work, such as in the notorious cement pits of Sachsenhausen, many met their ends through the sadistic acts of the guards. In Sachsenhausen the guards would take pot shots at men wheeling wheelbarrows into the clay pits, and one favoured tactic was to throw a man's hat against the electrified fence and order him to retrieve it. The man could then choose between electrification or shooting for disobeying the guards' order. See BENT. Others were used for 'medical' experiments during which they were castrated and injected with hormones. Although gay men were not shipped en masse to the death camps at Auschwitz, a great number were among the non-Jews who met their deaths there. Estimates vary as to how many gay men died in the Holocaust, but figures of between 50,000 and 100,000 are feasible. In addition, many German gay men who were not imprisoned were simply sent to the eastern front to die an inevitable death in battle. When at the end of the war the concentration camps were liberated, many gay men were not released but were returned to prison as 'legitimate' criminals. Nor were they considered eligible for compensation from the West German government. In fact, in May 1954 the West German Federal Constitutional Court upheld the constitutionality of the post-1935 Paragraph 175 on the grounds that it contained 'nothing specifically Nazi'. It was only in 1969 that the ban on male homosexual relations was lifted. In regard to lesbianism, the Nazis mooted the idea of specific legal sanctions, but dropped them in favour of promoting a restrictive idea of German womanhood that focused on children, kitchen and church. However, some records indicate that a number of lesbians were consigned to the camps, where they wore the BLACK TRIANGLE for antisocial behaviour. Since the holocaust gay people have had to fight not to have their suffering erased by historians, and even today there are few monuments to the men that died (*see* AMSTERDAM; NEUENGAMME). Yet the Holocaust is a reminder, and an ever more poignant one in the time of AIDS, that despite seeming acceptance within society such gains cannot be taken for granted. It is (or should be) indelibly imprinted on the lesbian and gay consciousness, and both the pink and black triangles have become the most common symbols of lesbian and gay liberation.

homintern Term originally coined by poet AUDEN to describe the international bonds that can exist between lesbians and gay men. It alludes to the fact that the idea of nationality is problematic for homosexuals, since they are often oppressed by the nations of which they are citizens. The links of community do not therefore necessarily respect national boundaries. The word was a play upon the Comintern, or communist international. The idea was also pertinent for straight society. The idea of queers forming a kind of secret society which cut across traditional patterns of alliance and posed a threat to national security has been a favourite of the right wing throughout the twentieth century. In Germany in 1907–09, during the EULENBERG AFFAIR, it was often alleged that homosexual politicians were allowing State information to leak to the arch-enemy, the French. Newspaper editor Maximilian Harden warned that gay men formed 'a comradeship...which brings together men of all creeds, states, and classes'. In 1913 the head of Austrian Intelligence services, Alfred Redl, was uncovered as both a double agent and a gay man, which added fuel to accusations that gay men form a security risk. The Redl case was cited by Joseph McCarthy in America (*see* MCCARTHYISM) as an example that showed the necessity for the campaign of terror that he launched against suspected homosexuals.

homo- Prefix which can be attached to words to indicate a specific reference to lesbian and gay sexuality and to social structures.

homoaffectionality Strong emotional links between members of the same sex. It is most often used to describe intense relationships within works of film, theatre and literature. Although homoaffectionality usually stops short of any physical or erotic contact, the lesbian and gay audience will often interpret such relationships as implying some erotic content. Thus the intense glances between James Dean and Sal Mineo in the film REBEL WITHOUT A CAUSE can be felt by the gay male audience to be sexual, while the straight audience is more interested in the heterosexual love plot of the film. Indeed, until the gains of the HOMOPHILE movements of the 1950s and 1960s and the GAY LIBERATION movement of the 1970s made it acceptable to depict explicitly sexual relations between members of the same sex, creative works had to limit themselves to homoaffectionality to remain acceptable and publishable. Thus it was only through homoaffectionate relations such as ROMANTIC FRIENDSHIPS or CONFIRMED BACHELORS that homosexual authors could make contact with their lesbian or gay audience.

homoeroticism Any creative work which suggests lesbian or gay sexuality or love can be termed homoerotic. Although homoeroticism should strictly be sexual in nature to distinguish it from HOMOAFFEC-TIONALITY, lesbians and gay men are so used to reading their sexuality between the lines of creative works that the hint of strong emotional feeling between two men or women can be seen as homoerotic. Thus they can easily identify with the feelings of characters in the BUDDY FILM genre, while the straight audience will probably view them as strictly heterosexual.

homogenic Term for homosexual created by the activist and theorist Edward CAR-PENTER, partly as a criticism of the word homosexual that was constructed out of both Greek and Latin roots. However despite these academic credentials, the term never gained currency.

homophile Term for homosexual, which became popular in the mid twentieth century in America. Since the root is the Greek *philos* for love, lesbian and gay activists at the time felt that it placed more emphasis on the emotional side of lesbian and gay relationships, rather than the purely sexual as in the word homosexual. It served in the title of many gay organizations of the time (*see* NORTH AMERICAN CONFERENCE OF HOMOPHILE ORGANIZATIONS). However, it lost widespread use in the 1970s for precisely the same reasons as it originally caught on. Activists in the more radical gay liberation years of the 1970s felt that it tried to present a sanitized, desexualized version of gay lives for mainstream consumption and acceptance.

Homophile Action League Lesbian and gay rights organization created in the late 1960s which was representative of the new militance in the queer movement. It urged lesbians and gays to confront their oppressors, rather than attempt the more downbeat strategies of lobbying and defensiveness. One of their usual forms of action was PICKETING.

homophile movement The epithet often given to the different organizations that made up the NORTH AMERICAN CONFERENCE OF HOMOPHILE ORGANIZATIONS, and contrasted with lesbian and gay liberation groups that took off after the STONEWALL RIOT. An implicit distinction is made between the explosive radicalism of post-1969 and the timid tactics of education and lobbying beforehand. However, while in the early stages at least education was the main aim, the success of the black CIVIL RIGHTS MOVEMENT gave the organizations a more militant edge. Moreover, given the climate of harassment that pervaded the lesbian and gay communities in the 1950s and 1960s in America, the later (direct) actions of the homophile groups, for example in their ANNUAL REMINDER at Independence Hall in Philadelphia, were extremely courageous. In addition, they introduced notions that were important to later lesbian and gay groups, such as the idea that there should be organizations that were devoted exclusively to lesbian and gay rights, without getting sidetracked by other political issues. Debates over the worth of COALITION POLITICS continue into the 1990s.

homophobia It is defined as the fear or hatred of homosexuals, and is colloquially used as the word for beliefs which explicitly or implicitly denigrate lesbians and gay men. Matters such as verbal assaults, physical attacks, the removal of the children of lesbian and gay parents, and discrimination in housing, employment, tax, pensions and immigration are all commonly ascribed to homophobia. However, there is debate about the usefulness of the term, because homophobia is defined as an irrational hatred. Both QUEER activists and lesbian feminists argue, from different positions, that straight people's hatred of lesbians and gay men is wholly rational. Lesbian feminists are working to overthrow the patriarchal social, economic, political and emotional structures which currently regulate and govern our lives. The hatred and fear that men, and women, feel for lesbians is then rational, because lesbians want to destroy their power by destroying patriarchy. Queer activists are also challenging the desirability of many of the structures of the heterosexual world, and hence attacking the way that heterosexuals organize their lives. Again, for heterosexuals to hate homosexuals in these circumstances is not necessarily irrational.

homosexual The term first appeared in an 1869 pamphlet by the Hungarian Karol Maria Kertbeny which put a case for the repeal of Prussia's anti-gay legislation. It initially caught on among scientific and academic publications, and gained widespread currency in the early twentieth century. Despite being criticized for being too clinical, for putting too much emphasis on the sexual, and for being a false construction from both Latin and Greek roots, the word has been the most consistently used throughout the twentieth century, and is still the preferred term for much of the straight media in the 1990s. From the 1970s on, lesbians and gays used the term far less, although they might resurrect it in a pejorative way to describe lesbians and gay men who are still highly closeted and whom the winds of gay liberation would have appeared to have passed by.

Homosexual Acts Lunchtime series of plays produced by the newly formed GAY SWEATSHOP theatre company in February 1975 at the Almost Free Theatre off Shaftesbury Avenue in London. The series included three plays: *Limitations* by John Roman Baker; *Thinking Straight* by Laurence Collinson; and *Ships* by Alan Wakeman. It was a great success, with people queueing round the block to get in. The season also included discussions, which gave many people the first chance to talk about their sexuality. Both *Thinking Straight* and *Ships* were later booked to play in Amsterdam.

homosexual exogamy Borrowed from the anthropological term for social systems in which marriage is entered into with individuals from outside a social group. The term was used to describe the phenomenon of gay relations in the pre-STONEWALL RIOT period where groups of gay men would prefer to have sexual relations with straight-acting or straight-identified TRADE, rather than amongst themselves. It tended to be a symptom of a negative attitude towards their sexuality by gay men, who sought 'real' men rather than their sisters. However, through it gay men were able to keep their social support networks intact without the tensions of sexual relations.

Homosexual Law Reform Society (1) British organization founded in 1958 with Kenneth Walker as the chair. It was formed in response to the government's lack of action over the recommendations of the Wolfenden Committee (*see* WOLFENDEN REPORT) in order to campaign for the legalization of gay sex. It had the joint focus of lobbying progressive MPs and opinionmakers, as well as trying to build up the pressure of public opinion. It was not radical, and was concerned with presenting a 'respectable' image of homosexuality that would not stick in the throats of the movers and shakers of middle-class 'public opinion'. Antony Grey, one of the main protagonists in the Wolfenden reforms, was secretary for a number of years from 1962. In 1970 the organization became the Sexual Law Reform Society. (2) Organization which sought to pressure for legalization of homosexual acts in the Australian Territories. It was set up after a much discussed case in Canberra in 1968 when a young man who was out cruising was stabbed but was still prosecuted for indecent assault.

honey Common term of endearment in camp argot, though it can be used to preface an admonition or a disagreement.

Honey, I'm more man than you'll ever *be* and more woman than you'll ever *get* *See* CARWASH.

Hooker, Dr Evelyn American sex researcher whose work argued against the notion that lesbians and gay men are likely to have psychological problems. Using subjects from homosexual societies such as the MATTACHINE SOCIETY, the first such report was released in 1957. In 1967 she was chosen by President Johnson to head a Task Force on Homosexuality for the

American National Institute of Mental Health. The report, published in 1969, recommended the decriminalization of homosexuality. Whilst ignored by the newly incumbent President Nixon, the report was used by lesbian and gay activists for campaigns such as removing homosexuality from the American Psychiatric Association's list of psychiatric problems, which it did on 9 April 1974.

hot Sexually exciting. The term can be used to describe either a particularly gorgeous person or an especially sweat-soaked sexual bout. American gay writer Edmund White sees the term as a sign of the post-liberation masculine ideal of the gay male community when he writes, 'Perhaps no other word so aptly signals the new gay attitude as *hot*. Whereas *beautiful* in gay parlance characterizes the face first and body only secondarily, *hot* describes the whole man, but especially his physique.'

hot-dogging Gay male sexual practice which involves rubbing the penis between the buttocks of the partner, without actually penetrating the ass. The metaphor is obvious when you remember the common term for the butt is buns.

Hot Living Edited by John Preston in 1985, this was the first collection of steamy safer-sex stories.

Hot Wire: The Journal of Women's Music and Culture This American magazine is published three times a year, and has a circulation of some 15,000 copies. It was founded in 1984, and contains news, features, letters, poetry and drawings related to women's theatre, writing, art, film and video.

Hothead Paisan The homicidal lesbian terrorist who appears in the comic strip by American cartoonist Diane DiMassa. Hothead, who lives with her cat, takes great pleasure in exterminating obnoxious straight men.

Hotlanta Annual gay party in the US city of Atlanta which began in 1979 as a river rave with rafting and water fights for a few hundred bright young things. After a decade it had become a huge event, and taken over the whole of Atlanta's swanky midtown gay ghetto, with queers rolling in from all over the south-east and midwest of America. It is an essential date on the calendar of the (white and wealthy) A-list gays.

how dare you presume I'm heterosexual Slogan that was used on badges and stickers in the 1970s by the GAY LIBERATION FRONT, and later by other organizations. The GLF put special emphasis on lesbians and gay men COMING OUT and challenging the easy assumptions that heterosexuals make that the entire world is as dreary as they are.

How to Have Sex In An Epidemic 1983 American AIDS education publication produced by a group of gay men, including some men with the syndrome. Whereas hitherto AIDS information had been produced by doctors, the publication of this forty-page booklet marked the start of gay men taking control of their response to the growing epidemic. Unsurprisingly, it also presented the most sensible reaction to the threat of AIDS thus far, focusing on making sexual activities safe, rather than telling people to abstain or cut down their number of sexual partners. Instead of wallowing in fear or guilt, it declared its challenge to be 'how we can have gay, life-affirming sex, satisfy our emotional needs, and stay alive!'

HTLV III Acronym for the human T-cell lymphotopic virus, known now as the human immunodeficiency virus (HIV) and probably the virus which leads to AIDS. It was first isolated in 1983.

Hudson, Rock (1925–85) American movie star. Hudson hit the headlines when in July 1985 he announced that he had AIDS. He was the first mainstream star to suffer from the syndrome, and his announcement sent shockwaves through America, despite the fact that by that time more than ten thousand Americans had already been diagnosed with AIDS. Hudson died in his home in Beverly Hills on October 2nd 1985.

Hughes, (James) Langston (1902–67) Black American poet and writer who was one of the leading figures in the HARLEM RENAISSANCE. His works include poetry: *The Weary Blues* (1926), *The Dream Keeper* (1932) and *Ask Your Mama* (1961); novels, *Not without Laughter* (1930); short stories, *The Ways of White Folks* (1934); as well as humorous sketches and a play. Strongly influenced by the ups and downs of black life in America, Hughes also employed the rhythms of blues music in his work. Some historians believe that Hughes had a relationship with the Howard University professor, Alain Locke, who helped to promote his career. The poetry of Hughes, as well as the rich culture of 1920s Harlem, was celebrated in the 1988 short film by British director Isaac Julien, *Looking for Langston*.

hung or **well-hung** Used to describe someone lucky enough to have a large cock.

The Hunger 1983 film directed by Tony Scott which follows in the LESBIAN VAMPIRE genre. It presents the rather weak storyline of a thousand-year-old woman, who has somehow managed to make herself look like Catherine Deneuve and who seduces a young woman doctor (Susan Sarandon) in an attempt to make the Sarandon character her eternal partner. The film has managed to attract a cult lesbian following despite the rather dubious political implications of predatory sapphism and the weak plot.

Hunter, Tab (1931–) Pin-up of yesteryear, built and boyish, who appeared in a clutch of films in the 1950s, such as *Battle Cry* and *Damn Yankees*. Hunter later made a comeback, not with megastar status, but in films such as John Waters' *Polyester*, where he is pursued by Divine's housewife character. To the joy of Hunter's gay fans of the 1950s, it was revealed that he is gay himself.

hunting In what passed as the gay subculture of the high middle ages, allusions to hunting were commonly used in writings both by and about gay people. It was possibly used in the sense that we use CRUISING today. The force of the term was probably strengthened by the fact that GANYMEDE, whose name was also commonly used to describe homosexuals, was himself a hunter when he was plucked up by Zeus. In addition, in the same period the HARE was an animal which was commonly associated with same-sex desire.

Huon of Bordeaux Early thirteenth-century French romance in the chanson de geste genre. One subplot tells how Ide, an early PASSING WOMAN, becomes a knight of the Holy Roman Emperor. Because of her military skill the Emperor, believing her to be a man, gives her his own daughter in marriage. Not knowing how to extricate herself she goes through with the ceremony, but finally confesses her sex to the princess. The Emperor condemns her to be burnt to death, but she is ultimately saved by a convenient last-minute transformation into a man.

husband American prison and working-class lesbian slang of the 1930s which described the BUTCH partner in a lesbian BUTCH/FEMME relationship. *See also* JOCKEY.

hustler American and Canadian slang for a male SEX-WORKER.

hwarang The hwarang was an elite class of male youth in ancient Korea, who were famed for their fine clothes and singing. They originated as male entertainers after there had been fights of jealousy between the female singers of the court. The young men also seem to have been involved in shamanistic rites. After about AD 350, the hwarang became a highly trained military elite which was probably held together by homoerotic loyalties.

hyacinth This plant in Greek mythology was named after the youth Hyacinthus was turned into one by his grieving lover, the god Apollo, who had inadvertently killed him while throwing the discus. It has therefore become associated with homosexuality.

Hyacinthus In Greek mythology, a youth who was beloved by Apollo, the god of music, poetry and archery. Apollo was so enraptured by Hyacinthus that he neglected his own activities in order to follow the youth everywhere. Tragedy struck one day as they were throwing the discus. Apollo lobbed the discus so that when Hyacinthus ran to catch it he was struck on the head and died. In his grief Apollo turned the drops of his lover's blood that fell to the ground into flowers.

Hyde Park Gays and Sapphics British lesbian and gay group which spreads the message for gay rights every Sunday at Speakers' Corner in London's Hyde Park.

hyena Animal which had an association with homosexuality in the middle ages. *See* THE EPISTLE OF BARNABUS.

Hymenaeus The ancient Greek personification of the marriage song who was reported in some traditions to have homosexual relations. He was represented in androgynous terms, with both male and female clothing, long curly hair and carrying fruit. Interestingly, he was said to lose his voice after the marriage ceremony. Thus some see him as a symbol of the same-sex rituals that marked the INITIATION period before marriage. He is also sometimes described as related to King Admetus (*see* APOLLO).

hysteconomy Women's forms of economic activity including both women's informal earning activities and women-only businesses. In the lesbian feminist movement of the 1970s the hysteconomy was emphasized as a means of giving women autonomy from patriarchal society, and allowing them to achieve separatism.

I, J

Invert

I am a boy Message written on slips of paper pinned to the frocks of drag queens in San Francisco in the 1950s. The police had attempted to arrest some of them under an out-of-date law that prohibited people posing as members of the opposite sex. In response they were encouraged by activist Jose SARRIA to wear these badges so that a conviction could hardly be obtained.

I Am What I Am Gutsy show number which was sung by Albin in the Broadway musical version of LA CAGE AUX FOLLES in 1982, though not in the film (a derivative version was sung over the credits of the third *Cage* film, *The Wedding*, in 1985). The song, written by Jerry Herman, is a celebration of self-acceptance – 'What I am needs no excuses' – which has become a gay anthem second only to OVER THE RAINBOW, and perhaps more appropriate for the times than its escapist sister. It was later recorded by disco diva (and alleged born-again homophobe) Gloria Gaynor from whence it became a gay disco staple, the perfect thing for an uplifting last number. In 1990 the post-Mardi Gras party in Sydney ended with practically every drag queen in Australia on stage together singing the song. Gaynor also recorded 'I Will Survive'. Although the later song is lyrically not as apt for the lesbian and gay experience, it has a pleasing get-out-of-my-hair upfrontness and provides an opportunity for wannabe divas to produce some dancefloor campery.

I became one of the stately homos of England Quentin CRISP in THE NAKED CIVIL SERVANT.

I forgive you for the sin which you have committed against me Words spoken by an eighteen-year-old Dutchman, Jan Ides, on hearing that he had been sentenced to death for sodomy. Ides was executed by strangling and burning in Zuidhorn in September 1731 as part of a huge campaign against gay men in Holland between

1730 and 1731 during which some 60 gay men lost their lives. The eighteenth century in Holland had seen a growth in the gay subculture similar to that of the MOLLY HOUSES in London: with cruising grounds, slang including the use of CAMP NAMES, and their own taverns known as lohuysen.

I hate straights! *See* QUEER MANIFESTO.

I keep my treasure in my arse, but then my arse is open to everyone From Mario Mieli, *Homosexuality and Liberation* (1980), while describing how the heterosexual male horror of being fucked in the ass makes it a subversive activity for gay men to engage in.

I'm as pure as the driven slush Tallulah BANKHEAD, quoted in the *Saturday Evening Post*, April 1947.

I never hated a man enough to give him his diamonds back The much married Zsa Zsa Gabor (1919–) in the British *Observer* magazine in 1957.

I've got my eyes on Billy's seat Campaign slogan of David Widdup who stood as an openly gay candidate for a seat in the Australian federal elections of 1972. He was standing against the Prime Minister, Billy McMahon, in an attempt to gain publicity for the gay rights message.

I want to be alone *See* GARBO, GRETA.

I was born a tomboy Such were the uncompromising opening words of the memoirs of Charlotte Cushman (1816–76), the American actress. Butch from the beginning, as a child Cushman cracked open her doll's head so that she could examine its brains. She had romantic friendships with a series of artistic women, including the American painter Rosalie Scully, the English poet Eliza Cook, whom she met whilst touring in England and who won her heart with love sonnets, and the American sculptor Emma Stebbins, with whom she had a committed 'friendship' lasting nearly twenty years.

I Was Born This Way 1975 disco single by Charles 'Valentino' Harris, on which he sang of his queerness.

I would attempt to come between them Answer given by the BLOOMSBURY GROUP member Lytton Strachey at his tribunal to register as a conscientious objector in the First World War when he was asked what he would do if he saw a German soldier try to rape one of his sisters.

Ibn Ammar Arab poet who lived in the eleventh century AD and attended the court of the King of Seville. The story of his gay relationship has entered Arab folklore. He became infatuated with al-Mutamid, the son of the King, who requited his desire, and the two were inseparable until the monarch banished the poet in anger. When al-Mutamid succeeded to the throne, he restored Ibn Ammar to the court and to his bed. The poet left in fear, however, after dreaming that his lover would be responsible for his death. When al-Mutamid eventually located him, he reassured him by making him an official at court. Ultimately the dream came to pass, and Ibn Ammar became involved in a rebellion which finally led to his death at the hands of the King.

Icebreakers British organization of the 1970s which grew out of the counter-PSYCHIATRY group of the GAY LIBERATION FRONT. It was specifically intended to provide a telephone helpline and befriending service for gay men who were coming to terms with their sexuality. The British lesbian and gay bookshop 'Gay's the Word' was an offshoot of this organization.

icon The precise reasons why anyone should become an icon for the gay community are multiple. Many become so for their historical significance, because they gave lesbians and gay men a public face and a visibility they had not had before. Oscar WILDE and Radclyffe HALL performed this role in the late nineteenth and early twentieth centuries for gay men and lesbians respectively in the UK. In the twentieth century the US-born lesbian writer Audre LORDE gave black lesbians a visibility which they had been denied even (or especially) within lesbian and gay publications, and also gave black lesbians words to describe themselves (*see* ZAMI). Others inspire because of their political work and commitment: for example, take Edward CARPENTER, Rita Mae BROWN and Harvey MILK. There is also a curious species of gay icon which is composed mainly of Hollywood screen goddesses, and balloon-fulls of hot air have been expelled to try and explain why. In truth, the reasons why are as intangible as a definition of CAMP. They are part of the jewellery box of intuitive lesbian and gay knowledge, and any such person can tell you why or whether anyone should be considered an icon. Perhaps the mere act of a lesbian or gay man declaring lifelong loyalty to a public figure is enough to confer iconic status. Stars such as Greta GARBO and Marlene DIETRICH appeal to both lesbians and gays because of their mystique and the androgyny which they projected in art as well as life, Mae WEST because of her command of the one-liner and her disregard for the strictures of sexual 'propriety'. Judy GARLAND, icon supreme, best fits the mould of the icon whose public glamour rides above her private turmoil. Others such as Theda Bara, Hollywood's first vamp and leading lady, and Joan Crawford, perhaps inspire because they were pure creations. Crawford particularly, as a poor girl from a mining town in Pennsylvania, showed that it was possible to cut a devastating figure from the humblest beginnings, and struck a chord with gay audiences who were discarding heterosexual stereotypes to create their identities, and who spent a lot of time in self-protective camouflage. Other lesbian icons tend to be more rationally chosen and strong women and out lesbians abound from BOADICEA to Martina NAVRATILOVA, from k.d. LANG to Bea in PRISONER.

Idylle Saphique The story of the affair between lesbian writer Natalie BARNEY and her lover Liane de Pougy, one of the most famous courtesans in Paris at the turn of the century. The memoirs were published in 1901.

if a bullet should enter my brain, let that bullet destroy every closet door Passage that was included in one of the living wills that the gay politician Harvey MILK recorded on tape before he was, in fact, assassinated. Milk had long had forebodings that his high-profile position as an openly gay man might result in him becoming a victim of violence, and he recorded a series of tapes which not only outlined who he wished to take on his mantle after his death, but also encouraged his associates to use his demise as a spur for further gay rights work.

If it be a sin to love a lovely lad, oh, then sin I. From *The Affectionate Shepherd* by the English poet Richard Barnfield (1574–1627).

If It Die André GIDE's memoirs written in 1920 but not published until 1926, under the title of *Si le grain ne meurt*. They detail his experiences of his trips to North Africa in 1893 and 1894–95. They also explicitly discuss his gay experiences and feelings, and were one of the most public comings out in history when they were published. Gide had published them partly in the effort to force discussion on the issue and, not surprisingly, they caused a huge furore.

if it feels good, do it Badge slogan of the 1960s.

If you're poor then you're a dyke Poem in *Lesbian Peoples: Material for a Dictionary* (1976) by Monique Wittig and Sande Zeig which ironically describes the different usages of the different terms LESBIAN, SAPPHIST and DYKE: 'If you're poor/then you're a dyke/if you're rich/you're sapphic/but if you're neither one nor the other/a lesbian, a lesbian is what you'll have to be.'

ILGA *See* INTERNATIONAL LESBIAN AND GAY ASSOCIATION.

immac Brand name of a British make of depilatory cream, essential for any drag queen to make sure there are no unsightly tufts poking out from her fishnets and which, unlike the razor, does not make her cleavage look like the Somme.

immigration In most countries it is next to impossible for a lesbian or gay man to apply for rights of residence on the grounds of a long-term relationship with a same-sex national of that country, however long they have been together. At present only Denmark, the Netherlands, Norway, Sweden, Australia and New Zealand have any legal provision. Canada has given permission for some multinational couples to remain together, despite having no official policy. In April 1994 a gay English immigration official, Mark Watson, was jailed for providing his Brazilian lover with illegal documentation to enable him to stay in England, because he knew that an application would be refused if he went about it officially. Meanwhile, nearly all countries have some provision for married couples to take up residence.

in the department 1950s queer slang to describe someone else who is gay. Could be used as a code to ascertain someone's sexuality without referring to it explicitly. *See also* HOCKEY TEAM.

in the life American slang, recorded as early as the 1930s, to describe those taking part in the lesbian and gay community, and thus had connotations of a reasonably well-adjusted homosexual. Used mainly within African-American communities.

Inclusa Pamphlet published in 1864 by the German sexologist Karl ULRICHS which aimed at setting forth a dispassionate discussion of homosexuality.

Indigo Girls Successful American dyke indie band, consisting of Amy Ray and Emily Sailers. Their records include *Strange Fire* (1987), *The Indigo Girls* (1989), *Nomads, Indians and Saints* (1990), *Back on the Bus Y'all* (1990), *Rites of Passage* (1992) and *Swamping Orphelias* (1994).

indorse Term for sex between men which was recorded as being used by gay men in London in the eighteenth century, according to *The London Journal*. It apparently derives from boxing slang, in which to indorse meant to strike someone on the

back, or knock them over upon their back. Its relevance to the act of gay sex is obvious.

Inga (d. 1943) Norwegian drag artiste who worked in drag bars in Oslo during the Nazi occupation of Norway. He was active in the resistance and carried information on Nazi marine movements across the border into Sweden while dressed as a woman to arouse less suspicion. Eventually his sex was discovered by Nazi soldiers who tried to rape him and he was executed. He was honoured posthumously by the King of Norway.

ingle Popular term in Elizabethan England (1558–1603) for a younger gay man who is usually passive in sexual relations. It had some connotations of effeminacy, and was often used to describe men who worked within the disreputable and unmanly milieu of the THEATRE.

initiation rites Anthropological studies of cultures worldwide have demonstrated an enduring link between initiation rites and same-sex erotic practices. Initiation rites mark the entry by a young man or woman into the status of full adulthood, and are often conducted within sex-segregated environments; the young person receives the knowledge of how to be an adult member of their own gender before being allowed to wield this new knowledge with a mixed-sex society. In many societies of the Pacific islands and Australasia, male initiation rites involve the ritualized anal penetration of the boy by an adult relation or by one who is chosen to be his mentor in the initiation process. Such rites are often related to notions within those societies of the significance of SEMEN as a fluid which contains the essence of masculinity; thus the implanting of semen in his rectum is a way of helping his masculinity to flower. Historians have suggested that the archaic forms of homosexual relation in SPARTA and CRETE represent a hangover from a similar ritual.

Inquisition The court which was established to inquire into offences against the Roman Catholic Church. It was fully established by Pope Gregory IX in 1235, and torture as a means of extracting confessions was first sanctioned by Pope Innocent IV in 1252. Although ecclesiastical, the Inquisition commonly sought the help of the State in its examinations. Those found guilty were handed over to the secular authorities of each land to be dealt with according to their laws, which in the case of stubborn heretics often meant execution. In 1451 the Inquisition was mandated by Pope Nicholas to investigate cases of SODOMY. Under the Portuguese Inquisition some 900 cases were prosecuted for the 'unmentionable sin', of which about fifty were burnt at the stake. This included lesbians until a ruling in the seventeenth century decreed that sodomy had to involve penetration and ejaculation. The notorious Spanish Inquisition was similarly cruel in its persecution of 'sodomy' cases. Between 1518 and 1616 fifty-two executions took place in the town of Seville alone. The Inquisition was also, of course, responsible for the burning of WITCHES in the middle ages. Such events were not unique. Throughout the whole of Europe, men and women were commonly prosecuted and often executed for 'sodomy' during this period, even if it was not done with the sanction of the Catholic Church.

Institute of Sexology German organization, based in Berlin, which was the centre of operations for the gay activist Magnus HIRSCHFIELD who founded it in 1919. It was dedicated to work on rights for women, lesbians and gays, on the legalization of contraception and abortion, and on sex education. It housed a counselling centre, a museum, space for educational activities as well as a comprehensive library of works on sexuality (*see* LIBRARY OF THE INSTITUTE OF SEXOLOGY).

Integrity Lesbian and gay religious organization which was set up within the Episcopal Church in 1974. It has more than fifty chapters in the United States as well as many others worldwide.

inter Christianos non nominandun Latin phrase, meaning literally 'not to be named

among Christians', which became a standard euphemism for homosexual relations specifically and all forms of non-procreative sex generally, well into the nineteenth century. Its first usage is not known, though it was a favourite expression of Sir Robert Peel.

intermediate sex The term used by Edward Carpenter for homosexuals, which was broadly similar to Karl ULRICHS' notion of a THIRD SEX, namely of a different category of gender which was placed between the conventional roles of masculine and feminine. Although Carpenter tried to question the stereotypes of homosexuals as bearing the characteristics of the opposite gender and although he suggested the term to promote the idea of homosexuality as a variation rather than as a degeneration, his linking of gender to sexuality meant that his theories were prone to be read in this way and were open to the problems inherent in the ideas of CONGENITAL INVERSION.

The Intermediate Sex 1908 book by the gay social activist Edward CARPENTER. The title was chosen to present the ideas that people with homosexual impulses were a harmless social variation, which occupied the middle ground in terms of gender. Within the book, Carpenter went further. Using the terminology of URANIANISM, he suggested that, in affairs of the heart, Urnings, with an understanding of both sexes, were in a privileged position. He wrote, 'It is probable that superior Urnings will become, in affairs of the heart, to a large extent the teachers of the future society.'

Intermediate Types among Primitive Folk 1914 work by the gay social activist Edward CARPENTER, in which he presented his case that in many traditional societies gay people occupied privileged positions and thus in many cases acted as forces that propelled those societies forward. He believed that Uranians, when they were freed from the necessities of procreation and with a spiritual wholeness and insight sprung of their knowledge of both genders, in seeking 'new outlet for their energies' became 'students of life and nature, inventors and teachers of arts and crafts...revealers of the gods and religion...became medicine men and healers...and so ultimately laid the foundation of the priesthood, and of science, literature and art'. Thus Uranians served an evolutionary purpose through their superior development, which was why they were to be found in all societies at all times. *See* URANIANISM.

international Mexican slang for a gay man who takes both an active and passive role in gay sex. Thus, as in many societies where gender roles are sharply dichotomized, active and passive roles are seen as mutually alien. *See* ACTIVE/PASSIVE SPLIT.

International Lesbian and Gay Association (ILGA) Describing itself as a worldwide organization fighting for lesbian and gay rights, the association was founded in the English city of Coventry in 1978, and was originally called the International Association of Lesbians/Gay Women and Gay Men (IGA). It was formed for four specific purposes: to provide information for campaigns against governments and international bodies; to coordinate the work of different national organizations; to promote the unity of lesbians and gay men worldwide through the dissemination of information; and finally to cooperate with other movements that support lesbian and gay rights.

The Intersexes: A History of Similisexualism as a Problem in Social Life 1908 work by Edward Stephenson, writing under the nom de plume of Xavier Mayne. It represented one of the first attempts to write about lesbian and gay life as it was lived, and contains much interesting information about lesbian and gay subcultures in European cities at the turn of the century.

intrafemoral sex Sex where the dick is pushed between someone's thighs, often used as a safe sex alternative to anal penetration where no condom is available. Also known as the PRINCETON RUB.

inversion Almost a standard term for homosexuality in the very late nineteenth and early twentieth centuries. However, it – along with the word invert – was more than a neutral word and contained an implicit judgement on same-sex eroticism, namely that it negated what was a 'natural' order of things. In addition, the word often carried connotations of reversing natural gender roles, and thus implied some form of psychological explanation. Nevertheless, some of the more 'progressive' sex researchers such as Havelock ELLIS and John Addington SYMONDS regularly used the term.

invert A man or woman who is believed to be, or believes that he or she is, a person who is CONGENITALLY INVERTED. Invert was popularly used as a name for homosexuals up to the 1950s.

Isherwood, Christopher (1904–86) English-born writer. In the early 1930s Isherwood lived in Berlin, the setting for the book *Mr Norris Changes Trains* (1935) and *Goodbye to Berlin* (1939), parts of which formed the basis of the film CABARET, and which are partly responsible for a gay fascination with the seediness of Weimar Berlin. After the rise of Nazism in Europe, Isherwood went to America, and in 1953 he began a relationship with Don Bachardy, who was later to carve no small renown for himself as a painter. His American writings increasingly emphasize homosexuality as a theme. *A Single Man* (1964) depicts a lonely Los Angeles gay man, while *Down There on a Visit* (1966) gives us a portrayal of a male hustler. Isherwood was also involved in both the gay rights movement (through the organization ONE INC.) and in the development of gay spiritual thought through his associations with fellow Brit Gerald Heard and with the Vedantist creed.

Isophyl Meaning lover of the same, it was the name suggested for lesbians and gays by the twentieth-century British philosopher, writer and gay theorist Gerald Heard. Freed from the conventional roles of society, Heard saw the isophyl as possessed of the flexibility and creativity, the prolonged adolescence, that was necessary for social and evolutionary advance. It was this flexibility, expressed through communality, as opposed to the family, which he felt that lesbians and gays should cherish, rather than in emulating social roles in an attempt to appear 'normal' and thus gain tolerance from an unworthy society. Influenced by Vedantism (a Westernized form of Hindu spirituality), he saw same-sex sexual behaviour as imbued with spiritual potential as it was not limited by the commitment to breeding. He also saw the greater freedom of lesbians and gays to transcend gender roles as a spiritual advance.

it is good to have pleasure with a woman, with a boy, with a camel Arab proverb which points to the gap that has historically existed between sexual practice and the sexual austerity of Islam in the Middle East.

It Is Not the Homosexual Who Is Perverse But the Society in Which He Lives 1971 film directed by Rosa von Praunheim. The film attacked those queers who wished to gain acceptance within the very system which oppressed them instead of attempting to overthrow it; the problems of the ghetto therefore become a function of internalizing straight societal mores. The film depicts the coming out of David and follows him through the various manifestations of gay life, including street cruising, bars, monogamy and a countercultural collective in which he discusses the nature of homophobia. *See also* ARMY OF LOVERS.

Jack and Jill parties Appeared on the lesbian and gay social scene in the late 1980s. They were essentially based on the JACKOFF parties which became popular among gay men with the advent of AIDS, and the closing down of BATHHOUSES, but with the addition of Jills, or lesbians, as well. Their existence indicated not only the coming together of some lesbian and gay communities in the 1980s, but also the deep pondering both had done about sex in that

time. Sex wars among lesbians and the changes in gay male sexuality as a result of AIDS had made such sexual arenas possible. Not infrequently, men who defined as gay would also have sex with women who defined as lesbian. While many couldn't see the difference between this and heterosexuality, others hailed it as the latest in QUEER, saying that the experience of both partners as sexual outsiders made sex qualitatively different, the lesbian was as likely to fuck the man with a STRAP-ON as to go bottom, for starters, and offered infinite chances to explore different roles.

jack off To wank. A jack-off party is therefore a get-together when a number of men will gather to masturbate themselves, usually while watching porn. Such parties became a feature of the American gay lifestyle in the 1980s when the threat of AIDS had become manifest.

Jack Straw's Castle The car park of this north London pub is a popular late-night taxi destination for those men looking for a bit of fresh air, since it is the gateway to the gay theme park that is HAMPSTEAD HEATH.

Jahrbuch für Sexuelle Zwischenstufen (Yearbook for Sexual Intermediates) One of the earliest journals of scholarly works on homosexuality, which was produced annually between 1899 and 1923. It was edited by Magnus HIRSCHFIELD, the German gay rights activist, and was published under the aegis of his Berlin-based SCIENTIFIC-HUMANITARIAN COMMITTEE. It carried articles about homosexuality, reviews of the literature then being produced, and commentaries on current events of interest.

jam American slang term of the 1940s which meant heterosexual. Its derivation is unclear.

James I (1566–1625) King of England from 1603, he had already been King of Scotland from 1567 (as James VI). His court was renowned for homoerotic goings-on. James had made little attempt to disguise the chain of close relationships with men that he had from an early age, including

Esmé Stuart, Earl of Lennox, and the Earl of Bothwell whom James embraced in public, causing the French ambassador to go for his smelling salts. In fact, when he ascended to the English throne a popular comment was said to be, 'Elizabeth was King, now James is Queen.' But James' great love was George Villiers, Duke of Buckingham. Their closeness caused such a raising of eyebrows that the Privy Council discussed the matter, and James delivered one of the first justifications of homosexual affection in history. In a speech which alluded to what appears to have been a popular understanding of the relationship between Jesus and ST JOHN THE EVANGELIST, James said, 'You may be sure that I love the Earl of Buckingham more than anyone else...Jesus Christ did the same, and therefore I cannot be blamed. Christ had his son John, and I have my George.'

Jarman, Derek (1942–94) British saint, activist, film-maker, public PWA and hero to many gay men. Jarman was canonized by the SISTERS OF PERPETUAL INDULGENCE as St Derek of Dungeness of the Order of Celluloid Knights. His films were: *Sebastiane* (1976); *Jubilee* (1977); *The Tempest* (1980); *Caravaggio* (1986); *The Last of England* (1987); *War Requiem* (1989); *The Garden* (1990); *Edward II* (1991); *Wittgenstein* (1992); *Blue* (1993); and *Glitterbug* (1994). All of them show a talent of vision, humour, furious intelligence, warmth and unashamed queerness. Jarman was revered in the gay community not only for his creative output, but also the strength of his political commitment. He publicly supported the aims and tactics of direct action groups such as OUTRAGE!, arguing that the 'respectable' side of gay politics was a dead end: 'Good-mannered city queens in suits and pinstripes, so busy establishing themselves, were useless at changing anything.' Change was to come when guilt and self-hatred were exorcized and when gay men could live a life of cultural heterodoxy and sexual freedom: 'Every orgasm brings its own liberty'. His queerness was evident in his films from

the homoeroticism of *Caravaggio* and *Sebastiane* to the staged OutRage! protest in *Edward II*. He lost his brave struggle against AIDS two days before the vote on the AGE OF CONSENT in the House of Commons in February 1994. Perhaps the most fitting tribute to him was the shrine of candles left opposite his flat in London's Charing Cross Road by the queer demonstrators who had just conducted an impromptu riot through the streets after the defeat of the amendment to reduce the age of consent from twenty-one to sixteen.

jazz The musical form which had its roots among black communities in the American south, and was developed in New Orleans, before reaching Chicago, where it got its name. It was associated in the early twentieth century with the black communities which were seen, though often in a voyeuristic sense by whites, as more sexually open. The writer F. Scott Fitzgerald styled the 1920s in America 'the jazz age' in reference to the hedonistic possibilities of the time. It was heavily influenced by the BLUES.

Jenny Lives with Eric and Martin Children's storybook, written by Susanne Boesche, which was the first English-language book that aimed to demystify the gay lifestyle for young readers. It tells the story of a weekend in the life of Jenny, a young girl who lives with a gay male couple, her father and his lover. It became the centre of a storm of protest in the 1980s in the UK when tabloid newspapers asserted that it was being routinely used in London schools. In fact, it was merely stocked in a teacher's resource centre. *See* POSITIVE IMAGES.

Jeremy British magazine of the late 1960s. Following the passage of the SEXUAL OFFENCES ACT in 1967 it was possible for such magazines to be open about their readership (*see also* SPARTACUS), and moreover it demonstrated the new openness which the whiff of freedom had given the gay subculture. Appealing to the consumerism which was taking shape in the subculture, Jeremy carried extensive coverage of the trendy and fashionable London scene, as well as travel articles, and the standard agony and advice.

Jesus In a Gnostic version of the Gospel of Mark which was found in the library of a Mount Sinai monastery, the Lazarus story is recast in what was said to be the original version. It tells that the young man coming from the tomb looked at Jesus, and begged him to be able to be with him. Jesus said that certain preparations were needed and when he later met the youth, who was naked apart from a linen cloth, he stayed the night and taught him the 'mysteries'. *See also* JOHN THE EVANGELIST, ST.

JO Abbreviation of jack off, to wank. Used in the language of gay CONTACT ADVERTS by men who are simply seeking manual relief. *See* JACK OFF.

jockey American prison and working-class lesbian slang of the 1930s which described the BUTCH partner in a lesbian BUTCH/FEMME relationship. *See also* HUS-BAND.

jockey brief Male underwear, and fetish object for gay men, especially the used variety. First developed in 1934 by the Jockey International Company as an alternative to the long johns and boxer shorts which were the usual type at the time. The fly front was added two years later.

jockstrap Athletic support. Fetish object for gay men, and handy too, since it gives open access to the ass. Invented at the turn of the twentieth century by a Finnish athlete, Parvo Nakacheker.

St John the Evangelist The beloved disciple 'whom Jesus loved' and who rested on Jesus' bosom at the last supper (John 13:23). Steamy.

Joseph and His Friend American novel published in 1870, by the poet Bayard Taylor. Dedicated to 'those who believe in the truth and tenderness of man's love for man', it was one of the first novels to imply gay sexuality. It tells the tale of an American farmer who, although entering into a heterosexual marriage, feels different from the people around him.

Julian and Sandy The regular characters on the 1960s radio programme ROUND THE HORNE, played by Kenneth Williams and Hugh Paddick, who were responsible for releasing a flood of the gay argot POLARI and of gay innuendo onto an unsuspecting listenership. The two, both former chorus boys, would appear each week running a new business, seeming to have a finger in just about any entrepreneurial pie – from Rentachap domestic help, to BONA tickets, Bona drag, to your actual Bona everything.

Just A Gigolo Cole Porter Song, in which the singer confesses to having a 'dash of LAVENDER'.

K

Kilts

kakila Term used in the KAMA SUTRA for the SIXTY-NINE position, when two partners go down on one another at the same time, when practised between men and women, two men or two women.

Kali The cult name of the Hindu goddess Durga, the wife of Siva, and a deity of death and destruction. She is sometimes known as the destroyer. Represented as black, blood-smeared with red eyes, four arms, matted hair, sharp fangs and a protruding tongue dripping blood, she is one of the deities associated with new age GOD-DESS worship.

Kaliardá The name by which the modern Greek gay slang system is most commonly known; it is also sometimes referred to as *latinika* ('Latin'), *vathia latinika* ('deep Latin') or *etrouska* ('Etruscan') amongst other terms. The term *Kaliardá* is itself derived either from the French *gaillard* or from a Romany term for gypsy. In the dichotomy that is made in Greek society

between the active and passive sexual roles (*see* ACTIVE/PASSIVE SPLIT), *Kaliardá* is associated with the passive gay man. As a slang system it is quite complex and almost forms a language in itself, incorporating words from other languages and using a minimum of Greek words.

Kalisaya Bar Gay bar in Paris at the turn of the century which was patronized by Oscar Wilde and his circle after Wilde's release from jail.

Kama Sutra The world's first sex manual and literary classic, written by the sage Vatsyana in the 4th–5th centuries AD, and compiled from verses of Sanskrit texts several centuries old. One chapter of the work, called AUPARISHTAKA, deals with oral sex. It would appear from the original work that auparishtaka has been widespread in some parts of India since time immemorial. For example, the *Shushruta*, a 2,000-year-old medical treatise, describes the wounding of the penis (*lingam*) with the teeth as one of the causes of certain diseases. In addition, lesbian activity is recorded as having been commonplace in the *anthapura*, or harem.

Kamia origin myth Among the Kamia tribe of America, it is related that the Kamia ancestors camped on the east side of Salton Sea, but were scattered from there when a female transvestite (*warharmi*) and two male twins appeared from the north. It was these three who introduced Kamia culture.

Kansas The epitome of mid-American dullness. For queers, Kansas has a special resonance in this sense due to the astute line of Dorothy in the camp classic, THE WIZARD OF OZ, 'Toto, I don't think we're in Kansas anymore.'

Kapok Doctor The name given to British doctor 'James' Miranda Barry (1795–1865) who spent forty years dressed as a man and working as an officer and surgeon in the British army. She was known for her flirting with women at army dances, and she conducted an affair with a Mrs Fenton. With the help of an elaborate pair of shoulder pads, she managed to keep her true sexual identity secret until after her death when her body was being prepared for burial.

Kaposi's Sarcoma (KS) A previously rare form of skin cancer which had been documented in Africa and amongst older men from the Mediterranean area, but which is one of the conditions particularly associated with people with AIDS. It causes a growth of blood-vessel walls, thereby creating red or purple lesions on the skin. It may subsequently be found inside the mouth, gut and lungs. For most people with KS the problem is mainly cosmetic, since the lesions can be disfiguring. Many undergo forms of chemotherapy to remove them. The condition is named after Moritz Kohn Kaposi (1837–1902) an Austrian dermatologist who first described the lesions. The American Centers for Disease Control set up a Kaposi's Sarcoma and Opportunistic Infections Task Force in 1981 to investigate the appearance of a number of cases of KS in gay men, which ultimately led to the identification of AIDS as a particular syndrome.

Kaposi's Sarcoma Education and Research Foundation Founded in 1982 by Mark Conant, a dermatologist affiliated to the University of California at San Francisco. Conant also established the first KS clinic in America in San Francisco. The foundation was one of the first organizations to be aware of the huge potential threat of AIDS and to campaign for funding for research. The activist Cleve Jones, who later founded the NAMES PROJECT, was also involved.

kathoey The nearest thing to a gay identity in traditional Thailand. Literally rendered as transvestite, the kathoey was the female-identified partner in relationships that were conceived of with reference to heterosexual partnerships. The kathoey would take the passive role in sex, while his partner who would be active was not thought of as having a sexual identity different from other men. Such relationships were not necessarily persecuted, and some 'men' and kathoeys would marry in Thai villages. With the influx of information into Thailand from Western gay communities, gay Thais have begun to reject such role-playing, and gay relationships which are not based round the dualities of masculine/feminine or ACTIVE/PASSIVE are becoming more common.

Kenric The British lesbian group which formed out of ARENA 3 in 1965, so called because the original members lived in the London boroughs of Kensington (Ken) and Richmond (Ric). The name Kenric has become synonymous with middle-class straight-acting white women who are resolutely non-political. As the nice face of British lesbianism, Kenric is still going throughout the country.

Kertbeny, Karl Maria (1824–82) Hungarian who was credited with the first use of the word HOMOSEXUAL in 1869.

Kettners Restaurant in the Soho district of London. It is famous in gay history as the place where Oscar WILDE would take his sexual contacts for dinner. He would make them a gift of a silver cigarette box, as a convenient way of paying for services rendered or about to be rendered.

Key West Resort area of the Florida Keys, and the southernmost point of the United States, which in the 1970s became one of the most popular tourist destinations in the country for holidaying gays. Considered less sophisticated than its New York counterpart of FIRE ISLAND, Key West attracted a more mellow type of gay visitor, and was quite popular with touring couples.

keys On the gay leather scene of the 1960s and 1970s keys, like HANKIES, were used to indicate a man's sexual preferences to those he was cruising or who were cruising him. Keys were used because they could be attached to the trousers on the left or right side. Thus, following convention, keys on the left indicated a TOP and on the right a BOTTOM. If they were attached in the middle of the back, they referred to someone who was willing to play either role.

Khajuraho Indian city famous for its ancient temples which have many explicit homoerotic pictures inscribed on the walls.

khush Hindi word which means happy. Used by some south Asian lesbians and gays to mean gay, or the ecstatic pleasure of queerness.

kiki Name given to women within the lesbian bar culture of the 1950s and 1960s who did not take on one of the BUTCH/FEMME roles. There would often be considerable animosity towards these women who refused to play by the rules. Kiki could also be used to describe a partnership between two butch or two femme women.

The Killing of Sister George In this 1968 film by Robert Aldrich, June Buckridge (Beryl Reid) is a cheery country nurse, Sister George, in her soap opera professional life and an aggressive, butch lesbian by night. Her alcoholic binging and loud outbursts, as well as the malicious influ-

ence of a nasty BBC executive, Mercy Croft (Coral Browne), make her lose both her job and her baby lover (Susannah York). The film sets up a tension between the closet and open lesbian lifestyles. To the queer viewer, Sister George is a strong woman who is unable to pretend to be what she is not, and it is for this which she is punished. The club scenes were filmed in the real and famous London lesbian GATEWAYS CLUB.

kilt A BUTCH frock. A tartan skirt worn by men as part of traditional Scottish dress, and co-opted by British men who were interested in tossing an altogether more sensitive caber in 1993 as the newest gay contribution to the male fashion world. Skirts were very much the thing that season, and south-east Asian style sarong affairs were also a common sight in London clubs. And if butch calfs in DOC MARTENS weren't sufficient, there was the added frisson that traditionally a Scottish man wasn't supposed to wear any underclothing to staunch the breeze. An ad by the Scottish AIDS Monitor group in 1994 showed that this wasn't quite the case, and that a little piece of latex was permissible.

King, Billie Jean (1943–) Great tennis player who acknowledged an affair with her secretary, Marilyn Barnett, in 1981. The declaration occurred after Barnett had sued King, alleging that the latter had promised to support her for life.

kings, queer *See* QUEER KINGS AND QUEENS.

King's Cross Area of Sydney, in Australia, which from the 1950s through the 1960s became the focal point of Sydney's growing gay subculture, having had a reputation for being bohemian throughout the two world wars. Hotel bars such as the Rex and 'The Quarter Deck' in the Chevron catered to a camp clientele, and the aptly named Hasty Tasty hamburger joint was a place for casual pick-ups. It also became the area for drag show clubs which proliferated in the 1960s, such as the Jewel Box and Les Girls, which is still operating today.

Kinsey, Dr Alfred (1894–1956) American sex researcher. Kinsey first became interested in the research of human sexual behaviour when he was elected to teach a university sex education course while on the teaching staff of Indiana University in 1937, ironically because he was seen as conservative and likely to give the 'right' message. When he began to research for the course, however, he discovered the paucity of works on the subject. In wonderment at this, he began his own research, which eventually entailed the interview of over 18,000 men and women about their sexual behaviours. In 1947 he founded the Institute of Sex Research to carry on researches into the subject. Much of the money raised from his bestselling reports was channelled back into the Institute. His reports on sexual behaviour among men and women were published in 1948 and 1953 respectively. (*See* SEXUAL BEHAVIOUR IN THE HUMAN MALE; SEXUAL BEHAVIOUR IN THE HUMAN FEMALE.) They included the (shocking) revelations that some 4% of male and 2% of female interviewees identified themselves as exclusively homosexual, while 37% of men and 13% of women had enjoyed homosexual activities at least once. These findings were eye-openers to a society which had not realized that queers were everywhere.

Kinsey six Slang term for someone who is exclusively homosexual. It derives from the pioneering sex research of Alfred KINSEY, who used a scale of nought to six to measure the sexual orientation of his subjects. Those who were exclusively heterosexual earned a zero, while those with any degree of homosexual leaning scored a mark along the scale up to six, for completely homo.

kinshon Boys in American prisons of the early nineteenth century, who served as sexual partners for the older inmates. In return for their corporeal favours the boys would be handsomely rewarded, and on occasion the relationship would become semi-permanent, with the lovers sharing the same room. One report of the time declares, 'The Sin of Sodom is the vice of prisoners, and boys are the favourite prostitutes.'

Kiss of the Spider Woman Novel by Manuel Puig, adapted for the screen in 1985. It tells the story of the prison relationship between Molina, a gay window dresser who is jailed for molesting a minor, and Valentin, a left-wing journalist imprisoned for political activities. Molina spends his time telling stories from old movies for Valentin, who tries to raise Molina's political consciousness. Ultimately the two have sex and Molina, for love, dies for Valentin's cause. The film leaves out the elements of Puig's original novel in which Valentin attacks Molina's destructive identification with the subordinate female in cinema. William Hurt won an Academy Award (Oscar) for his portrayal of Molina, the first actor to do so for a gay role.

kkoktu kaksi Traditional puppet play of Korea. In the play, the hero Pak ch'omji, a satire on the idle provincial gentleman, spends his money on a pretty boy, Midongaji, which gives rise to several coarse jokes about their gay relationship.

Knights of the Chameleons Private gay club in the Australian city of Sydney started in 1962 and still in existence. Such clubs (also the Boomerangs and the Polynesians) organized dances, picnics and parties.

Knights of the Clock Los Angeles group for interracial gay men formed in 1951. Unfortunately short-lived.

Knights Templars Medieval military Christian sect which was founded in 1119 and had attained great influence by the fourteenth century. They became subject to one of the greatest sex scandals of the middle ages when in the early 1300s, Philip IV of France, nervous of their influence and coveting their wealth, got informers to denounce them as sodomites who had initiation rituals in which novices were forced to kiss members on the buttocks, anus and mouth. Many of the

Knights were tortured, though few owned up to such activity.

knitting Slang term for masturbation.

Kopay, David (1942–) American baseball player who played for the San Francisco Forty-Niners, the Detroit Lions and the Washington Redskins among others. He came out to a stunned public in 1975.

korophilia Erotic attraction of an adult woman for a young girl. It derives from the Greek word for a young girl. A lesbian version of PAEDOPHILIA, it represents an attempt to delineate different forms of lesbian attraction. It never really caught on though. *See also* PARTHENOPHILIA.

kosher US gay slang for a circumcised cock, derived from the Jewish term for food which is prepared in accordance with religious law.

Kowalski case Legal case in America. In November 1983 Sharon Kowalski was injured in a car accident, becoming quadriplegic and suffering severe brain damage. Her parents refused to give their daughter's lover, Karen Thompson, full access to Kowalski, or even input into her care. In fighting for these rights, Kowalski campaigned to make lesbians and gay men aware of the need for them to legally document the rights they wish their lovers to have over them in similar circumstances.

Krafft-Ebing, Richard Freiherr von (1840–1902) German-born Professor of Psychiatry at Vienna who was pivotal in the changing attitudes in Europe to homosexuality at the end of the nineteenth century and who was one of the main figures responsible for the MEDICALIZATION OF HOMOSEXUALITY. In his 1882 bestselling work *Psychopathia Sexualis*, he presented examples of a huge variety of uncommon sexual behaviours, including SADISM, MASOCHISM, TRANSVESTISM and UROLAGNIA. Everything, it seems, was perverse unless it led to pregnancy. It was the first time that many of these activities had been widely discussed. In his theories on 'antipathic sexual instinct', or homosexuality, he initially declared that homosexuals

manifested a 'diseased condition of the central nervous system', but as the work went through different editions more emphasis was placed on congenital causes, a hereditary 'taint'. He usually expressed this 'taint' in terms of the 'wrong' gender predominating (*see* GENDER DYSPHORIA). That is not to say that all homosexual acts were thus caused. He drew a distinction between pre-pubescent same-sex play or homosexual acts in single-sex environments and 'true' or congenital inversion. It is difficult to assess the historical impact of his work. He himself was probably more positive about homosexuality than many of his contemporaries, and he supported the campaign for the repeal of PARAGRAPH 175. By a year before his death he wrote in an article for the JAHRBUCH FÜR SEXUELLE ZWISCHENSTUFEN that, although homosexuality is an aberration, it is not necessarily prohibitive of mental health. However, the bulk of his popular writing stressed the idea of sickness, and he was not able to control the ways in which anti-homosexual people might use this to justify the continued repression of homosexual activity, not to mention the devastating psychological impact it had on lesbians and gays who read his works only to find out they were sick. And yet the debate that surrounded his writings focused attention on sex and a homosexual identity, and was partly responsible for the setting up of organizations such as the SCIENTIFIC-HUMANITARIAN COMMITTEE of Magnus HIRSCHFIELD. It can be argued that such developments were necessary to the twentieth-century lesbian and gay liberation movement.

Krafft-Ebinger After the German sexologist, some people who recognized themselves as lesbian chose to name themselves after him and his theories (*see* SIND ES FRAUEN?).

Kramer, Larry (1935–) American gay writer and AIDS activist who has kept what at times was a one-man running commentary on the American government inaction in response to the AIDS epidemic. Originally unpolitical – 'Like many others, when Gay Pride marches started down Fifth Avenue at the end of June, I was on Fire Island' –

Kramer drew fire from gay liberationists when his novel *Faggots* was published in 1978. They saw the book, which criticized the sterility of lives built on sexual promiscuity, as a guilt-ridden attack on the gains of 1970s sexual liberation. When the AIDS epidemic started, Kramer's social group was among the first to be affected, and he was a founder member of GAY MEN'S HEALTH CRISIS, only to be pushed out when his abrasive style conflicted with the development of the organization into a semi-official body. He kept writing about the epidemic – 1985 saw the first production of THE NORMAL HEART – and in 1987 was key among the founders of ACT UP. *See also* 1,112 AND COUNTING.

Die Kreis/Le Cercle Swiss periodical which was originally called *Schweizerisches Freundschaftsblatt* (Swiss Friendship Bulletin) when it was founded in 1933 by a Swiss lesbian who went by the name of Mammina. In 1943 the magazine and the society which sponsored it became all men, and the name was changed to DER KREIS. It lasted until 1967, by which time French- and English-language sections had been added.

KS *See* KAPOSI'S SARCOMA.

Kwell American brand name for the gamma benzine hexachloride lotion which is used for treating scabies or CRABS.

KY jelly Brand name of a popular lubricant,. marketed by the medical firm Johnson & Johnson, used widely by gay men for easing up the anus for fucking. The brand became increasingly popular during the 1980s when condoms became de rigueur for safe sex during the AIDS epidemic. It eclipsed other brands since, being water based, it did not rot condoms like other popular brands of oil-based lubricants. Some men liked to put some lube in the condom before sex to increase sensitivity, although health workers worried that this might make it more likely that the condom would come off during sex.

L

lesbian sex radicals

The L-shaped Room 1962 film based on the book by Lynne Reid Banks and set in a rooming house with two gay characters. One, Johnny (Brock Peters), is in the grips of a tortured unrequited passion. Also in the house lives a kind old vaudevillian, Mavis (Cicely Courtneidge), full of song and dance, who constantly refers to a 'friend' who was once her partner. When asked if 'he' was also a performer, she takes from the mantelpiece a small photo of a woman. 'This is my friend', she says, 'it takes all kinds, you know, dearie.' Slightly patronizing means of showing that even we have feelings, but progressive for the cinema screen of the early 1960s.

Labouchere amendment Popular name for Section 11 of the British Criminal Law Amendment Act of 1885, taken from the name of its proposer, Henry Labouchere. It was in many ways a conservative reaction both to the formal abolition of the death penalty for buggery in 1861 and to the dif-

ficulties of gaining a conviction for buggery, which had led to the acquittal of the defendants in the BOULTON AND PARK AFFAIR. Whereas HENRY VIII'S BUGGERY LAW was only focused on anal sex, the new amendment made all homosexual acts illegal, and punishable by up to two years' hard labour. It earned the nickname 'the blackmailer's charter' for the severity of its scope, since there was concern that it would lead to an increase in blackmail against wealthier gay men because they would fear prosecution under it. The most famous victim of the new law was Oscar WILDE. While lesbian sex was not originally covered by the law, in 1921 there was an attempt to bring it within the scope of the amendment. This failed in the House of Lords because of the worry that it might bring lesbianism to the attention of women who had never heard of or contemplated it. The Labouchere amendment was finally repealed by the 1967 SEXUAL OFFENCES ACT.

labrys Double-headed axe, often used as a symbol for lesbianism, and worn in jewellery form around the neck of many a dyke. It appears in ancient Greek art carried by members of AMAZON armies, and was associated with the goddess Demeter.

The Ladder The magazine of the lesbian organization the DAUGHTERS OF BILITIS, which was set up in 1956. Like the Daughters, the magazine started off fairly non-political, keeping more to cultural pieces, and for much of its life it tended to an assimilationist editorial line, urging women to behave and dress in an 'acceptable' manner, so as not to alienate support. When the lesbian activist Barbara Gittings assumed the role of editor in 1962, it took on a more strident political air, but with the advent of GAY LIBERATION it was increasingly unable to appeal to the new radical lesbians who were active by the early 1970s. In 1970, with arguments among the feminist movement causing divides, the magazine split from the Daughters, but only carried on until 1972.

The Ladies of Llangollen Affectionate nickname for Eleanor Butler (1739–1829) and Sarah Ponsonby (1755–1831), two upper-class Irishwomen who left Ireland together in 1778 and set up home together in PLAS NEWYDD, a cottage in Llangollen Vale in Wales. This was the second time they had attempted to elope, and they had to do it in male clothes so as not to be too conspicuous on the route. Their families realized they could not be stopped, and eventually gave them small stipends. Although their relationship occasioned some criticism, mostly as a result of Eleanor's butch appearance, on the whole they seemed to be accepted by society at the time, because their relationship was assumed not to be sexual, and because they were deeply conservative in most other respects. Referring to the biblical story of DAVID AND JONATHAN, their relationship was called a 'Davidean friendship' by the poet Anna Seward, known as the SWAN OF LICHFIELD, who herself had had an extremely passionate romantic friendship. Eleanor's diaries, which detail their lives together, provide rare documentation of what amounted to a same-sex marriage.

ladslove The sap of this saucily named plant is said to smell of cum. English poets of the nineteenth and early twentieth centuries sometimes referred to the plant to connote homosexuality.

lady Term used by BUTCH lesbians within the lesbian bar subculture of the 1950s and 1960s to describe their FEMME partner, but recorded as early as the 1930s as part of prison slang. Family-based metaphors were common within this scene (*see* HUSBAND; WIFE), and butch dykes would even refer to their partners as 'the family'. Such metaphors gave fuel to later lesbian-feminist arguments that the BUTCH/FEMME scene was merely a mimicking of heterosexual patterns of relationship.

lambda The Greek letter 'λ' for liberation. It was chosen in 1970 by the GAY ACTIVISTS ALLIANCE to serve as a symbol of gay liberation, and in 1974 was adopted as the international symbol for lesbian and gay rights by the International Gay Rights Congress meeting in Edinburgh, Scotland. Whilst it never caught on in the same way as the PINK TRIANGLE, it has had its uses. Many organizations, especially in America, have used it as a way of signifying lesbian and gay concerns together. It has also been worn in jewellery form by lesbians and gay men to draw attention to their sexuality to others that are in the know, and thereby to facilitate 'contacts'.

lambda delta lambda The first lesbian sorority at an American university, it was founded in 1988 at the University of California at Los Angeles (UCLA). Its goals were declared to be to highlight awareness of women's, gay and other minority issues.

Lambda Literary Award Prestigious American award established in 1989 recognizing excellence in lesbian and gay literature; the trophy is presented annually. The award is organized by the *Lambda Book Report*, a bimonthly non-fiction journal which reviews lesbian and gay books and authors.

lang, k.d. (1961–) Androgynous, Canadian, lesbian pop star who has produced four albums: *A Truly Western Experience* (1984); *Angel at My Lariat* (1986); *Shadowlands* (1988); *Absolute Torch and Twang* (1989); and *Ingénue* (1992). A committed macrobioticist and animal lover, lang's name has been linked with that of Martina Navratilova. Infamously, she and Cindy Crawford were featured on the cover of the magazine *Vanity Fair*, with Cindy lasciviously shaving the butched-up k.d. She starred in Percy Adlon's film *Salmonberries* (1991), which did very well at lesbian video parties. She is one of the few out lesbian stars who has been able to move over to mainstream success, and is both cult icon and major pop star.

latex love Safer sex. That is, fucking using a (latex) condom to act as a barrier to the transmission of the HIV virus. It now includes the use of dental dams and latex gloves. When HIV became prevalent in the 1980s, the decade was declared the era of latex love.

lattie British slang for a room or flat, derived from the gay argot, POLARI.

lavender Colour often used to denote homosexuality. The historical roots of this association are not clear. Some say that as a fusing of the colours red and blue, traditional female and male colours respectively, lavender represents the fusing of genders which is held to be within the homosexual psyche. The purple gemstone amethyst has also been used in this way because of its colour. Lavender became popular in American lesbian circles in the 1930s, as a colloquial term for other lesbians.

Lavender Couch Published in 1985 and written by San Francisco therapist Marny Hall, this was the first detailed consumer's guide to therapy and counselling issues for lesbians and gay men; written from a positive and out gay perspective, and trusted by thousands.

lavender herring The scare tactic used by regressive-minded critics in their attempt to put people off sexually progressive movements and to weaken those movements by declaring that only queers would want to participate in them. For example, the feminist movement has been accused throughout its history of being a cradle of lesbianism, and all those who participated in it were labelled as lesbian. Such distortions both slowed down the feminist movement and made it difficult to establish lesbian issues at the centre of the movement.

Lavender Jane Loves Women Album, produced in 1974 by musicians Alix Dobkin, Kay Gardner and Patches Attom on the Women's Wax Work label, which was a politically inspired collection of lesbian-feminist tunes. Exhorted women to ride the lesbian train. Part of the new WOMEN'S MUSIC.

lavender menace Betty Friedan, the founder of the American National Organization for Women (NOW), and her henchwomen used this term to describe lesbians active in NOW. They feared that an association with lesbianism in the public mind would undermine the organization. Some of the lesbians active in the GAY LIBERATION FRONT played on these fears when in 1970 they took over the stage of the Second Congress to Unite Women, and delivered speeches about the difficulties of lesbian lives. The women all wore T-shirts emblazoned with the words lavender menace. However, on 6 September 1971, NOW did vote in favour of recognizing lesbian concerns as central to the concerns of the feminist movement. Alluding to the common term 'red menace', used throughout the Cold War to describe the perceived communist threat, lavender menace has been used both by homophobes to describe the threat represented by queers to their idea of social harmony and by queers to mock the irrationality of the homophobes' fears.

lavnecks Lesbian slang, an abbreviation of lavender rednecks. It was used by critics of

1970s radical feminism to describe what they saw as the reactionary nature of the orthodoxies of lesbian feminism which imposed a politically correct terror and which did not allow any dissent. It was a term which alluded to 'rednecks', the stereotypical reactionaries of middle America, substituting 'lavender', which was a colour traditionally associated with queer sexuality.

League for Civil Education Short-lived organization for lesbian and gay rights which was founded in the early 1960s in San Francisco. The league assisted people who were involved in legal cases concerning gay civil rights. An associated group . also promoted the political ambitions of Jose SARRIA in his campaign for election to the San Francisco board of Supervisors.

leather The wearing of black leather clothing has been de rigueur among certain sections of the gay community for some fifty years. It is particularly associated with men and women who take part in SADO-MASOCHISTIC sex, although since the 1960s the black leather jacket has become a common fashion item among lesbians and gay men who only know the taste of VANILLA. 'Real' leathermen and women would spurn such affected wearing of leather however, since for them it is still a badge of transgressive sexuality. Indeed, many of them have stayed off the leather bar scene which they don't see as serious enough. Other items often worn include leather trousers, jackets, chaps, caps and harnesses. Ever since Brando in *The Wild One*, cowhide has had associations of rebellion, and it was an obvious choice for sexual outlaws. Of course leather's erotic feel and smell, as well as the butch and shady look it gives its wearer, has contributed to its sustained popularity.

Leather and Lace Los Angeles lesbian SM organization of the 1980s.

leather bar The first leather bars in America were seen in the 1950s. Of course, at this time, the bars would simply be used to cruise for men who might be interested in SM activities, rather than actually doing it

on the premises, as became possible in the 1970s. A series of codes were used by leathermen to facilitate their cruising. If a MASTER stood with his left arm against the right arm of another man, it meant that they were partners. If he stood with his left arm on the outside, away from the other man, it meant that he could be approached. To approach a man you stood with your left side against his right side. By the 1970s bars and clubs had become far more risqué, employing effects to create the LEATHERSPACE which focused attention on sexual possibilities.

leather closet Term used within LEATHER and SM communities to refer to the additional barrier they face in being open about their interests in SADOMASOCHISM, even if they have COME OUT about their sexuality. While we wouldn't expect much more than narrow-mindedness from straight society towards more radical forms of sexual expression, unfortunately lesbian and gay communities themselves have often been intolerant about SM. Thus, when coming out as a leather person, lesbians and gays have had to come out of two closets: their sexuality and their SM interests. Many LEATHER QUEENS stay within the second closet.

leathermen Butch queens dressed from top to bottom, as it were, in black LEATHER have been visible on the gay scene since the end of the Second World War. Many of the first leathermen took to the style because of the associations of rebellion which matched their perceptions of themselves as outcasts, either because of their wartime experiences or because of the rejection of homophobic society. In addition, they have traditionally been associated with the wilder side of queer sexuality such as SADOMASOCHISTIC practices. As such, they have not always found acceptance even among the lesbian and gay community, which at times has been more preoccupied with projecting a 'respectable' image to straight society, than in celebrating the sexual diversity which makes it unique.

leatherspace Term first used by the SM writer Geoff Mains in his book *Urban Aboriginals*. It refers to both the physical space where leathermen and SM practitioners congregate such as leather bars and clubs, and the mental space they create in isolation from mundane concerns which allows them to concentrate fully on sexual role-play. In reality, the two meanings are intertwined since leather clubs employ effects to disrupt ordinary consciousness – and the inhibitions that stem from it – to place attention on the men and women within and the seriousness of their intent. Walls and floor tend to be dark and plain, natural light excluded and music repetitious so all attention is focused on sex. The creation of the mental leatherspace occurs during sex play. Many scenes will start with prolonged periods of bondage, of hooding or other forms of sensory deprivation, progressing on to whipping, cutting, paddling or piercing.

leatherwomen Women who enjoy dressing in leather clothing but, more specifically, women who are part of the SM communities. Leather as a major element in the lesbian communities occurred much later than that for gay men. In particular, the lesbian feminist movement of the 1970s objected to the implications of leather on a number of grounds, most obviously because of the power relations they decried in SM sexuality. In addition, leather itself went against the ecological consciousness of many lesbian feminist communities. Although some lesbians were participating in the leather scene in the 1970s (there were, for example, women's nights at the CATACOMBS), it was not until the 1980s with the debates about sexual expression within lesbian communities that lesbian leather took off. Some of the most visible leatherwomen are the DYKES ON BIKES groups which head PRIDE marches in America.

Leaves of Grass Anthology of poetry by American poet Walt WHITMAN. First published in 1855, it was revised practically every year until his death. It was in the CALAMUS section, which was added in 1860, that Whitman elaborated the idea of ADHESIVENESS, or the kind of pure and uplifting comradely love that he saw as existing between men. As he wrote, 'I proceed for those who are or have been young men/To tell the secret of my nights and days/To celebrate the need of comrades.' Although the poetry is not specifically erotic, sections describe close relations between men, such as when Whitman wrote, 'For the friend I love lay sleeping by my side...his arm lay lightly over my breast – And that night I was happy.' These were sufficient to cause a sensation and to get Whitman sacked from his job as a clerk.

Lemon case Legal case in the UK in July 1977, when champion of public standards Mary Whitehouse brought a prosecution against the editor of GAY NEWS for blasphemy. It occurred after the newspaper had printed a poem by Professor James Kirkup, called THE LOVE THAT DARES TO SPEAK ITS NAME, which described the sexual feelings felt by a Roman centurion for Christ on the cross. The prosecution won, the first successful blasphemy case in fifty-five years.

Leopold and Loeb Two American law students, Nathan Leopold (1906–71) and Richard Loeb (1907–36), who together murdered a young boy in 1924. They both received a life sentence for the crime. Their story was the inspiration for the play *Rope's End* by Patrick Hamilton. As *Rope*, this play was adapted for the screen by Alfred Hitchcock in 1948, in which the two anti-heroic lovers, Shaw Brandon (John Dall) and Philip Granillo (Farley Granger), believing themselves to be above the dictates of common morality, hold a cocktail party over the trunk in which they have hidden the corpse. The two were also the basis for the 1959 film *Compulsion* directed by Richard Fleischer, and the 1991 film *Swoon* directed by Tom Kalin.

lesberado The kind of lesbian who spends a peripatetic life on the road in a beaten-up van driving between different women's communes.

lesbian The word refers to the Greek island which was the home of the poet SAPPHO. It has been used since the rediscovery of Sappho in the renaissance to denote 'women like Sappho of Lesbos'; the question is whether 'women like Sappho of Lesbos' meant women who have sex with women. Whether the meaning of 'lesbian' was *not* this is hard to tell. However, by 1732 (in William King's *The Toast*) lesbian was explicitly meant as referring to sex between women. Dictionaries usually give the first use of lesbian as the reference in a periodical *The Alienist and Neurologist*, in 1883; it perhaps shows the biases of compilers that they date lesbianism from its first pathological and medical use. The American group RADICALESBIANS famously answered the question 'what is a lesbian?', with the answer, 'A lesbian is the rage of all women condensed to the point of explosion' (1970). The title of the publication in which this definition appears, *The Woman Identified Woman*, provided a further definition of a lesbian: a woman whose primary emotional, sexual, social and political commitments lie with women. A more lesbian-feminist analysis is that offered by Adrienne RICH in *Compulsory Heterosexuality and Lesbian Existence* where she suggests that a lesbian is a woman who resists and rejects male power and male exploitation, and that the sexual nature of lesbianism becomes inessential. On the other hand, pro-sex dykes argue that sexual desire must be the defining characteristic of lesbian. While these questions are interesting, they do seem to miss the point: no one is going to solve the riddle of lesbian identity before you are beaten up on the streets.

Lesbian and Gay Black Group The first organization in the UK that allowed black lesbians and gay men to work together substantially. It was formed from the Black Gay Group, which in turn had been formed from the British Gay Asian Group, and was initially dominated by gay men. Lesbian representation has increased however. In 1992 the group opened a Black Lesbian and Gay Centre in London.

lesbian and gay movement General term for the many different strands of lesbian and gay politics, although whether or not it has ever composed a unified movement other than at a few crucial moments is doubtful. History is replete with examples of individuals declaring their own sexuality to be NATURAL for them and resisting the coercion of heterosexual society, but the roots of an organized movement are usually seen in the work of Magnus HIRSCHFIELD at the turn of the twentieth century in Germany. In America sporadic attempts such as the SOCIETY FOR HUMAN RIGHTS were the only examples of organized gay politics until the formation of groups such as the MATTACHINE SOCIETY, DAUGHTERS OF BILITIS and ONE INC. spelt the beginning of the HOMOPHILE MOVEMENT. In the UK the situation was similar, with impetus provided by reformist groups pushing for legal change, such as the HOMOSEXUAL LAW REFORM SOCIETY. While such groups provided a solid background of activism, it was not until the 1970s that many lesbians and gays personally felt the decisive changes that turned the decade into one of lesbian and gay LIBERATION. However, the cooperation between lesbians and gays in organizations such as the GAY LIBERATION FRONT was short-lived, and by the mid-1970s the dominant theories of the lesbian community were those of LESBIAN FEMINISM, while the gay male communities were more interested in pushing a campaign for sexual liberation in the 1970s, and responding to the terrible burden of the AIDS epidemic in the 1980s. Further, people with additional political concerns, such as black lesbians and gay men, usually felt the need to organize separately. Although the different communities could come together for specific campaigns such as those against the BRIGGS INITIATIVE in California and against CLAUSE 28 in the UK, and although lesbians have contributed magnificently to the fight against AIDS, in Britain particularly there has been no sustained period of cooperation on a movement level. (In America organizations such as the NATIONAL GAY AND LESBIAN TASK FORCE have had more success.) The QUEER groups of the 1990s are felt by most lesbians to be male dominated and male oriented in their agenda, and by many black lesbians and gays to be composed predominantly of white activists. However, such speedy periodizations and divisions belie the greater complexity of specific lesbian and gay communities. For example, in the UK there has never been much cross-over between the social scene and the political movement, whereas in San Francisco the experience of police harassment led many bar-owners to be active in the political struggle. And all along political organizations have only ever managed to mobilize a small section of the communities, other than on the annual PRIDE marches. While the growth of lesbian and gay community institutions continues, and the quality of life improves, such a situation looks set to remain.

lesbian and gay studies Political and academic movement which began in the 1970s and achieved a critical mass to enable it to be taken seriously in the 1980s. The City College of San Francisco became the first college in America to have a department of gay and lesbian studies in 1989, and even now it is more widespread in America than in other countries. In the UK, for example, although some courses on lesbian and gay history are available in some universities, only the University of Sussex has a lesbian and gay studies department. Whilst in the 1970s lesbian and gay studies concentrated primarily on CLAIMING historical homosexuals, by the 1980s it had two major focuses. First, it sought to redress the heterosexist bias in other college courses, such as history, by aiming to describe how people were able to manage their same-sex desires in the past. Second, it sought to focus on subjects which were of especial concern to lesbians and gay men, such as AIDS prevention, or the legal framework for lesbian and gay relationships. Extremely rigorous, the ideas of SOCIAL CONSTRUCTIONISM have come out of lesbian and gay studies to challenge the easy assumption that homosexuals in the past or in different societies have viewed

their sexuality in the same way as lesbians and gays within large gay communities can do now. With the growth of lesbian and gay publishing, the number of lesbian and gay studies books seems to have increased exponentially.

lesbian archives Lesbians have generally suffered more than gay men from the process of ERASURE from history resources, and it has been important for them to create their own organizations to collect lesbian publications, personal statements and photographs, to preserve the contributions they have made to their culture. In the UK, the first lesbian archive was created in London in 1984 to do just that. It was criticized however for failing to address the lives of black lesbians sufficiently. Thus in 1989 it employed a black lesbian project worker to redress this imbalance. The New York Lesbian Herstory Archives was founded in the mid-1970s and houses a large and growing collection of lesbian literature, art and memorabilia.

Lesbian Avengers Lesbian direct-action political group that was formed initially in New York in the 1990s to provide a focus for lesbian activity which would utilize the confrontational tactics employed by groups such as ACT UP and QUEER NATION. A chapter of the Lesbian Avengers was set up in London in 1994.

lesbian bar Lesbian drinking and meeting place. Until the establishment of a diverse commercial scene in the late twentieth century, bars were the linchpin of the lesbian community. Evidence suggests that working-class women in America were beginning to visit saloon bars by the 1920s, which would have been impossible in the nineteenth century. Thus it was probably among working-class lesbians that a bar subculture began to emerge. For much of the twentieth century, lesbian bars, known in the 1950s as gay bars, needed to be very discreet since their clientele could not risk discovery.

lesbian bed death Term used by some lesbians to describe the phenomenon of sex petering out during the course of long-term relationships. Many PRO-SEX dykes have blamed it on the strictures against women taking control of sexual matters imposed by the lesbian-feminist movement.

lesbian boys A term which was used by the American photographer Della Grace as the title of a photograph showing semi-naked butch lesbians wearing STRAP-ONS. This oxymoron is indicative of the queer framework used by Grace, which celebrates the breaking-down of stereotypes and the challenging of orthodoxies, in this case the 'boring' stereotype on lesbian sexual practice as non-phallic and unaggressive. The whole idea of lesbian boys has been challenged by feminists because it seems that lesbians really want to be gay men and do 'male' sex. Grace's earlier work is collected as *Love Bites* (1991).

lesbian chic The term given in the 1980s to the way in which lesbianism became a badge of glamour, associated with a kind of sexy and attractive rebelliousness. Pop stars implied that they were involved with women. MADONNA, for example, hinted that she was having an affair with performer Sandra Bernhard, while supermodel Cindy Crawford was photographed on the cover of *Vanity Fair* 'shaving' lesbian singer k.d. LANG. This was all very shallow, and the media folk who promoted it had no intention of actually exploring the difficulties of lesbian lives. It was not, however, an entirely new phenomenon. In the 1920s bisexual experimentation among women also became chic.

lesbian communes With the growth of lesbian separatism in the 1970s there was a movement to create women-only communities. Some of these were in cities, but many lesbians created rural communes away from the male values of urban life. Often, however, such Swiss Family Robinson life was not easy for our valiant sisters, and few of the communes outlived the 1970s.

lesbian connection The lesbian connection was a shorthand way of describing the debates which took place in the early 1970s in the feminist movement in America as to whether lesbian issues were necessarily part of the feminist agenda, and whether a public association with lesbianism could harm the feminist cause. *See also* LAVENDER MENACE.

Lesbian Connections Women's periodical, circulated free in the 1970s.

lesbian continuum A phrase first used by Adrienne RICH in her influential *Compulsory Heterosexuality and Lesbian Existence* (1978). Rich, a poet and lesbian feminist, uses the term to refer to the 'range – through each woman's life and throughout history – of woman-identified experience, not simply the fact that woman has had or consciously desired genital sexual experience with another woman'. The lesbian continuum then marks the entire range of relationships between women and not just those between dykes. Implicit in the idea of a lesbian continuum is the belief that there is an essential essence to all woman–woman relationships, and that being a dyke is a more extreme version of being a best friend. Rich's study is extremely important in that it stresses the similarities in experience between lesbians and heterosexual women, particularly in relation to male power. However, it has been challenged on two points: first, because it seems to imply that any female relationship is lesbian, regardless of whether that relationship is a sexual one; and, second, for its emphasis on male power and PATRIARCHY as the most defining and crucial element of all women's experience.

lesbian fairbody Arbitration body proposed by lesbians of the 1970s as part of a non-formal system of resolving disputes between members of lesbian communities. Chosen and agreed upon by the disputants, this lesbian non-formal legal system was mooted as a way of appropriating autonomy from a male legal establishment.

lesbian feminism While many lesbians subscribe to the basic ideas of feminism, there are very important differences between being a lesbian who is a feminist and being a lesbian feminist. Lesbian feminists subscribe to a particular analysis of society, this analysis being lesbian feminism. The fundamental principle of lesbian feminism is that the root inequality which is the cause of all oppression in all contemporary societies is woman-hating. Lesbian feminism argues that all crime, inequality and distress are the effect of men trying to enforce their rule over women. The key way that men maintain their power as a group, lesbian-feminists argue, is via the institution of heterosexuality. It is through the mechanism of heterosexuality that women are made subordinate and cowed into good behaviour. Patriarchal societies ensure women enter heterosexuality by stigmatizing, devaluing and applying sanctions to all alternatives. 'Love' and 'romance' are viewed as problematic because they produce a form of false consciousness which obscures from women the facts of male domination, aggression and violence. Once women are in heterosexual relationships they come under the control of men who ensure their good behaviour by threat or enactment of sexual violence, physical violence, economic sanctions, abuse of children, stigmatization as frigid and so on. If women try to leave, they lose their jobs, their children are taken from them, and they are subject to physical and verbal abuse. Having achieved the compliance of women through COMPULSORY HETEROSEXUALITY, patriarchy then works to appropriate all wealth and advantage for men. Given this system, it is impossible to be heterosexual and a feminist, because you are actually controlled by, and sleeping with, the enemy. For lesbian feminists then, choosing to be a lesbian is to choose to undermine heteropatriarchy; it is a political decision, hence the name POLITICAL LESBIANS. Lesbian feminists advocate a spiritual and moral separatism from patriarchy and male values, and various groups of lesbian feminists have tried to establish both small-and large-scale SEPARATIST communities. The aim of lesbian feminism is to destroy the system of heteropatriarchy and end the oppression of women by men, by withdrawing their support from the system and actively working to undermine it. Lesbian feminism was very strong in the 1970s and early 1980s (perhaps 20,000 lesbian feminists in the UK at the peak), but is increasingly under attack for a number of reasons. By insisting on the fact that the basic state of society is the class of women oppressed by the class of men, lesbian feminism has ignored the very real differences between women (and men), particularly class, sexuality and race. Many black women have argued that their racial identity is more important than the fact they are women, and do not believe that their basic interests are served by uniting with women against black (and white) men, but in uniting with black men to combat racism. Similarly, many lesbians feel that their interests lie as much with gay men in combating HOMOPHOBIA as with heterosexual women. In particular, it seems that racism and classism cannot be completely explained in terms of gender. In academic terms lesbian feminism fails as a global theory because it has no independently establishable causal links, and because it endows a huge geographically, linguistically, economically and culturally diverse group of men with a single monolithic identity and conscious agency; it can offer no evidence for how patriarchy makes decisions or acts. Nor can it offer external evidence to support the belief that compulsory heterosexuality is such a strong and pernicious force; if it was, surely we would all be straight? Many lesbians reject the idea that you can choose to be a lesbian as a tactical strategy in a political battle – with the implication that come the revolution and the overthrow of heteropatriarchy we can all go and sleep with the boys. In the same vein, PRO-SEX LESBIANS have argued that the concept of political lesbians is intrinsically flawed because it breaks the links between lesbianism and sexual desire for women. According to the lesbian feminist view, one is a lesbian if one detaches from men and becomes a WOMAN-IDENTI-FIED-WOMAN; it is not necessary to have sex with women. Key lesbian-feminist theorists include Mary Daly, Sheila Jeffreys and Janice Raymond.

lesbian feminist (1) A woman who analyses the world according to LESBIAN FEMINISM and who uses this analysis to develop her public politics and personal morality. (2) Used as a description of a woman's style and dress. In the straight media this is hashed out as hatchet-faced, fat, bald, no make-up, dungarees and boots. Among the lesbian and gay community a woman is usually described as a lesbian feminist if she does not respond to the fashion demands of the high street but sticks to short hair, no make-up, sensible shoes, trousers and no frills. Lesbian feminists do not wear leather trousers (too SM), high heels (too disabling) or cropped tops (too hetero-sexy).

lesbian (in)visibility Lesbians have historically suffered more from the process of ERASURE than gay men, since history (as opposed to HERSTORY) has usually been concerned with men and their actions. This has been something of a mixed blessing. Since lesbians were invisible, they were not subject to the same legal sanctions (although they were not immune to legal action by any means, and their freedoms were already constrained by the lack of autonomy that financial dependence on a male provider meant), and institutions such as ROMANTIC FRIENDSHIPS were allowed with the blessing of a society that did not imagine anything untoward going on between two devoted female friends. However, even in the twentieth century the process continues. Magazines and newspapers which supposedly represent the entire community give more attention to gay male issues, and political groups are overwhelmingly male. Thus, lesbian activists who believe that political progress cannot be made until lesbian lives and relationships are acknowledged and frequently seen have made the call for lesbian visibility central to their political strategy.

A popular post-STONEWALL RIOT slogan is, 'Lesbian visibility is lesbian survival.'

a lesbian is the rage of all women condensed to the point of explosion Political definition of lesbianism that made clear the experiential and theoretical links between it and feminism. The line was derived from the document that was presented by the RADICALESBIANS group in their LAVENDER MENACE zap of May 1970 on the Congress to Unite Women, a conference of women's liberationists from the East Coast which was taking place in New York City. The definition was part of the theory of WOMEN-IDENTIFIED-WOMEN which sought to change the way lesbianism was defined.

Lesbian Line British phoneline, based in London but with branches elsewhere, which offers support and information to lesbian callers.

Lesbian Mothers Resource Network Organization founded in 1974 in the American city of Seattle to deal with the issues of child custody, visiting rights, donor insemination (AID) and adoption. Its remit is to work so that any court cases deciding custody and visiting rights of parents over children are conducted without consideration to sexuality and instead are judged solely on the basis of giving the best settlement for the children concerned. It offers lesbians information, emotional support and access to friendly legal representation.

Lesbian Nation The Utopian objective of 1970s lesbian feminists who initially sought to create communities of women based on feminist values that together would then form a powerful space, a Lesbian Nation, which was not run by the destructive rules of testosterone. Lesbian Nation would be a reconstitution of the matriarchies which lesbian feminists believed had existed in prehistory.

lesbian pulp fiction Thrived in the 1950s despite a prevailing hostility to queer people. Such novels were allowed to be published because most of them were intended to be salutary reminders that lesbian sexuality ended in tragedy and death. Nonetheless, they were read widely by lesbians of the period, because they offered at least some recognition of lesbian sexuality which was otherwise unavailable. *See also* BRINKER, BEEBO.

lesbian safe sex An area of considerable controversy. There have been very few cases where woman–woman transmission of HIV seems to have occurred. Lesbians are of course at risk from HIV through other activities, such as intravenous drug use or sex with men. However, there seems to be almost no risk attached to sex between women, which does not involve cutting or blood loss. Oral sex seems to be fine except possibly when a woman is menstruating. There have been a number of safer-sex campaigns aimed at lesbians which have suggested the use of latex gloves and dental dams. The take-up on these has depended on a woman's erotic preferences.

lesbian separatism Political creed, common since the 1970s, a radical strand of lesbian feminism which declared that not only should women be women-identified, but also they should live entirely independently of men within women-only communities and women-only spaces. Separatism was extended to gay men, who were seen as socialized into the same roles as straight men.

Lesbian Sex This modern classic, written by JoAnn Loulan and published in 1984, is an essential text for any lesbian determined to create the sex life she wants – as Loulan says, 'to see sex as integral to who we are and how we interact'. Practising the details sustains sex in any long-term relationship.

Lesbian Sex Mafia (LSM) New York-based lesbian radical sex organization, founded in 1980 by Jo Arnone and Dorothy Allison, who placed adverts in the *New York Native* magazine. It was initially defined as a group for women into all forms of radical sex such as SM, fetishes, role-playing and use of sex toys. Like the GAY MALE SM

ACTIVISTS, with which it was contemporary, it helped to revolutionize the American SM scene. Although predated by the SAMOIS organization, LSM had an open membership rather than the referral system of recruitment which had prevailed throughout the 1950s and 1960s. In this sense LSM represented an unabashed upfrontness articulated by the SM community. This was especially significant for lesbians, since the lesbian feminist movement had traditionally characterized SM as antithetical to the aims of feminism and had associated it with patriarchal violence.

lesbian sexual radicals Alternative term for the PRO-SEX LESBIANS of the 1980s who sought to use porn, role-playing, SM and other juicy techniques to fan the lesbian sexual flames. This enraged the lesbian feminists who saw these activities as allowing male notions of power to enter the equal world of lesbian relationships. Lesbian sexual radicals argue however that women taking control of their sexual pleasure is a political act in itself, since women have traditionally been denied such control. *See* RADICAL SEX.

lesbian subculture Network of lesbian social venues and social life. In America, the subculture among working-class lesbians was already becoming considerable by the 1920s as many women moved into urban areas to find work.

lesbian thrillers Genre of lesbian fiction that took off in the 1980s, with works such as KATHERINE V. FORREST's *Amateur City* (1983) and *Murder at the Nightwood Bar* (1987); Barbara Wilson's MURDER IN THE COLLECTIVE; Iona McGregor's *Death Wore a Diadem* (1989); and Mary Wings' SHE CAME TOO LATE and SHE CAME IN A FLASH. The lesbian thriller is a spacious vehicle combining lesbian romance with a discussion of feminist themes and issues, and usually elaborating a theory of justice that is filtered through feminist thinking. Acts of violence are usually perpetrated by men providing exemplification of the injustices and social abuses of patriarchal society. The novels also revise the role of the detective to make it one that is more fitting with the lesbian role in society.

Lesbian Tide Journal of the Los Angeles section of DAUGHTERS OF BILITIS, which split from the main organization in 1973 because it felt that it was too conservative and did not fit the new radicalism of the decade.

lesbian vampires Since the characterization of lesbians and gay men as predatory infects straight discourse, it is unsurprising that such a notion should receive explicit depiction in horror films. In *Dracula's Daughter* (1936) Countess Alesca has a special attraction to women. Roger Vadim's *Blood and Roses* (1960) and Joseph Larraz's *Vampyres* both deal with lesbian vampires. Roman Polanski's *The Fearless Vampire Killers* (1967) features a viciously stereotyped gay vampire. These titles are included here, not for any progressiveness, but because they are indicative of the wonderful power of queer people to upset the straight world-view.

lesbians ignite Slogan of the GAY LIBERATION FRONT in the 1970s, still often worn on badges and stickers.

lesbophobia Homophobia that is directed specifically at lesbians, and which is equally likely to emanate from gay male communities and from heterosexual women as straight men. In the theories of LESBIAN FEMINISM, lesbophobia is not 'irrational' but part of the programme of patriarchy to ensnare women and control their lives in the male interest. Thus lesbophobia is a symptom of the problem, the solution to which is not found in educating individuals out of their views, but in women coming together to defy patriarchy.

Lesbos Greek island, not far from the coast of Turkey, which was the location for SAPPHO's educational establishment for girls, and thanks to the Greek poet has given its name to the most common word for a woman who loves other women. As a result of its heritage, Lesbos has become a fascination for lesbians. Natalie BARNEY and Renée VIVIEN journeyed there in 1904,

in the hope of founding a colony of women poets in honour of Sappho. Although their scheme didn't come off, the island is a popular tourist resort for lesbians, and women's camps are held there every year.

lesions The characteristic symptom of KAPOSI'S SARCOMA. In the early years of the AIDS epidemic, lesions were often the first sign that a person had the syndrome. Thus for some gay men the examination of their own body for the first sign of a lesion became a daily ritual, and the examination of the bodies of their potential sexual partners became almost obsessive. As a badge of having AIDS, the disfiguring marks unfortunately led to some gay men being ostracized within their communities.

Levi's Brand of jeans made by the San Francisco Levi Strauss company. Levi's particularly, but other makes of jeans as well, became essential as the epitome of masculine fashion within the BUTCH gay male communities in the UK and America in the post-liberation era, forming an essential part of the clone look. Some excitable men have even turned them into FETISH items, having a special erotic attraction to men wearing them (*see* LVs), desiring to keep them on during sex, and even taking them to the grave.

LIAHO Gay CONTACT ADVERT abbreviation for 'let it all hang out'. It is used by men who want to meet men interested in exhibitionist and uninhibited sex.

Lianna 1983 film directed by John Sayles about a wife and mother who leaves her family for another woman. Her coming out is not a smooth affair, and the film has been criticized for presenting a gloomy picture of lesbian love, as well as presenting a disinfected representation of lesbian sexuality. However, it remains one of the most well-known cinematic representations of lesbianism.

liberation, lesbian and gay Term that is usually used to describe the changes that occurred in lesbian and gay communities at the beginning of the 1970s, derived from the GAY LIBERATION FRONT and other liberation movements of the time. With the growth of lesbian and gay subcultures and institutions, and the development of large political groupings, it was felt that a great process of change was taking place in the lives of lesbian and gay people. It does not, however, mean that liberation has actually been attained, and the term has also been criticized by lesbian feminist critics on the grounds that it was a mainly male agenda which predominated and which concentrated on sexual freedoms as its goals.

library One of the main sites of self-discovery for lesbians and gay men, usually through the books but sometimes (mainly for the men) through the washrooms. Many of us, particularly in the dark days before the STONEWALL RIOT, remember going in to libraries to check for references that would give some validity to the vague stirrings inside us we knew marked us out as different. Starting with dictionaries, where we could check the words we were beginning to learn, we could go on to other works to find images or descriptions of others like us. Often such a search has been depressing, and sometimes the only books which even touch upon same-sex eroticism are those which exist to warn us off it, but the mere act of looking serves as a catalyst for the formation of identity.

Library of the Institute of Sexology Based in the Berlin headquarters of gay activist Magnus HIRSCHFIELD's Institute of Sexology was a phenomenal library of works relating to same-sex eroticism and love. In one of the greatest acts of philistinism in modern history, the library was seized by the Nazis in 1933, and many works were burned, including manuscripts by Karl ULRICHS and Richard von KRAFFT-EBING. In fact, the often seen photographs of Nazi book burning show the conflagration of May 1933 in which much of the Institute's collection was destroyed.

Lighthouse *See* LONDON LIGHTHOUSE.

lilies of the valley Camp slang for the unglamorous condition of haemorrhoids. Also known as grapes.

Lilith According to rabbinical writings, Lilith was the first woman; she was created simultaneously with Adam, and from the same clay. She was also the first bolshy woman, and was driven from the Garden of Eden, for refusing to be subservient to Adam. The same name is given to a vampiric night monster of Babylonian origin who attacks children in particular. Her name means night.

lily pond Name given by British lesbians and gay men to the tearoom (not in the toilet sense) on the first floor of the former Lyons Corner House in London's Piccadilly Circus. It became popular first with gay men who used to take afternoon tea there on Sundays, and then among lesbians as well.

Lippincott, Andy Character in the Doonesbury cartoon series drawn by Gary Trudeau. He came out in 1976, while he was fending off the romantic overtures of Joanie Caucus. He later died from AIDS-related illnesses.

lipstick lesbian Term coined in the 1980s for a lesbian who played around with her gender by rejecting the lesbian feminist proscriptions against the patriarchal regime of cosmetics. Sometimes used pejoratively by politically active lesbians to refer to a STRAIGHT-ACTING woman, whose lesbianism is not obvious. *See also* GLAMOUR DYKE.

lipsynching Gay pastime which involves mouthing and camping along to a backing track and described by actor Scott Thompson as 'the most popular gay sport after figure skating'. It is one of the staples of the DRAG QUEEN act. Often done poorly to schmaltzy numbers to disguise a lack of talent, when it is produced with artistry, as by the fabulous LYPSINKA, it can provide a masterly exploration of different cultural images. Lypsinka describes it as 'like watching a movie and believing in the characters. It's grand illusion, but it's real.'

Lister, Anne (1791–1840) The upper middle class, educated and unmarried mistress of Shibden Hall, Yorkshire. She left diaries written in code which were rediscovered and translated by Helena Whitbread and subsequently published as *I Know My Own Heart* (1988) and *No Priest but Love* (1992). These diaries describe not only how Anne ran her estate and her knowledge of the politics and culture of the period, but also her sexual relationships with women. For instance, in January 1825 she wrote, 'I soon took up her petticoats so as to feel her naked thighs next to mine. Then after kissing with my tongue in her mouth, got the middle finger of my right hand up her and grubbled her longer and better than ever.' Anne was clearly a dyke, and the existence of her diaries is problematic for those historians who argue that before the sexologists showed them the way, *c.* 1900, there were no lesbians but lots of non-genitally oriented ROMANTIC FRIENDS.

The Little Review Journal founded by the lesbian couple, Margaret Andersen and Jane Heap, in Paris in the 1920s. It contributed towards a literary renaissance in the city, and helped the careers of several lesbian writers including that of the poet BRYHER, whose real name was Winifred Ellerman. Andersen also wrote a defence of homosexuality in the article 'Two Points of View' which appeared in the journal. Andersen and Heap hosted literary salons in their Paris flat.

The Living End 1992 film directed by Gregg Araki, in which a gay writer (Craig Gilmore) teams up with an explosive drifter (Mike Dytri) after they have both learnt that they are HIV-positive. The two are forced to hit the road after Dytri's character shoots a police officer, and they embark on an odyssey which often includes sex and violence. The film, with its exploration of the turmoil of HIV and its projection of an atmosphere of grim desolation in which there is no room to be sentimentally self-indulgent (or, indeed, to deny oneself satisfaction), was hailed as the epitome of the new QUEER CINEMA.

lobbying Political tactics which involve targeting people in positions of authority with campaigns of persuasion to pressure them to use their position for purposes of change. Usual lobbying tactics involve letter-writing campaigns and petitions. Although lobbying campaigns can be huge in scope (for example, the British AGE OF CONSENT campaign in 1993–4 used mass letter writing to Members of Parliament), they do not have the same empowering effect on communities suffering injustice as DIRECT ACTION because they see authority figures as the primary agents of change, with communities serving to request their support. However, it is not always easy to draw a clear distinction between the two. For example a petitioning campaign will often serve as a vehicle for a number of activists to confront people on the streets about their prejudices against lesbians and gay men and thus acts as a small-scale direct action. Moreover, given that lesbian and gay liberation will necessarily involve legislative change at some point, lobbying is necessary; yet necessity will not lead to any thoroughgoing social change that will directly affect the lives of lesbians and gay men. In the history of the lesbian and gay movement, a historical division is often drawn between the pre- and post-STONEWALL RIOT period with lobbying being seen as the dominant form of action before 1969 and direct action sharing the spotlight thereafter. In the UK in the 1990s the lesbian and gay movement in London at least centres around the dual organizations of the STONEWALL GROUP which utilizes lobbying techniques, and OUTRAGE!, which espouses direct action and community initiatives.

Lola 1970 song by the British pop group, The Kinks, which tells of the attraction of a man for 'Lola', who it turns out is a transsexual; the discovery does not, it seems, dampen the singers' ardour. As one of the first popular songs which even touched on issues of homosexuality, 'Lola' became known as the 'gay song' for most of the 1970s, and was still being used as backing music for gay story-lines in British television in the 1980s.

London Lesbian and Gay Switchboard Usually known as Switchboard. It was set up by those involved in GAY NEWS in 1974, partly as a way to relieve the newspaper of the need to deal with calls from those seeking advice and counselling. Despite the fact that Switchboard offers a huge range of information, support, referral and services such as accommodation finding, it is equally known for being extremely difficult to get through to. Rumour has it that the phone got kicked off the hook back in the 1970s which hasn't yet been realized.

London Lighthouse Usually known as the Lighthouse. A London-based residential and support centre founded in 1988 for people with HIV and AIDS, the Lighthouse provides services for people throughout the entire experience of living with HIV, from diagnosis to bereavement counselling, as well as providing a useful social environment. It holds an annual fundraising sponsored cycle ride, called 'To the Lighthouse'.

Longtime Companion 1990 film directed by Norman Rene which was the first mainstream celluloid handling of the AIDS epidemic. It follows a mainly gay group of friends through ten years of the crisis, from the first chilling portents of the suffering to come, through the fear and helplessness when a number of them are struck by the syndrome, to the growth of community response to the crisis, the PLWA movement, and the beginnings of AIDS activism. Although eschewing anything too shocking for a straight audience, the film didn't pull any punches in regard to the emotional burden that the 1980s presented as gay men watched their lovers die. Set in a gay milieu, it also managed to communicate a sense of the strength and value of community.

longtime companion Gender non-specific term for a lover which became fashionable at the beginning of the 1980s, and was taken on by some lesbians and gays who wanted a way to describe their partnerships which did not have the transitory connotations of lover or boy/girlfriend. Before the 1980s it had been a stock phrase in obituaries and histories which allowed writers to avoid all mention of the homosexuality of their subject.

Lord Longyang (Longyang Jun) A character in the Chinese historical classic, the *History of the Warring States* (*Zhan Guo Ci*). Lord Longyang was a minister of the Prince of Wei and had a gay relationship with his master. From then on his name was used in Chinese writings to denote male homosexuality. The Longyang Club is a British organization for East Asian lesbians and gays.

Lorde, Audre (1934–92) American writer who was author of more than a dozen books of poetry and prose, as well as a founding member of Kitchen Table: Women of Colour Press. Having grown up in poverty in Harlem, Lorde's writings are all imbued with her political view of the world, and she has taken on the status of ICON for many black lesbians. In *The Cancer Journals* (1980) she gives a moving account of her own battle with breast cancer, as well as talking about the treatment she got, as a black lesbian, at the hands of the medical establishment. In her 'bio-mythography', *Zami: A New Spelling of My Name* (1982), she gave black lesbians new vocabulary to describe themselves. Lorde's work was always sensual, since she was always convinced of the power that being in touch with their eroticism gave to women. She responded to debates within the feminist movement over whether pornography was necessarily oppressive by arguing that women's own control of their erotic feelings should be separated out from patriarchal exploitation of women's erotic potential.

Love him...love him and let him love you. Do you think anything else under heaven really matters? Line from James Baldwin's novel, GIOVANNI'S ROOM.

the love that dare not speak its name The epithet for homosexual love is derived from the poem *Two Loves*, by Lord Alfred DOUGLAS, the youthful lover of Oscar WILDE. The work describes the wanderings of the poet in a strange waste garden, where he sees two youths: one 'did joyous seem' and sings of the love between men and women, while the other 'full sad and sweet' has the appearance of delicate sorrow. Both claim to be called Love, until the second eventually concedes and declares, 'I am the love that dare not speak its name.' A latecomer to the garden, the second love is called Shame by his companion. Used during the WILDE TRIALS, the epithet has been a standard reference to gay love throughout the twentieth century. In the mouthy aftermath of Stonewall it was commented on ironically, as *Time* magazine declared in October 1969, 'The love that once dared not speak its name now can't seem to keep its mouth shut.'

Loving the Fragrant Companion (Lian Xiangban) Chinese play, written by the Ming dynasty writer Li Yu (1611–80). In it a young married woman, Shi Yunjian, falls in love with the talented young woman Yunhua. To ensure that they can remain together, she arranges for Yun to become her husband's concubine.

LSD *See* ACID.

lube Lubricant, essential to smear on the dick and/or ass for smoothing one's way to an easy entry for anal sex or fisting. In the 1970s, the most prevalent types of lubricants tended to be oil based (*see* CRISCO, VASELINE) and were known generically as grease. After application, men were said to be greased up, or pregreased. With the advent of AIDS, however, water-based lube (such as KY) became essential since it did not weaken the rubber of condoms. A lube job is when partners oil their bodies and rub them together to achieve orgasm.

Lucian (*c.* AD 120–200) Greek satirist and wit. A free thinker, he was known in his own time as the blasphemer. His *Dialogues* include several passages spoken by lesbians which provide a defence of lesbianism. Lucian's lesbians are, however, bound

by gender stereotype; one boasts of being 'a man in every way'.

ludus Latin for game, the word was commonly used in the middle ages in writings which referred indirectly, or through punning, to gay sex. It was possibly a code word specific to homosexual circles as a way of referring to their sexuality without drawing explicit attention to it.

lunch Gay male slang term, popular in Australia, for a man's crotch. Probably developed because it would be something you'd want to get your mouth round.

luppy A young professional lesbian. The term was derived from the American neologism of the 1980s, yuppie. While lesbians have not had the same career opportunities as their GUPPY counterparts, a significant number of these well-heeled dykes have become a fixture. Related to, though not synonymous with, GLAMOUR DYKE, designer dyke and LIPSTICK LESBIAN.

LVs Abbreviation used within gay CONTACT ADVERTS by men who have an erotic interest in men who wear jeans made by the California-based Levi Strauss company (*see* LEVI'S).

Lypsinka American drag queen, the gay community's leading expert in LIPSYNCH-ING. Her frenetic show consists of a dizzying pastiche of nostalgic American iconography of women from club chanteuses through TV hostesses to B-movie heroines; not always meant to be recognizable other than in type. Lypsinka has become somewhat of an icon in her own right. Her glamorous svelteness has been seen modelling gowns by Valentino for the US magazine *Esquire*, in advertisements for the clothing chain Gap, and wearing Joan Crawford's clothes when they were auctioned at Christie's in New York, as well as performing with entertainer Sandra Bernhard.

M

M Abbreviation sometimes used in gay CON-
TACT ADVERTS. Rather confusing, it can refer
to either a MASTER or a MASOCHIST.

Mädchen in Uniform 1931 film directed by
Leontine Sagan and adapted from the play
Yesterday and Today by Christa Winsloe,
itself a version of her novel *The Child
Manuela*. Set in a Potsdam boarding school
for the daughters of poor Prussian army
officers, it depicts the love of Manuela, a
sensitive student, for her sympathetic
teacher Fräulein von Bernbourg. The film
was shown with one of two alternative
endings. In one, Manuela, having been
punished for disclosing her secret, intends
to throw herself down the central stairwell
of her school, but is saved by her school-
mates. In the other, she jumps from the top
of the building, and dies at the feet of her
devilish oppressor, the headmistress. The
film not only attacks convention through
its lesbian plotline, but also, since it is
directed by a woman, shows an understanding sensibility of women's relations
with one another.

Mademoiselle de Maupin Novel by
Théophile Gautier, published in 1835.
Rallying under the aesthetic slogan of
EPATER LE BOURGEOIS, it set out to challenge
comfortable bourgeois notions of gender
and sexual propriety by presenting a lesbian protagonist who projected a perfectly
androgynous appearance, a young woman
who was as attractive when dressed as a
man. Gautier explains that she is a member
of a third sex with 'the body and soul of a
woman, the mind and power of a man,
and…too much or too little of both to be
able to pair with either'. The novel created
the archetypal exotic lesbian that was to
figure so often in French decadent literature in the nineteenth century. There was a
historical Mademoiselle de Maupin who
provided inspiration for the novel. She
was a seventeenth-century French singer
who performed in male roles. She eloped

with a young woman who, on discovering her real gender, denounced her, and she was arrested. Although she was sentenced to death, a campaign led to her reprieve, and she went back to performing.

Madonna (Ciccone) (1959–) American pop singer, dancer and actress who has become the nearest thing that the late twentieth century has produced in the style of a real gay icon. Her remarkable influence over popular culture of the 1980s and 1990s is testified by the fact that she inspires either intense devotion or revulsion in practically everybody. Her fans, which include most gay men, admire her fabulous glamour, her tightly choreographed stage shows, and her ability to reinvent her image at will – from the be-bangled ingenue of *Holiday* to the sexually self-possessed dominatrix, Dita – of *Erotica*. Audiences have seen Madonna (almost literally) inside out after her 1992 book *Sex*, which explored her sexual fantasies, where she was not coy about shucking her clothes for the camera. And yet the high-octane image changes have served only to disguise Madonna as a real person – fortunately perhaps since the human touches of her film, *In Bed with Madonna* (1991), show her as a bit of a spoilt self-obsessive. Her detractors denounce her as brainless hype who, for all her sexual emancipation, is no real role-model for women. But she's got the money – so does she care? More recently she has cultivated a bisexual image, through her woman to woman snog in the video of *Justify My Love* (1990) and the rumours of her dalliance with lesbian comic Sandra Bernhard.

Madrigal, Anna The transsexual landlady in Armistead Maupin's TALES OF THE CITY, played by Olympia Dukakis in the television production. The lady of the anagrammatical surname, who gives each of her cannabis plants a name and each of her tenants a joint, has become a by-word for the mother-figure in gay circles.

mag-darling Tagalog term used in the Philippines, which literally means 'like darling' and is used to refer to a young woman who has a crush on another female.

Magazine of Experimental Psychical Studies German scientific periodical which in 1791 published a study of two homosexual men, believed to be the first scholarly work on the subject.

The Mahabharata Indian literary classic written 800–500 BC by Vyasa. It contains references to two female realms ruled by Alli and Pavazha Kodi, both female monarchs. A verse in the *Mahabharata* also refers to women sexually stimulating each other, and condemns them for using a dildo. Two references to HIJRAS also occur in this work. First, the work describes how the shikhandi or peacock, a symbol of sexual energy, was a hermaphrodite or eunuch. Second, it relates the story of Arjuna who after defeat in a game of dice is exiled for twelve years of which one year must be spent incognito. Having been sentenced in a previous encounter with the goddess Urvasi to lose his manhood for a year, Arjuna spends one year as a hijra. He is described as 'wearing bangles made of white conches, braiding my hair like a woman, and clothing myself in female attire'.

Mahmud of Ghazni (971–1030) Reigned over Khorasan and Ghazni from 997. The Sultan had a torrid relationship with a slave boy, Ayaz. Their relationship has become as celebrated in Arab literature as that between Hadrian and ANTINOUS in Western gay mythology.

mahu Originally meaning feminine, mahu is the name given to a particular class of men within Tahitian society, who adopt the dress of women and who perform work that is thought appropriate to women. They also seem to have a particular role of offering oral sex to Tahitian men who are not identified as mahu. The men who go to them for sex do not see it as conflicting with their heterosexuality, and often remark that the mahu give better head. Far from being outcasts like transsexuals within Western societies, the mahu were customarily given a privileged position, and traditionally the chiefs of particular areas would take them as 'wives'. There is also some evidence to indicate that in the past mahu played the role of SHAMAN within Tahitian society. Although some mahu still exist in contemporary times, the 'modernization' of Tahiti has meant that the role has declined and that younger Tahitians do not regard the institution as positively as their elders.

Maitrikarar Indian legal term for a marriage of friendship, a legally recognized form of relationship which was originally developed for businessmen to formalize an extramarital relationship. When in 1987 two policewomen in Bhopal, Lila Namdeo and Urmila Srivastava, registered their relationship in such a way, several other lesbian couples elected to do the same.

Making Love 1982 film directed by Arthur Hiller which tells the story of a young doctor who leaves his wife after realizing he is gay. It presents a reasonably positive, if a little oversanitized, view of the comfortingly middle-class relationship between the doctor (Michael Ontkean) and his novelist boyfriend (Harry Hamlin).

Malleus Maleficarum Book published in 1484 by Heinrich Krämer and Jakob Sprenger which gave instructions on how to identify a witch, and how to torture her to the point of confession. The work played a part in the sometimes hysterical witchhunts and mass murders which led to the deaths, according to some estimates, of some three million European women from the 14th to the 17th centuries. It was very often single or strong women who bore the brunt of these accusations, and they have been claimed by feminists as among the victims of patriarchy. The last trial for witchcraft in England was in 1712.

mamma American prison and working-class lesbian slang, first recorded in the 1930s. It referred to the FEMME woman within a BUTCH/FEMME lesbian relationship.

Man and Society The journal of the British organization, the ALBANY TRUST, which first came out in 1961. Following the findings of the WOLFENDEN REPORT, its editorial line tended to work the negative argument that the State should not extend its interference into matters of private sexuality if it could be demonstrated that these matters did not concern wider society.

man's man Among heterosexuals the phrase refers to a man of unimpeachably straight credentials. Among gay men the mere raise of the eyebrow can transform it into an entirely opposite reading. Highlights the odd fact that the same men who beat us up because we are gay also seem to want to spend all their time in male company.

manang bali Literally meaning man transformed as woman, the name was given within the Iban society of north-west Borneo to a man who had been instructed in dreams by supernatural forces to adopt the dress of a woman and to engage in homosexual relations with other men of the society. Such men were often called upon to act as SHAMANS or healers. Similar classes of men were common to many societies throughout south-east Asia.

manicure Apart from being compulsory for cutically conscious queens, the manicure is a necessary part of FISTFUCKING scenes. The fister's manicure involves cutting the nails very short, then filing down the remainder until they are entirely smooth. This ensures that there are no nasty snaggy parts of the fingernails which could tear rectal or vaginal tissue during fisting. Apart from being more comfortable, the practice has a health logic, since it means less likelihood of blood, and therefore less likelihood of transmission of any STDs. Fisters will also remove any jewellery before plunging in, for the same reason.

mannish lesbian A prototypical BUTCH lesbian. With the growth of the ideas of SEXOLOGISTS about homosexuality and gender at the turn of the twentieth century, lesbians were assumed to exhibit male characteristics, and wear male dress. Many lesbians themselves appeared to accept these notions, the most notorious being the

English writer Radclyffe HALL and the protagonist of her novel THE WELL OF LONELINESS, Stephen GORDON. From the privileged position of the late twentieth century, such women have been criticized for aping male ideas that an independent woman, or WOMAN-IDENTIFIED-WOMAN, must necessarily want to be male. Some historians have argued however that, in the absence of women-controlled discourses about sex, the 'mannish' image was necessary for women who wanted to demonstrate that their relationships with women were sexual, and not the platonic stereotypes of ROMANTIC FRIENDSHIP. In that sense mannish lesbians were the prophets of lesbian visibility and the stigma bearers for the negative reaction that was bound to entail.

mantee American prison and working class lesbian slang of the 1930s which described the BUTCH partner in a BUTCH/FEMME lesbian relationship.

Mapplethorpe, Robert (1947–89) Gay photographer, some of whose works depict homoerotic or sadomasochistic scenes; he is particularly noted for his portraits of black men. In 1989 there was a rumpus when the Corcoran Gallery in Washington DC cancelled a planned exhibition of his work. Protests from artists and gay activists followed, until the gallery apologized for the incident. A gallery official in Cincinnati was, however, later arrested for refusing to cancel the same exhibit.

Mardi Gras Festival, known as Shrove Tuesday on the Christian Calendar, but linked to the ancient festival of Candlemas, when people would burn a straw figure to symbolize the end of winter and to wake the sleeping earth. The festival was also part of a period of 'turning everything upside down', and participants would dress in the clothes of the opposite sex. Thus, the lesbian and gay festivals of Mardi Gras, which involve their gaudy costumes and cross-dressing, would seem to have long historical links. See SYDNEY LESBIAN AND GAY MARDI GRAS.

Margery Term that at the beginning of the nineteenth century was used as a generic term for gay men, though it was particularly applied to the transvestite male sex-workers who plied the streets of London. It probably derived from the CAMP NAMES that gay men would use between themselves. The word was common currency as late as the 1920s. Marge was sometimes used in the later part of the twentieth century in the lesbian communities to indicate a BUTCH dyke.

maricon Spanish slang term for a gay man, usually used pejoratively and with connotations of effeminacy, but sometimes adopted by those Latino faggots themselves.

Marie-Antoinette, Josephe Jeanne (1755–93) Queen of France. One of the incitements which led to the French Revolution was a series of political pamphlets accusing Marie-Antoinette of lesbianism. The pamphlets began to circulate early in the 1780s, and even outlasted the unfortunate Queen herself. One, published in 1792, was entitled 'A list of the persons with whom the Queen has debauched liaisons' and, among the list of over thirty persons, about half were women. Marie-Antoinette was also renowned for her circle of close female companions, among whom relationships similar to ROMANTIC FRIENDSHIPS were common. While the accusations were probably informed more by disquiet at the extent of Marie-Antoinette's power within the court, the mud stuck, and the rumours spread outside France. Anne LISTER mentions them in the diaries of her time in Paris.

mariposa Spanish for butterfly, sometimes used to refer to gay men. It echoes the other Spanish term maricon, but with added overtones of effeminacy and flightiness.

Marlboro Man Referring to the all-male models used in Marlboro cigarette advertising campaigns, the term was used to describe the new masculinity found on the gay scene in the 1970s. As a footnote, the original Marlboro Man was queer.

Marlowe, Christopher (1564–93) English poet and the greatest dramatist in Elizabethan England before Shakespeare, he revolutionized the art of tragedy in the theatre. Marlowe's life displayed reckless irreverence and disdain for convention, and he was for his time remarkably open about his same-sex attraction. In fact, when he was stabbed in the eye in 1593 in a tavern in Deptford, London, he was already heading for arrest for treason, and the charge of sodomy was not unlikely, since evidence had been collected against him. Richard Baines had reported that Marlowe had uttered the timeless opinion that 'all they that love not Tobacco and Boyes are fooles'. And Baines also alleged that Marlowe had repeated what seems to have been a common heresy of the time that Jesus and ST JOHN THE EVANGELIST shared the same bed, and that Christ used John 'as the sinners of Sodoma'. Homosexual love also appears as a theme in Marlowe's work. EDWARD II (1593) has become a text of gay liberation. In *Dido, Queen of Carthage* (1594), which is sometimes attributed to him, GANYMEDE demands jewels and a brooch from Jupiter (Zeus) before he will 'hug' him. In his poem *Hero and Leander* (1598), it is Leander who is described in the most erotic terms: his 'dangling tresses' of hair 'Would have allur'd the vent'rous youth of Greece/To hazard more than for the Golden Fleece'. Marlowe stands out as one of the few pre-twentieth-century individuals who not only admitted, but justified, his attraction for the same sex.

marriage Given the ubiquity of heterosexual marriage as a traditional building block of society, it is not surprising that, to a greater or lesser degree of seriousness, lesbians and gay men have constructed their relationships with reference to the holy institution. In the letters between JAMES I and George Villiers, Duke of Buckingham, the former seems to have taken on the role of the husband, addressing his epistles to his 'sweet child and wife', and declaring that he 'had rather live banished in any part of the world with [him] than live a sorrowful widow-life without [him]'. It would be too much to simply accuse such men of aping heterosexual forms of relationship; the use of the term marriage for sex in the MOLLY HOUSE subculture of the eighteenth century shows that even in less enlightened times, gay people were capable of subverting heterosexual life in a humorous and self-conscious way. In the WHITE SWAN in London in the early nineteenth century, marriage ceremonies were held between the male clients with a real chaplain, the Rev. John Church, in attendance. While these ceremonies may have mainly been bawdy send-ups, with the entire congregation consummating the match in the several beds that had been placed in the 'chapel', it is also likely that the Rev. Church saw a serious side to it. His letters indicate that he believed the love between men to be a spiritually uplifting emotion that was not exclusive of Christian sentiment, and while Church was accused of and prosecuted for sodomy, he never abandoned his ministry. In the modern lesbian and gay rights movement, activists differ over whether marriage rights are an important political goal. Some claim that lesbians and gay men are quite capable of defining their own relationships without needing the approval of straight society. At present the only country to offer legal recognition of partnerships on a par with heterosexuals is Denmark, under its 1989 partnership laws (although these did not include the right to adopt children). However, the METROPOLITAN COMMUNITY CHURCH does offer rites of blessing of relationships, which it sometimes performs in mass ceremonies at lesbian and gay pride festivals.

Mars symbol The symbol (♂) of the Roman god of war or the planet, Mars is now the most easily recognized symbol for men and masculinity. Like the VENUS symbol for women, it passed from astrology through the disciplines of biology and psychology into general usage. Since the 1970s, two interlocking Mars signs have been used to represent male homosexuality. Groups of the GAY LIBERATION FRONT in America in the early 1970s also superimposed the male and female symbols to serve as a sign for the common lesbian and gay movement.

Martin, Violet *See* SOMERVILLE AND ROSS.

martyr The French writer André GIDE bemoaned the lack of them: 'We have had WILDE, Krupp [*See* CAPRI], MacDonald, EULENBERG...Oh, victims! Victims as many as you please! But not a single martyr. They all deny it; they will always deny it...To try to establish one's innocence by disavowing one's life is to yield to public opinion.'

Mary 1788 novel which was an account of the relationship between Mary Wollstonecraft (1759–97), the English feminist and author of *Vindication of the Rights of Woman* (1792), and her romantic friend Fanny Blood. The two women opened a school in London's Newington Green which was successful. Nevertheless, Mary believed that Fanny's constitution was too weak for this, and persuaded her to marry a mutual friend who could take her to Portugal for her health. Fanny died in childbirth in 1785.

Mary-Ann British term for a male homosexual which originated in the mid nineteenth century and was the most commonly used word for a gay man in the Victorian period. A professional Mary-Ann was a male SEX-WORKER, the life of one of whom is most vividly described in the book SINS OF THE CITIES OF THE PLAIN.

masochism The deriving of (sexual) pleasure from the receiving of pain. The term is derived from the name of the Austrian novelist Leopold von Sacher-Masoch (1836–95), who depicted this form of sexual pleasure in his works VENUS IN FURS and *The Legacy of Cain* (1870–77). It takes two to tango however, and the practice has been incorporated into the consensual activities of SADOMASOCHISM.

masons and orders American lesbian slang for BUTCHES and FEMMES respectively.

master The TOP in bondage or SM sex.

masturbate To satisfy oneself sexually, usually with the hand, but also with SEX TOYS. The precise etymology of the verb is not known. There are two possibilities, both derived from Latin. The first is that the word is a combination of the Latin mazdo meaning penis and turba meaning agitation, the second is that it is a mixing of manus meaning hand and stuprare meaning to defile.

Mata Hari (1876–1917) Born Gertrud Margarete Zelle MacLeod to a wealthy Dutch family, she became Mata Hari, which means eye of the dawn, when she left her husband. She was part of Natalie BARNEY's chic set in Paris at the turn of the century. She was executed in 1917 after being convicted of working as a German spy.

Maternas The name of the lesbian society in Katherine Forrest's 1984 novel *Daughters of a Coral Dawn*. Unlike the egalitarian communities of other lesbian utopian literature (*see for example* THE WANDERGROUND), Forrest presents an unsettling view of a society ruled by one 'Mother', to whom the entire community is biologically related.

Matlovich, Leonard *See* GAY VIETNAM VET.

matriarchal calendar System of counting years developed by lesbian feminists in the 1970s which rejected what they saw as the male Christian calendar and instead began its counting from 8,000 years earlier when, according to the book *When God Was a Woman*, goddess worship was still the prevalent religion and women were powerful social actors. *See* MATRIARCHAL SCHOOL.

matriarchal school A group of nineteenth- and twentieth-century scholars who endorsed matriarchal theories of human social origins. The theories were first formulated by J. J. Bachofen in 1861 in *Das Mutterrecht* (Mother-right). All agree that matriarchy preceded patriarchy as the dominant form of social organization.

Mattachine Action Committee Short-lived organization that was set up by the New York chapter of the MATTACHINE SOCIETY in

July 1969 to placate the radical young lesbians and gays who wanted the organization to harness the energy that had been generated by the STONEWALL RIOT. However, when Dick Leitsch of the Mattachine Society suggested a silent vigil in Washington Square, it was immediately clear that the two groups had different agendas, and the younger activists broke away to put their energy into the GAY LIBERATION FRONT.

Mattachine Review Magazine of the MATTACHINE SOCIETY which began publication in January 1955 and reflected the changes in the organization which had ousted many of its founders and taken a far more assimilationist position on lesbian and gay politics. It ceased to appear after the dissolution of the society in 1964.

Mattachine Society Gay rights organization founded in 1950 by five men in Los Angeles, among them the inspirational activist Harry HAY. The men had been members of the Communist Party, which was reflected not only in their tactics, but also in the radicalism (for the time) characteristic of the organization in its initial years. The group had a cell structure, to which new members were recruited through discussions sponsored by the Mattachine Foundation, the public face of the organization. It was formed to 'liberate one of our largest minorities from...social persecution'. One of Mattachine's first activities was to defend one of their membership, Dale Jennings, who had been arrested by police on soliciting charges whilst out cruising. The subsequent acquittal was the first time that an openly gay person had been acquitted on lewd-vagrancy charges. The name of the society was taken from a type of music group found in parts of France and Spain in the twelfth and thirteenth centuries. The groups were composed of men that dressed as women, and their leader was always known as Mother Pig. The members were usually educated city folk, who would put on masks whenever they appeared in public. The name therefore referred to the need of homosexuals to mask their true sexual identity. The society had an initiation ceremony where members would hold hands and vow that no gay person need ever again enter the world and feel alone and unwanted and rejected. However, a convention in April 1953 in Los Angeles marked the takeover of the society by a more assimilationist strand of gay thinking, and the end of involvement by many of the original founders. In fact, the new leaders threatened to turn over to the FBI the names of any members who were also members of the Communist Party, unless they resigned. From then on, until the organization dissolved in 1964, Mattachine was far less radical, and its membership decreased.

Maurice Novel by E. M. Forster (1879–1970), finished in 1914 but not published until 1971, after his death. It depicted the love between a middle-class Cambridge graduate and the groundsman who worked on the estate of his former university colleague and platonic lover. It compared the satisfaction of open gay love to the sterility of a sham marriage. As it dealt with gay love, and what's more had a happy ending, Forster believed that the public would not be able to stomach it. It was later made into a film by the glossy Merchant-Ivory team.

Mayor of Castro Street The unofficial title of Harvey MILK, who ran his successful campaign for election to the San Francisco board of supervisors from his camera shop on the CASTRO, a shop which also served as a centre for the gay community of the area. It was also the title of Milk's 1982 biography by writer Randy Shilts, which is due to be made into a film.

McCarthyism Period of American history, 1950–54 which was dominated by the influence of reactionary Senator Joseph McCarthy (1908–57). In 1950, when he was chair of the Senate Government Operations Committee, McCarthy initiated an anti-communist witchhunt. Employees within the US State Department were hounded out of their jobs and saw their lives destroyed, and workers within the Hollywood entertainment industry, branded a subversive hotbed, were also targeted. The campaign was also extended to include suspected homosexuals, and continued until McCarthy was subject to a vote of censure in the Senate in 1954. Since his death in 1954 of hepatitis, many have testified that McCarthy was himself gay. The period was representative of the reactionary forces at work in American society in the 1950s. Yet, while McCarthy sought to persecute queer people viciously, the constant emphasis upon them of the period gave many a strengthened sense of their own identity, and of the political imperatives to organize which faced them.

McKellen, Sir Ian (1935–) One of the greatest British actors of the twentieth century, McKellen has recently taken his presence to the stage of gay politics, having come out in a flurry of publicity during the campaign around CLAUSE 28. As one of the leading lights in the lobbying organization the STONEWALL GROUP he was highly public in their campaign for an equal AGE OF CONSENT. Awarded a knighthood in 1991, McKellen provoked an argument by accepting the honour from a homophobic government, for which he was publicly criticized by Derek JARMAN among others.

McLean, Sharley (1923–) Lesbian activist and saint. Born in Germany, she has had a finger in one campaigning pie or another since she arrived in the UK in 1939, from the feminist movement to working as a counsellor for the TERRENCE HIGGINS TRUST. She has also stood outside for countless Sundays regardless of the weather to spread the word as a member of the HYDE PARK GAYS AND SAPPHICS. And along with all that she is a mother of two. Her commitment to the cause was recognized when she was canonized by the SISTERS OF PERPETUAL INDULGENCE in June 1993.

McTavish, Stoner Fictional lesbian detective, McTavish jointly owns a Boston travel agency, and is the eponymous hero of Sarah Dreher's novel *Stoner McTavish*.

MDA Hallucinogenic drug with stimulant properties commonly taken on the queer scene in the 1970s.

meat rack Any area which is bustling with gay men CRUISING for sex.

medicalization of homosexuality The name given by historians to the process which took place throughout the nineteenth and early twentieth centuries as the power to talk about sex and sexuality was passed from the Church to the scientific and medical establishment; homosexuality therefore went from being a sin to being a sign of pathology, a physiological and psychological aberrance. The term most often refers to the writings of the nineteenth-century SEXOLOGISTS, but also extends to the work of Sigmund FREUD and to the intervention of psychiatry into the explanation of lesbian and gay sexuality. The process was begun as early as the 1830s. In 1838 Sir Alexander Morison wrote in *The Physiognomy of Mental Diseases* that homosexuality was a 'monomania [or excessive preoccupation with one thing] with unnatural propensity'. He recommended the treatment of huge doses of camphor. As with many of the changes associated with the sexologists, controversy rages as to how positive a process this actually was, although given the depth to which scientific notions have informed the way in which we view sexuality it is difficult to envisage how things could have progressed differently. Not only did it usher in a period in which homosexuality was viewed as a medical 'problem', and thus open to 'treatment' through often barbaric means, but it also meant that negative explanations of same-sex sexuality were able to persist despite the waning of religion as a strong force in Western societies in the twentieth century. However, despite the fact that the notions of science in the nineteenth century hinged on simplistic constructions of sexuality and gender, with often negative consequences, it is arguable that without the idea of homosexuality as a particular individual characteristic (or pathology) the history of homosexuality in the twentieth century, including the rise and limited success of a lesbian and gay rights movement, would not have been possible (*see* CONGENITAL INVERSION).

Mediterranean homosexuality Often used as a way of referring to societies in which the social evaluation of male homosexuals largely depends on whether they take the active or the passive role in sexual intercourse (*see* ACTIVE/PASSIVE SPLIT). The phenomenon is particularly associated with the countries that border the Mediterranean Sea, although it is also observed in Asia and South America.

Megara In the Ancient Greek (present Turkish) city of Megara it was reported that an annual contest was conducted where young boys had to kiss the lips of an examiner who would rank them according to their snogging skills. The contest was possibly related to ancient male initiation rites connected with the worship of the god DIONYSUS.

Mehmed II (1429–81) Ottoman Turkish ruler who developed a 'child tax'. The Sultan's envoys would travel to all the villages in the European section of the Turkish empire once every four years and select the most attractive boys for the army corps, the palace pages' school and the labour corps. In addition many were procured for sexual purposes.

men's symbol *See* MARS SYMBOL.

Merioola A Victorian mansion in Edgecliff, Sydney, Australia which housed as its tenants many of Australia's principal artists from the mid-1940s, including a number in the forefront of the Australian avant garde. It became known as buggery house, because numerous residents were queer.

Metropolitan Community Church Non-denominational church founded for the lesbian and gay community by the Rev. Troy Perry in Los Angeles. The very first meeting of the church took place on 6 October 1968 and had a congregation of just twelve people. Now, in the 1990s, there are churches worldwide. The MCC has been no stranger to the homophobia of those who, we presume, consider themselves such real Christians that they have a licence to negate the freedom of worship of others. Two choir members were shot during practice in Kansas City, the San Francisco church has been burnt down, and anti-gay demonstrations have been common.

Michigan Womyn's Festival One of the largest and most popular of the WOMEN'S FESTIVALS that were organized in America in the 1970s and 1980s. The festival was first held in 1976, and took up some 600 acres of fairly wild Michigan land. Lasting four days, it provided a feast of women's music, as well as the space for women to live together in a women-only space for the duration. In the early 1980s controversy raged at the festival when a number of lesbians attempted to set up SM workshops, but were harshly criticized by other women. In 1982 the organizers bought up some land for the festival, which gave it an assured future.

Midnight Cowboy 1969 film which depicts Jon Voigt as a hustler trying to raise money to take his dying friend (Dustin Hoffman) to Florida. It was popular with gay audiences despite the antipathy that the two protagonists maintained towards 'faggot' values.

Midnight Masquerades Extremely popular costumed balls which were held weekly at the Haymarket Theatre in London from 1717, organized by John Heidegger. It was common for men to come in full drag, while women could explore their BUTCH aspects as sailors, soldiers and clergymen. The masquerades were popular among the MOLLY subculture, and gave the mollies a chance to take their fabulous 'masquerade habits' into the streets. The balls became known as dens of homosexual iniquity.

midwives to the lesbian subculture Name given by historian Lillian Faderman to the nineteenth-century sexologists, who, she argues, gave lesbians definitions around which they could begin to construct identities, and the communities based upon those identities.

Mikael 1924 film adaptation of Hermann Bang's novel *Mikael*, directed by Carl Theodor Dreyer. It is a gay love story in which a renowned painter, Zoret (Benjamin Christiansen) falls in love with his young (nude) male model Mikael (Walter Slezak). Although the young man is an ungrateful parasite, the painter bequeathes him his possessions, and dies happily, knowing that he has experienced great passion. It's that simple.

militance Within the different liberation movements, it is a relative concept; one woman's boat-rocking militancy is another's overly cautious moderation. Militants tend to be the people who are shouting louder than you are; though perhaps real militance is in maintaining the energy to keep struggling. As Audre LORDE said, 'It means doing the unromantic and tedious work necessary to forge meaningful coalitions...it means fighting despair.' Outside of liberation movements, it is a confused concept; as Emmeline Pankhurst put it, 'Why is it that men's blood-shedding militancy is applauded and women's symbolic militancy punished with a prison cell and the forcible feeding horror?'

military One of the major demands of some sections of the lesbian and gay movement, particularly among the mainstream groups in America, is the right of out lesbians and gay men to enlist in the armed forces. This was particularly relevant recently since it was one of the promises offered by Bill Clinton during his presidential election campaign in 1992 in return for the support of the lesbian and gay communities. Public disquiet at the thought of faggots in the army led to something of a botched compromise when the new President took over. That is not to say that lesbians and gay men haven't been there all along. Personnel discharged for their sexuality during the SECOND WORLD WAR formed the backbone of many of America's largest urban lesbian and gay communities. In addition, many lesbians chose to carry on in the military, or enlist, even after the end of the war since it gave them a chance to be in a women's environment, and allowed a career and travel that they would find difficult to achieve otherwise. While times were hard and any women who were exposed as lesbians were certain to be discharged, they developed their own networks to inform each other if an investigation was taking place, and ironically many lesbians were better at keeping their sexuality secret than naive straight women who were flummoxed by some of the authorities' questioning.

Milk, Harvey (1930–78) Legendary American politician and gay activist. He became an icon for the gay communities as a symbol of the fact that, in sufficient numbers, lesbians and gay men could exert political power and demand their own representatives. Milk had a fairly inauspicious start: he grew up on Long Island and served in the navy, after which he worked as a teacher and later in an investment company. He settled down into a marriage-like relationship with his lover, Joe Campbell, and then with Craig Rodwell, who was later to be active in the groups springing up after the STONEWALL RIOT. He was also conservative politically; until, that is, the whirl of liberalism caught him in the late 1960s, and he became active in the anti-VIETNAM WAR and COUNTERCULTURAL movements, finally quitting his job. He moved to San Francisco where he opened a small camera shop on the CASTRO in 1973, which served less as an enterprise than a community centre, and as the Castro increasingly became the centre of gay life, he began to realize that gay people were there in sufficient numbers to elect their own chosen officials. After several unsuccessful attempts, he was elected to the San Francisco board of supervisors on 8 November 1977, the first 'out' gay to be elected to public office in America, perhaps the world. He used his position on the board not only to protect the rights of the lesbian and gay communities (for example, against the BRIGGS INITIATIVE), but also to champion the people of downtown San Francisco against the powerful corporate interests that seemed intent on moving in. However, his was to be a tragically short period of office. He was murdered on 7 November 1978, by fellow supervisor Dan White, along with the liberal mayor George Moscone. His death came as a desperate blow to a community that had been seeing real gains, and the travesty that was Dan White's trial rubbed salt into the wounds. Gay people were excluded from the jury, and White was only convicted of manslaughter. Community outrage led to the WHITE NIGHT RIOT when a crowd of several thousand besieged the City Hall.

milk run In American gay slang of the 1970s to make a milk run meant to go cruising for sex, usually in public toilets or TEA-ROOMS. The term played upon the routine travels of a milkman, implying that such cruising was correspondingly habitual, and likewise involved a traipse around a circuit of venues to find an acceptable partner. A similar term, with the same meaning, was to go Christmas carolling.

Millthorpe House near Sheffield in the UK where gay social activist Edward CARPENTER lived with his lover George Merrill. The two met after cruising each other on a train, and Merrill moved in with Carpenter in 1898, and lived there for the next thirty years until he died in 1928. The house became a pilgrimage site for all manner of social activists, including Gandhi who paid a visit there to discuss vegetarianism and pacifism. After Merrill died, Carpenter could not bear to remain alone in their house, and he moved to Guildford where he lived in a bungalow until he died a year later.

Mineshaft A New York two-storey late night sex club that hosted nightly SM play. Internationally notorious as a public sex palace, it drew pilgrims from across the world eager to chart the wilder shores of sexual expression. Its many rooms were home to every variety of sexual play, although it occasioned criticism from 'real' leathermen who felt that many of the patrons were predominantly into VANILLA sex but with a few leather trappings. It was perhaps the pre-eminent ongoing leather

establishment from its opening in 1976 until it was closed in 1985, partly as a result of the hysteria which was attendant on the advent of the AIDS epidemic. The club was celebrated in the 1990 collection, *Mineshaft Nights*.

Minorities Research Group Early British lesbian organization, founded in 1963 by Esme Langley and Diana Chapman. It initially concentrated its work on counselling isolated lesbians and holding lesbian gatherings in pubs. From 1964 it began to publish the magazine ARENA 3, and the social meetings petered out.

Minority AIDS Project Los Angeles AIDS service organization which caters for black people infected and affected by HIV.

minority consciousness The understanding that one is part of a distinct group in society, with its own specific needs. Of course, minority consciousness usually only comes to those who are subject to oppression for one particular facet of their identity. Straight, white men see themselves as only part of a general population. Lesbian and gay assertion of their minority status was a late developer as a whole and only really began in the twentieth century after the SEXOLOGISTS had marked them out as a distinct category, and with the growth of urban subcultures in which they elaborated their own institutions that made their differences manifest. Even today however, there are those who claim that lesbians and gays are only a collection of individuals, rather than a distinct group.

A Mirror Ranking Precious Flowers (Pinhua Baojian) Chinese anthology dating from the nineteenth century which describes the same-sex trysts between male actors and their patrons.

Mishima, Yukio (1925–70) Japanese nationalist and writer whose works *Confessions of a Mask* (1949) and *Forbidden Colours* (1951–3) explore his homosexuality. *Confessions of a Mask*, a collection of the experiences of his youth and adolescence, is similar in a sense to the Western COMING OUT NOVEL, and describes the creation of an identity formed by a sense of difference: 'It was precisely what people regarded as my true self which was a masquerade.' *Forbidden Colours* was less successful critically. It portrayed the gay subculture of 1950s Tokyo and the initiation of the protagonist Yuichi into this life, and as such was one of the first works by a mainstream author that described the actualities of gay existence. Mishima was passionate about Japanese traditionalism, and was wary about the creeping process of Westernization that he saw taking place in Japan. His attitudes to homosexuality were similarly rooted in Japanese tradition, and he idealized the inspirational value of love between older and younger men which he saw as part of Japan's SAMURAI and Buddhist tradition. In November 1970, Mishima and four companions took control of the military headquarters in Tokyo, where he gave a speech attacking the constitution that had been forced on Japan by the Allies following the Second World War. He then committed ritual seppuku suicide by disembowelling himself, followed by the suicide of a young follower, who according to some was his lover.

Miss Furr and Miss Skeene Short story by the American writer and lesbian, Gertrude STEIN, which was published in *Vanity Fair* in 1922. It showed the huge sea-change that had occurred in public knowledge of the possibility of lesbian sexuality since the beginning of the century. Whereas twenty years earlier emotional relationships between women could have been written about with the general public seeing them as ROMANTIC FRIENDSHIPS which they did not imagine could be sexual, by 1922 Stein was aware that lesbian sexuality would be imputed to such relationships. Since in this depiction of the relationship between Georgine Skeene and Helen Furr it was precisely lesbianism that she wanted to write about, she was aware of the need to use covert signifiers to make the story publishable. Thus she talked about the women as GAY, a way of referring to lesbianism that only women within the lesbian subculture would recognize. This was the first published use of the word gay to refer to homosexuality.

Miss Thing The all-purpose epithet of American camp gay argot, Miss Thing can be used with the range of meanings that SNAPping has, and the two are often done simultaneously, e.g. when summoning another queen across the bar, when berating her for acting up and frightening away the stud you were cruising, or when trying to extract the story from her of the stud she was cruising the night before – it is Miss Thing to whom you are talking.

missionary work Slang term for the seduction, or attempted seduction of an ostensibly straight person by a lesbian or gay man, otherwise known as RECRUITMENT. The term plays on the often expressed fear by homophobes that lesbians and gay men are anxious to draw as many people into homosexual practices as possible, especially the young. The thing is that it is all true, but all lesbians and gay men worth their salt know that it is a case of redemption rather than damnation.

mist and moon studios Chinese poetic euphemism for the male brothels which flourished throughout the Chinese empire during the Sung dynasty.

Mister X 1975 play by Roger Baker and Drew Griffiths, and performed under the aegis of the GAY SWEATSHOP theatre company. It portrayed the kind of gay person who is willing to take part in the scene or visit gay plays, but who is unwilling to add a voice to the calls for gay liberation, and as such was intended to challenge its gay audiences. The play was first performed at a conference of the CAMPAIGN FOR HOMOSEXUAL EQUALITY in Sheffield, where it was rapturously received, and a tour of local CHE groups followed.

Miwa, Akihiro (1935–) The grande dame of the Japanese theatre, Miwa is a female impersonator and an openly gay man. His big break came when, while working as a waiter, he met Yukio MISHIMA and in 1968 was cast in Mishima's film adaptation of Rampo Edogawa's play *Black Lizard* about a glamorous empress of crime (Miwa) who will stop at nothing to get the precious rocks she craves – until she falls in love with the detective who has been hired to apprehend her. Miwa has also made a name as a chanteuse, especially known for his Japanese versions of French classics. Although the ONNAGATA or female impersonator is a standard role in traditional Japanese kabuki theatre, there was initially much resistance to Miwa's cross-dressing. His subsequent fame has helped to familiarize the Japanese population with the fact of gay sexuality.

moderne At the turn of the twentieth century, it appears that the word moderne could be used as a code way of indicating lesbian sexuality when approaching other women whose sexuality was uncertain. In *A Beautiful Girl*, an unpublished story by Harriet Levy, a friend of Alice B. TOKLAS, written at that time, the narrator relates an incident where she is approached by a woman in Paris. The woman is apparently requesting intimacy, and goes on to state that the narrator looks 'moderne'. Although the narrator understands her request, she feigns ignorance. The term is perhaps referring to the category of NEW WOMEN who, through the feminist movement, were demanding education and employment which women had traditionally been denied. It therefore draws a link between the gains of the early feminist movement and new opportunities for lesbian sexual expression.

Mohave origin myths According to Mohave mythology, Hanos, or transvestites, have been present since the beginning of the world. The Mohave also believed that in the early period of the mythical era the sexes were undifferentiated.

molly or **mollying cull** (1) British term for a homosexual man which had become popular by the beginning of the eighteenth century. Although used as a generic term for any gay man, the word is particularly associated with the subculture of MOLLY HOUSES that thrived in London at the time, and the

very definite social identity of the men within it. Even when not in the taverns, mollies had developed sophisticated ways of making contact with one another, especially for the purposes of cruising for sex. The subculture of the mollies appears more like our modern gay subculture than that of the intervening period. It involved sophisticated sending-up of heterosexual institutions as well as gender roles. Yet this appears to have been self-consciously done. For example, although mollies used female names and occasional transvestism, there was not the sense that a molly relationship need take place between a male-identified man and an effeminate one, nor that sex roles (active or passive) need necessarily inform social roles. Indeed, records indicate that mollies might switch from the active to the passive role for different sex acts. Finally, the court records following purges of the molly houses show no sense of shame or sin. Fear, certainly, at the possible penal implications of prosecution, but the mollies seem on the whole not to have let the anti-gay arguments of moral purists affect their self-image. The word seems to have been one of the first terms for gay men which was actually popularized from within the subculture, rather than having been co-opted from the pejorative vocabulary of heteros. It was probably derived from the Latin *mollis* meaning soft, which makes it apt for the camp world the mollies created for themselves. (2) Molly was sometimes used in the later twentieth century among lesbians, when a FEMME lesbian might be termed a molly dyke.

molly houses The centrepiece of London's vibrant gay subculture around the turn of the eighteenth century, molly houses were taverns where homosexual men from the whole range of professions in the lower-middle and lower classes would gather to be together and to have sex. The appearance of molly houses was a watershed point of gay history because they marked the first time that homosexuals came together as a distinctive minority to create their own social institutions. While cruising for gay sex had gone on since time immemorial, the molly houses were as much about socializing with other similar men as they were about finding sexual opportunity, although the danger of arrest for sex in public made them far safer than the other options. Moreover, unlike gay subcultures of the nineteenth century, the mollies did not on the whole marry, and there is a sense that there was great integrity in their lives. Transvestism was common in molly houses, especially when the mollies were due to go to a costumed masquerade. One account reads, 'Some were completely rigged in gowns, petticoats, headcloths, fine laced shoes, furbelowed scarves and masks.' At a trial in 1732, witnesses gave evidence that one John Cooper, known as Princess Seraphina, 'us'd to wear a white Gown, and a scarlet Cloak, with her Hair frizzled and curl'd all round her Forehead; and then she would so flutter her Fan, and make such fine Curt'sies, that you would not have known her from a woman.' While transvestism had been common in England for some time, and had been remarked on in Elizabethan times, the mollies were different in that they were not intending to deceive anyone as to their gender; they all knew the others were men, but were using dressing-up as we might drag up today – to look fabulous, and as part of their parodies of heterosexuality and heterosexual institutions. For example, they would use CAMP NAMES to address one another (*see* FEMALE DIALECT); would invent their own sexual versions of popular dances; and if two men went off to have sex with one another they were said to be going to marry, while the bedroom they went to was called the chapel. They even went to the lengths of holding mock births, known as a lying-in, complete with harassed midwife, groaning mother, hot water, clean towels and a wooden baby (or even the occasional infant cheese). But these were still dangerous times to express any sexual heterodoxy, and molly houses were so visible that they came under the attack of the SOCIETIES FOR THE REFORMATION OF MANNERS. Informants were paid to lead

police to the establishments, and in 1726 there were purges, including the premises of MOTHER CLAP. As a result some nine people, including Mother Clap herself, were brought to trial, and three were hanged. This did not, however, kill the molly subculture. In fact, on occasion they fought back. When the peace officers (the police of the day) attempted to raid a molly house near Covent Garden in December 1725, the twenty-five men within resisted, and a few of them were able to escape. Who said resistance began with the STONEWALL RIOT? In addition, the fanaticism of the moral purists seems to have backfired, and after the pogroms of the early eighteenth century the power of the societies declined and prosecutions for sodomy decreased. The molly houses probably began to decline in popularity in the mid eighteenth century, ceding predominance to more organized forms of male prostitution. Those that remained tended to become more covert, and less is known about them.

Molly myth The huge popularity of Molly Bolt, the saint-like hero of RUBYFRUIT JUNGLE, has made her a figure of lesbian folklore, even for women who have not read the novel. Her sense of justice in the face of everything has struck a chord both with many readers who respond to what she faces and with many women who are just recognizing their sexuality. As Sadie Benning says in her short video, *Me and Rubyfruit*, 'I had read *Rubyfruit Jungle* for the first time when I was thirteen or fourteen – [I] started reading it and I was like "I'm just like this character".'

mollying cull *See* MOLLY.

Mona's San Francisco working-class lesbian bar which was opened in 1936 and was one of its first queer joints. Situated on Columbus Avenue, it later had an awning on which was printed, 'where girls will be boys.' Women who went there to drink adhered to BUTCH/FEMME roles.

monasticism The ideal of monasticism, of drawing closer to God through seclusion which developed in ancient Egypt, has had a long history of association with both male and female homosexuality, which is unsurprising given the sex-segregated communities which it fostered. St AUGUSTINE warned nuns that they should love each other spiritually, not physically; whilst a sixth century abbot, Paul Helladicus of Elusa, wrote of the imperative to maintain a guard over the expression of lesbianism in convents. Other writings of the first few centuries AD also warn of the need to maintain a godly distance between monks. This association persisted through the middle ages, with successive Lateran councils placing stringent penalties on any clergy who were found to have engaged in homosexual conduct, and still exists today.

The Monocle Gay bar in Paris in the 1930s, owned by the lesbian 'Lulu'.

monotony Lesbian and gay reworking of the word monogamy which they saw as a tedious restriction of sexual freedom and adventure.

Montagu–Wildeblood affair Notorious British legal case of the 1950s which was responsible for creating a swing in public opinion towards some form of legal reform. The aristocrat Lord Montagu of Beaulieu had already been subject to an inconclusive trial in October 1953 for 'serious offences' involving two boy scouts. The attendant publicity spurred some MPs to request an inquiry into the criminal law regarding homosexuality. The affair gathered momentum, and in January 1954 Montagu, his cousin Michael Pitt-Rivers, and journalist Peter Wildeblood were charged with conspiring to incite two airmen to commit indecent acts. The tactics that the crown used in preparing its case were brought into question: the apartments of the men had been searched without authority, and the three men had not been given adequate access to legal advice after arrest. Although they were found guilty, public opinion had come round in their favour: crowds at the court expressed their support, while the *Sunday People* declared that the affair had 'exposed the

complete failure of our so-called "civilisation" to find any remedy for sexual perversion to replace cruel and barbaric punishment'. A number of MPs expressed their concerns, the government announced the setting up of a departmental committee to examine the 'problem', and a few months later the committee that would produce the WOLFENDEN REPORT was established.

monty Became a term for a gay man in the UK of the 1950s after the public spectacle of the MONTAGU-WILDEBLOOD show trial in 1954.

moral majority Term used generically for those lucky souls who hold what they believe to be 'traditional' moral values. The term was particularly used in Reagan's America to describe the right-wing bigots who had brought him to power and who opposed any form of liberal reform, from abortion rights to gay rights. Jerry FALWELL, who reached a new nadir when he declared that HIV and AIDS were the mysterious workings of his (presumably married and mid-American) god, set up an organization with the name in 1979. As a popular badge slogan of the day remarked, 'The moral majority is neither.'

Morocco 1930 film starring Marlene Dietrich, in which she kisses a woman on the lips. Unfortunately, the reason in the plot is to whet Gary Cooper's appetite, but nonetheless, the shot has entered lesbian cinematic iconography.

Mosaic British group for black lesbians of a mixed racial descent which was formed at the second ZAMI conference in Birmingham at the beginning of the decade. In 1993 Mosaic held its own first conference.

Mother Clap The proprietor of the very popular MOLLY HOUSE in Field Lane, London in the early eighteenth century. Margaret Clap's house was raided by peace officers (the police of the day) in 1726, and she was brought to trial. At the hearing, Samuel Stevens, a witness from the SOCIETIES FOR THE REFORMATION OF MAN-

NERS, described what he had seen when he had infiltrated her establishment: 'I found between 40 and 50 men making love to one another, as they called it. Sometimes they would sit in one another's laps, kissing in a lewd manner and using their hands indecently...Then they would hug, and play, and toy, and go out by couples into another room on the same floor to be married.' Needless to say, 'marriage' for the mollies meant something altogether more sensual and transitory than that other sacred institution. Clap was found guilty of keeping a disorderly house, and was sentenced to stand in the pillory, to pay a fine and to spend two years in prison. Her motives for providing such hospitality to gay men are not clear – maybe she was an early FAG HAG.

Mount Love Secret name of a mountain resort in California, actually called Bankhead Springs, which became the planned site of a lesbian and gay community in 1971, when a lesbian, Pat Love, suggested the buying of a mountain resort there. She kept the name of the place secret to avoid any action against the plan. It never became reality, since there were not enough people to put up the initial investment. *See also* ALPINE COUNTY.

Mousa Paidiki Collection of poems by the second-century Greek poet Strato of Sardis which concentrated on the love of the poet for young boys. The poems shared a number of attributes. Very often they were laments, either because the particular object of desire was felt to be unattainable or because of the process of ageing which would eventually destroy the boy's hairless good looks. Finally, a number of the poems compared the love of boys to the love of women, and found the latter wanting. For example, 'What!...Compare the rouge which disguises women's faces to the fresh complexion of young men.' The collection was known in Latin as *Musa Puerilis*.

Mouse Nickname for Michael Tolliver, the endearing every-gay inhabitant of Anna MADRIGAL's rambling shack in the TALES OF THE CITY series, spurned as low-life by the HAMPTON-GIDDES. Michael's search is for the one true love, a love he finds, loses, then finds again with Dr John, the suave gynaecologist. Sexily played by Marcus D'Amico in the television series.

Mr Benson Novel by John Preston which was first serialized in the mid 1970s in the American leather magazine *Drummer* and was the first blockbuster amongst modern leathermen. The two main characters, Aristotle Benson and Jamie, are respectively a top and a bottom. Benson is older, wealthier and more educated than Jamie, and communicates with other topmen, the underworld and law enforcement personnel which enables him to create a network of surveillance around his slave. The book depicted 'real' SM practitioners who played their roles all the time, rather than for the occasional sex scene.

Ms Title for women proposed by the feminist movement in the 1970s as a replacement to Miss or Mrs, both of which measured a woman's position by her relation to men. However, those who proposed it underestimated the ideological forces which bolster the language that men use about women, and the ability of those forces to respond to feminist innovation. Thus, rather than replacing other titles, Ms tended to get listed as a third alternative title on forms, thereby creating a new category whereby men could recognize feminists or lesbians.

mugawe Name given within the Meru society of Kenya to a male religious leader. The relationship between the twin authorities of religion and politics is conceived of as a relationship between male and female. Thus, as politics is male, religion is female, and the mugawe adopts female dress. He also engages in homosexual relations, and sometimes marries a man. *See also* SHAMAN.

Murder in the Collective 1984 LESBIAN THRILLER novel by Barbara Wilson in which two women, Pam and Hadley, set themselves up to investigate an outbreak of violence in two collective businesses, Best Printing and the lesbian separatist B.

Violet Typesetting. During their investigations Pam, who previously identifies as heterosexual, falls in love with Hadley. As a detective novel, coming out story and vehicle for discussing some of the issues of lesbian politics, the book is representative of the complexity of the lesbian thriller in general. Wilson also wrote *Gaudi Afternoon* (1991), *The Dog Collar Murders* (1989), and *Sisters of the Road* (1987).

Musa Puerilis Collection of epigrams dedicated to the pleasures of the love of boys, written by the second-century Greek poet Strato.

muscle Mary A gay muscle fiend. The kind of gay man who spends hours in the gym pumping his biceps to the size of watermelons, and creating the kind of cleavage of which Faye Dunaway would be envious, before rushing home to slam a quiche in the oven.

musical Music, like theatre, has been one of those areas of human life to which queers seem drawn. Whether we are naturally more creative, or whether it is because the arts exercise a more liberal regime, is unsure. Probably both. The nineteenth-century sex researcher Havelock ELLIS noticed this phenomenon in his STUDIES IN THE PSYCHOLOGY OF SEX. He writes, 'As regards music, my cases reveal the aptitude which has been remarked by others as peculiarly common among inverts.' As a result, along with words such as temperamental and creative, 'musical' served as a covert signifier for homosexuality in the less-enlightened 1940s and 1950s. Thus in film, theatre and television, characters with these less than manly characteristics could be read as queer by discerning audiences. The terms also came in useful for people to refer to themselves while subtly dropping a few hairpins to others, in order to make contact.

mutual masturbation Sexual act between two or more people in which both partners masturbate the other simultaneously or consecutively. In the 1980s, with the advent of HIV, it became the most common sexual activity between gay men.

It is often assumed that lesbian sex (without a dildo) is mutual masturbation by definition, but this assumption ignores the wonderful activities lesbians actually carry out in bed and elsewhere.

My Beautiful Laundrette 1986 film directed by Stephen Frears, and written by Anglo-Pakistani playwright Hanif Kureishi. Set among London's South Asian community, it explores questions about racism and assimilation, by portraying the love between a young blonde punk with a right-wing past (Daniel Day Lewis), and the son of a Pakistani writer (Gordon Wainecke), who jointly open a laundromat.

my name is going to head the list Response by Second World War WAC Sergeant Johnnie Phelps to General Eisenhower, who had made a request for her to disclose the names of all the lesbians in her battalion. She added that he'd also need to round up half the battalion, some of whom had been decorated. Eisenhower cancelled the order.

my only books were women's looks The description used by Natalie BARNEY of her schoolgirl days. She went on, 'At twelve I knew exactly what I liked and I firmly decided not to let myself be diverted from my tastes.' The rhyming phrase was actually used by Irish musician Thomas Moore (1779–1852) in *Irish Melodies* (1807).

Mykonos Greek island, and popular tourist destination for gay men. With its nightlife, nude beaches and gay hotels, Mykonos vies with SITGES to be the European equivalent of FIRE ISLAND.

The Myrmidons Play by the Greek playwright Aeschylus, written about the fifth century BC, which unfortunately has been lost to posterity. However, references to it are found in the writings of others. The play dealt with the relationship between Achilles and his lover Patroclus who was killed during the Trojan war. The aggrieved speech of Achilles following Patroclus' death was reportedly particularly memorable.

myrtle Another plant which has been used to indicate homosexuality. The myrtle appeared in a wreath with another plant, CALAMUS, in the symbol used by members of the late-nineteenth century gay organization THE ORDER OF CHAERONEA. Myrtle also appears in a poem in THE THOUSAND AND ONE NIGHTS, being held by an attractive boy who is the object of the poet's desire.

mysophilia Technical term for a sexual interest in mud and dirt.

myth of lesbian impunity Contrary to popular belief, lesbian sex has historically been prohibited and punished with the same or similar laws to those dealing with gay male sex. The most notable exception to this is the UK, where lesbian sex has never been legally prohibited. However, in France, Spain, Italy, Germany, Switzerland and America, lesbian sex has usually been punishable under the sodomy laws. Nevertheless, records do suggest that prosecutions for lesbian sex were much more rare than for gay male sex. These were much more likely to occur when the women accused were passing women, economically powerful or using a dildo. In the early 1990s a British lesbian was jailed for fraud when she had sex with women whilst allegedly passing as a man, which shows how the social strictures against lesbianism can be implemented even when 'lesbianism' is not a crime.

Narcissus

NACHO *See* NORTH AMERICAN CONFERENCE OF HOMOPHILE ORGANIZATIONS.

naff Meaning bad in the gay slang POLARI, the term has become popular in the 1980s to refer to something déclassé. The derivation is unclear. Three possibilities are a reversal of fanny/fan, from the initials of not a fuck or not available for fucking, or from the French word for navel.

The Naked Civil Servant 1968 autobiography of Quentin CRISP which details his odyssey from screaming outcast to stately homo, his tribulations in 1930s and 1940s Soho, and the support of other blue-rinsed queens. The book was filmed in 1975, with John Hurt in the lead, which launched Crisp into stardom. The film, shown several times on British television, provided support for many a homo-in-distress, and a role model of courage and kindness. The title derives from his stint as a live model for art classes. Oh, and he throws out a rope of hope for those among us who are challenged by cleaning, when he says, 'There was no need to do any housework at all. After the first four years the dirt doesn't get any worse.'

Names Project The initiative which seeks to celebrate the lives of the many people who have been lost to the AIDS epidemic through the huge and moving project of the AIDS quilt. It started in 1986 when gay activist Cleve Jones, feeling despair over the death of a best friend, sat on his patio with another friend and began painting the names of friends they had lost on a large piece of cloth. The process enabled him to work through many of his feelings, and he found it so therapeutic that he asked other friends to do the same. Many people contributed 3 x 6 foot panels, and the quilt steadily grew. It was displayed in the Capitol Mall in Washington DC in October 1987, where it covered a space larger than two football fields, and has been shown in many other cities in

America and abroad since. It demonstrates the human impact the AIDS epidemic has had, allows survivors a creative means of expressing their grief, and also raises funds for AIDS initiatives. Similar quilts have been initiated in other countries worldwide.

namsadang troupes Korean all-male theatre groups which seem to have functioned as homosexual communes. The troupes performed music, acrobatic acts and puppet plays, and were composed of about 40–50 homeless males. They were divided into groups of Sutdongmo (butch) and Yodongmo (queen). All newcomers belonged to Yodongmo. Until new members were promoted to become junior performers, they were expected to wear women's dress and behave as females within the group. There was often great competition for good-looking newcomers among the other performers. The newcomers would sometimes sleep with servants in the village where the performance was taking place.

nancy One of those female names which has historically become attached to gay men. Common in Britain and North America in the nineteenth century, it is still common in the UK in the twentieth century. 'Miss Nancy' was the nickname earned by early nineteenth century US Senator William Rufus de Vane King, due to the rumours circulating about his sexuality and his putative relationship with James Buchanan. In Britain 'nancy-girl' was sometimes used in the mid-twentieth century to refer to lesbians. The word is also recorded in the nineteenth century as a term for the butt.

napkin ring *See* COCK RING.

Narcissus In Greek mythology a beautiful youth who was loved by the nymph Echo, but was indifferent to her charms. As recompense he was similarly fated to fall hopelessly in love. Stopping to drink at a fountain one day, he saw his own reflection and fell head over heels in love with himself. Unable to kiss his own image, he jumped into the fountain and died. When the nymphs came to bury him, all they found was the purple flower which bears his name. It is from this myth that the term narcissism for self-devotion is derived, a word which is often applied to lesbians and gay men by clever souls who imagine that just because we go for the one half of humanity that bears the same genitals we are infatuated with ourselves.

nasha devka Russian phrase, literally meaning our girl, which is used by gay men within camp Russian slang to refer to a fellow gay man. Similar to the English usage of 'she's one of us'.

National Coalition of Black Lesbians and Gays American organization, based in Washington DC which was founded in 1978 to work at a grass-roots level to empower local communities of black lesbians and gay men. It has also worked around the issues of HIV and AIDS in black communities.

National Lesbian and Gay Task Force American lesbian and gay rights organization founded in 1973 to lobby, educate and advocate for lesbian and gay rights. It also organizes at a grass-roots level. Since 1990 the organization has funded two full-time lobbyists situated in Washington DC, one of whom specifically works on health issues, particularly AIDS. It has also targeted homophobic violence and the repeal of the sodomy laws of some American states for particular campaigns.

National March on Washington for Lesbian and Gay Rights Huge annual lesbian and gay march held in Washington DC. The first such march was held in October 1979, and attracted up to 100,000 participants.

National Organization for Women, The (NOW) American feminist organization, founded in 1966, with about 300,000 members; it rubbed up against LESBIAN FEMINISM in 1970 and 1971. *See* LAVENDER MENACE.

National Viewers and Listeners Association British society headed by the 'moral' crusader Mary Whitehouse (1910–), that campaigns against the representation of violence and sex in films, theatre and television. It was formed from her 'Clean Up TV' Campaign, which began in 1964. Whitehouse was worried about the growing acceptance of lesbian and gay sexuality, and thus the society was particularly fond of attacking any representation of homosexuality. In 1977 she successfully prosecuted GAY NEWS (*see* LEMON CASE). In 1981 the association launched a legal case against the play *Romans in Britain* by Howard Brenton, showing at the National Theatre, which featured a simulated act of anal rape by Roman soldiers. The lawsuit actually tried to prosecute the play under public decency legislation on the grounds that such acts would not be permissible in public places. The case was swiftly dismissed. Sadly, Whitehouse resigned as head of the association in 1993.

natural A construct which is wielded by those who have power over the institutions of society. Thus lesbian and gay sex is contradictorily condemned as unnatural on the grounds that it is both like and unlike nature; it is the base lust of the animal world, and yet at the same time it is something that is found only amongst humankind (an assertion which is incidentally not true; there have been cases of same-sex relationships between lions, giraffes and swans, among others). Many lesbians and gays have responded by asserting that they did not choose their sexuality, it chose them, and it is the most natural thing for them to follow their own desire in seeking pleasure. As Joe Orton said, 'I've never outraged Nature. I've always listened to her advice and followed it wherever it went.' Of course, once we realize that we are equally part of nature, nothing that we do willingly is unnatural, the door is opened to the possibility of reinventing nature; for Kinsey, the idea of unnatural sex was a contradiction in terms: 'The only unnatural sex act is that which you cannot perform.'

Nautilus Make of weights machine which featured heavily on the gay male scene in the 1970s, when gays suddenly discovered that bodies were plastic and if they couldn't have the hunk they fancied just yet, they could turn themselves into him. The Nautilus-toned body was an essential part of the BUTCH look of the time.

Navajo origin myths In the social origin mythology of the Navajo tribe of Native Americans, homosexuals are described as being rich and having control of all wealth. As a consequence they were usually put in charge of the household. Another Navajo myth tells of how the men and women of the tribe quarrelled with one another and went to live on opposite sides of a river. They were reconciled by the mediation of a supernatural berdache figure. This myth points to the special position of lesbian and gay people in reconciling the opposing gender roles within society.

Navratilova, Martina (1956–) Czech-born American tennis phenomenon and lesbian pin-up. Navratilova was already a rising star of the grass court when she visited America in 1973. In 1975 she defected, and has since reigned over tennis like no other, capturing the Wimbledon title no fewer than nine times. As if those muscly legs in those little tennis skirts wasn't enough for the legions of dyke fans that follow her around, Navratilova has always been quite open about her lesbianism – with only one slight blip. When she applied for American citizenship, she described herself as bisexual, in the hope that this would make her application more acceptable. In 1978, a relationship began with Rita Mae BROWN after she had arranged a meeting to research a character in a book she was writing, but media publicity about the affair made Navratilova resign as head of the Women's Tennis Association. Her later affair with Judy Nelson provided positive images for dykes worldwide as Navratilova would routinely climb into the crowd to snog her lover after winning games. In recent years she has stepped up her campaigning work for lesbian and gay rights, speaking at the march on Washington DC in April 1993, and filing a law suit against the enactment of the homophobic Amendment 2 in Colorado which bans legal protection for lesbians and gays in the fields of housing and employment. In 1994 she announced her retirement before playing a final, fabulous semi-final at Wimbledon.

NAZ project Founded in 1991, a self-help and social care group for people within the South Asian and Muslim communities in the UK who are living with or affected by HIV and AIDS. It also offers counselling and support facilities.

necklace For much of the twentieth century any necklace worn by a man was judged to be a sign of gayness. Within the COUNTER-CULTURE of the 1960s many men (straights included) also chose to wear neck adornments as part of their unisex look, which sent out rather confusing signals.

necktie, red One of the items of clothing used by gay men in the 1920s and 1930s, according to the gay activist Harry HAY, to covertly indicate their sexuality to other gay men. According to Hay another way to 'spot one' was if they were wearing a hankie that matched their tie. A prototypical HANKIE CODE.

nelly Either an effeminate gay man, or any activity or thing considered to be slightly on the swishy side. According to *The Oxford English Dictionary*, the term has been used since the beginning of the 1960s, and derives either from the female name or from the rhyming slang, Nelly Duff for puff (originally meaning breath of life, but the extension is obvious). More popular in America (the British preferring NANCY), the word has been claimed by gay men as a sign of their subcultural difference. *See* GOD SAVE US NELLY QUEENS.

Nero (AD 37–68) Roman emperor who is notorious for fiddling while Rome burnt. He was also reported to have married a castrated slave boy in a public wedding ceremony.

Nestle, Joan (1941–) American lesbian writer and activist, Nestle co-founded in the mid-1970s the New York Lesbian Herstory Archives, which for a long time shared her home. Through her work at the archives she has documented the experi-ence of lesbians as it was actually lived. In particular, she has become known through her writings for 'reclaiming' BUTCH and FEMME relationships from lesbian feminist critics who criticized the roles as aping het-erosexual values and perpetuating male-identified power relations. In *Butch-Femme Relationships: Sexual Courage in the 1950s* she argued not only that butch and femme lesbians were self-consciously role-playing with their gender, rather than being trapped within the paradigms of hetero-sexual gender identification, but also that these lesbians were the trailblazers and stigma-bearers for the lesbian communi-ties by virtue of their visibility: 'Butch-femme women made Lesbians visible in a terrifyingly clear way in a historical period when there was no Movement protection for them.'

Neuengamme German site of a Nazi con-centration camp, and also of a small memorial stone, which was the first monu-ment laid to the memory of gays who died during the Second World War. It was paid for by a Hamburg lesbian and gay organi-zation.

new age leathermen/women Term for leatherpeople who seek to combine their leather and SM interests with a search for spiritual meaning. They point out that during SM play the altered state of con-sciousness achieved is comparable with the ecstasies and raptures of religious transformation. They also assert that SM not only explores the full range of sensory stimulation, but also allows the practi-tioner to reconnect with elements of the psyche which are displaced by the enforced rationality of 'civilized' life. Thus it allows a completeness which is spiritual in scope. Although the term, like many other new-ageisms, is more properly a phenomenon of the 1980s, leatherpeople throughout the decades have pointed to the transformative implications of their sexuality.

New Alliance for Gay Equality Organization set up in 1978 by Californian lesbians and gay men in order to fight the homophobic BRIGGS INITIATIVE.

the new woman (1) The title is particularly associated with a phenomenon of the late nineteenth and early twentieth centuries in America and Europe. The new woman took advantage of the new possibilities for women's education, had a professional career and led an independent life. (2) The name has also been given throughout the twentieth century to the women who have been at the forefront of the new lifestyles which had become acceptable for them. Thus, in America after the First World War, when an influx of immigrants brought a diversity of cultures which helped to relax social mores, and after suffrage for women had been won, those women who wore less restricted clothing, who put off marriage and who lived a fuller life than that of wife or mother were also known as new women. The term has also been used in the twentieth century for (heterosexual) women who are assertive about their sexuality.

New York Lesbian Food Conspiracy Food cooperative, set up with the objective of moving towards women's self-sufficiency in the 1970s. It distributed food at cost price to women's credit cooperatives, which could then distribute the food to their members. The lesbian feminists involved wanted to create women's economic as well as cultural and political autonomy, so that separatism would become a real possibility.

New York Native Weekly newspaper for lesbians and gay men which was founded in 1981. Although based in New York, it carries local and national news.

Ni-chome The district in Tokyo where the majority of the capital's gay bars are found. It is part of the Shinjuku neighbourhood which hosts both swish stores and restaurants and the seedier stratum of Japanese life in the form of the many massage parlours and sex shows. The bars in Ni-chome, all thrown on top of one another, are remarkable for the way in which they divide themselves to cater for clientele with every conceivable preference. There are bars for teenagers, bars for every different foreign nationality, bars for CHUBBIES (though are their chasers allowed in?), as well as karaoke joints and drag shows. There are, however, relatively few places for lesbians. The bar scene was a legacy of the social venues that were created to service the Tokyo Olympic Games in 1964.

nick vamps 1950s British lesbian prison slang for women who are not necessarily lesbians on the outside but when they go to prison they go after the BUTCH dykes inside.

Night of the Long Knives On 30 June 1934, Hitler ordered the secret police, the Gestapo, to destroy the stormtroopers, or Brownshirts, under the control of the gay Ernst Röhm, whom Hitler considered to have gained too much power. Some 200 people were rounded up and executed, many of whom were accused of homosexual behaviour. *See also* PARAGRAPH 175.

Nighthawks 1978 film directed by Ron Peck, about a gay teacher who cruises in bars and clubs and who has casual sexual encounters by night. The teacher begins to realize that he is leading a double life, and comes out to his students when they ask him if he is 'queer'.

nightsweats Like LESIONS, nightsweats were symptoms attached early on to the onset of AIDS-related illnesses, and gay men in the early 1980s sometimes induced sweats by their fear of having one. In gay fiction of the 1980s and 1990s the mention of sweating and sodden sheets is usually enough to indicate the presence of HIV.

Nilsen, Pam Lesbian detective in Barbara Wilson's *Murder in the Collective*. Nilsen works in a printing collective in Seattle, Washington.

No. 96 Popular Australian soap opera, first screened in 1971. Revolving around a group of residents of a Sydney block of flats, the show was renowned for its liberal depiction of sex and nudity. This liberalism extended as far as homosexuality and, as well as lesbian characters, the regular Don Findlayson, a nice guy popular with the audience, came out as gay, and embarked on a series of gay relationships and one-night stands. The ratings for the show were consistently high, and it spawned imitators which also had gay characters. The show helped make gay sexuality a talking-point in Australian society.

no glove, no love Slogan used in SAFER SEX education in South Africa.

nonoxynol-9 Chemical, found in most spermicides, which is effective in destroying the HIV virus. This property was first identified by Bruce Voeller, of the Mariposa Foundation in California.

Norma Trist, or Pure Carbon: A Story of the Inversion of the Sexes 1895 novel by Dr John Wesley Cahart. Its heroine Norma is physically attracted to other women. Norma murders a former lover who is about to be married. While not exactly a happy story, it is notable for the fact that Norma considers her sexuality to be entirely natural for her, and gives a spirited defence in the witness box. Thus it introduces the idea that what is not 'normal' for a majority might be normal for a minority.

normal Can refer to what is statistically more common, but is often confused by heterosexuals to refer to whatever it is that they condone morally. Lesbians and gay men often echo this confusion by stressing the findings of sex researchers such as Alfred KINSEY to demonstrate the potential size of lesbian and gay communities. Others argue that only the individual can decide what is normal for them and that it need not be what is normal to others. An early version of this argument was adopted in 1895, by the lesbian heroine of the novel NORMA TRIST. Such a conception is essential to the development of MINORITY CONSCIOUSNESS.

The Normal Heart Play by gay AIDS activist Larry KRAMER which opened at New York's Public Theatre in April 1985,

and at the Royal Court in London in 1986. Not known for his grasp of understatement, Kramer produced a vehicle for his polemics against both the establishment reaction to the AIDS epidemic and the effects of gay liberation in the 1970s. Set in the early years of the epidemic, its protagonist Ned Weeks argues forcefully against Government sloth in responding to the growing crisis, and communicates the sense of emergency of which Kramer was one of the first to be conscious. Yet he also aims his criticisms at the hedonism which characterized gay male communities in the 1970s, declaring, 'the gay leaders who created this sexual-liberation philosophy in the first place have been the death of us...Why didn't you guys fight for the right to get married instead of the right to legitimize promiscuity?' And get married Weeks does. He finds the 'normal heart' of the title in a melodramatic final ceremony with his dying lover. It was this aping of heterosexual values and condemnation of sexual liberation which many other gay activists did not feel was particularly helpful at a time when bigots were joining hands worldwide to denounce AIDS as the wages of sin.

North American Conference of Homophile Organizations (NACHO) Set up after a conference of lesbian and gay groups in Kansas City in the summer of 1966, and pledged to 'the improvement of the status of the homosexual'. A loose federation, more a consultative body, of different groups throughout America, including some chapters of the MATTACHINE SOCIETY and THE DAUGHTERS OF BILITIS. Sharing the unfortunate experience of too many lesbian and gay organizations, NACHO acted at first as a battlefield for tensions between different groups and individuals concerning their ideas of what the 'homophile' movement should be. It was disbanded in 1970 after acrid disputes at a convention in San Francisco between the more 'respectable' homosexual activists and the more radical forces of gay liberation which had been unleashed in the aftermath of the STONEWALL RIOT. NACHO was also attacked for the small number of lesbians involved.

North-Western Homosexual Reform Committee Founded in 1964 in a miner's cottage in Lancashire it was one of the nationwide support groups of the British HOMOSEXUAL LAW REFORM SOCIETY. It was always the more radical of the groups that formed the 1960s law reform movement. Many of its members were quite public about their sexuality, and in 1967 the group declared that homosexuality was not a medical problem but a problem of society's. It later evolved into the Committee for Homosexual Equality (*see* CAMPAIGN FOR HOMOSEXUAL EQUALITY).

Northstar Gay comic superhero who first zapped a baddy in 1980.

nouveau pauvre Those members of radical lesbian and gay communities which emerged in the 1970s who emphasized their working-class roots to indicate their impeccable political credentials. Also called downwardly mobile.

nouvelle lesbian Term that is used within the LESBIAN FEMINIST movement to describe a woman who comes to realize her sexual desire for other women through the sense of closeness and sustenance of participating within the women's movement. Thus, although a woman's lesbianism has a clear sexual dimension, her choice of sexuality has been made with political considerations.

NOW *See* NATIONAL ORGANIZATION FOR WOMEN, THE.

nudity From gay cruising beaches to lesbian music festivals, nudity often functions as a way of stripping away the artifice of clothed appearances and drawing the community together. Nudity has been idealized by some writers as recreating the links between humans and nature; Walt WHITMAN wrote a paean to Greek culture which suggested that 'the highest height and deepest depths known to civilization...came from their natural and religious idea of nakedness'.

nuns, lesbian *See* CARLINI, BENEDETTA; ST TERESA OF AVILA.

Old gays

O Tercier Sexo (The Third Sex) Brazilian novel written by Odilon Azevedo in 1930. In it, lesbian workers unite to remove men from power.

Oakland's gente That lesbian favourite, a dyke's SOFTBALL team. This one was set up and comprised of black lesbians, and offered them a safe space for socializing amongst themselves.

odd girls Name given for most of this century to lesbian lovers. Indicates the difficulties which a hostile society had in coming to terms with lesbian passion. Employed particularly in the sensational LESBIAN PULP FICTION of the 1950s and 1960s which dealt with lesbian relationships.

Of the New Woman and Her Love: A Book for Mature Minds German novel published in 1900, written by Elizabeth Dauthendey. Its plot revolves around Lenore, a woman of her time, who rejects heterosexual marriage on the grounds of her incompatibility with men. She has a ROMANTIC FRIENDSHIP with another woman, Yvette, but does not see this relationship as equatable with the 'impure' sapphists. Historian Lillian Faderman cites this as important evidence that women at the turn of the twentieth century were able to have close emotional and physical relationships with other women without necessarily seeing them as lesbian.

off-Broadway (And later, when off-Broadway was assimilated into the mainstream, 'off-off-Broadway'.) The name given to the New York fringe theatre of art house theatres, café venues and studio spaces. The more provocative productions posed a great challenge to the safe mores of mainstream theatre, and allowed a platform for more interesting handling of social issues. Predictably, it was in this milieu that the first non-conventionally damning portrayals of lesbian and gay life were to be found.

oh my dear sir, if you knew how little I care for your sex, you wouldn't get any ideas in your head. Statement by French painter Rosa Bonheur (1822–99), who is best known for her nature paintings, including animal ones. She was given legal permission to dress in male clothing on the grounds that it was inconvenient to wear women's clothes while painting in farmyards. She made her statement in response to a man who asked her whether she was not concerned about going out in society alone. She also declared that she would rather paint bulls than men. Bonheur lived with her lover Nathalie Micas for over forty years, and the two are buried in the same vault.

oh, you mean I'm homosexual! Of course I am, and heterosexual too, but what's that got to do with my headache? Response by Edna St Vincent Millay to a psychoanalyst at a Greenwich Village party who, when asked to suggest the cause of her headache, suggested that it may be the response of sublimating latent sexual urges.

OHL *See* ORAL HAIRY LEUKOPLAKIA.

Old Compton Street Street in the SOHO area of central London which from the late 1980s was becoming the focus of gay life in the capital. The growth in the number of gay bars in the city at the time, as heterosexual bars closed due to economic conditions and owners reoriented their venues to the recession-proof gay clientele, made the area increasingly gay. By the 1990s the street had become one of the few in London where men in KILTs outnumbered bemused straight TOURISTS, where leatherwomen could snog other LEATHERWOMEN without so much as an eyebrow pencil being raised. A Valentine's Day carnival in the street organized by the lesbian and gay rights group OUTRAGE! in 1993 rechristened it Queer Street.

An Old-Fashioned Girl 1883 novel by Louisa May Alcott, which describes a BOSTON MARRIAGE between Rebecca, a sculptor, and Lizzie, an artist, who are described 'as happy and independent as birds; real friends, whom nothing will part'. The work illustrates how such a nurturing relationship between two women can assist the work of both of them, especially within a society which still considered marriage a woman's ultimate goal. This novel demonstrates Alcott's firm commitment that any woman who wanted to progress professionally could best do it within such a relationship with a woman. Her conclusion is unsurprising. Living in Boston, such relationships were very much part of her milieu. She herself firmly avoided heterosexual marriage, preferring, as she said, to 'paddle her own canoe'.

old gays Rather patronizing name given to those lesbians and gays who came to their identity before the blooming of lesbian and gay activity of the last few decades. Name given by those who imagine (erroneously) that healthy queer life only began with the STONEWALL RIOT.

olisbos Ancient Greek word for a leather-covered DILDO. Some commentators maintain that the word is used with this meaning in a fragment of the poetry of SAPPHO.

Olivia (1) 1951 film, scripted by Colette and set in a Paris boarding school. It was the only film of the 1950s to deal with lesbianism, although, with convention, it rejected such love as a valid emotional option. It featured dark dealings in school corridors and ended in the traditional tragic circumstances. Given sensational hype as a film on 'the subject talked about in whispers'. (2) The pen name of Dorothy Strachey Bussy, the sister of Lytton STRACHEY, gay author and member of the BLOOMSBURY GROUP. She used the name when writing about her own lesbian experiences.

Olivia Records Women's record label. The company was established by a ten-strong collective of lesbian feminists in 1973, and became a major force in the growing field of women's music. It sponsored music festivals and tours. It also acted as a women's economic unit, the objective of lesbian separatists, by employing only women and with pay based on need.

omipaloni Term from the British gay slang POLARI for homosexual, derived from 'omi' meaning man, and 'paloni' meaning woman. The word could be used to refer to lesbians, though sometimes the similar 'paloniomi' was used.

On Our Backs Lesbian sex magazine first published in 1984 with the aim of encouraging sexual exploration and sexual empowerment for lesbians. Its title is a play on that of the radical feminist publication *off our backs*.

onanism Masturbation or coitus interruptus. Any activity which does not put sperm to its procreative use. The word derives from Onan, Judah's son in the Book of Genesis, who committed the sin of ejaculating on the ground. The inimitable Dorothy PARKER called her budgie Onan, because he kept spilling his seed on the floor.

once, a philosopher; twice, a sodomite From the French writer Voltaire (1694–1778), who apparently once slept with an (unknown) Englishman, as a scientific experiment, when he was attending the court of Frederick the Great in Berlin to see if he would like it or not. When he heard that the same man had repeated the act, Voltaire upbraided him for going beyond the bounds of legitimate bisexual investigation.

One One man play by Jeffrey Hagedorn which received its initial showing in Chicago in August 1983. It was the first play about AIDS.

One Inc. Early American gay organization founded in Los Angeles in October 1952. The name derives from a statement of Thomas Carlyle that 'a mystic bond of brotherhood makes all men one'.

One Magazine: The Homosexual Viewpoint American periodical that ran from 1952 to 1969 and which was founded by members of the organization ONE INC. Although it had to get a Supreme Court decision in 1958 to get the postal service to distribute it, the magazine had a circulation of some 5,000 at times. It carried news items as well as features of scholarly interest.

1,112 and counting Article by Larry KRAMER which appeared in March 1983 on the front page of the NEW YORK NATIVE, in which he berated the lack of response to the AIDS epidemic from political and medical establishments, and from the gay communities themselves. The figure of 1,112 was the number of people who had died or who had been diagnosed with AIDS by that time. Kramer wrote, 'If this article doesn't rouse you to anger, fury, rage and action, gay men may have no future on this earth.' Although attacked by some as being too alarmist, the article changed the framework in which gay men conceived of the syndrome, and (along with the PLWA MOVEMENT) marked the beginning of the political response to AIDS.

only connect An injunction which appears in E. M. Forster's *Howards End* , 'Only connect!...Only connect the prose and the passion...and human love will be seen at its height.' It has been used by gay people to talk about the need to come out and to allow one's sexuality to influence other areas of life, rather than to keep everything in separate compartments. It was also used as the title for a 1979 British television play, in which a student who is writing a thesis on Edward CARPENTER realizes the connection between post-liberation gay politics as he knows it, and British gay history as it existed before the GAY LIBERATION FRONT ever burst onto the scene.

Only Yesterday 1933 film with Franklin Pangborn, the archetypal SISSY of the 1930s American screen in his most overtly gay role. He attends a party with a male date, discussing the drapes in shop windows as they make their way, 'That kind of blue just does something to me.' The film attempts to contrast the flippant concerns of gay men and women as Pangborn and his date join the women in frivolous gossip while the 'men' discuss the 'manly' stock market crash. As always, though, an ironic reading of 'male' power structures is possible.

onnagata The male actor in traditional Japanese kabuki theatre who plays only female roles. In the eighteenth-century theatrical manual *Ayamegusa*, the essence of the onnagata role is described: 'Unless the onnagata lives as a woman in his daily life, he is unlikely ever to be considered an accomplished onnagata'. Thus the homosexual implications of the role appealed to writer Yukio MISHIMA who wrote a short story called *Onnagata* in 1957 which drew on his friendship with Akihiro MIWA, and with the famous onnagata Utaemon. The story deals with the realization by an apprentice to a kabuki company of his attraction to the onnagata actor in the company.

opera queen A gay opera fanatic. With the combination of pure musical passion and a theatricality that sometimes borders on the absurd (who can act when they are belting out the libretto from their very diaphragm?), opera has been a medium that has historically appealed to gay men. The love-torn characters have entered gay folklore (*see* CAMILLE; VISSI D'ARTE), and convinced opera queens declare a devotion to some of the divas (*see* LA DIVINA; LA STUPENDA) that is every bit as strong as that inspired by cinematic ICONS. The strength of opera queen devotion is so legendary that an article in the New York magazine CHRISTOPHER STREET declared, 'There is no position so absurd that an opera queen won't defend it.' With their sizeable gay clientele it is not surprising that many opera houses have become renowned cruising areas. The toilets in the Bolshoi in Moscow are about the nearest thing that city has to a gay bar, while the balconies in New York's Metropolitan were so heaving that gay men were reputed to wear trousers with an opening at the back in order that they need not miss any of the first act whilst being shafted.

oral hairy leucoplakia (OHL) An infection caused by the EPSTEIN–BARR VIRUS which causes white, hairy-looking marks on the side of the tongue. The condition is not thought to be infectious.

Oranges Are Not the Only Fruit 1985 novel by British lesbian writer Jeanette Winterson which, like RUBYFRUIT JUNGLE, presents the battle of a protagonist (Jess) recognizing her sexuality and (successfully) fighting to express it in spite of the odds. The heterosexual establishment in this case is the evangelical church, typified by Jess' mother, whose restriction to the church's dogma is symbolized by the fact that when Jess is in hospital she determinedly brings the same fruit each day. Jess' relationships with women cause a rumpus in the tabernacle, the implication being that the two cannot be combined. Such a conclusion is offset somewhat by the almost forgiving humour with which Jess' mother and fellow evangelicals are portrayed. The novel was very successfully televised in 1990, the first modern lesbian novel to be so adapted.

orchid This species of flower got its name from the Greek word for testicles, since the bulb of the plant is said to resemble a man's balls. *See* ORCHID EATER.

orchid eater Nineteenth-century euphemism for a gay man who enjoyed performing fellatio on other men. *See* ORCHID.

Order of Chaeronea Secret British homosexual society of the late nineteenth and early twentieth centuries. It appears to have acted as a network of homosexuals (male, although some reports suggest that Radclyffe HALL and Una Troubridge attempted to join) who lent each other support, and who also put pressure on people in positions of authority to argue for the cause of homosexual emancipation. Its name was derived from the battle of the same name (*see* CHAERONEA, BATTLE OF), and it used the date of the battle (338 BC) as the starting-point for its own unique calendar, the Year of the Faith, for communication between members. Its symbol was the 'seal of the double wreath', which had an outer wreath of CALAMUS, probably in reference to WHITMAN'S LEAVES OF GRASS, and an inner one of MYRTLE. In the middle of the wreaths was a chain to symbolize the unity of the society and the letters Z, L and D for zeal, learning and discipline.

Organization of Women of African and Asian Descent (OWAAD) British black women's organization that acquired this name in 1979. The Organization of Women of African and Asian Descent had been founded one year earlier, but the ˙new name represented the desire for all black women to work together on the issues that concerned them, such as racist violence, deportation and enforced sterilization. The organization was the first national association of black women, and as such was extremely influential, even though relatively short-lived. It folded in 1982, largely as a result of arguments about feminism and sexuality. The organization always involved a large number of black lesbians, although at times they had to fight to have their sexuality adequately represented.

The matchless Orinda Nickname for the the English poet Katherine Philips (1631–64), who had a ROMANTIC FRIENDSHIP with Anne Owen. She first adopted the name in her correspondence with Sir Charles Cotterell.

Orlando 1928 novel that Virginia Woolf wrote to her friend and sometime lover Vita SACKVILLE-WEST. The first edition was illustrated with photographs of Vita and her ancestral home, Knowle. The book follows the life of Orlando, who was originally born as a sixteenth-century nobleman but was subsequently transformed into an eighteenth-century noblewoman, amongst other gender confusions. *Orlando*'s appeal to the gay reader is twofold. First because of Orlando's changing sex, her love affairs always contain elements of homosexuality; her sex is never true. Second, the very changeability of Orlando's sex undercuts the 'naturalness' of sex and gender. The filming of *Orlando* by Sally Potter in 1992 with the queer additions of Tilda Swinton as Orlando, Quentin Crisp as good Queen Bess, and Jimmy Somerville as an angel exploited Orlando's relationship to the gay community.

Ormond, or the Secret Witness Novel by the American Gothic author Charles Brockden Brown published in 1798, which provides important evidence of the institution of ROMANTIC FRIENDSHIP in that country during the eighteenth century. It portrays the relationship between Sophie and Constantia, with whom she had been brought up. Although the two are separated by Sophie's travels and marriage in Europe, Sophie finally travels to America to collect Constantia and sets off with her to England where they will live, presumably in a ménage à trois. Heterosexual relationships in the novel are presented as Gothic horrors, such as the evil suitor who Constantia kills, or as sanguine affairs, such as Sophie's marriage. All tears and sighs are devoted to the relationships between women.

Orton, Joe (1933–67) British playwright, author of *Loot*, and ENTERTAINING MR SLOANE. He was murdered on 9 August 1967 by his lover Kenneth Halliwell. No stranger to the COTTAGES of London, Orton kept a diary relating his sexual experiences. *See also* PRICK UP YOUR EARS.

Oscar Wilde Memorial Bookstore Gay bookstore opened by gay activist Craig Rodwell, one-time lover of Harvey MILK, in 1967 in Mercer Street, New York. It was the first openly gay business in the city. It also served as a community centre, producing its own newsletter, *The Hymnal*, which called for gay people to register on the electoral roll, and to put pressure on political candidates to work for gay rights. The shop was later moved to CHRISTOPHER STREET.

Other Countries Annual American journal for black gay men which was founded in 1986. It carries features, reviews, fiction, poetry, drawings and photography. It has a circulation of 3,000 copies.

Out and Outraged Massive direct action demonstration which took place on 13 October 1987 to protest against the decision of the US Supreme Court in the HARDWICK CASE to uphold the constitutionality of the anti-sodomy laws of the state of

Georgia. Some 840 people were arrested as they descended in waves to protest on the steps of the Supreme Court.

out of the closets and into the streets 1970s lesbian and gay liberation slogan which stressed the need for queer people to announce their sexuality as a way of showing the size of the lesbian and gay communities.

Out on Tuesday Name of a lesbian and gay magazine programme broadcast on Channel 4, which frequently showed independent work and alternative documentaries. It was the first regular lesbian and gay broadcast in the UK. Now replaced with 'Out'.

outing Term given, according to queer writer and activist Michelangelo Signorile by *Time* magazine, to the practice of publicizing people's homosexuality against their will. The practice gained media prominence in the 1980s and 1990s as radical lesbian, gay and QUEER activists threatened to publicize the names of lesbian and gay public figures who were either responsible for homophobic laws or church attitudes, or who, through their silence, refused to use their positions to advance the cause of lesbian and gay rights. Less radical members of the lesbian and gay communities, along with the hetero press, have condemned the practice as infringing individuals' rights to privacy. In the case of the straight press, their outrage is a remarkable piece of hypocrisy since they have delighted in revealing the sex lives of the famous since the year dot. Others wonder why we would want to admit that the usually contemptible targets of outing campaigns share our sexuality. In their defence queer activists have argued that individuals have a responsibility to the community which through its courage has made their lives easier, that the private/public divide is a bogus one as lesbians and gays have their privacy routinely denied by homophobic practice in employment and housing, and that ultimately the lesbian and gay movement is fighting for the right to be public, not pri-

vate, about our sexuality. Moreover, since the advent of AIDS, the homophobic denial of the health needs of gay men from governments worldwide has created life and death imperatives for the movement, next to which the right to privacy has low priority. The Eulenberg Affair is a very early case of outing. In 1989 a gay US Congressman threatened to reveal the names of gay Republicans if they persisted in their homophobic attacks on Speaker Tom Foley. In the summer of 1991 a British group, FROCS (Faggots Rooting Out Closet Sexuality), threatened to out some 200 public figures, only to reveal at a press conference that it was a hoax. For some it was a climbdown, for others an expert way of demonstrating the hypocrisy of the press who, while condemning outing when done by queers themselves, arrived at the conference in their droves, droolingly contemplating a good scandal. In 1992 pop creation Jason Donovan won a court case against *The Face* after the magazine had reported an attempt to out him. Gay writer Armistead Maupin described the word outing as 'a nasty word for telling the truth'.

OutRage! This British direct-action group is the one most closely associated with QUEER politics. The organization was set up in May 1990 in direct response to the death by queerbashing of actor Michael Boothe, and to the lack of police action in similar cases, and it has been in the forefront of British queer politics since. Committed to direct action and civil disobedience to defend the dignity and human rights of lesbians and gay men, the group has added not only confrontational tactics to the British scene, but also a much-needed dose of theatricality and humour. Always with an eye to the media-worthy, the ZAPs and behind-the-scenes paper-pushing have been mixed with a mock-burning at the stake during the enthronement of the Archbishop of Canterbury, the crucifixion of a lesbian activist at London's Westminster Cathedral, an exorcism of the demon of homophobia from the Church of England, Urban Glamour Assaults by uppity drag queens on London's shopping malls, a mass trouser-dropping outside Parliament to display the legend 'Equality now!' printed over the boxer shorts of a lovely line-up of young(ish) hopefuls, a mass turn-in for 'sex crimes', queer weddings, queer family Christmases and homosexuality promotion drives.

Outrageous! 1977 film directed by the out gay director Richard Benner. It deals with the story of a Toronto hairdresser (Craig Russell) who dreams of donning the frock as a female impersonator. Sacked from his job for appearing as Bette Davis in a local bar, he heads for New York to carve out a new life. The film, which was a big hit, examines the tensions within the gay community between the macho gays and the fabulous queens.

Over the Rainbow Judy GARLAND's plaintive evocation of the lullaby land where 'skies are blue' and 'troubles melt like lemon drops' has been termed the 'gay national anthem' by the lesbian singer Holly Near. This is not just because it was part of the soundtrack of the cult/camp classic THE WIZARD OF OZ (but was nearly dropped from the film, if you can believe it), but also because it and, indeed, the whole film have become a neat encapsulation of the lesbian and gay desire to flee the sorrows of hostile heterosexuality for a place where queerbashing, the loss of custody and, let's face it, work don't exist and where passion can be given full rein. But the song, and the film, are also a reminder that such escape is in reality only the stuff of fairy tale, and that our Oz's have to be built at home, however unpromising the material.

OWAAD *See* ORGANIZATION OF WOMEN OF AFRICAN AND ASIAN DESCENT.

Oxford Street Street in the Australian city of Sydney which became a centre for the city's gay life in the 1960s, and increasingly so throughout the 1970s. Home to a variety of queer venues, the street began to be known as the 'Glitter Strip', or 'Golden Mile', in the 1980s. The area as a whole was referred to as the 'GHETTO'.

paddy US Latino slang for archetypal blond, blue-eyed Anglo men.

Paglia, Camille (*c.* 1945–) American academic who seems to have come from nowhere to be the voice of Anglo-American lesbianism in no time at all. She is the author of *Sexual Personae* (1990) and a collection of essays, *Sex, Art and American Culture* (1993). Her current position as lesbian par excellence is puzzling since she seems to believe that men, masculinity and phallic power are the basis of creativity and culture and that lesbians, by denying themselves access to this life-force, are stunting their lives emotionally, sexually, and creatively. A cynic might suggest that it is precisely because of this stance, not representative of other lesbians, that she has received so much media attention; she is that ultimately unproblematic novelty – a masculinity-worshipping lesbian.

pancake Black American lesbian slang of the 1950s and 1960s to describe a STONE BUTCH who had been FLIPPED.

Pandora's Box (Die Büchse der Pandora) 1929 German film directed by G.W. Pabst and featuring probably the first explicit lesbian character on screen. The film starred Louise Brooks as Lulu, a woman 'driven by insatiable lusts', and Belgian actress Alice Roberts as her passionate lesbian admirer, Countess Geschwitz. The countess demonstrates her love by embarking on a heterosexual blackmail ploy to raise money for Lulu. The British censors deleted the Countess from the film, and she did not appear in the initial version of the film in America.

pansies' charter for freedom Name given to the decision in 1958 to remove the absolute veto upon the discussion of homosexuality on the British stage. As the Lord Chamberlain, who was responsible for judging what was, or was not, to be shown, suggested, 'The subject is now so widely debated, written about and talked over that its complete exclusion from the stage can now no longer be regarded as justifiable.' The name derives from the fact that the Lord Chamberlain generously agreed the use of the word pansy, but not bugger. The decision did not lead to a growth of gay-inspired theatre. This came only with the enactment of the Theatres Act of 1968, which gave the stage the precarious safeguard of a transcendent notion of the 'public good' (similar to the Obscene Publications Act) that could override the sensibilities of the censor. Only then were playwrights freer to explore what had hitherto been disallowed.

pansy Usually pejorative term for a gay man, especially an effeminate one, though some gay men have willingly taken on the word as a term of reference for gay men who are entirely out. The flower has reportedly been explicitly associated with homosexuals from the early years of the twentieth century, though writer Judy Grahn suggests it has a history longer than this; she reminds us that the flower which Puck collects for Oberon in Shakespeare's *A Midsummer Night's Dream*, and which when squeezed into the eyes will make those affected fall in love with the first creature they see, was probably a pansy, while the flower that sprang from the blood of HYACINTHUS is not the hyacinth we know, but could also have been the pansy. In film the flower became a useful way of signifying homosexuality without mentioning it. In the opening shots of Samuel Goldwyn's *Palmy Days*, a swishy SISSY rushes into a cake shop to order a cake. When the assistant asks him if he wants it decorated with roses, he replies, 'No. Pansies!', and disappears from the film. The implications were obvious. *See also* VIOLETS.

pansy without a stem Gay male slang for a lesbian, from PANSY, without the rather obvious and unsubtle stem or dick.

Paragraph 16 An attempt by the British conservative government in December 1990 to portray lesbians and gay men as unfit foster parents because of their lifestyles. A paragraph of the guidelines to the 1989 Children Act stated, 'Equal rights and gay rights have no place in fostering services.' After a vigorous campaign by the lesbian and gay movement, the offending passage was removed, leaving control of fostering services with the local authorities concerned.

Paragraph 175 The clause in German law which prohibited homosexual relations. In 1935 it was revised under the order of Hitler to include kissing, embracing and even gay fantasies, as well as genital acts. Hitler's administration later also ordered the compulsory sterilization of gay prisoners. The West German government did not revise or repeal the law until September 1969, and for that reason many gay men who had been imprisoned in camps were not even released after the end of the Second World War.

Paris Is Burning 1991 documentary film directed by Jennie Livingston which brought the VOGUEING style of black communities of Harlem and the Bronx to a public which knew of it only through MADONNA's highjacking of the form the previous year. The film, which was distilled from hours of footage shot in the vogueing balls, demonstrated how vogueing was used to create a sense of community.

Parisex The pen-name used by American gay activist Henry GERBER in writing his essays advocating rights for homosexuals.

park queen A gay man who enjoys cruising for sex, and engaging in sex, in public parks. Synonymous terms include green queen, bushie moll, nature lover and a member of the shrub club. A park where cruising goes on is sometimes known in America as a teagarden, after TEAROOM.

Parker, Dorothy (1893–1967) American writer, probably better remembered for her grasp of the caustic one-liner than for her poems and short stories. It is for this reason that she has become an icon for gay men, despite the fact that she was not a stranger to fairly unsound remarks, especially when she was having problems with her husband, Alan Campbell, who was rumoured to be gay. Among her memorable quips are: 'And where does she find them?' when told that her arch-rival Clare Booth Luce was always kind to her inferiors; 'She runs the gamut of emotions from A to B' in a review of Katherine Hepburn's acting and 'How can they tell?' when told that President Calvin Coolidge had died.

Parris Island Island in the American state of South Carolina which houses a base for American marines. In 1988, the military authorities conducted a virtual witchhunt there in their effort to unearth lesbian servicewomen. During their investigations they used such enlightened tactics as interrogating one woman in the presence of her ex-husband, and threatening her with the loss of custody of her child unless she agreed to name other lesbians. In the end, some 10 per cent of drill instructors were either discharged or jailed. Such tactics are unfortunately all too common in the American military.

parthenophilia Erotic attraction felt by a woman for an adolescent girl. Derived from the Greek parthenos, meaning virgin. It was probably created by German gay activist Magnus HIRSCHFIELD in the early 1900s in order to differentiate the different forms of lesbian attraction. *See* KOROPHILIA.

Parting Glances 1985 film written and directed by Bill Sherwood which included one of the first celluloid portrayals of a person with AIDS who refused to take on the status of victim. The film showed a day in the lives of a triangle of gay Manhattanites: Michael (Richard Ganoung); his worthy but dull lover, Robert (John Bolger), who is off to Africa to do good works; and his ex, Nick (Steve Buscemi) who has AIDS and with whom Michael is still in love. The film was criticized at the time for concentrating on the upwardly mobile gay communities.

partying Enjoying a combination of drugs and disco, as they did in those far-off, heady days of the 1970s.

passing the love of women The phrase which describes the joys of gay male love is taken from the biblical story of DAVID AND JONATHAN. It has been reworked by lesbians to describe the superiority of their love, most notably in the title of the ovarian work by the historian LILLIAN FADERMAN, *Surpassing the Love of Men*.

passing women Female transvestites who chose to dress as men for a variety of reasons. In nineteenth-century America many working-class women elected to live as men because of the advantages at work, higher wages and freedom of travel to which men were privileged. Owing to restricted dress codes of the time, such women could 'pass' as men relatively easily.

patent leather bar Gay slang for a bar that has LEATHER or SM pretensions but whose clientele falls on the effeminate side of butch.

pathic Term for a passive homosexual which came into vogue, like INGLE, in Elizabethan England. In *Sejanus His Fall* (1603), the playwright Ben Jonson called Sejanus (a Roman statesman, d. AD 31) 'the noted Pathick of our time'. The word remained in use throughout the eighteenth and nineteenth centuries. It derives from the Greek term for passive.

Patient Zero Name given to Gaetan Dugas, a French-Canadian airline steward, by some of the people involved in the early stages of identifying the cause and means of transmission of AIDS. Dugas was one of the first North Americans to develop AIDS. Moreover, back in those far-off seeming days when the names of people who had died or who were with AIDS could be fitted onto one blackboard, he seemed to have been involved with many of the men who first developed the symptoms, and he was seen by some as one of the early agents of transmission of HIV. In his book AND THE BAND PLAYED ON Randy

Shilts turned Dugas into a Gothically sinister figure who knowingly went to bathhouses to infect other men with 'gay cancer'. Critics found this rather too simplistic a piece of scapegoating which ignored the fact that Dugas himself suffered and died as a result of AIDS. Patient Zero was given a posthumous right-to-reply in the 1994 movie *Zero Patience* by Canadian director John Greyson.

PC (1) *See* POLITICAL CORRECTNESS. (2) Physical Contact; the PC Law was a vicious apartheid concept in South Africa – forbidding PC between different ethnic groups. Lesbians and gays had always defied this law in their bars and clubs.

PCP *See* PNEUMOCYSTIS CARINII PNEUMONIA.

pederast Term specifically for PAEDOPHILIA, but often extended to refer to homosexuality in general. It was first recorded in 1613, when English traveller Samuel Purchas wrote of his travels to Sicily, 'He telleth of their Paederastie, that they buy Boyes at a hundred or two hundred duckats, and mew them up for their filthie lust.'

pederasty The homoerotic attachment of an older partner for a younger one. Pederasty was the sexual norm in ANCIENT GREECE, and it is often assumed that its meaning is similar to what we would now understand by paedophilia, namely sex with children. However, in ancient Greece the younger partner was typically a young adolescent, and the pederastic relationship was often held to be beneficial to the youth's upbringing.

peg-house Slang term for a male brothel. It is commonly thought to have originated from the shipboard practice of having a young cabin boy sit on a peg to dilate his anus. In actual fact, the term may have its source in the boy-harems of Ottoman Turkey. Benches have been found, which look like school benches with pegs of various sizes on which boys were evidently required to sit. The lads presumably progressed from smaller to larger pegs whilst at the same time they studied Turkish literature and song to enhance their abilities as 'entertainers'.

penetration Since penetration, both vaginal and anal (though *they* don't like to talk about the latter), is a staple activity of heterosexual intercourse, blinkered straights (and indeed some lesbians and gays) have for a long time assumed the same to be true of lesbian and gay sex. Although sexologists such as Havelock ELLIS argued that male homosexuality did not necessarily entail anal sex, he still believed that the answer to the question of what lesbians do in bed still had to use the word dildo. It was only really when the myth of the vaginal orgasm was shattered by Masters and Johnson in the 1960s that clitoral sexuality was widely acknowledged by men. Penetration became a bête noire of the FEMINIST movement of the 1960s and especially the LESBIAN FEMINIST movement of the 1970s. It was argued that cultural fixation on the penetrating phallus was both symptomatic and perpetuating of a conception of sexuality that focused on (male) power, and that saw the orgasm as the sole legitimate goal, thereby dismissing all other sex acts. It was believed that in shifting attention from penetration to different activities and other erogenous zones there was a possibility of creating sex that was more egalitarian and more concerned with the emotional needs of the partners, one that not only could be controlled by women, but was also ultimately more pleasurable for them. Not all lesbians or gay men were entirely happy with this POLITICALLY CORRECT SEX, and in the 1980s particularly many LESBIAN SEX RADICALS readvertised the joys of STRAP-ONS, as well as SM and other activities. Meanwhile, the gay male communities went in somewhat the opposite direction. They diverged from lesbian feminism in the 1970s when they seemed to be more concerned with pushing back the frontiers of sexual expression. In this sexual heyday, fucking as well as FISTING and the use of SEX TOYS were all staples of the gay scene. With the advent of AIDS however, penetrative activities were seen as those which entailed the most risk and many gay men eschewed fucking for a regime of wanking, body rubbing and sometimes oral sex.

Pensées d'une Amazone Book by Natalie BARNEY, who was the centre of a circle of chic lesbians in the Paris capital in the early twentieth century. It was a collection of thoughts on homosexual love.

pentamadine Drug that is commonly used for the treatment and prophylaxis of PNEU-MOCYSTIS CARINII PNEUMONIA.

Penthesilea Warrior queen who, according to Greek myth, led AMAZON troops into the Trojan war, in order to fight for Troy. She was slain by the hero ACHILLES.

per scientiam ad justitiam Latin for 'justice through knowledge', this slogan was used by the German gay campaigner Magnus HIRSCHFIELD, who aimed to use the newest scientific arguments about the congenital nature of homosexual desire to argue that there was no choice, and therefore no crime, in a homosexual orientation. He believed that widespread dissemination of these theories would ultimately lead to greater tolerance and pressure for legal change.

personal is political Slogan of 1960s lesbian feminist movement. They believed that women with a commitment to feminism had to live out that commitment by refusing to engage in sexual relationships with men, since it was men who were responsible for their oppression.

Personal Rights in Defense and Education (PRIDE) Los Angeles-based organization which in 1967 coordinated gay demonstrations against the harassment which gay men faced at the hands of the Los Angeles Police Department.

Peter Pan Seen in the light of the dubious sexuality of its author J. M. Barrie, the 1904 children's drama becomes a celebration of the flight from a restrictive world and its enforced heterosexuality. The little hero runs away when he hears his parents talking of his future, which includes work and marriage. He goes to live with the fairies,

the boy ones being dressed in mauve, a colour which was associated in the public mind with Oscar WILDE, who had been disgraced only a decade earlier. Some fairies don't even know what sex they are. The naming of Never Land might be seen however to function as an ironic commentary on the possibilities for escape.

phallos Concept used by some Jungian psychologists to refer to what they see as the darkly masculine part of the male collective unconscious. According to them, this prick-worshipping, ritualistic image of the masculine has been denied men by the historical association of maleness with rationality and spirit, rather than the body and nature. Some SM theorists assert that the ritualistic possibilities of SM and the homosocial environments of gay leather clubs shove the phallos back into the scene, and allow gay men to celebrate a complete masculinity.

Philadelphia 1993 film directed by Jonathan Demme which was the biggest budget and most mainstream film with an AIDS-related theme since LONGTIME COMPANION. It cast American actor Tom Hanks as a lawyer with AIDS who has to go to court to fight for his right to maintain his job, and is replete with courtroom set pieces to discuss the merits of homosexuality. It was criticized by many as presenting an anodyne view of AIDS – including an improbably harmonious relationship between Hanks and his family – as well as being about a decade too late. However, it did serve to increase awareness of the syndrome among mainstream movie-goers. Hanks won an Academy Award for his part, in a long tradition of Oscar winners for 'afflicted' roles.

picketing Common demonstration tactic of the early lesbian and gay rights movement in the United States. The first such picket was organized in 1963 by the HOMOPHILE ACTION LEAGUE of New York, and took place at the Whitehall Draft Induction Centre. The twelve activists who took part were protesting about breaches of confidentiality regarding the military draft record of homosexuals. Many such demonstrations followed. Dressed in smart clothing, the demonstrators concentrated very much on projecting an image of respectability to authority, so as to allow lesbians and gays access to mainstream society.

Pierre et Gilles French photographic duo who create a camp world of androgynous and innocent men and women set amidst magical or fantastic backgrounds which often draw elements from Indian and Catholic iconography. Their photos, which have been used by fashion designers such as Thierry Mugler and pop artists such as Marc Almond and Dee-Lite, as well as appearing in their own exhibitions, have become so ubiquitous in the 1990s that they seem the predominant aesthetic of the age among the gay communities, and even in heterosexual advertisements. This is not inappropriate, since the fantastic and androgynous subject matter is consonant with the challenges of QUEER THEORY. The two photographers have woven myths around themselves too, for example by refusing to use their surnames.

pink As a colour associated with homosexuality, pink is an example of the arbitrary associations of gender roles. Before the First World War, pink as a form of red was linked with masculine action, while it was actually the blues which were soppy and female. As well as the connotations of effeminacy, pink has a particular association with the gay communities because of the use of the PINK TRIANGLE in the HOLOCAUST. Pink is now used as a prefix in many forms (for example PINK POUND and PINK PRESS) to refer to the institutions of the lesbian and gay communities.

pink pound The economic muscle of lesbians and, more so, gay men. With the appearance of LUPPIES and GUPPIES in the 1980s, the lesbian and gay communities were increasingly talked about as a major force on the market. It was assumed that without children the majority of queers would be able to ride the recession more smoothly. To some extent this was borne out: many straight yuppy wine bars turned into gay bars when the bottom fell out of the market, and there was a growth in areas like lesbian and gay publishing when surveys revealed how much more likely lesbians and gay men were to buy books. Some activists called on the pink pound to be used as a political force, either to pressurize straight business to improve its services to lesbians and gays, or to direct the pinkies into enterprises owned by lesbians and gays. Others felt that all this concentration on the pink pound overlooked the question of the pink overdraft, and the real problems of poverty experienced by those sections of the community who weren't doing quite so well as their white, middle-class and often male counterparts. The pink pound is sometimes known as 'homecon', after COMECON (Council for Mutual Economic Assistance), the economic organization of Soviet-bloc countries set up in 1949.

pink press The lesbian and gay media.

pink triangle The most well-known symbol for homosexuality. It dates from the Nazi HOLOCAUST, when the thousands of gay men who were shipped off to concentration camps for their sexuality were required by the Nazis to wear an inverted pink triangle badge on their clothing to indicate the reason for their internment. In the 1970s, activists within the gay liberation movement resurrected the symbol both because it was easily identifiable, and because it drew attention to the oppression which lesbians and gay men still faced within society. The direct action group ACT UP also used the symbol in the 1980s, now with the point of the triangle facing upwards, to draw attention to the holocaust which the AIDS epidemic represented for gay male communities. Although the pink triangle is usually used to indicate the lesbian and gay movement, the lesbian equivalent has been the BLACK TRIANGLE. In Mel Brooks' 1983 film *To Be or Not to Be*, the gay dresser Sasha pointed out another downside of the pink triangle, 'I hate it. It clashes with everything.'

pinkie ring A pinkie ring or ring on the little finger of the hand, particularly the left hand, has come to be used by both lesbians and gay men as a discreet way of drawing attention to their sexuality.

pinning up your bobby pins 1950s slang meaning to act straight or, if impossible, at least inconspicuously. A bobby pin was a kind of flat hairpin and the phrase alluded to putting your hair up and acting respectably.

pirates, lesbian See BONNEY, ANNE.

piss-elegant Gay slang term popular since the mid twentieth century for any slightly affected airs held by a gay man which are not based on any manifest superiority. OPERA QUEENS, with their disdain for the musical subspecies of disco, are often accused of holding piss-elegant disdain for the B-list gays.

piss scenes Term for sexual scenarios that involve WATERSPORTS.

pitcher Borrowing from a baseball analogy, this BUTCH American slang term refers to the active partner in anal sex. See CATCHER.

Plas Newydd Name of the cottage in Llangollen Vale, Wales, which was bought in 1780 by Sarah Ponsonby and Eleanor Butler, who are better known as THE LADIES OF LLANGOLLEN. The two lived there, in what the local papers referred to as 'the Fairy Place of the Vale', for fifty-three years. They decorated the cottage themselves, established an impressive garden and received many guests. The cottage assumed mythical importance for women of the time and later generations who either lived in their own ROMANTIC FRIEND-SHIPS, or desired to but were constrained by financial circumstances. Its importance is comparable to that of MILLTHORPE for gay men at the turn of the twentieth century.

Plato (c. 427–c. 348 BC) The Greek philosopher whose SYMPOSIUM provided some of the earliest justifications for homosexual relations. Plato was himself aware of the sexual nature of pederastic relations, and wrote that the rituals of CRETE and SPARTA had a sexual nature. The headship of his famous Academy near Athens was reported to have been passed down from lover to lover for some three generations.

platonic love The term for sex-free passion was founded on a passage in the SYMPO-SIUM where Plato was eulogizing not love between the sexes but the loving affection which Socrates had for young men, which was supposedly pure.

play space Like LEATHERSPACE, the physical and mental freedom to engage in radical sexual activity such as SADOMASOCHISM, BONDAGE or FISTFUCKING. The physical space can be anywhere, as long as the conditions are suited to concentrating attention on the scene. The mental space involves both partners preparing, for example through role-playing, to achieve the sense of isolation and excitement necessary.

Playa del Ingles Canary Islands resort area which serves as one of the hot centres for the gay tourist – with a nude beach, busy backrooms and sand dunes behind the beaches where you can get someone to lick off any excess suntan lotion.

PLWA (person living with AIDS) movement The PLWA movement, which began in the early 1980s in America, marked the early political response of people affected by the growing AIDS epidemic, and their desire to take an active role in governing their treatment and their lives. It rejected the notion, peddled through the media, that an AIDS diagnosis was just a prelude to a death certificate, and asserted that PWAs could still have fulfilling lives. The inception of the movement was when, in 1983, a group of PWAs presented the Denver Principles to a conference on lesbian and gay health in the American city of Denver (see PWA). The document recommended that 'people with AIDS...form caucuses to choose their own representatives, to deal with the media, to choose their own agenda, and to plan their own strategies...People with AIDS have the right to die and to live in dignity.' While the movement was crucially important in allowing many PWAs to take control of their lives, it was perhaps born of a notion of individual worth that was most prevalent among white, middle-class, gay male communities, and its insistence that PWAs form a common constituency perhaps obscured some of the ways in which class, ethnicity and gender might filter the experience of living with the disease. The movement also drew an implicit distinction between the concerns of those with HIV and those with AIDS, in contrast to Europe where the BODY POSITIVE form of organizing was more prevalent.

pneumocystis carinii pneumonia (PCP)
The most common opportunistic infection associated with AIDS, PCP was the first illness that led to the identification of the syndrome as a specific condition. PCP is found in most people, but it is usually kept in check by the body's immune system and it is only in those with damaged immunity that it develops serious symptoms. Caused by the fungus pneumocystis carinii, symptoms include shortness of breath, a dry cough, night sweats and chest pains. However, it is one of the infections which is increasingly better treated, and prophylaxis, involving Septrin tablets or pentamadine inhalations, is useful in keeping it at bay.

polari British underground slang that was particularly associated with the gay community. It was probably derived from the eighteenth- and nineteenth-century argot of itinerant showpeople and actors, as well as that of tramps, known as 'parlyaree'. The version that became established as the underground means of communication for gay men seems to have been passed from men in the merchant navy, initially to the dockside pubs and eventually to the gay pubs and meeting places. A fabulous gay artefact, it functioned as a means of protection, to communicate messages about identity and sexuality, or just gossip, in a hostile environment, as well as a way of taunting that hostile culture. It was a complex system. Some words were taken from the Romance languages from which it was derived: 'bona' meant good, great, it's fine

or anything related; 'omi' was a man; 'paloni' a woman; and 'varda' was to look at. Some came from rhyming slang, such as 'barnet' (fair) for hair, others were words reversed such as 'ecaf' for face or 'riah' for hair (again). But there was also 'lals/lallies' for legs, 'dish/Nancy' for the ass, 'ogles' for the eyes (and 'ogale fakes' for glasses), 'bats' for feet, 'slap' for make-up, especially when worn as part of drag (a word also used in polari), NAFF for anything bad and 'bijou' for anything small but stunning. 'Trolling' was to hunt for sexual contacts, and 'tipping the velvet' was to work as a prostitute. Many terms characterized gay men as feminine or used female names: 'Nancies' and 'Mariannes' were gay men, while 'Aunt Nell' meant to listen, and could be attached to the beginning of a sentence as an injunction. Many words were used along with polari, and are still used routinely today: 'cruising', or COTTAGING for those looking for sex, 'auntie' for an older gay man, and 'queen' for a self-evident one. The slang was popularized by JULIAN AND SANDY on the massively popular 1960s radio show *Round the Horne*, and soon the nation's drawing rooms were reverberating with 'ooh's and 'eek's and 'varda's. Many gay men seized upon it as part of their heritage, and in the 1990s the occasional 'bona' is still to be heard in gay clubs and bars.

poli-sex *See* POLITICALLY CORRECT SEX. Stems from 'personal is political' approach which argues that even what you do in bed is fraught with political significance.

political correctness (PC) Term developed within the feminist and lesbian-feminist movements to describe the kinds of lifestyles and attitudes that were believed to be consonant with the radical feminist consciousness. At its most extreme, political correctness could involve most aspects of life, including sexual behaviour, language use, dress, use of money, food, consciousness of race, class and ecological issues and political activism. While the concept represented an attempt to thoroughly apply a lesbian-feminist critique in order to build social institutions that were in no way oppressive, it was not without controversy. Many women felt that it could become overly dogmatic, and resented the sometimes cold treatment of women who were deemed to be politically incorrect (PI). Such arguments are still current, for example in the debates between POLITICAL LESBIANS and PRO-SEX LESBIANS. By the late 1980s, however, political correctness was more associated with a particular movement within American academic establishments to raise consciousness of issues of race, sexuality and gender politics, especially in respect to the assumptions that lie behind language. The prospect of hitherto silent minorities finding their own voices and challenging images of themselves has caused something of a furore in the mainstream press which has condemned it as the 'tyranny of the left'.

political lesbian Term that is used by LESBIAN FEMINISTS to describe a woman for whom lesbianism need not be based on sexual desire at all, but who uses the term lesbianism to describe any relationship between women which brings them together and away from men. Within LESBIAN FEMINISM there have been many women who describe themselves as lesbian and who do not have sexual relationships with women but who are WOMAN IDENTIFIED in every other way. Such a definition of lesbianism has been criticized by some PRO-SEX LESBIANS, who see sexual intimacy between women as fundamental to any true lesbian identity. *See also* HISTORIC LESBIAN; LESBIAN CONTINUUM; NOUVELLE LESBIAN.

politically correct sex In the 1970s many lesbian feminists began to criticize the conventions of what they saw as male sexual behaviour, which concentrated on the orgasm. They advanced instead the exciting regime of hugging and kissing, emphasizing equal touching time, and frowning upon power games such as role-playing or SM into sex. Many foolish souls still carried on wanting to have orgasms.

polymorphous perverse Term originally derived from the psychoanalytical writings of Sigmund FREUD. It refers to the mind before it is socialized (the id) and which remains in some part in the subconscious to be revealed in dream. Freud believed that the undeveloped person contained sexual impulses which were undifferentiated in terms of gender, and that it was the socialization process which created widespread heterosexuality by repressing the homosexual urge. The all-embracing sexuality of the undeveloped mind was termed the polymorphous perverse.

Pompeii The evidence of one of the earliest homosexual subcultures is preserved in the Roman city in the form of the explicitly gay graffiti which has been found there. It includes such choice quotes as 'Phoebus the perfume-maker fucks excellently', 'I want to be fucked by a man', and 'Autus fucked Quintius here'. Much of these prototypical toilet scribblings were found in the BATHHOUSES which had by the Roman period replaced the Greek gymnasium as the centre for gay activity.

poof/pouf British term for a gay man which was first recorded in the mid-nineteenth century, and originally referred to men who picked up male SEX-WORKERS. While generally used as a pejorative, it has been adopted by some gay men as an affectionate epithet for others. The longer version, poofter, which became rare in the UK until it was reintroduced from Australia in the 1960s, is used to describe any man who does not live up to the rugby-playing male stereotype, gay or not.

popes, queer *See* QUEER POPES.

poppa American prison and working-class lesbian slang of the 1930s which described the BUTCH partner in a lesbian BUTCH/FEMME relationship.

poppers The drug amyl nitrate, a stimulant which raises the heartbeat and creates a powerful, if rather short-lived, sense of euphoria. It is produced in liquid form in capsules or bottles, and inhaled straight from the bottle or when soaked into a hankie. Usually taken during sex or in clubs, it provides a little artificial kick to sexual excitement or to jazz up a dance-floor dirge. The name comes from the capsule form which needed to be popped open before use. Apart from the headaches, its most obvious deleterious side-effect is to make a club smell like a changing room with no extractor fan.

pornography Literally meaning writing about prostitutes, pornography or the representation of anything from human nudity to actual sex acts on film, photography or art is one of the areas where the lesbian and gay male communities have traditionally been at loggerheads. Until the late twentieth century, pornography was practically always in the hands of men, so it is not surprising that gay men have an easier relationship with it. In the nineteenth century pornographic novels such as *The Power of Mesmerism* (1891), *The Romance of Lust* (1876), and *My Secret Life* (1890), as well as TELENY, the novel sometimes attributed to Oscar WILDE, included feverish gay scenarios, which can still get a rise today. Of course, censorship was a problem and some people argued that art could not be descriptive of the human experience if it was not allowed to depict such a large part of it. E. M. Forster wrote, 'Nothing is more obdurate to artistic treatment than the carnal, but it has to be got in. I'm sure: everything has to be got in.' Throughout much of the twentieth century, pornographers such as BLADE circulated their works privately, while less explicit physique mags found a wide 'readership' of one-handed readers. Porn never seemed out of step with the objectives of gay male sexual liberation of the 1970s. In the late twentieth century, although British obscenity laws forbid the representation of an erect dick, American gay porn is such a huge industry that its stars such as Jeff STRYKER have become minor celebrities. Even in the decade of AIDS, while many porn stars were quickly affected, the industry has adapted to a new role: condoms feature heavily in the

scenes, and porn has been at the centre of new avenues of safe sexual expression such as JACK OFF parties. The lesbian relation to pornography has meanwhile been far more problematic, and heavily informed by the critiques that have evolved within the feminist movement. Concentrating on the representation of women within male-controlled porn, which is 'designed to dehumanize women' (Susan Brownmiller), feminists have argued that porn is a vital link in the chain that perpetuates male power and violence over women. Andrea Dworkin, who along with Catharine MacKinnon proposed an amendment on pornography for the Minneapolis City Council which provided for compensation from pornographers for women victims of violence, writes, '[Pornography] is the ideology that is the source of all the rest; it truly defines what women are in this system – and how women are treated issues from what women *are*.' (*Right-Wing Women*, 1983). Drawing from this, radical-feminist and lesbian-feminist anti-pornography campaigners have critiqued all pornography as legitimizing power differentials because, in the objectification of people that porn represents, even if there are no manifest power differences between the models, there is between the viewer and the viewed. In the 1970s, and particularly the 1980s, this led to serious conflicts between anti-porn lesbian feminists and some PRO-SEX LESBIANS such as Pat CALIFIA and Gayle Rubin who made the charge that campaigns against porn colluded with a right-wing and anti-lesbian agenda to repress all heterodox forms of sexual expression, and that only a lesbian-controlled pornography could challenge the patriarchal suppression of women's own sexuality. Meanwhile, photographers such as Della Grace and Tessa Boffin and magazines such as ON OUR BACKS championed the free expression of lesbian sexuality. Gay men also chimed in on these 'sex wars', reminding that historically censorship legislation has disproportionately affected the representation of lesbian and gay sexuality, since the kind of people we have managed to entrust to execute such laws are usually the kind of people who find any mention of queer sexuality 'pornographic' whether or not it is explicitly sexual. The arguments rage on. *See* FEMINISTS AGAINST CENSORSHIP.

Poseidon According to the Greek poet Pindar (522 or 518–438 or 432 BC), Pelops, the King of Pisa in Elis, was, when young, abducted by Poseidon, the Greek god of the sea, in much the same way, and for the same purpose, as GANYMEDE was abducted by Zeus.

positive images One of the fashionable expressions of the 1980s lesbian and gay movement, the term referred to the campaign to create more widespread visibility of lesbians and gay men in ways that presented them as valued and valuable members of society, rather than the child molesters and neurotic, promiscuous killers that had hitherto been the norm. In particular, lesbians and gay men argued that school textbooks should include positive lesbian and gay characters to create role models for young lesbians and gay men, and to educate other schoolchildren about the validity of lesbian and gay lifestyles. The movement made little headway despite the positive stance of some authorities, such as the Inner London Education Authority, and despite the claims of the tabloid presses that schools were being overrun with gay proselytizing. Right-wing fears over such campaigns were one of the factors behind the introduction of CLAUSE 28 by the Thatcher administration. *See also* JENNY LIVES WITH ERIC AND MARTIN.

pre-cum Seminal fluid that is produced by the dick during sex, before the whole wad is ejaculated. Men produce different levels of the stuff. A man who produces a lot is known as a drip queen. Pre-cum has problematized the practice of oral sex in the age of HIV. It is relatively easy to withdraw the dick from the mouth before orgasm, but less easy to prevent any pre-cum entering the mouth. Thus, whilst any risk is not terribly high, AIDS educators have recommended that a condom is used for oral sex,

or that men at least refrain when they know that they have any cuts in the mouth.

preppie bars Descriptive of a certain kind of gay bar, which is distinguished by its young upwardly mobile clientele. From the American slang usage of prep to indicate an undignified upper-class college student.

pretend family The way in which the Thatcher government in the UK of the 1980s chose to characterize any domestic set-up which was not organized around the two parents, the 2·4 children and the semi-detached in suburbia, and used particularly to reject the claims by lesbians and gay men that they should have the right to foster and adopt, and to bring up children if they so wish, and to deny the validity of the domestic arrangements that we were making.

pretty policeman British slang for any plain-clothes police officer who is sent into public toilets to act as an agent provocateur in order to arrest and charge with indecency any men who attempt to solicit him for sex. The word pretty refers to the police practice of choosing goodlooking officers for the task, who would often be dressed in 'gay' clothing, such as ripped jeans and leather jackets. Although by the 1990s widespread campaigning by gay organizations to end the practice had succeeded in theory, with London's Metropolitan police supposedly putting an end to all plain-clothes operations, there are still many reports of entrapment taking place.

The Price of Salt 1952 novel by Claire Morgan which related the story of two lovers, Carol and Therese. It differed from other lesbian novels of the time by actually having the two women ending happily together. As such, it offered an important boost for many lesbian readers.

Prick Up Your Ears 1987 film, directed by Stephen Frears, which dramatized the life of British playwright Joe ORTON.

Pride Lesbian and gay demonstration which is held annually in many cities worldwide at a point in mid-June to commemorate the STONEWALL RIOT. Although the march remembers the coming out of the lesbian and gay political movement, many of the marches held have taken on more of a carnival taint, and have become less political. The first Pride marches were held in 1970 in New York and four other American cities. In New York a small crowd gathered in Waverly Place near Sheridan Square in the Greenwich Village ghetto and bravely headed out of the village up to Central Park where they found that 2,000 or more co-protesters had joined en route. In Los Angeles some 1,200 people turned out to mark the occasion. In Britain the first Pride march was held in August 1971 when a small crowd, organized by the GAY LIBERATION FRONT, marched from Marble Arch to Trafalgar Square. Marches have been held annually since then.

PRIDE See PERSONAL RIGHTS IN DEFENSE AND EDUCATION.

primordial soup Any place that is crowded with heterosexuals. Somewhat stifling for members of more developed life-forms.

Princeton rub US slang term for sex between men when the dick of one is rubbed either between the thighs or on the stomach of his partner. How the name of Princeton was associated with these particular positions is unclear; possibly it was the invention of sneering students of another university.

Prisoner: Cell Block H The essential lesbian cult TV show, set in the all-women environs of Wentworth Detention Centre in Australia and detailing the lives of the be-dungareed women on the inside. First screened in 1979, *Prisoner* struck a chord somewhere, and has been shown in some forty countries in twelve languages worldwide. The show provides a pantheon of pin-ups. There is 'Queen' Bea (Val Lehman), crafty and not averse to using force but always with the interests of the girls at heart. Lehman has made something of a second career touring lesbian clubs in the UK. Judy Bryant (Betty Bobbitt) remains cool even when working the steam press, while the sinister form of Joan 'the Freak' Ferguson (Maggie Kirkpatrick) stalks the corridors – her sadistic glee perhaps the hardened front of an embittered heart. But then there's the nice screw, Meg (Elspeth Ballantyne), to offset the grip of Ferguson's leather glove. The roost is ruled with a fist of iron and acting of wood by Erica 'Davo' Davidson (Patsy King). Oh, and there's the gay male favourite, Lizzy Birdsworth, the dizzy old crimmo with the complexion of a PG Tips chimp. While the whole scenario is fraught with lesbian undertones, there have been some explicit lesbian storylines. Judy deliberately gets herself banged up in order to be with her lover Sharon, while in her previous job Ferguson was said to have beaten up a prisoner for killing her lover. The theme tune to the series, with the plaintive cry that 'the sun and rain are prisoners too', has been a dyke favourite as a slow number to end a dance. It has the same longing for a better world that has made OVER THE RAINBOW a gay anthem.

La Prisonnière (The Captive) 1926 play by Edouard Bourdet, first shown in Paris. It was about a Frenchwoman, daughter of a diplomat, who is 'seduced' into a lesbian relationship. As an interesting note, the use in the play of a bunch of violets to symbolize the lesbian relationship led to a huge drop in the sale of violets from Parisian florists when the play was shown.

pro-healing policy Code of conduct implemented by some women's music festivals in the 1980s to ban the display of SM equipment, or the activities of women producing lesbian pornography. It was argued that many women felt damaged by living within a violent male society, and such displays exacerbated this psychological damage.

pro-sex dykes See PRO-SEX LESBIANS.

pro-sex lesbians A challenge to the lesbian feminist orthodoxy which emerged at the 1982 Barnard conference on sexuality in America. Pro-sex lesbians criticized the concentration of lesbians and lesbian feminists on the evils of hetero patriarchy and the joys of romantic friendship and woman bonding, and their ignoring of sex between women. The core of being a lesbian, the pro-sex lesbians argued, is that you want to fuck women, not admire them. An important issue for pro-sex lesbians was anger at the rejection and denigration of 'old-style' (pre-1970s) dykes by politically motivated lesbian feminists. The 1980s were marked by the 'lesbian sex-wars' between lesbian feminists and pro-sex dykes, centring particularly on pornography, SM and BUTCH/FEMME. In the 1990s these debates lessened, mainly, it seems, because a new generation of lesbians have appeared who are more prepared and more able to judge lipstick, dildo and feminism. The most famous advocates of pro-sex are the Americans Amber Hollingbaugh, Gayle Rubin, Joan NESTLE and Pat CALIFIA, and in Britain Nettie Pollard and Cherry Smith.

A Problem in Modern Ethics John Addington Symonds' essay on (male) homosexuality, first published in an issue of fifty copies in 1891. In it he sought to establish that homosexuality was simply a harmless sexual variation, and was not incompatible with mental or physical health. In answer to the idea of Richard von KRAFFT-EBING that homosexuality was the result of a hereditary 'stain', Symonds argued that there was no one in Europe who had not inherited such a stain, and thus since everyone was potentially open to inversion Krafft-Ebing's analysis was merely academic. The work was also important in that it drew an explicit link between theories of homosexuality and the legal changes which Symonds saw as necessary to prevent the 'unjust' criminalization of an innocent class of people. He was not, however, concerned with the question of lesbianism, and it was only at the insistence of Havelock ELLIS that female inversion was included in the joint venture which became SEXUAL INVERSION. After Symonds' death in 1893, his writings on homosexuality were suppressed by his family, although pirated editions of *A Problem in Modern Ethics* did appear in 1896 and 1901.

The Problem of Homosexuality Less than enlightened declaration by the Church of England Moral Welfare Council in 1954. While still arguing the sinfulness of gay sex, the report did however argue that it was not the business of the law, and was one of the factors that led to the legalization of gay sex in England and Wales in 1967 (*see* SEXUAL OFFENCES ACT).

Project Inform San Francisco-based organization which was founded in 1985 to act as a centre for any information about alternative treatments for AIDS and AIDS-related illnesses in order to empower PWAs over their own treatment. It runs a hotline which gives out information on any treatment which seems to be promising. It also campaigns with America's Food and Drugs Administration to speed up the process of testing drugs for general use.

promote homosexuality Slogan used by radical groups such as QUEER NATION and OUTRAGE! on literature and placards in their campaigns. The concept of the promotion of homosexuality has significance on both sides of the Atlantic since it was used in the wording of both the HELMS amendment and CLAUSE 28.

Proposition 6 *See* BRIGGS INITIATIVE.

prostate The gland situated in male mammals around the neck of the bladder, which provides the fluid element of cum. Massaging the gland, which can be done via the rectum using either the hand or the dick can lead to orgasm in itself, which gives a conclusive lie to any heterosexual theory that the ass was not intended for use as a sexual organ.

Prove It On Me Blues Blues recording by singer Ma RAINEY, who exploited the interest aroused by her bisexuality. The record dealt with a bold woman loving women, who sang 'Went out last night with a crowd of my friends/They must've been women, 'cause I don't like no men.' The sleeve showed a black woman in BUTCH drag chatting with two FEMME women, and watched by a policeman, which served to hype the scandalous attraction of Rainey's sexuality.

Psappha The alternative spelling of SAPPHO which was invented by the French poet Pierre Louÿs, the author of LES CHANSONS DE BILITIS. The spelling was adopted by lesbian poet Renée VIVIEN, who met Louÿs shortly after arriving in Paris at the beginning of the twentieth century and who considered him as a mentor.

psychiatrists Described by Peter Maxwell Davies in GAY NEWS of June 1973 as 'the true inheritors of the mantle of the Holy Inquisition and the Witch Hunters'.

psychiatry Lesbians and gay men have not always had an exactly harmonious relationship with the discipline of mind-medicine. Many psychiatrists have used their simplification of Sigmund FREUD to justify attempts to treat people for their homosexual 'condition'. In London, the Counter-Psychiatry Group, fashioned after the anti-psychiatry movement of R. D. Laing, was set up in 1971 in order to challenge the assumptions of the profession regarding lesbians and gay men. The group held demonstrations against practitioners and David Reubens' 1969 book *Everything You Always Wanted to Know About Sex*. In America, the work of Evelyn HOOKER provided impetus for the campaign to get the American Psychiatric Association to remove homosexuality from its list of conditions.

The Psychogenesis of a Case of Homosexuality in a Woman 1920 study by Sigmund FREUD in which he specifically discusses lesbianism. It is the case-study of an eighteen-year-old woman, Dora, and he ascribes her lesbianism (which has never reached genital expression) to the desire to be impregnated by her father, and to envy of her brother's penis. He also describes her 'masculinity complex', which he puts down to this penis envy; yet her supposed masculinity is simply her feminist unwillingness to take on the traditional role of woman. In effect, her envy is of her brother's privilege as a man. Dora describes her love for women in terms of a 'purity' which is redolent of the ROMANTIC FRIENDSHIPS of the nineteenth century, but the case-study shows how such relationships were no longer able to exist without sexual interpretations being cast on them.

public school In England and Wales, confusingly, a private school. Usually sex-segregated, public schools are notorious for the extent of homosexual relations that are supposed to exist within them. After the conviction of Oscar WILDE, W. T. Stead reported in the *Pall Mall Gazette* that 'if all persons guilty of Oscar Wilde's offences were to be clapped into gaol, there would be a very surprising exodus from Eton and Harrow, Rugby and Winchester [public schools] to Pentonville and Holloway [prisons]'. Rumour has it that the reason the British Parliament is so loathe to grant lesbians and gay men their civil rights is because most of them haven't quite reconciled themselves to their school days.

puer aeternus From the Latin, and meaning eternal youth. The goal of men in the ever-so-slightly ageist gay male scene of the 1970s up until now. A lot of blood, sweat and staples were expended in keeping that skin taut and those bodies firm, to resist the dirty work of Madame l'Age.

pueri Alexandrini Literally means Alexandrian boys. After the Greek conquest of Egypt, the city of Alexandria became famous for its hedonistic lifestyle and the variety of sexual pleasures that could be had there. It achieved such a reputation in the ancient world for its male prostitutes that in Rome the slave boys who were kept by their masters to render sexual services were known as Alexandrian boys. An alternative form was pueri Aegyptii or Egyptian boys.

punk Prison/vagrant slang term for a younger man who plays a sexually submissive role for his older partner.

Der Puppenjunge (The Hustler) 1926 novel by writer, anarchist, and champion of man/boy-love John Henry Mackay (whose nom de plume was Sagitta). It portrayed the relationship between a closeted gay man and a Berlin rent-boy, set within the gay life of 1920s of that city. The novel was translated into English and published in 1985.

purple hand Short-lived symbol for gay liberation which was popular in San Francisco in the 1970s. It was a camping up of the name of the New York 'black hand' mafia gang, and was said to have been born after a gay demonstration at the offices of the *San Francisco Examiner* newspaper to protest a homophobic editorial. When an employee poured purple ink on the protesters, they imprinted the side of the building with their hands.

Purple String Bangkok-based gay dance troupe, it has developed various dance routines, employing traditional Thai dance, to use as educational material to teach the gay population and the rent boys of the city about AIDS and SAFE SEX.

pussy Slang term for the female genitals. Recorded as early as the sixteenth century, the term derives from the use of the word pussy to refer to women in general. It is also used by gay men to refer to their mouth or anus.

PWA (person with AIDS) Term that was developed in the early years of the AIDS epidemic, to counter the terminology of AIDS 'patient' or 'victim' which was being employed by the media in their reports. It was felt that such terms emphasized the helplessness and passivity of people who had HIV and AIDS and denied the possibility of an active response to the syndrome. The term gained currency after a group of PWAs issued a document at a 1983 conference on lesbian and gay health in the American city of Denver, which declared, 'We condemn attempts to label us as "victims", which implies defeat, and we are only occasionally "patients", which implies passivity...We are "people with AIDS".' The document, which became known as the Denver Principles, became the manifesto of the PLWA MOVEMENT.

Pythias *See* DAMON AND PYTHIAS.

Quaalude US trade name since 1973 for methaqualone, a sedative drug that was used by many as a sleeping pill since it had a similar downing effect to barbiturates. It was a common feature of the drugs scene in the 1970s American gay subculture.

Quaint Honour Play by Roger Gellert, produced in London in 1958. It described the outbreak of 'gay panic' in a private school for young men, as a relationship between a prefect and a fourteen-year-old boy is revealed. The prefect is expelled, but does not express the conventional tortured guilt of such exposure. Perhaps a little trop for a 1950s London audience, the play failed.

Quatrefoil 1950 novel by American writer James Barr. It deals with the story of a young naval officer, Phillip Froelich, and his relationship with an older and more experienced gay man. So far so much the same. What made this novel more exceptional, however, was the way in which it sought to subvert the unwritten publish-

ing laws of the time which demanded that any story with a gay theme should end in suicide or murder (*see* THE CITY AND THE PILLAR). Although there is tragedy, in *Quatrefoil* it comes as an accident, and for its time the novel provided a positive note for its gay readers.

queen The popular self-referential slang term for gay men derives not from the powdered and wigged monarch herself, but from the word quean, itself derived from old English, which came to mean a sexually promiscuous woman, or female sex-worker. Thus, like GAY or FRUIT, a term for a prostitute has evolved to refer to gay men.

Queen Christina The story of the lesbian Swedish monarch CHRISTINA, whose one love was for the beautiful Countess Ebba Sparre, was adapted into a 1933 film version directed by Rouben Mamoulian and starring that lesbian and gay icon, Greta Garbo, as the monarch. The screenplay included a passionate kiss between Garbo and Elizabeth Young as the Countess. When harried by a minister to marry and produce an heir, she stubbornly refuses and, dressed in riding attire, declares, 'I shall die a bachelor!' Disappointingly, and departing from history, she has an affair with Antonio (John Gilbert), although interestingly he first falls in love with her because he thinks that she is a man.

Queen of Bithynia Epithet applied to Julius Caesar, who was alleged to have played the passive sexual role to Nicomedes, King of Bithynia. The affair is described by Cicero.

queens, queer *See* QUEER KINGS AND QUEENS.

queer (1) As a term for a lesbian or gay man, it is recorded in this usage as early as the 1920s in the UK, though terms such as 'queer cull' for a fop or fool were in use as early as the eighteenth century and might represent a prototypical form of the modern usage. While the term has more often been used pejoratively, it was also the chosen word of self-reference for many gay people within the subculture for much of the twentieth century. As the word GAY grew more popular, many British men still preferred queer, since they felt that gay was a middle-class term that did not represent the network of working-class bars. (2) The word came back into vogue at the turn of the 1990s when it was hailed as the chosen term for QUEER POLITICS, seen by some as the new paradigm in the lesbian and gay movement. In this sense queer was said to refer equally to lesbians and gay men, and the slogan 'Dyke + fag = queer' was common. However, since the new queer politics remained mainly under gay male control, many lesbians complained that the term was just as much part of the problem of LESBIAN INVISIBILITY as any other 'joint' effort. When used as a self-referential term in the 1990s queer implies a membership of, or agreement with, the radical queer political groups. (3) In disciplines such as literary criticism, the word is used to describe the way in which lesbians and gay men are packaged for the heterosexual audience. This usage borrows from the pejorative use of the word, and indicates that a heterosexual author is wanting to communicate to their readers the idea that something is sexually amiss.

queer as fuck Slogan, worn on T-shirts and badges within the groups associated with QUEER politics of the 1990s. Emphasizing the confrontational strain of queer, the slogan was designed to be as offensive as possible to sensitive heterosexuals.

queerbashing Messy, usually nocturnal experience which, unlike a wet dream, is far from pleasant. It has been used since the 1970s to refer to an unprovoked attack on a lesbian or gay man by homophobes, or queerbashers. The threat of queerbashing has become routine for lesbians and gays, especially those living in urban areas. With their usual talent for turning the horrific into the comic, gay men sometimes call a man who has been queerbashed a crushed fruit or a sister in distress, and have even named gay social events queer bashes (after bash meaning party).

queer bird American lesbian slang, which became widely used in the 1930s, to refer to other lesbians. The phrase probably began its life in women's prisons, from where it travelled to others in the life.

queer cinema Generic term for many of the films by gay (male) filmmakers in the 1990s, including Gus Van Sant's 1991 *My Own Private Idaho*, the works of Derek Jarman (particularly EDWARD II), *Swoon* (*see* LEOPOLD AND LOEB), PARIS IS BURNING, TONGUES UNTIED and Constantine Giannaris' 1991 *Caught Looking*, which were held to be the cinematic response to the same sense of anger (fuelled by the AIDS epidemic) that gave rise to QUEER POLITICS, and which were informed by the same in-your-face sense that the time for putting our argument respectably had passed. The main exemplar of the often macho and violent genre is sometimes held to be Gregg Araki's THE LIVING END which asserts that life must be countered head-on. Rather like queer politics itself, queer cinema is not marked by a uniform sensibility or philosophy but rather by a common desire on the part of gay film-makers to take control of their own celluloid representation.

queer corner 1960s American HUSTLER slang for a particular area where male SEX-WORK-ERS would congregate whilst they were waiting to be picked up by a customer.

queer highwaymen The nineteenth-century highwayman Tom Rowlandson dressed as a woman and robbed his victims of their jewellery.

queer kings and queens of England Among those bejewelled British monarchs reported to have enjoyed a little same-sex sceptre crossing behind the back of court, as it were, are William II (*c.* 1060–1100), Richard I The Lionheart (1157–99), Edward II (1284–1327), James I (1566–1625, James VI of Scotland), William III (1650–1702) and Queen Anne (1665–1714).

queer manifesto Document that first appeared in June 1990 during New York's gay PRIDE week. Printed on newsprint, it consisted of several anonymously written essays, with the headline 'Queers read this', which were instantly resonant for lesbians and gays who had had it up to the teeth with campaigning all the time with little appreciable change in the attitudes of straight society. Copies of the manifesto were faxed across the Atlantic, and found their way onto computer bulletin boards. The manifesto represented for many the start of (one aspect of) the QUEER movement as an important strand of the lesbian and gay movement. One essay, entitled 'I hate straights!', was intended to bring forth the RAGE which had been building up within lesbian and gay communities. It demanded, 'LET YOURSELF BE ANGRY. Let yourself be angry that the price of our visibility is the constant threat of violence, anti-queer violence to which practically every segment of this society contributes', and preached a new form of angry SEPA-RATISM, telling queers to tell their straight friends to 'GO AWAY...until YOU can change'.

Queer Nation A series of radical DIRECT ACTION groups that burst on the scene in different cities throughout America in 1990, which first brought QUEER politics to widespread attention. Rather than an entirely new development in lesbian and gay politics, Queer Nation enjoyed the legacy of 1970s groups such as the GAY LIB-ERATION FRONT, but with the slick, media-conscious presentation that political action had acquired through AIDS groups such as ACT UP. The name of the group embodies the ambiguities present in queer politics with its overtones of a discrete, even sepa-ratist community. Some prefer to see the 'nation' as the cultural territory occupied by those whose lifestyles do not fit the het-erosexual standard. Many Queer Nations, including the founding New York and San Francisco groups, went the way that broad political groups seem to go so often, and imploded under the weight of different factions less than two years after they had been founded. However, others, such as Chicago, carry on.

queer politics Term used from 1990 to refer to a new force in lesbian and gay politics which was associated with organizations such as QUEER NATION in America and OUT-RAGE! in the UK. However, with our fin-de-siècle capacity for declaring new phenomena before they have coalesced, queer was represented as a coherent ideo-logy in the media, both pink and naff, before it really stabilized. People currently understand it in two sometimes contradic-tory ways. First it is simply seen as the chosen term of radical and confrontational lesbian and gay activists who have har-nessed some of the anger and energy of the AIDS activist movement to the general lesbian and gay movement, and whose chosen tactics are those of DIRECT ACTION and CIVIL DISOBEDIENCE. The activists choose the word queer as a way of reclaim-ing the language used by anti-gay bigots, to disarm their vocabulary and throw it back in their faces. This in itself is nothing new: DYKES and FAGGOTS have often flexed their linguistic muscle by coopting the lan-guage of bigotry. Christopher ISHERWOOD also preferred queer for the same reasons: 'It makes heterosexuals wince when you refer to yourself by these words if they've been using them behind your back, as they generally have.' But the word also serves to communicate the idea of subcultural difference, with sometimes SEPARATIST and ESSENTIALIST implications. 'Queer' (dyke and fag) culture is marked out as different from straight culture, as a way of demarcating the battle lines for the movement, and the fight is between queers and straights. Amongst other things, this easy polarization of society leaves little room for bisexuals to play any part in the struggle for sexual freedom. The second strand of queer thinking also uses the idea of subcultural difference, but plays with it to more subtle effect, to draw out the conflict as one between the institutions of heterosoc and anyone who dissents from the norms of that society. It celebrates sexual difference, but also sees sexuality as socially constructed and thus more mutable under different circumstances. As Peter TATCHELL wrote in 1993, 'In a society where there were no pressures or privileges associated with being straight, a lot more people would be queer or bisexual.' Thus homophobia is as restrictive of options for the heterosexually defined as it is for the civil rights of lesbians and gays. Some people have even taken this idea of sexual plasticity to the confusing lengths of proclaiming sex between lesbians and gay men as the queerest of the queer (see JACK AND JILL PARTIES). This rendering of queer politics ultimately leads to the rejection of separatism; to quote Peter Tatchell again, 'If everyone is potentially queer and queer freedom is in everyone's interest, then it is obvious that we should all be fighting for queer liberation, side by side, regardless of sexuality or gender.' In this case, the battle becomes one between those who define as queer and the institutions of heterosexuality which limit sexual expression. Neither strand of 'queer' thinking is entirely new, however, but carries a huge legacy from other groups in the history of the LESBIAN AND GAY MOVEMENT.

queer popes Several popes are said to have been divine in both senses. Among them: John XII (937–64), who was alleged to have organized a brothel from the Vatican; Benedict IX (1020–55) who held huge queer orgies in the Lateran palace; Paul II (1417–71) who wore a huge glamorous tiara and who allegedly died while being fucked by a minion; Sixtus IV (1414–84) who unhappily allowed the beginning of the Spanish INQUISITION; Leo X (1475–1521) who bankrupted the papacy in his search for ever more gorgeous robes; and Julius III (1487–1555) who was more interested in watching for the coming of his cardinals than that of the Lord.

queer Roman emperors History implies that it was wholly straight emperors who were somewhat in the minority. Among those who are reported to have enjoyed same-sex activities are Augustus (63 BC–AD 14), Tiberius (14 BC–AD 37), CALIGULA (AD 12–41), Claudius (10 BC–AD 54), NERO (AD 37–68), Otho (32–69), Domitian (51–96), Nerva (30–98), Trajan (53–117), Hadrian (76–138), Commodus (61–92), and Heliogabalus (205–22). The Roman consul Julius Caesar (100–44 BC) was also reported to have enjoyed same-sex activities.

queer ships When the Second World War ended and the US military command, freed from the necessity of retaining personnel, began to persecute lesbians and gays within the forces once more, hundreds of them were packed onto such ships and offloaded at the nearest port. What they didn't predict, however, was that these discharged personnel would often stay in these ports rather than go home and give up the freedom they had grown used to. Thus they became the backbone of queer communities in coastal cities such as San Francisco, New York and Boston.

queer space A safe space in which QUEER people can feel open and uninhibited about their sexuality. The notion points out some of the contradictions inherent in queer politics, since queer is explained by some as a non-separatist political praxis, yet a queer space is often defined as exclusively lesbian and/or gay, and sometimes but not always bisexual.

queer subculture In effect a totality of different subcultures, each subject to different forces. The factors of gender, race, class and age are particularly important in defining how individual queers view their sexuality, and how they choose to express it socially. It can exist, however, as a political entity, since homophobia is not interested in differences between different groups of queers, however much some queers might like to pretend that they are more acceptable than others.

queer theory A term more usually used to describe the work of particular theorists than a cohesive body of work. Notable queer theorists are Judith Butler, Eve Kosofsky Sedgwick, Cindy Patton, Diana Fuss, and Richard Dyer. Generally, no assumption should be made that those doing queer theory are gay. The things which unite these theorists are an emphasis on interdisciplinary writing and conceptualization incorporating Marxism, feminism, political theory, history and film theory and a stress on the body, lived experience and subjectivity. To describe it in queer theory terminology: queer theory seeks to que(e)ry what is apparently straight(forward). Such theory is often criticized as untranslatable into everyday English and therefore only of interest to other academics, and impossible to transform into practical politics and therefore self-indulgent. There is certainly no clear relationship between the work of queer theorists in the academy and queer activists campaigning on the streets.

queerarchy 1990s term for the categorization of people that sometimes occurs within the political groups associated with QUEER politics. Within the queerarchy the queeristocrats are those who conduct any meaningful acts in their lives entirely within the queer community, and who are entirely open about their sexuality and politics on the occasions that they venture into BREEDER society.

queers bash back 1980s slogan which sought to challenge the belief by lesbians and gay men that violence was necessarily a part of their lives. It was used by those who believe that lesbian and gay communities should take matters into their own hands to deal with the problem of queerbashing when the police cannot be relied upon; and if that means vigilante groups, then so be it. Queers Bash Back was the name of a British group that went out to gay cruising areas to guard against, and repel, queerbashing attacks.

Querelle of Brest 1953 novel by Jean GENET which most perfectly demonstrates the gay fascination with sailors as well as the special type of seediness and promiscuity that they exhibit in gay fantasy. While on shore leave, Querelle's fantastically beautiful body becomes the focus of frustrated desire, the site of fantasy fulfilled or a temptation leading to death or disgrace for several men. Yet, in his odyssey through a mainly male world of violence, inarticulacy, power games and stunted emotions, Querelle begins to find a transcendent self-knowledge through allowing himself to be fucked and through his first mouth-on-mouth kiss with another man, the police chief Mario. The novel was filmed in 1982 by gay director Rainer Werner Fassbinder whose creation of the world of exaggerated masculinity resembled an animated TOM OF FINLAND. Both novel and film have been seen as metaphors for the alienation created by Western society and, given Genet's known fondness for the underworld of crime and prostitution as the repository of certain innocent truths and passions unbridled by the sophistications of society, this is possible. As the *Spectator* said in its review of the novel, 'The characters in Genet's books all share a burning, tempestuous passion to live.'

The Quilt Popular name given to the huge memorial quilt that was started by the NAMES PROJECT to commemorate the many lives that have been lost to the AIDS epidemic.

The Quilt Short story by Indian writer Ismat Chughtai, published in India in 1944. Its lesbian theme provoked a scandal and, with echoes of Radclyffe HALL, Chughtai was tried for obscenity. It is the story of the relationship between an Indian woman whose husband refuses to let her leave the house, and her female servant, told by her niece who discovers these rum goings on beneath the quilt while staying with her.

Quim British lesbian magazine which was set up in 1989 by a collective of black and white lesbians. It was particularly intended to discuss all issues of lesbian sex and sexuality, and was accused by some members of the lesbian community as being little more than soft porn which glorified SADOMASOCHISM. It has also been seen as an organ of white lesbians which does not address the concerns of black lesbians equally. In 1994 there was a special edition guest-edited by black lesbian performer Leonora Rogers-Wright which devoted the majority of space to black lesbian voices.

radical fairies During the 1970s many gay men felt the need for elaborating a gay spirituality and communality within a nurturing environment. They felt that the gay movement was concentrating too much on law reform, and on the material aspects of the gay scene, not on developing specifically gay forms of social institution. Such men felt that there existed a form of gay psyche which was greatly different from the heterosexual consciousness. They believed that if gay men created an internal revolution to rid themselves of the detritus of living within a homophobic society, they could establish this psyche as a dominant force. At the same time gay historians such as Arthur Evans were re-examining myth and folklore to construct a history of heterodox spirituality. In his work *Witchcraft and the Gay Counterculture*, Evans explored the relevance of European myth regarding fairies to the modern gay movement. He argued that they symbolized the remnants of ancient Celtic tradi-

tions of matriarchal society and nature worship after they had been forced underground by patriarchal conquerors. As such they represented part of a continuous tradition of 'heretical' spirituality, a tradition shared by the WITCHES who were persecuted in the middle ages. Since the accusations levelled against witches often included those of licentiousness and sexual impropriety, the sexual heretics of today – lesbians and gay men – can also locate themselves within this tradition. Out of these two forces the radical fairy movement developed. Gay men took on the label as a way of examining their folkloric heritage, and challenging the spiritual norms of heterosexual society. They often congregated together to create lifestyles to put this knowledge into practice (*see* SPIRITUAL CONFERENCE FOR RADICAL FAIRIES). Their movement was paralleled by the lesbians who were exploring eco-feminism and claiming witches as their spiritual predecessors.

radical sex Sexual behaviours which fall outside the conventional, or VANILLA forms of sexual expression. The term is generally used to describe activities such as BONDAGE AND DISCIPLINE or SADOMASOCHISM, and on occasion role-playing, such as BUTCH/FEMME or COTTAGING. Radical sex indicates the political implications of diverse sexual activities which their practitioners see as challenging the control which heterosexual society seeks to place over our lives. It argues that sexual radicals have an ability to carve their own sexual pleasures which is denied those who are bound by paradigms of monogamy and simple penetration. It is not without controversy, however, and has come under criticism from within both the gay male communities and particularly the lesbian-feminist movement for implying creating a hierarchy of sex ('radical' as opposed to 'conservative') which sees radical sex as better.

Radicalesbians A group of feminist lesbians who formed in late 1969 in New York when they found that lesbians were being ignored in feminist organizations like the National Organization of Women and the REDSTOCKINGS, and by gay men within post-STONEWALL RIOT organizations such as the GAY LIBERATION FRONT. They wrote *The Woman Identified Woman* in 1970, and led the LAVENDER MENACE action against the National Organization of Women. Rita Mae BROWN is the most famous of the lesbians who was involved with the group.

rage Like anger, rage is a legitimate response to oppression, and a way of demonstrating continued resistance. It is 'about living and not just surviving' (Yvonne Flowers). Although the feminist movements have used the term since the 1970s, it has become particularly associated with the late 1980s and the 1990s when many lesbian and gay activists, sensing little change on the part of the heterosexual establishment twenty years after the STONEWALL RIOT, and with the experience of AIDS to demonstrate that gay lives are not considered worthy of Government money, have found even anger too weak a term,

and talk of rage as more suited to their feelings.

Rainbow Coalition In America the coalition between different identity, class and issue-focused groups into a voting-block with a coherent progressive agenda. The coalition typically works within the Democratic Party to push progressive candidates in the primary elections, and to negotiate platforms acceptable to the member groups in the final elections. Although lesbians and gays are included in the coalition, such alliances are not entirely welcomed by some activists, since they see individual identities being submerged for the sake of promoting a unified idea of 'economic justice'. Thus alliances between different identity groups are known as rainbow alliances. It is often thought that the RAINBOW FLAG is a symbol of such alliances, but in fact it is specific to the lesbian and gay community.

rainbow flag As a symbol for the lesbian and gay movement, the rainbow flag has been with us since 1978, during which time it has been through several incarnations. At a meeting in 1978 for the San Francisco Gay Freedom Day Parade the idea of a rainbow flag as an enduring symbol for gay pride was mooted. The idea borrowed from symbols used within the hippie movement and black civil rights groups. San Francisco artist Gilbert Baker produced the prototypes, which had eight stripes in pink, red, orange, yellow, green, turquoise, indigo and violet. Two huge flags in these colours were flown in the 1978 parade. By the 1990s the flag had been simplified to six stripes of red, orange, yellow, green, blue and violet. A diverse set of variations have been seen however, including flags based on the American stars and stripes, with the red and white stripes replaced by rainbow colours, and flags with the PINK TRIANGLE or LAMBDA symbol superimposed. Another version has a black strip to commemorate those we have lost to AIDS. In the 1990s the flag is a common sight in lesbian and gay marches worldwide, and flies in gay neighbourhoods in many cities.

Rainey, Ma (1886–1939) Black blues singer who performed such songs as PROVE IT ON ME BLUES in 1920s Harlem, and who cultivated a bisexual image.

Ramayana Indian literary classic written by Valmiki. One episode describes how Hanuman sees women in passionate embraces in the palaces of Lanka 'as if they were making love to their male lovers'.

Rat Mort Bar in the Place Pigalle in Paris at the turn of the twentieth century which by night served as the stamping ground of many Parisian sex-workers, who were quite open about the lesbian affairs they had with one another. Because of the outré atmosphere, it became the favoured haunt of many French writers and artists of the time.

rave (1) Common term used at the turn of the twentieth century in English girls' schools and women's colleges to describe passionate crushes felt by one girl for another, which involved a more or less erotic content. They were distinguished from simple friendships by the intensity of the feeling involved. (2) In the late 1980s and 1990s in the UK it came to mean a huge all-night one-off club, usually housed in a large building such as a warehouse or aircraft hangar, for young things high on ECSTASY.

re-gaying AIDS The unforeseen (by gay activists at least) effect of the mid-1980s effort at DE-GAYING AIDS was that the bulk of funding for AIDS information and education in the UK and America was channelled into materials produced for a 'general public' that was, in effect, heterosexual society. Meanwhile, the majority of people who were being exposed to HIV were still gay men. As a result, in the late 1980s and early 1990s AIDS activists and gay men began to pressure for the re-gaying of AIDS. What they wanted was not only the recognition that gay men were still disproportionately affected by the epidemic, but also the targeting of government funding and education to these communities.

Read, Mary *See* BONNEY, ANNE.

Reagan, Ronald (1911–) American President throughout the initial years of the AIDS epidemic. However, Reagan was unwilling to provide any leadership to confront the growing crisis that HIV and AIDS represented. He did not see fit to even mention the word 'AIDS' in public until September 1985, by which time more than 10,000 Americans had been diagnosed with the syndrome. When he set up a presidential commission on AIDS in July 1987, it did not include a single expert on the subject and contained only one openly gay person. The result was that the commission was denounced as a fiasco. Much to everyone's surprise, the report of the commission was progressive, advocating the banning of discrimination against people with HIV/AIDS, the maintenance of confidentiality about HIV status, and the expansion of education about HIV. Less surprisingly, the report was largely ignored by the Reagan administration.

Rebel without a Cause 1955 film classic featuring pin-up James Dean as a disaffected youth. Sal Mineo also features in the SISSY role of Plato who is brought up by a cloying maid in place of his father, and who looks to Jim (Dean) as a sort of older-brother figure. Dean returns his friendship, and, for the queer audience, the sparks fly.

recruitment *See* MISSIONARY WORK.

red Colour used within gay HANKIE CODES and CONTACT ADVERTS to indicate an interest in FISTFUCKING.

Red Hot and Blue 1990 record and video in which an eclectic selection of modern rock stars, from Iggy Pop to Jimmy Somerville, rehashed some of Cole Porter's finest tunes in the interests of raising money for International AIDS Day 1990. Erasure and k.d. LANG also appeared on the record.

red ribbon Red ribbons are worn commonly in a loop pinned to the lapel as a sign of concern over the AIDS epidemic, and a passive indication of solidarity with those who are affected by the crisis. They were first developed within the fashion industry to echo the yellow ribbons worn as a token for soldiers who went off to fight in the Gulf war, and gained prominence when many performers wore them during the Academy Awards ceremony in 1991. Many committed AIDS activists have argued that wearing ribbons is an ineffective and token way of salving the individual conscience without challenging government apathy over the crisis, and, on AIDS demonstrations, chant, 'Red ribbons are not enough.' An alternative form was seen at the première of Derek JARMAN's film BLUE in 1993 when people wore blue ribbons instead.

Red Stripe condom First condoms produced in the UK which were recommended for anal sex.

Redl *See* HOMINTERN.

Redstockings Radical-feminist group in New York in the late 1960s. The organization was originally called Group One, but the name Redstockings was coined by feminist writer Shulamith Firestone in 1969 to suggest a combination of two traditions, that of the BLUESTOCKINGS and the red of revolution and radical activity. In its principles the group stated, 'We do not ask what is radical, revolutionary, reformist or moral – we ask: Is it good for women or bad for women?' Established around a cell-like structure of CONSCIOUSNESS-RAISING GROUPS, the organization campaigned on issues such as abortion. According to some lesbian members such as activist Rita Mae BROWN and Karla Jay, Redstockings, like many other mainly heterosexual radical groups, was not always willing to take on the lesbian cause, and was slow to recognize the political significance of events such as the STONEWALL RIOT.

Relax *See* FRANKIE GOES TO HOLLYWOOD.

religion Although the organized religions have not historically been the most welcoming institutions for lesbians and gay men to express their sexualities – the INQUISITION springs to mind – many lesbians and gay men have remained believ-

ers, and continue to assert their right to worship and to deal with the morality of their sexuality as they choose. Religious groupings include: Affirmation – United Methodists for Lesbian and Gay Concerns; Affirmation – Gay and Lesbian Mormons; American Baptists Concerned; Brethren/Mennonite Council for Lesbian and Gay Concerns; DIGNITY; Friends for Lesbian and Gay Concerns (Quaker); Hineinu (Jewish organization); INTEGRITY; Julian Fellowship (for Catholic women); Lesbian and Gay Christian Movement; METROPOLITAN COMMUNITY CHURCH; New Ways Ministry (for lesbian and gay Catholics); Odinshof (heathen religious and educational charity); Presbyterians for Lesbian and Gay Concerns; Quaker Lesbian and Gay Fellowship; Quest; Seventh-Day Adventist Kinship International; Unitarian/Universalists for Lesbian and Gay Concerns; United Church Coalition for Lesbian and Gay Concerns; Universal Fellowship of Metropolitan Community Churches; and finally the SISTERS OF PERPETUAL INDULGENCE. Of course, there are also many other lesbians and gays who bond with others of their sexuality within their own religions without creating separate organizations.

rent boy A male sex-worker. The term renter has been used at least since the nineteenth century. Oscar WILDE wrote in a letter to Alfred DOUGLAS, 'I cannot listen to your curled lips saying hideous things to me. I would sooner be blackmailed by every renter in London.' Now often abbreviated to just 'rent'.

Rents Play by Michael Wilcox, first produced in 1979, which blew away the cobwebs of furtiveness which had characterized depictions of male sex-work. The two gay youths, Phil and Robert, eke out their incomes on the game, but manage throughout to maintain a sense of humour and cynicism about their clientele.

respectability Usually means the aping of the lifestyles and attitudes of heterosexual society. A vexed question in lesbian and gay politics has always been to what extent we should present ourselves as respectable in order to win support for campaigns such as legal reform. Some see it as pragmatism, others as a no-win ploy that could only ever win limited freedom for those who are willing to pretend to be straight without attacking the root cause of oppression. Describing the takeover of the MATTACHINE SOCIETY by more moderate activists, Harry HAY said that the movement 'became more interested in being respectable than self-respecting...They believed we were just like anyone else.'

retail therapy The time-honoured gay reaction to the sling-backs and arrows of outrageous fortune is to spend money. It seems that any problem, romantic, professional or financial, can be removed, or at least displaced, by a trip to the sales. The gloomiest brow can be cleared by the gentle swish of plastic through the electronic scanner, and the faraway sound of the bank manager having apoplexy. Who needs Sigmund when you can have Harvey Nicks?

Revolutionary People's Constitutional Convention Conference held in the American city of Philadelphia in September 1970 by the black liberation group, the Black Panthers, in order to draft a constitution that would 'represent all oppressed people'. On the advice of Black Panther leader Huey Newton, representatives from the newly formed GAY LIBERATION FRONT were invited. Newton had recently demanded that militant black leaders confront their 'insecurities' about homosexuality, and had suggested that 'we should try to unite with them in a revolutionary fashion', the first time that COALITION POLITICS between the black and lesbian/gay movements had been explicitly suggested in America. However, the convention, which attracted over 10,000 people, showed the problems with such coalitions immediately. There was no specific workshop for the lesbian delegates to draw up their statement of rights, and many of them left in disgust.

RFD: A Country Journal for Gay Men Everywhere A magazine which was produced in a gay farmhouse community in Iowa, USA, from 1974. It was aimed at, and in large part written by, the many gay men of the 1970s who went into the American countryside seeking to create rural FAIRY communes and escape urban gay ghettos. It was in rural life, rather than the hectic metropolitan centres, that they hoped to create truly alternative ways of life and remain in touch with their own spirituality. Packets of pansy seeds were attached to some issues. Contemptuous gay men in urban gay ghettos developed the term RFD queen to refer to a naive gay man in a rural backwater, a gay hick.

rhubarb and custard A cocktail of barbiturates and ecstasy produced in tablet form which is popular on the gay club scene. It is regarded as fairly toxic.

rice queen Dubious slang term for a white gay man who is erotically attracted to men of East Asian descent. *See also* BEAN QUEEN, DINGE QUEEN, FROG QUEEN, SNOW QUEEN. Rice pudding is US gay slang for semen, especially when ejaculated by an East Asian man.

Rich, Adrienne (1929–) American lesbian-feminist poet and essayist. Her status as poet has enabled other lesbian poets to move towards, if not into, the mainstream. Her prose work such as *Of Woman Born* (1976), *On Lies, Secrets and Silence* (1980), and *Compulsory Heterosexuality and Lesbian Existence* (1980) have been very important in defining a lesbian feminist agenda. Her position as a mother has also been important in opening out motherhood to include lesbians.

Richard I (1157–99) King of England. Better known as Richard Lionheart (Richard Coeur de Lion), for his valour in the Third Crusade. The *Chronicles of Henry II* (his father) suggest that all was not as straight as an arrow with young Richard. They describe his close relationship with Philip II, King of France, who 'so honoured him for so long that they ate every day at the same table and from the same dish, and at night their beds did not divide them'. Richard's name has also been linked with the French minstrel Blondel, who is said to have accompanied the King to Palestine and, after his capture on the way home, to have located him in prison in Austria, using a song which they had jointly composed.

rimming The practice of licking or sucking the anus of your partner. In the early years of the AIDS epidemic rimming was seen as fairly risky by some educators, although this probably said more about their distaste for the act itself. In effect, unless the partner being rimmed has blood around the anus, there is very little risk, and even less if a DENTAL DAM is used.

risk group In the early days of the AIDS epidemic, health professionals, as well as the media, talked about societal groups 'at risk' from HIV and AIDS, including the FOUR H'S. While it was true that the vast majority of people living with HIV and AIDS in Europe and North America were drawn from such communities, the implication was created that these communities were inherently more at risk, rather than that individuals within them put themselves at risk through certain behaviours, thus reinforcing the notion that AIDS was the problem of various marginalized and 'undesirable' groups. People with HIV, as well as some professionals argued that 'risk behaviours' was a more appropriate term.

ritual prostitution Many historians have claimed that male-cult prostitution was a common feature of religious ceremonies in the archaic civilizations of the Mediterranean lands. Indeed, it seems that male prostitutes practised in the Temple of Solomon in Jerusalem. Although the evidence is unclear, it would appear that both male and female prostitutes operated within the temple, according to the Hebrew Bible. We can assume that the male prostitutes were expected to have sex with men, since homosexual eunuchs are recorded throughout the Babylonian and Assyrian civilizations (*see for example*

ASSINU). This proposition is interesting since in the Hebrew Bible fears are expressed that the Hebrews were adopting practices of prostitution from their neighbours, and its prohibitions on homosexuality, which have been responsible for the later attitude of the Church towards homosexuality, can be seen in this light as an attempt to clear up this particular problem.

Roaring Twenties Name given to the 1920s in America, which saw a general loosening of social mores, and a greater expression of diversity, including sexual. Despite prohibition of alcohol, SPEAKEASIES were found in every town. In areas like Harlem, socially and sexually adventurous clubs and parties were held. It was here that lesbians and gay men found a place they had not had before.

The Rocky Horror Show The cult rock musical which campily spoofs horror film conventions. It deals with the corruption/redemption of all-Americans Brad and Janet, and features Tim Curry as Dr Frank N Furter, the embodiment of deviant sexuality who blasts in with a gutsy 'I'm a sweet transvestite from Transsexual, Transsylvania' and who proudly displays his latest creation, the muscle-bound Rocky, whom he marries. A glorious celebration of unrestrained sexuality, the film has also allowed generations of college kids to drag up in fishnets and stillies, the innocent little angels.

Rohm, Ernst (1897–1934) Friend of Adolf Hitler, founder of the Nazi party in Germany, and in charge of Hitler's army of fascist Brownshirts, or Sturmabteilung (stormtroopers). His homoerotic escapades were widely known within the party. He enjoyed Hitler's confidence until the Führer began to fear him as a rival, and he was arrested and shot on the NIGHT OF THE LONG KNIVES on 30 June 1934.

Rollerina Camp fixture in New York's Greenwich Village streets in the 1970s, and example of the marvellous insanities of gay life. Rollerina was a Wall Street businessman by day and rollerskating drag granny at nights and weekends.

Resplendent in frock, bonnet and glisten-ing specs, she wove in and out of the traf-fic, casting blessings hither and yon with her wand. Greeted always by appreciative laughter from gay onlookers and bewilder-ment from straight tourists, she was an example of why the ghetto is the most fun place to be.

Roman Emperors, queer *See* QUEER, ROMAN EMPERORS.

romantic friendship A close relationship between two women which was seen up to the late nineteenth century in America and Britain as a positive institution, an edifying experience for women which allowed them to express emotional commitment before, of course, the ultimate experience of marriage. American author William Cullen Bryant talks of women in Vermont who 'slept on the same pillow and had a common purse, and adopted each other's relations'. There was a great growth in such relationships towards the latter half of the nineteenth century when move-ments among women for suffrage and employment gained impetus. This allowed some middle-class women to find, often for the first time, the economic indepen-dence to resist matrimony and devote themselves to women-oriented relation-ships. While these relationships involved a high degree of emotional closeness, the extent to which any were erotic is difficult to establish. Society, which had little con-cept of the lesbian as a category of women, could only see them as non-sexual, and it would be dangerous for any women to commit any evidence of sexual closeness to paper. Societal approbation for such friendships diminished with the growth of the ideas of sexology which made the hall-marks of romantic friendship – sleeping in the same bed, writing affectionate letters, holding hands – suspicious in terms of sexual contact.

Rome Although the Roman civilization is not as celebrated as that of Greece for its liberalism regarding same-sex sexuality, and although it has not provided us with the wealth of literary material that we have received from Greece, there is ample evi-dence that same-sex eroticism was a common part of Roman lives. We must be wary however not to make the assumption that homosexuality was defined in the same way that it is in the twentieth cen-tury. In Rome same-sex relations were fil-tered through societal class roles. For example, it seems to have been common for masters to have sexual relations with their slaves; as Seneca records, 'Unchastity is...an obligation for the slave'. Sexual rela-tions with slaves form some of the subject matter for writers such as Plautus and Horace. Like Greece, a sharp distinction was made between the active and passive roles in sex, with the penetrator considered as unimpeachably masculine. However unlike Greece, it appears that boys who were to become citizens were not consid-ered appropriate as passive partners in anal sex. Male prostitution appears to have been institutionalized in Rome; male sex-workers even had their own holiday and had to pay a tax to the State. In terms of the Roman literary heritage, we have poetry from Catullus and Tibullus describing the joys and sorrows of loving boys, while Virgil's *Eclogues*, based on the works of the Greek writer Theocritus, include the char-acter of CORYDON, the lovesick shepherd. Juvenal satirized Roman same-sex prac-tices in accusing aristocratic Romans of demeaning themselves in their attractions to lower-class boys. Petronius' SATYRICON is a work of some sexual explicitness, while Martial depicts the entertainers (*cinaedus*) who were known for their sexual services. In total, attitudes towards homo-sexual relations were more mixed in Rome than in Greece, largely because they did not share the Hellenistic notion of ped-erasty as an edifying part of a young man's upbringing.

Roosevelt, Eleanor (1884–1962) Wife of American President Franklin D. Roosevelt, who had an affair with journalist Lorena Hickok, which had already started by the time of FDR's inauguration in 1933, at which Eleanor wore a sapphire ring which Lorena had given to her. Hickok covered the White House for Associated Press, and was asked by the President to examine the social effects of the Great Depression.

rooster This bird was associated with male same-sex eroticism in ancient Greece. Paintings on vases show older male suitors presenting the birds to the young objects of their affections. They were also linked to the bisexual god Dionysus.

Rose is a rose is a rose is a rose Line by Gertrude STEIN from the poem 'Sacred Emily' which was written in tribute to the painter Sir Frederick Rose. It alludes to the fact that a thing might be perfect in itself, yet inexplicable other than by reference to itself. The line became somewhat of a logo for Stein's relationship with Alice B. TOKLAS, and was written on a number of their belongings.

Roseanne American television comedy show, aired since 1989, which serves as a platform for the take-no-hostages style of the wisecracking mother (Roseanne Arnold) in her daily battles with husband and children. The show has included gay characters in the form of Leon, Roseanne's boss at the shopping mall diner, and her friend Nancy (played by cult lesbian comedian Sandra Bernhard). It hit the headlines in 1994 when Roseanne visits a lesbian bar and engages in a mouth to mouth kiss with Mariel Hemingway. When American TV networks refused to air that particular episode, Roseanne threatened to pull the plug on the entire series unless they relented.

Rosebud The word which Pat CALIFIA suggests in *Sapphistry* as the SAFE WORD for use in SM and sexual role-playing. For those times when 'no' presumably doesn't mean no, 'rosebud' can mean no instead.

rough trade Slang term for the sort of man who becomes violent during a casual sexual encounter. Typically, a working-class man who would identify himself as straight, and who would only take the insertive role during any sex.

Round the Horne Tremendously popular British radio show that had the nation's families clustered round the wireless regularly between 1965 and 1969. The show featured a bizarre population of characters from the wartime lovers, Dame Celia Molestrangler and 'ageing juvenile' Binkie Huckaback, to the uppity Australian feminist Judy Colibah. What was guaranteed was a thick spread of sexual innuendo, not only from the satyriasis-suffering folk singer Rambling Syd Rumpo but also from the self-evidently gay JULIAN AND SANDY. The programme was a staple for gay audiences as one of the few that allowed any affirmation of their lives to slip through.

Royal Exchange One of the most popular cruising grounds for men out for dick in London, used for this purpose as early as 1700. The Exchange was home to a variety of traders as well as men who were seeking casual labour. It also attracted men who went there to find ROUGH TRADE. *The London Spy* of January 1699 records, 'We then proceeded and went on to the Change...and Jostled in amongst a parcel of Swarthy Buggerantoes, Preternatural Fornicators...who would Ogle a Handsome Young Man with as much Lust, as a True-bred English Whoremaster would gaze upon a Beautiful Virgin.'

rubber queen Gay slang for a gay man with a fetishistic attraction to latex, whether latex clothing, sheets or other items.

Rubyfruit Jungle 1973 novel by Rita Mae BROWN which became a lesbian favourite due to the damn-near perfection of its hero Molly Bolt, who demonstrated the self-image gains the LESBIAN FEMINIST movement had made for its members. It was described by its publishers as a book 'about growing up lesbian in America – and living happily ever after'. Athletic, intelligent, drop-dead gorgeous and with leadership qualities, Molly goes on a picaresque odyssey through life battling against a multitude of ills: heterosexual women who dabble with lesbianism; straights who can't see the lesbians for the stereotypes; CLOSETed lesbians; and the exploitative wealthy. Through all this she emerges victorious, with her sense of righteousness unbashed, as an unrelentingly positive role-model who is too good for any man (*see* MOLLY MYTH). No prizes for the significance of the title: 'When I make love to women I think of their genitals as a, as a rubyfruit jungle...women are thick and rich and full of hidden treasures and besides that, they taste good.'

Rule, Jane (1930–) American writer. She is the author of a number of novels, including the impressive *The Desert of the Heart* (1964), which was the basis for the film *Desert Hearts*. Rule also wrote the groundbreaking *Lesbian Images* (1975), which examines fiction by and about lesbians including the work of Ivy Compton-Burnett, Elizabeth Bowen and May SARTON.

run the fuck To be the dominant partner within the sexual act, and control the way in which sex progresses, (1980s slang).

Russell, Colin Character in the British soap opera EASTENDERS, who appeared regularly from 1986 to 1989, played by Michael Cashman, a gay actor who has since become known for his work in the British gay rights organization STONEWALL. Colin was the only gay character to be beamed into the nation's salons for such a length of time, and as such he served a positive role in demystifying gay lives, and as a positive role model for other gay men. The only problem was, he was so horribly, annoyingly nice that it would be no surprise if the entire nation now thinks we are all middle-class, quiet and with a sense of humour that must have been left in the office 'up West'. He had two relationships: with the unprepossessing barrow-boy, Barry Clark (Gary Hailes), who ditched him for the closet; and with Guido Smith (Nicholas Donovan), with whom a snog gave the nation's media apoplexy, and an excuse for the headline 'Eastbenders'.

After an HIV scare, Colin left the square because he had developed multiple sclerosis.

Russian Revolution Contrary to popular belief, the Russian Revolution did briefly spell a period of lesbian and gay freedom. The Bolsheviks, with the rationale that the State should not interfere in sexual affairs, legalized divorce, abortion, birth control and homosexuality. A period of lesbian and gay creative activity followed, only to be sharply repressed when Stalin became dictator in 1929, and everything went horribly wrong.

Russian River Picturesque resort area sixty-five miles from San Francisco around the town of Guerneville which has been a popular destination for revelling queers since the 1970s. They bought houses and cottages and founded bars and restaurants in the queer boom town, and went there at every opportunity they had to leave the whirl of the metropolis. Resorts were given bucolic titles such as the Woods or the Willows, and cater for all comers. The Russian River Lodge was even known as Folsom-in-the-Woods for the number of leather holidaymakers it attracted (*see* FOLSOM STREET). Along the meandering curves of the river swimming, sunbathing and, of course, cruising are all possible.

Ruth and Naomi Held by some to be an example of a biblical lesbian relationship. When Naomi tried to persuade Ruth to return to her family after the death of her husband, Ruth said, 'Intreat me not to leave thee, or to return from following after thee; for whither thou goest, I will go; and where thou lodgest, I will lodge.' (Ruth:16). And she followed Naomi to her homeland. It is a popular inclusion in ceremonies to celebrate lesbian relationships, and is an obvious lesbian clue in the film *Fried Green Tomatoes at the Whistlestop Café*.

S

Sailors

S Abbreviation sometimes used in gay CON-
TACT ADVERTS. Rather confusingly, it can
refer to either a SADIST or a SLAVE.

Sa'di Iranian poet, and author of the
Gulistan (Rose Garden) and the *Khubsiyyat
va majalis al-Hazl* (Impure Things and
Facetiae). The latter consisted of crude
pornographic pieces. Sa'di writes of the
power of the beautiful boy, 'with whom
the souls of pious men are inclined to com-
mingle', and of the 'soft-fleshed and fine
skinned boy' who is the best to have as a
catamite.

Sacher-Masoch, Leopold von (1835–95)
Author of the novel *Venus in Furs*, who
gave his name to the practice of
MASOCHISM.

Sackville-West, Vita (Victoria) (1892–1962)
Aristocratic British writer who had numerous passionate relationships with women
while being married to Harold Nicolson
(who had a penchant for young men).

Sackville-West is most famous for her love
affairs with Violet Trefusis and Virginia
Woolf. A manuscript describing her relationship with Trefusis was found by her
son Nigel Nicolson in a locked bag after
her death. It was subsequently edited and
published as *Portrait of a Marriage*.
Sackville-West's relationship with Trefusis
(from 1918 to 1921) apparently involved a
considerable amount of dressing up with
Sackville-West passing as a man so that
she could publicly caress Trefusis. The
affair nearly destroyed both their marriages; the lovers eloped to, and travelled
in, Europe for several months before their
respective husbands succeeded in dragging them home. Both Sackville-West and
Trefusis wrote (heterosexualized) accounts
of their affair: *Challenge* (1924) and *Broderie
Anglaise* (1935) respectively. While
Sackville-West was not fighting on the bar-
ricades like Radclyffe HALL, she was privately clear about her love for women and
went to no particular lengths to hide it.

When a petition was being drawn up protesting against the ban on *The Well of Loneliness* in 1928, Virginia Woolf told Sackville-West that she would not be asked to sign it because her proclivities were too well-known. Woolf's love for Sackville-West was embodied in ORLANDO (1928), the first edition of which was illustrated with photographs of Vita and her ancestral home, Knowle. ORLANDO has been described as the longest and most charming love letter in English literature. But Sackville-West does seem to have been pretty irresistible. 'She shines in the grocer's shop in Sevenoaks with a candlelit radiance, stalking legs like beech trees, pink glowing, grape clustered, pearl hung', wrote Woolf in 1925. Sackville-West is today remembered more for *Portrait of a Marriage* (especially after it was filmed as a glossy aristocratic love story for the BBC in 1990), and for the garden she created at Sissinghurst than for her novels which were very successful in her lifetime, particularly *The Edwardians* (1930) and *All Passion Spent* (1931).

Sacred Band of Thebes Ancient Greek army unit, founded in 371 BC, which was composed entirely of couples of male lovers, some 150 of them. The rationale was that men fighting along with their lovers would not wish to show shame, and would fight ferociously to the end. The Band was decimated at the Battle of Chaeronea by Philip of Macedon and his son Alexander the Great.

sadism Deriving (sexual) pleasure from the giving of pain. The word is derived from the name of the French author, Donatien Alphonse François, Comte de Sade (1740–1814), known as the Marquis de Sade. His life was punctuated by a number of prison sentences as a result of his chosen form of sexual expression. His often disturbing works, such as *120 Days in Sodom* are also the creations of a mind excited by the suffering of others, and were banned by French courts as recently as 1957. Modern sadists have found ways of incorporating their desires into the consensual practices of SADOMASOCHISM.

sadomasochism The giving or receiving of pain within sexual play. The word, a fusing of SADISM and MASOCHISM, was first introduced by the sexologist Richard von KRAFFT-EBING in his 1886 work *Psychopathia Sexualis*. In the process, sadomasochism was characterized as a discrete, and pathological, form of sexual behaviour, rather than a potential of all sexual play. The term refers to a whole wealth of possible acts, including verbal abuse, humiliation, spanking, PIERCING, cutting, BONDAGE, asphyxiation, wearing of uniforms and role-play – in fact, any activity which can be perpetrated by one DOMINANT agent on their SUBMISSIVE partner. Thus what is at issue is the allocation of POWER into sexual situations. That is not to say that sadomasochistic pleasure does not have a biological basis. In fact, the experience of pain spurs the release of ENDORPHINS, a natural opiate-like substance created in the brain, which heightens sexual ecstasy. Although the two roles within sadomasochism are reversible, serious practitioners argue that the most exquisite sex can be performed only by those people who have extended experience of the art of either role, and within serious sadomasochistic communities people will become known as particularly talented in one specific role. While concerned with the giving of pain, responsible sadomasochistic practice is extremely safe. Partners will often set limits to play beforehand, and have a SAFE WORD which the submissive partner can use to terminate the sex. Although not a specifically gay or lesbian form of sex, sadomasochism has contributed to the greater choice of sexual expression that can be found on the whole within queer communities, and gay LEATHER communities have been relatively able to find a place within gay communities. However, there are many lesbians and gays who ally themselves with a sexually blinkered mainstream in condemning sadomasochism as unnatural and likely to 'give us all a bad name'. In fact, sadomasochism has often been decried by the lesbian feminist movement as capitulating to male systems of power and militating against the practice of egalitarian forms of sex. However, in their defence, sado-masochists, including LESBIAN SEX RADI-CALS, argue that, since power is a facet of society, sadomasochism is in fact a more honest and complete form of sexual expression because it addresses all parts of the psyche, as well as all forms of sensory experience. It allows partners to acknowl-edge societal patterns of power and to work through them within safe and agreed sexual role-play. SM has a long history, but before the liberating winds of GAY LIBERA-TION blew away many of the cobwebs of sexual conservatism, it tended to be a clan-destine affair, and any clubs or parties practised an exclusive entry system, usu-ally through personal referral. In the 1970s, SM practitioners began to be less ashamed of their activities, and politicized the recognition of the legitimacy of their sexu-ality as a rightful part of the lesbian and gay movement. Nonetheless, many of the men who had been on the leather scene in the 1950s complained that too many men were coming on to the scene who were interested only in dabbling in mild SM. The SM scene received a setback in the 1980s as AIDS hysteria tended to condemn any flavours of sexual expression other than VANILLA. However, the liberation of the 1970s ensured that sadomasochism could never quite fit back into the LEATHER CLOSET.

safe sex or **safer sex** The range of sexual behaviours or adapted sexual behaviours that was recommended by health educa-tors to reduce the risk of transmission of HIV. In the very early days of the epidemic, when the cause of AIDS was not known, complete sexual abstinence was the only entirely safe regime. As medical knowl-edge increased, safe-sex education focused on avoiding 'the exchange of body fluids', a phrase which became common in gay communities. Specifically, this meant avoiding the introduction of the blood, sperm or vaginal fluids of one partner into the bloodstream of another through the walls of the vagina, rectum or mouth. Thus safer sex was broadly defined as fucking only with a condom, and abstaining from

oral sex, or using a condom or DENTAL DAM if the fellator/cunnilinguist had cuts or sores in the mouth. In addition, efforts at EROTICIZING SAFER SEX suggested a whole range of sexual activities that could be tried, which had no, or low, risk of HIV transmission. Records of the incidence of other STDs demonstrated that gay men adapted to safer sex far more readily than their straight counterparts. Indeed, many report that as well as being just as hot as any other sex, safer sex helps create a sense of community, since men who practise safer sex demonstrate a care for their part-ners, whether long-term or a casual pick-up. By the 1990s safer sex had become second nature to many gay men.

safe-sex clubs In the 1980s, as a result of the AIDS epidemic and the panic which closed down the BATHHOUSES, gay men were left with few venues for mass sexual activity. To a point such public sex was also frowned on within communities as some gay people blamed AIDS on the excesses of the 1970s, while much official HIV education confused information about safe sex with moralizing about promiscuity and monogamy. The strain of anxiety and caring for the sick also took its toll on the collective libido. By the mid-1980s gay men were recovering from the assaults of the moralists, and with empha-sis on EROTICIZING SAFER SEX were control-ling fears about HIV within a healthy sexual attitude. At about this time safe-sex clubs appeared in many American cities.

safe-sex hankie A new addition to the gay male HANKIE CODE, the safe-sex hankie was invented in 1984 by a gay male group in Texas. In black and white check it indi-cated that the man wearing it was only interested in safe-sex practices. Whilst it drew criticism from some AIDS educators for constructing safe-sex as a category dif-ferent from other types of sex, rather than as a form of all sexual activities, it did con-struct safer sex as a positive choice for gay men.

safe word A word agreed on by both part-ners in an SM scene which, when used by the submissive partner, will immediately terminate play. A special word is needed since protestations are likely to be ejaculated routinely as part of the scene. Thus most safe words are ones that are never likely to come up otherwise, and sometimes even the words 'safe word' are used. Safe words demonstrate that amongst experienced practitioners, SM is extremely responsible.

SAGE *See* SENIOR ACTION IN A GAY ENVIRONMENT.

Sagitta Nom de plume of the writer, anarchist and champion of man/boy-love John Henry Mackay (1864–1933). Although born in Scotland, he was brought up in Germany. He wrote a few works which set out the virtues of love between men and boys (*see* DER PUPPENJUNGE). Most of the books were designated immoral by the German government in 1909, and burned. Those that survived were clandestinely reissued by their author.

sailors The stuff of many a gay male sexual fantasy, based mainly on the commonly held idea that in those long hours aboard ship, with only other men for company, the old salts were not averse to a bit of bunk-hopping. The fantasy also engages the idealization of sailors as hyper-masculine, exemplified by Jean GENET's QUERELLE OF BREST. On a final note, they also provide an opportunity for many seamen/semen puns.

St George Work by the Florentine sculptor Donatello (*c*. 1386–1466) which became one of the earliest gay male pin-ups, along with Michelangelo's DAVID. St George was completed between 1416 and 1420, and presented a vision of male beauty. Donatello was himself attracted to boys, a fact known to his liberal patrons in the relaxed atmosphere of early-fifteenth-century Florence.

St James's Park A London cruising ground with a venerable history. Court records indicate that men were already using Birdcage Walk to find sex with one another in the late seventeenth century.

The bushes have been crowded ever since, and despite the best efforts of our illustrious constabulary they are still used for this purpose today.

Salome 1923 film version of Oscar WILDE's work by Alla Nazimova which reputedly had an all-gay cast as a tribute to Wilde. As with many good things, the film was a financial and critical failure, but it looked marvellous since sets and costumes were based upon illustrations by Aubrey Beardsley.

Sam American slang term from the 1970s to describe the little bit of masculine that is in all of us, in whatever proportions. Thus, when a gay man suddenly talks low and starches his wrists rigid when foraying into straight territory, or when a lesbian starts to get possessive about her girlfriend, it is said that the Sam in them is coming out. *See also* JANE.

Samois The first successful lesbian SM organization in America which began in 1978 in San Francisco. It broke up in the early 1980s. SADOMASOCHISM had a much harder time finding a welcome within the lesbian community since the orthodoxies of lesbian feminism from the 1970s onwards asserted that SM sexuality capitulated to the power playing of patriarchal society and therefore SM play ran counter to the aims of the feminist movement.

Sampson, Deborah (1760–?) One of the most famous PASSING WOMEN in American history and the most famous woman soldier in the war of independence. She always showed great gusto in the wearing of male clothing, and in going off on drinking bouts, but first achieved notoriety in her town of Plympton, Massachusetts when she was excommunicated from her local Baptist church for taking on the male persona of 'Timothy Thayer', filling herself with drink and taking another woman to bed. She later styled herself 'Robert Shurtlieff', and joined the American continental army, where she was acclaimed for her bravery. Her story is marred by the fact that she later went on to marry and have children.

samurai Japanese elite who rose as a class following the Heian period (794–1185) when power was devolved to local warrior families. The samurai would receive land in return for military service to such families. The samurai would enter battle accompanied by a page (wakashu), who tended to range in age between thirteen and nineteen. Sexual relationships thrived between the samurai and their pages, and literary accounts imply that bonds of romance often blossomed between the two, to the point that samurai were known to fight duels on behalf of the wakashu. The literature does not condemn such relationships, nor does it indicate that they represent anything other than masculine feelings.

San Francisco The California city that is viewed by lesbians and gay men world-wide as their own Emerald City. The city is relatively small, and thus the lesbian and gay community is actually smaller than in cities like New York, but their concentration in San Francisco has given them a visibility they don't have elsewhere. From the start, the city has had a gay subculture among the bohemians and adventurers that formed its early population; small all-male bars were founded among the early brothels along the Barbary Coast. In the 1850s the city saw huge numbers of new-comers, who were predominantly men, and in such circumstances expediency usually wins out. By the late nineteenth century it had already earned itself a reputation; Oscar WILDE noted that 'anyone who disappears is said to be last seen in San Francisco'. But it was the SECOND WORLD WAR which really began the history of San Francisco as a gay Mecca, as the centre from which thousands of service people departed for the Pacific theatre, and a place to which many of them returned after discharge, honourable or otherwise. Unable or unwilling to return to their isolated hometowns, many lesbians and gay men decided to remain in the city among people who were like themselves. As its reputation grew, more arrived, populating areas such as the CASTRO, and making a gay-friendly environment that scarcely existed elsewhere.

San Sebastian Painting by the Italian eclectic painter Guido Reni (1575–1642), which is illustrative of the homoerotic potential of the ST SEBASTIAN story, and of artistic representations of the saint. The painting shows Sebastian as remarkably alive, despite the two arrows piercing his body; a cloth is loosely tied around his loins. It also shows the different gender associations of Sebastian: his beardless face and long hands are a little effeminate, while his body is muscular. The painting was a favourite of Oscar WILDE who saw it on a trip to Genoa in 1877 and who described Sebastian as 'a lovely brown boy, with crisp, clustering hair and red lips'. It was also referred to in the novel *Confessions of a Mask* by Yukio MISHIMA.

Sang Hyang Toengyal Balinese deity combining the characteristics of both sexes, who, in Balinese cosmology, predated the separation of male and female. Also known as the 'solitary', the deity is highly esteemed.

Santa Maria del Carmine Monastery in Naples which was the final resting place of Conradin (1252–68), the last Hohenstaufen ruler, and his lover Frederick of Baden. The two died in an attempt to regain for the Hohenstaufens the crown of Sicily which had been seized by Charles of Anjou when he invaded Italy and slew Conradin's uncle in battle. Conradin was captured by Charles, tried as a traitor and beheaded. Frederick, in an act which has made their love affair the stuff of legend, requested to be executed along with him. The church in the Neapolitan monastery has become a site of pilgrimage for some gay lovers.

sapphism Woman-to-woman eroticism. The term was derived from the name of the Greek lesbian poet SAPPHO. Although the term was not used in mainstream published works until the 1920s, it had been used in the medical literature since the end of the nineteenth century, and it is probable that it had been used for some time by women who had read the classics with a specifically erotic sense (rather than just referring to Sappho in a general sense); the problem is one of documentation. Although less commonly used than LES-BIAN, there are many women who prefer the term as less obvious and more dignified. In the 1970s it was also used to talk about erotic desire between women without the political implications that lesbian had as a result of its use within the lesbian-feminist movement. Related terms include sapphic, meaning 'as of or pertaining to Sappho'. Again, the moment when Sappho became a synonym for lesbian is uncertain, but it probably has always been the case that to choose to describe a relationship between women as sapphic was to choose to define it as something more than simply a close friendship. Emma Donoghoe's work shows that by 1762 'Sapphic lovers' meant women who have sex with women and that, indeed, 'Sappho's feelings for the women of Lesbos seem to have been well known among the educated'. Sapphist means one like Sappho, i.e. a lesbian.

Sappho (1) Greek citizen (610–580 BC) who earned fame as a teacher, poet and lesbian. Her home was the island of Lesbos, from where she was exiled. She wrote numerous poems celebrating lesbian love, and was given the title of the 'Tenth Muse' by Plato. Unfortunately, in AD 380 in one of those cultural tragedies to which Christian zealots seem inexorably drawn, her books were ordered to be burnt by St Gregory of Nazianzus. In 1073 much of the surviving work was similarly destroyed by Pope Gregory VII. Despite the fact that a number of her works were discovered lining coffins by archaeologists in Egypt, posterity has given us only some 5% of her work. (2) London-based lesbian organization formed in 1972 (from the remains of ARENA 3 which organized social events and published a magazine of the same name, to which women subscribed from all over the world. Unlike earlier British lesbian organizations such as Arena 3, Sappho quickly identified as a feminist organization and was involved in actions by the GAY LIBERA-TION FRONT as well as independent zaps. It also organized insemination by donor for lesbians. Although the magazine is no longer published, Sappho still holds regular meetings in London.

Sappho was a right-on woman Slogan that was carried on placards on the very first lesbian and gay PRIDE march in New York. It was also the title of a 1972 book by Sydney Abbott and Barbara Love, which gave a history of the emergence of lesbians within the feminist movement.

Sarria, Jose Drag queen, amateur opera diva, gay activist, self-termed Dowager Widow of Emperor Norton, Empress of San Francisco and Protectress of Mexico, and the first openly gay person to run for public office in American history. Sarria's love of frocking-up was encouraged by his family from childhood – but he had to content himself with a small stage until his 'discovery', belting out arias from *Carmen* in San Francisco's BLACK CAT BAR. He remained there until it served its last Pina Colada in 1963, serving as something of a protectress for the gay crowd in the dark days of the 1950s. In 1961, police harassment had finally got too much and, switching his frock for straight DRAG, our hero marched into the San Francisco City Hall to file a petition to run for the board of supervisors, the city's governing body. He maintained a low-key campaign, explaining later that he didn't possess the respectable clothes necessary to go out shaking hands and kissing babies, but spread his message by word of mouth: this was a campaign against police harassment. In the final count, Sarria polled an incredible 5,600 votes. He didn't win, but he showed that the gay vote in the city was not to be underestimated. His candidacy was to serve as inspiration for later gay activists such as Harvey MILK. Indeed, Sarria was the first to sign Milk's candidacy papers for the election of supervisors while moderate lesbian and gay figures were warning Milk not to rock their relations with progressive straight politicians.

Sarton, May (1912–) Belgian-born writer whose large collection of work has established her reputation as America's leading lady of letters. Since 1939 she has produced some sixteen collections of poetry, nineteen novels, two children's books and ten journals. She first came out in print about her sexuality in 1965 with *Mrs Stevens Hears the Mermaids Singing*, in which the Mrs Stevens of the title declares that, 'We have to be ourselves, however frightening or strange that may be'. In addition since then, other works have explored issues of sexuality and gender: *Anger* (1982) looks at the different ways in which men and women express emotions, while *The Education of Harriet Hatfield* (1990), apart from the main plotline of a woman in her sixties asserting her independence, also took a look at issues of AIDS, homophobia and bereavement within the context of a lesbian relationship. Despite suffering a stroke at the age of seventy-four, Sarton has kept on writing.

Satyricon Latin work probably by the first-century writer Gaius Petronius (d. AD 66), who was known as the arbiter of elegance (*arbiter elegantiae*) at the court of the Roman emperor Nero (reigned AD 54–68). A fragmentary manuscript which describes the adventure of the narrator and lover in southern Italy, it luxuriantly details the excesses and vices of the Roman Empire.

Satyrs The first gay motorcycle club in America. It was formed in southern California in 1954, and indicated the first growth of the gay LEATHER communities. Other motorcycle groups were formed soon after, such as the Oedipus Club in Los Angeles and the Warlocks in San Francisco.

Savage, Lily (Paul O'Grady, 195?–) An old favourite in London pubs and clubs, she became in 1993 the most visible face of British drag and, faster than you could touch up your roots, she was packing out major theatres, producing best-selling videos and making more celeb appearances on British television than you could shake a lipstick at.

Savage Nights (Les Nuits Fauves) 1992 film directed by French director Cyril Collard, which deals with the reaction of Jean (played by Collard himself) to his diagnosis as HIV-positive. At first his reaction is to live fast – playing loud music, driving too fast and screwing around with both sexes – until he meets and falls in love with Laura, at which the film becomes the story of their doomed romance. In portraying such scenes as a bisexual man having unprotected sex with his girlfriend in the knowledge that he is HIV-positive, the film came under some criticism from AIDS educators and from those who saw it as likely to fuel the idea that bisexuals are the bridge by which AIDS is transferred from the gay communities to heterosexual society. Yet it is precisely because of this that the film is able to present the turbulence which an HIV diagnosis creates, rather than any sanitized version of living with HIV, and which contributes to the film's strength. Collard died of AIDS-related illnesses only three days before the film was awarded four French César awards.

Save Our Children Campaign Name of the organization founded by the Florida anti-queer campaigner Anita BRYANT.

scat From the Greek root *skat* meaning dung, scat refers to any sex practice that involves faeces. It can range from a voyeuristic pleasure at watching someone else shit to one partner passing shit over the body or in the mouth of another. Gay male slang terms for a gay man who enjoys scat include kaka QUEEN, shit queen and brown lipper. *See also* AUTUMN COLOURS; BROWN.

scene The queer venues, bars and clubs which are on offer in any particular place.

science fiction The genre has caught on among lesbian and feminist writers far more than gay male ones, interestingly since the mainstream of sci-fi writing tends to be sexist, but its roots should perhaps be seen in feminist utopian literature rather than the male science fiction. Its devices offer women a way of examining sexual relations in our societies and exploring other possibilities for social relations. Particular tools which are commonly used are the construction of a utopia, where sexual antagonism has been ended, such as Sally Gearhart's THE WANDERGROUND (1979), or of a dystopia, where the tensions within our society are taken to their conclusion such as in Margaret Attwood's *The Handmaid's Tale* (1986), in which women have become state-controlled wombs and any that disagree or are infertile are carted off to a radioactive wilderness. Like mainstream sci-fi, aliens often show the way things could be done differently, for example in J. Saxton's *Queen of the States* (1986) where the protagonist communicates with alien life through an out-of-the-body experience. Meanwhile, gay men have little more than the possible crush the computer HAL has for Dave in *2001: A Space Odyssey*. Thanks.

Scientific-Humanitarian Committee (Wissenschaftlich-Humanitare Komitee) German organization formed in 1897 to create debate around lesbian and gay issues and to push for the repeal of PARAGRAPH 175 of the German penal code, which criminalized homosexual activities. The committee was run by Dr Magnus HIRSCHFIELD, the German gay rights activist, until it was disbanded in 1933 by the Nazis. In 1897 the committee prepared a petition for the Reichstag to request the abolition of Paragraph 175, which was signed by names such as Albert Einstein, Thomas Mann and Leo Tolstoy, although the petition was not actually presented until 1922.

scissors In American lesbian slang, to make scissors of your partner is to manually stimulate her anus and clitoris at the same time. So called because of the position of the thumb and finger. Also called holding a BOWLING BALL.

Scottish Minorities Group Scottish organization which was founded in 1969 to campaign for the legalization of gay sex in Scotland. The legalization of gay sex in England and Wales under the 1967 SEXUAL OFFENCES ACT did not apply to Scotland

until 1980. The group also organized social events such as the Saturday night 'Cobweb' bash.

SCUM The Society for Cutting Up Men, produced its manifesto in 1968. The society set itself the aim of destroying the male sex. The manifesto, written by Valarie Solanas, described SCUM as 'dominant, secure, self-confident, nasty, violent, selfish, independent, proud, thrill-seeking, free-wheeling, arrogant females, who consider themselves fit to rule the universe'.

seal of the double wreath *See* ORDER OF CHAERONEA.

Sebastian, St (d. AD 288) Early Christian martyr who was put to death by the Roman Emperor Diocletian. Sebastian had served as a commander of the Emperor's private bodyguard. He was also a closet Christian, and when Diocletian learned of this he had him bound to a stake and shot at by archers until 'he was as full of arrows as an urchin is full of pricks'. Contrary to myth, he did not die, but recovered to the point that he was able once again to confront the Emperor about his persecution of Christians. This time he was stoned and dumped in the sewers. Sebastian has also become a gay icon. This is partly because the artistic depictions of his shooting have enabled generations of artists to produce pictures of the male nude, but also because of the fact that he was described as the 'beloved' of the Emperor, who dressed him in a girdle of gold. In addition, some have suggested that the story of his shooting by arrows is merely a symbolic representation of a mass rape, the prick of the arrow serving as a symbol of another type of prick. Thus in artistic representations Sebastian became increasingly effeminate-looking, whilst his 'executors' are represented as virile. The Sebastian story was reworked in the 1976 film SEBASTIANE, by another saint, the filmmaker Derek JARMAN.

Second World War Watershed event in the history of America's lesbian and gay community. It had a great impact on many women, leading to their self-identification as lesbians. It brought many women together in an atmosphere of independence from men, and with the close contact of women's barracks relationships naturally developed. Meanwhile, back at home, women were mobilized into traditionally male occupations to help the war effort. Dormitories and hostelries for women workers were opened in cities, where they could live in a women-only environment. Now many could earn a salary independently of men, something they had not been able to do before. For lesbians it created new freedom to live autonomous lives without having to marry for financial security. The war served to bring lesbians and gay men from widespread locations and backgrounds together. Although after the war an attempt was made to return to the status quo, too much had changed to turn the clock back. Women refused to go back to a life of domesticity, and many lesbians and gay men refused to return to the isolation of their places of birth. Instead they joined the swelling lesbian and gay communities in America's port cities.

Section 28 *See* CLAUSE 28.

see what the boys in the backroom will have *See* DIETRICH, MARLENE.

self-fulfilment ethic It rose in the Atlantic nations in the 1970s as the Protestant ethic declined and sanctioned the gratification of a range of inner needs and desires

semen Or sperm, cum, jissom (gissom), wad, load. However it is termed, sperm is one of those fluids that, for gay men at least, you just can't ignore, especially if your hog of a partner has pushed you over onto the wet patch. Worldwide, sperm has an importance in many societies as the giver of life and as proof positive of entry into adulthood, and often plays an important role in homoerotic INITIATION rites. In New Guinea and parts of Melanesia it is believed that a boy will not mature physically unless semen is implanted in his body by an adult, and anal sex is a way of transmitting valued male characteristics. Interestingly, in the early days of the AIDS

epidemic, safe-sex educators found that for many gay men the interchange of sperm played a similar significant role as a token of emotional closeness, which led them to resist barriers such as condoms.

The Semiramis Bar Gay bar in Paris at the turn of the twentieth century. It was described in a short story by one of its patrons, the French lesbian writer COLETTE, who described the place as home to a crowd of 'long-haired young lads and short-haired girls', and who described the women dancing together.

Senior Action in a Gay Environment (SAGE) American intergenerational social welfare group providing information and education on the issues faced by older lesbians and gay men, as well as providing direct services. It was founded in 1977.

sensuality and mutuality Reworking of the initials S and M (for SADOMASOCHISM) which became popular among LEATHER communities in the 1970s. It marked a newly positive attitude to the physical pleasures of SM which was possible in the liberated sexual climate of the 1970s after years of living clandestinely within the LEATHER CLOSET, as well as a new spirit of activism on the part of SM practitioners which sought to challenge the negative images of sadomasochistic sexual expression prevalent even within lesbian and gay communities. In addition, the word mutuality addressed the criticisms emanating from the lesbian feminist movement that SM refused to challenge the workings of patriarchal systems of power. Instead, leather people argued that SM sex could be just as egalitarian as POLITICALLY CORRECT SEX. *See also* SEX MAGIC.

separatism The political belief that one needs to organize separately from the usual form of organization. In terms of lesbian politics this means, at the very least, organizing separately from men. In its weakest form it is just the belief in women-only spaces and caucuses; in its strongest form it is the belief that women should completely cut themselves off from men, male organizational forms and male values. In the latter form there is an explicit or tacit belief that the way of life generated by women is morally superior to that created by men, for example more nurturing, peace loving, green, animal loving and so on. Lesbian separatism is inevitably a product of the wider politics of LESBIAN FEMINISM. Separatism as an explicit political philosophy of withdrawal was probably first explored within the black CIVIL RIGHTS MOVEMENT in the 1960s, before being taken on extensively by the FEMINIST movement. Separatism has never really been a major strand of the gay male movement, although some of the politics of the GAY LIBERATION FRONT in the 1970s and the radical politics of the 1980s and 1990s (*see* QUEER) have verged on it. Separatists of all persuasions differ over where they see it leading. Some view it as a temporary measure in order to raise consciousness, to provide an environment to heal the wounds of living in a racist, patriarchal or homophobic society, and to build the strength to challenge the prevailing system. Others see it as a permanent measure to create exclusive communities. In the long run, the latter approach may well be doomed since the individual identity is informed by a number of factors including sex, race, class and sexuality, and separatist communities have a tendency to atomize into the smallest units. Separatism is anathema to those who uphold ASSIMILATIONIST or COALITION politics, and is often denounced by the latter as the politics of the GHETTO.

separatist One who practises SEPARATISM.

serial monogamy The practice of having one reasonably long-term relationship after another, and being monogamous within each. Often associated with lesbian relationship patterns.

Seth and Horus Ancient Egyptian deities. Seth was the envious brother of the god Osiris, while Horus was originally a sun god who later became merged with the son of Osiris and Isis. Egyptian myth records that the two gods enjoyed sexual relations.

sex-change *See* GENDER REASSIGNMENT SURGERY.

sex circuses Sex shows produced in the black communities of Harlem in the 1920s. Such shows were for paying customers and would take place in BUFFET FLATS.

Sex Education Society British organization founded in 1947 which, similar to the older WORLD LEAGUE FOR SEXUAL REFORM, sought to enlighten public attitudes towards sexuality, and to lobby for legal reform in the field of sex. It included lesbian and gay rights as part of this platform. In addition, it published the *Journal of Sex Education*, the first issue of which carried reports of the sex findings of American researcher Alfred KINSEY and which, through its pages, offered succour to many lesbians and gay men of the time. Bringing the latest research to the attention of the British public, the society had a great influence on general opinion. The organization folded on the death of its chair, gynaecologist Norman Haire, in 1952.

sex magic Term that developed among SM communities in the UK and America in the 1980s to recast the initials S and M with a positive connotation. It marked the sense of activism that had led SM practitioners to challenge negative stereotypes since the 1970s. It also indicated the new spiritual movement within SM communities which described the ecstasies of sadomasochism as an almost religious experience.

sex toys Somewhat of a euphemism for any implement that can be used to give, or aid, sexual satisfaction. The most common are the DILDO and vibrator, although any household implement or even vegetables can be used. The majority tend to be phallus shaped in order to penetrate the anus or vagina. Hairbrush handles and courgettes are the sort of thing you could put your hand on easily. However, some men get a rise out of placing their dick in any vacuum cleaner attachment (on suck), and syringe-like devices have also been developed to stimulate the dick or nipples, while women have been known to enjoy sitting on the washing machine (on spin).

Sex toys are also commonly incorporated into sex play for two or more people, but AIDS educators recommend that if they are to be used for penetration it is probably wise either to put condoms over them or to clean them thoroughly between insertions.

sex-work, lesbian Although it has existed, whether explicitly or covertly, in the form of wealthier lesbians visiting lesbian bars and paying their way into the sexual favours of other clients, lesbian sex-work has neither been widespread nor particularly well-organized, and of course such exploitation of another woman would be anathema to feminist and lesbian-feminist women. In American slang Jane is used as a term for the lesbian client of a female sex-worker.

sex-work, male The male branch of the oldest profession has a long and venerable history. Historical records suggest that RITUAL PROSTITUTION was a common feature in religious ceremonies in the ancient Near East, and has been part of the ritual practices of SHAMANISM in cultures worldwide. In England there are records of the existence of male prostitution from as early as the sixteenth century. John Marston, in his 1598 *Scourge of Villainie*, condemns 'male stews', or brothels, in London. In the sixteenth and seventeenth centuries, brothels were probably not organized in the sense that we know today. They were more likely to have been inns where men could entertain their clients. In addition, moneyed gentlemen were probably able to gain the sexual favours of their male servants without even stepping out of the home, as the CASTLEHAVEN AFFAIR indicates. The MOLLY HOUSE scene of the eighteenth century also included a fair number of impecunious men eager to make pennies from penises. From the eighteenth century, the Guards also became notorious as a group of men who were sexually available. Sometimes they would solicit for themselves, often it was more organized. In THE SINS OF THE CITIES OF THE PLAIN, which gives us a detailed view of the nineteenth-century world of prostitution, one soldier, Private Fred Jones, announces, 'So

far as I can see, all the best Gentlemen in London are running after soldiers.' According to the book, a Mrs Truman ran a tobacconist shop near the Albany Street Guards barracks in Regent's Park and would take 'orders' for the men. The WHITE SWAN affair and CLEVELAND STREET SCANDAL also show how organized nineteenth-century sex-work could be. However, throughout this period it was not always easy to define exactly what was sex-work. It was never a profession in any full-time sense, and where sexual relations existed between men of different classes, as was common in the nineteenth century, it was expected that one partner would provide gifts for the other, no stigma being attached. In addition, since most of the historical documentation we have is from frequently hostile observers outside the subculture, we must be sceptical of their labelling men as 'bawds' or 'he-strumpets'. Since the vocabulary of prostitution was the only one they had to describe unorthodox sexuality, it is likely that many gay men who were not involved in any financial contracts were thus labelled. This introduces an interesting note: the historical linkage of male homosexuality and female prostitution. Many of the words that have been used to describe gay men (fruit, queen, gay) have actually evolved from terms for female sex-workers, and in Britain the same legislation (i.e. the Vagrancy Acts) has been used to cover both homosexuality and sex-work. The WOLFENDEN Committee was actually set up to examine both 'problems'. From this angle, it is interesting that the centre of gay life in contemporary London is Soho, which is also famous for its heterosexual fleshpots. That is not to say that female sex-worker communities and gay communities have always been on the best of terms. Some of the worst mud-throwers of gay men at the pillory (for example, in the White Swan affair) have been the prostitutes who blamed male homosexuality for their business drying up, and it was reported that the prostitutes were jubilant when it was heard that Oscar WILDE had been convicted. Yet they are both communities of the night, and perhaps this provides some bonds.

sex-worker Term developed in the 1980s to replace the word prostitute. It rejected the dismissive usage of the word prostitute to degrade the person to which it was applied. It is used along with the term sex industry to refer to the sizeable economy which the buying of sex has historically represented.

sex-workers, lesbian relations among In nineteenth-century America, sex-workers had their own system of ROMANTIC FRIEND-SHIPS, which protected and sustained them in the face of being labelled deviants from society.

sexologists The name given to the many different writers from the nineteenth century who wrote about same-sex sexuality as a scientific 'question', thus contributing to the process of the MEDICALIZATION OF HOMOSEXUALITY. The main figures are Havelock ELLIS, Richard von KRAFFT-EBING and Karl ULRICHS, although J.A. SYMONDS and Edward CARPENTER were also influential. These figures differ in the positivity with which they viewed homosexual relations – Carpenter, Ulrichs and Symonds were gay themselves – and in the terminology they employed, but their contributions fit broadly into a similar discourse of CON-GENITAL INVERSION, whereby a homosexual disposition was innate and involved a departure from biological gender. The writings of the sexologists were phenomenally successful, and works such as Richard von Krafft-Ebing's *Psychopathia Sexualis* sparked off countless debates in academic journals and the press, gradually filtering into the consciousness of the general public.

Sexual Behaviour in the Human Female The published findings of American sex researcher Alfred KINSEY into women's sexuality, which appeared in 1953. The report found that some 2% of the study were exclusively lesbian during their adult lives, while 13% engaged in lesbian sex at least once. Like the earlier SEXUAL BEHAVIOUR IN THE HUMAN MALE, the report caused a great sensation in the heterosexual press by suggesting an incidence of sex between women which had not been conceived of previously. It also gave succour to many lesbians who were now shown as a community that was potentially huge. The report only measured sexual acts, however, not the meaning or significance of those acts to the person concerned, nor close but non-sexual relationships. Thus the report was unable to discern the relationships between women which in the 1970s would be conceived of as lesbian, if not erotic. However, with the implication of a natural state of bisexuality for most people, the report paved the way for lesbians to construct their sexuality as a political choice.

Sexual Behaviour in the Human Male The first of the pioneering pieces of sex research published by the American researcher Alfred KINSEY, which appeared in 1948. His findings included the revelations that some 4% of men identify as exclusively gay, and 37% of men have at least one homosexual experience in their adult lives, figures which were much higher than most people thought. His conclusion was that, since many persons had obviously engaged in homosexual acts, yet would not identify themselves as homosexual, there were no homosexuals but only homosexual acts, and thus homosexual should only be used adjectivally. In this he aligned himself with Freud's theories that everyone has the propensity to engage in sexual acts with members of both sexes. As well as causing a shock on first being published, the Kinsey report had a long-term effect in that it gave the nascent lesbian and gay movement the ammunition to argue that anti-gay laws persecuted a sizeable and potentially powerful minority, and the faith that, if all lesbians and gay men were to COME OUT and assert their rights, gains could swiftly be made. The corresponding SEXUAL BEHAV-IOUR IN THE HUMAN FEMALE was published in 1953.

sexual endogamy Borrowed from the anthropological term for sexual relations which take place within a social group. It refers to the post-STONEWALL RIOT pattern of gay male behaviour where self-identified gay men would have sexual relations with other self-identified gay men. It indicated a healthier attitude among gay men towards their sexuality, in opposition to the phenomenon of homosexual exogamy.

Sexual Inversion The collaborative work by sex writers Henry Havelock ELLIS and John Addington SYMONDS, which eventually appeared in 1896 under Ellis' name as *Sexual Inversion*, and formed volume two of his seven-volume *Studies in the Psychology of Sex* (1896–1928). It argued for more progressive attitudes towards inversion. The two men had decided to work together in 1892, after Symonds had contacted Ellis as a result of an essay the latter had included in his first book, *The New Spirit* about Walt WHITMAN, who was something of a hero for both men. The work, which was originally published in Germany, included Symonds' essay *A Problem in Greek Ethics*, but when an English edition appeared his executor demanded the retraction of Symonds' name. This was not the end of the controversy. When the Legitimation League displayed the book in their offices, the secretary of the society was arrested for a 'lewd, wicked, bawdy, scandalous, libel'. He pleaded guilty, and copies of the book had thereafter to be published in America. As a result of all the publicity, the work was brought to the attention of many lesbians and gays who wrote to Ellis for support. In addition, it influenced liberal and intellectual attitudes towards homosexuality for much of the twentieth century. Sometimes such influence was not entirely positive. For example Radclyffe HALL relied heavily on Ellis' ideas in her often criticized depiction of Stephen Gordon in THE WELL OF LONELINESS. However, in its calling for the reform of anti-gay laws, the work can be seen to have played some part in the eventual development of the lesbian and gay movement.

Sexual Law Reform Society *See* HOMOSEXUAL LAW REFORM SOCIETY.

Sexual Offences Act The British legislation that in July 1967 finally, and not before time, provided limited legalization of sex between men. Lesbian sex was never explicitly included within the remit of British law, and by default it is subject to the same regulation as straight sex. The act broadly took up the recommendations of the WOLFENDEN REPORT, but it had taken ten years since the report for campaigning efforts and the changes in public opinion attendant on the crumbling of the puritan sexual morality of the 1960s to lead to government action. The law allowed for legal consensual sex between men over the age of twenty-one. It only applied however to England and Wales (sex between men did not become legal in Scotland until 1980, and in Northern Ireland until 1982), and had no force within the British armed services or the merchant navy. Moreover, it made the law against sex with minors and for importuning more stringent, and amendments by backward politicians judged that only sex 'in private' was to be allowed. In effect the definition of privacy was ludicrously narrow, and ruled out sex with any more than two people or sex where there was a chance of others witnessing. So if you weren't behind a reinforced iron door, tough. *See also* AGE OF CONSENT.

sexual politics Phrase introduced into popular currency by the book of the same title published in 1970 by American feminist Kate Millet. Initially, it referred specifically to the political implications of gender: the way in which gender is constructed socially which bears little or no relation to its biological importance (*see* GENDER GAP), and the way in which this construction is used to limit the power and freedom of women's lives. More recently, the Men's Movement has taken on the term in its work on the construction of masculinity. Finally, lesbian and gay theorists have used it to discuss the interplay between sexuality and politics, and the consequences of sexuality on social role. The term is also used by bookshops as a way of lumping together all books about women, lesbians and gay men on one discreet shelf.

sexualized society Description of America in the 1970s with what seemed like a sudden exploration of sexual behaviours by practically the entire populace.

sexually transmitted diseases (STDs) The various illnesses which can be transmitted through sexual contact have no regard for the sexuality of their carriers. However, given the particular nature and frequency of gay male sexual contacts, STDs tend to be more common among gay male communities, while lesbian sex tends to be less likely to lead to infection. The most common STDs in gay male circles are: gonorrhoea (the clap, the drip or GC), which can affect the eye, rectum, the throat or the urethra and which is usually recognized by a burning sensation whilst urinating and a penile discharge (although these are the same symptoms as for the less serious non-specific urethritis, aka NSU); syphilis, which is usually first recognized by an ulcer at the point of sexual contact and which can be extremely serious if left untreated; herpes, a virus which causes painful blisters or ulcers in the mouth, throat, vagina, on the penis or around the rectum; hepatitis-A (heppie), an inflammation of the liver which is found in fecal matter, which can be spread through RIMMING and which causes headaches, fever and jaundice; and hepatitis-B, similarly an inflammation of the liver but far more serious, transmitted in the same way as HIV, not always accompanied by symptoms, and best detected through blood tests. However, SAFER SEX, to protect against HIV, is effective against the transmission of many of these conditions, and the last decade has seen a fall in the incidence of STDs among gay men.

shakti In Hindu cosmology, Shakti is the principle of active feminine strength, or female energy. It is also the name given to a British South Asian lesbian and gay group.

Shamakami A group for South Asian feminist lesbians and bisexual women. The name was taken from the Bengali language and means 'love for one's equal or same'. The group provides a free newsletter, and thereby allows lesbians and bisexual women within South Asia to come together.

shaman Many traditional societies had an institution of a man or woman who was seen to have a heightened spiritual position in relation to the rest of the population. Such people, who are generically known as shamans (originally from a Sanskrit term for religious exercise), were seen to be able to communicate with the spirits, both good and evil, that made up the cosmology of those societies. This was seen to give them special powers, and they were often called upon as fortune-tellers or as healers. In those societies where particular social roles existed for individuals who wore clothing or engaged in activities thought appropriate to the other sex, or who engaged in sexual relations with members of their own sex, it was often those individuals who were called upon to act in a shamanistic role. Sometimes the role of shaman determined the transgenderal nature of the person (see TRANSVESTISM). Often however, the transvestite or homosexual was seen to have a particular knowledge of the cosmos by dint of their understanding the nature of both genders. Examples of such figures include the BERDACHE of North America, the MAHU of Tahiti and the BASIR or MANANG BALI of Borneo. Such figures have been held up by writers, such as the American lesbian author Judy Grahn, as well as those within the RADICAL FAIRY movement who seek to demonstrate the spiritual heritage of the lesbian and gay position within society, as a tool for their criticisms of the material values of heterosexual society.

Shanghai Lily As Marlene DIETRICH tells stuffy Clive Brook in the film *Shanghai Express*, 'It took more than one man to change my name to Shanghai Lily.'

Shanti Project An organization formed in Berkeley, California in the late 1970s which sought to provide support for those who were facing the likelihood of death. It based its approach on the works of Elizabeth Kubler-Ross. In the early days of the AIDS epidemic it started a self-help group for people who were suffering from KAPOSI'S SARCOMA. As the epidemic spread, it became increasingly involved in providing volunteers to befriend and provide services to those people who were affected. In 1982 it was given a grant by the San Francisco board of supervisors to provide counselling and personal support through the world's first AIDS clinic.

She Came Too Late and **She Came in a Flash** Published in 1986 and 1988 respectively, these two LESBIAN THRILLER novels by Mary Wings focus on the adventures of the articulate, fashion-conscious and glamorous amateur sleuth, Emma Victor. Emma is successful in her investigative activities, but does not always follow the right trail in the realm of love. In *She Came in a Flash*, Emma investigates the death of an old school friend in the Vishnu Divine Inspiration Commune, and the novel investigates the attraction for women of new ageism, as well as an exposé of some of the more cynical side of such establishments. In good, old thriller convention, Emma has various amorous encounters with both villains and goodies.

shoes In the nineteenth century in Britain, to wear patent leather on your hooves was to give away the secret that you were less than all man. The twentieth-century equivalent was suede, and in the 1930s wearing suede shoes was tantamount to frocking-up in public – it was a sign that you were 'that way'. Of course the blue version were saved from such aspersions by Gene Vincent, but even in the 1950s and early 1960s brown suede was still a closet-opener. Lesbians have meanwhile been stereotypically drawn to sensible (comfy and chunky) footwear. By the late twentieth century, DOC MARTENS in both boot and shoe form seem to have satisfied both halves of the community – unless you are of the SLING-BACK tendency, that is.

showtunes Numbers from stage musicals are extremely popular among older gay men, functioning as a form of plebeian opera librettos. From *The King and I* to *My Fair Lady*, through *Calamity Jane* and *South Pacific*, a test of how well a man knows the lyrics (especially from the schmaltzy numbers) is as accurate as knowing his Kinsey number.

shudo Japanese term for pederasty, which has a long tradition in Japan. *See* CHIGO; SAMURAI.

sidekick In many ways the female cinematic equivalent to the male SISSY. In the 1930s and 1940s it was a common custom to pair the leading lady off with a female best friend before fulfilling her destiny by getting her man at the end of the film. The sidekick was characterized by being far too self-assured to get any man, and compensating for this by her wit and strength of character.

significant other Partner. The term developed in the 1970s when lesbians and gays became frustrated with the paucity of vocabulary to describe the people who shared their lives. Irritatingly enough, the phrase also caught on with trendy heterosexuals, so you couldn't always be sure of the sexuality of the person you were talking to.

signifiers for homosexuality In the British and American theatre before the liberalization of the late 1950s and 1960s, it was not deemed appropriate to deal explicitly with gay characters. Instead, an elaborate series of signifiers, or signs, were evolved which suggested a gay sexuality in conventional terms. Gentle and poetic, nervous and artistic, emotional and temperamental male characters were thus recognizable as 'unmale', and very likely gay. While these signifiers worked on the level of societal stereotypes, they would also be picked up by gay members of audiences, and indeed terms such as musical, temperamental and nervous were used by gay men in the 1940s and 1950s as code words to refer to themselves in order to draw attention to their sexuality for the purposes of communicating to other gay men.

sil American lesbian slang, common in the 1930s. An abbreviation of silly, it referred to a woman with a crush on another.

silence = death The most famous slogan to appear from the gay activist response to the AIDS epidemic, used to remind gay people that they need to be vocal to pressure governments to provide sufficient care for themselves and their community. It first appeared on posters flyposted around New York in 1986, produced by the Silence = Death Collective, a group which went on to attend the founding meeting of ACT UP. The slogan appeared in white lettering beneath a PINK TRIANGLE which had one point facing up. The triangle was an inverted version of the one used in the GAY HOLOCAUST to indicate that the gay community was actively fighting back, not passively resigning itself to its fate. Along with a later version of ACTION = LIFE, which was produced with the same pink triangle design, the slogan silence = death has been used on posters, badges and stickers produced by ACT UP since 1987.

similsexualist Late-nineteenth-century term for homosexuality. Never really gained currency.

The Simpsons In the second series of the American hit cartoon television show, Karl, Homer Simpson's secretary, was palpably gay. His silky voice was produced by gay playwright Harvey FIERSTEIN.

Sinclair, Matt New Orleans antiques dealer turned private dick who lives with his lover Robin and became embroiled in murder and intrigue in Tony Fennelly's *The Glory Hole Murders* (1985) and *The Closet Hanging* (1987).

Sind es Frauen? (Are These Women?) 1903 novel by Aimée Duc which shows the influence of the writings of the nineteenth-century sexologists such as Richard von KRAFFT-EBING. The plot deals with women who prefer a professional fulfilment to the questionable joys of marriage. One is a doctor, others are studying for PhDs. They all reject romantic love to maintain their professional freedom. They acknowledge that such wayward behaviour can only mean one thing in the light of the sexological theories of the day, that they are CONGENITAL INVERTS. They adopt this label happily because of the independence it gives them, and refer to themselves as Krafft-Ebingers.

Sinister Wisdom Tri-annual American magazine for radical lesbian feminists edited by the activist and writer Elana Dykewomon. It was founded in 1976 and is published from Berkeley in California.

The Sins of the Cities of the Plain Or, The Recollections of a Mary-Anne. Fictionalized memoirs of a hustler who worked the streets of London in the late nineteenth century, published in 1881. It described such places as brothels where moneyed gentlemen could be fixed up with soldiers in the Foot Guards, and glamorous transvestite balls.

Sirporium A second-hand store that was owned and run by the SOCIETY FOR INDIVIDUAL RIGHTS, a gay rights group based in San Francisco.

sissy (1) Slang term of abuse for an effeminate male or a male who enjoys activities which are not quite macho, which for young hets rules out most things that don't involve pretending to kill people. It is most often employed to refer to young men who, like their TOMBOY counterparts, refuse to 'live up to' the gender roles expected of them, but it is sometimes used as a pejorative term for older gay men. The term is derived from the word sister and recorded as early as the nineteenth century. Many gay men remember being called a sissy long before they were aware of their sexuality, and the appellation is sometimes the first portent of a life to be lived outside the mainstream. (2) The older sissy became a stock character in film throughout the twentieth century, usually portrayed as a nervy shop assistant, clerk or hair stylist, or other such unfoundedly stereotypical gay career. The archetype of the genre was the American actor Franklin Pangborn whose whole career seemed to revolve around playing anxious shop assistants and clerks. (3) The word has been incorporated ironically into the slang of BUTCH gay men. Thus a sissy suck is an apprehensive and unenjoyable act of oral sex.

Sister Gin 1975 novel by June Arnold representative of the literature that had been made possible by the gains of the lesbian feminist movement. It is not a novel about lesbianism which seeks to justify or explain love between women, but the lesbianism of the protagonist just is. That is not to say that it is not important; the central character is a journalist and finds that being open about her lesbianism allows her to write with a greater honesty. Yet the novel also deals with the themes of dealing with middle age, with the menopause, with the need for black women to find their own voices, and 'finding oneself' in a more general sense. June Arnold also wrote *The Cook and the Carpenter* (1973).

sisterhood Feminist term (1) The community of women. Sometimes it is used to describe the entire female population, and sometimes just the section which is politically active within the feminist movement. (2) The emotional, spiritual, practical and political bonds that unite women. The term has specific connotations of political activity, to describe the solidarity between women involved in the movement, and the responsibility that feminists argued all women had to develop those bonds.

Sisterhood Is Powerful Title of 1970 book by Robin Morgan. Morgan was also the originator of the phrase 'Pornography is the theory, rape is the practice'.

Sisters Journal of the San Francisco chapter of the American lesbian organization DAUGHTERS OF BILITIS. The journal was aimed at inculcating an unabashedly open lesbian identity. It stated, 'Lesbian is a strong, proud word. As women-loving-women, proud of who and what we are, we must think of ourselves in strong, proud terms.' It also urged women to

reclaim the word DYKE, and to transform it into having positive connotations.

Sisters of Perpetual Indulgence Worldwide order of gay male nuns. The original Sisters, such as Sister Boom Boom and Sister Sadie the Rabbi Lady, began to appear on the scene in San Francisco in the 1970s, where their visible mix of habits and facial hair on demonstrations, with their motto of 'Give up the guilt' helped boost the eccentric image of the city. In the 1980s, with the emotional burden imposed by AIDS, their ministering was desperately needed, and they were known for their hospital visits as well as their efforts to spread the safe-sex message. In the UK, the sisters conducted Operation Rubber Habit in 1994 to take the good news about condoms into London gay clubs. They have also conducted exorcisms of places and institutions possessed by the demon of homophobia. A bit of a sticking point for the media, which though fascinated never seem to appreciate the joke: the phrase 'homosexual men dressed as nuns' doesn't quite communicate their sheer fabulality.

sisters of the road Community of American women travellers which burgeoned due to economic hardships in the Great Depression of the 1930s. Such women, while subject to a hard life, had freedoms of dress and travel which were otherwise difficult for women to attain. Not surprisingly, women travelling together for safety would commonly engage in lesbian relationships.

Sitges Spanish resort area in Catalonia, on the east coast, which vies with Mykonos as the centre for European gay tourism. With gay bars, restaurants and a (slightly inaccessible) nude beach as well as a sauna, backrooms and some al fresco cock in the woods behind the beaches, it has practically everything for the discerning gay traveller.

sixth man Term for a gay man which became current in the 1950s. It referred to the six-point scale that sex researcher Alfred KINSEY used in his studies on human sexuality.

sixty-nine Sexual position where both partners perform oral sex on one another simultaneously. The term is derived from the similarity of the position to the figures 69. More stylish queens prefer to call it *soixante-neuf*, which is the French translation. Unstylish queens in the British navy, however, developed 'swaffonder' or 'swassonder', corruptions of the French.

size queen Gay man who places a lot of importance on the cock size of his potential partners.

skeet shooting From American gay slang of the 1970s. To masturbate a partner to orgasm and to catch the jet of semen in the mouth.

slap British gay slang, used in the argot POLARI for make-up, especially when worn by a man in DRAG.

slave The BOTTOM in bondage or SM sex.

Sleep 1866 painting by Gustave Courbet (1819–77), which has become one of the most famous artistic representations of physicality between women. It depicts two naked women, supposedly asleep, in a position in which sleep would probably be furthest from their minds. The two lie side by side, one 'sleeper' with her leg draped over the other, who is caressing it. The second sleeper has her head on the breast of the first. A string of pearls is thrown over the bed, and a decanter rests on a table nearby. The picture is illustrative of the exotic way in which the love between women was depicted in France following the movement of EPATER LE BOURGEOIS, and the publication of such works as LES FLEURS DU MAL.

sling-back The footwear equivalent of Bri-Nylon. The kind of shoe that seems nowadays only to be worn by the Queen Mother and Princess Margaret – as well as drag queens who can't find stilettos big enough for their hooves. Possibly because they are simply nasty, they have become the standard reference for any footwear in camp argot, although pumps (in America) and stillies (stilettos) come a close second and third.

slogans Pithy statements to express huge issues. Worn on badges, T-shirts, shaved into the hair, tattooed onto the skin, shouted on demonstrations, printed on stickers stuck guerrilla-style throughout the streets, graffitied on walls, slogans have been the pulse of lesbian and gay politics since the 1960s. They include: ACTION = LIFE; ACT UP, FIGHT BACK, FIGHT AIDS; An army of lovers cannot lose; Avenge Oscar Wilde; Be peculiar; Better blatant than latent; Better gay than grumpy; Born-again lesbian; Bum sex; Chaste makes waste; Closets are for clothes; Copulate, don't populate; Don't ask, demand; Down with pants; DYKE POWER, FAG POWER, QUEER NATION; DYKE with attitude; End heterosupremacy in our lifetime; Equality for homosexuals; Fuck patriarchy; Fucking is better than killing; GAY IS GOOD; Gay Power; God is a lesbian; THE LORD IS MY SHEPHERD AND HE KNOWS I'M GAY; God made me gay/queer; Homophobia's got to go; Homosexuality is not a four-letter word; How dare you presume I'm a stereotype; HOW DARE YOU PRESUME I'M HETEROSEXUAL; I can't even think straight; I like boys; I own my body, but I share; If it moves, fondle it; If we can send one man to the moon, why not send them all?; I'm a faggot, and I'm proud of it; It takes two heterosexuals to make a homosexual; It's a bitch being butch; Keep my body off your ads; Keep your laws off my body; Lesbians have natural rhythm; Lesbians ignite; Lesbian visibility is lesbian survival; Make love, not babies; Mean Mother; The moral majority is neither; Mother Nature is a lesbian; MSchief; Never go straight, always go forward; Never going underground; No one knows I'm a lesbian; Now you have touched the woman, you have struck a rock; OUT OF THE CLOSETS AND INTO THE STREETS; People with AIDS are under attack, what do we do? ACT UP, fight back; Phallic symbols arise; Pray to God, She will hear you; PROMOTE HOMOSEXUALITY; QUEER AS FUCK; Queer with attitude; QUEERS BASH BACK; SAPPHO WAS A RIGHT-ON WOMAN; Screaming queen; Sexism is a social disease; SILENCE = DEATH; SISTERHOOD IS POWERFUL; Smash monogamy; Stop crucifying queers; STOP THE CLAUSE; Stroppy queen; Tradesman's entrance at rear; Two, four, six, eight, gay is just as good as straight – Three, five, seven, nine, lesbians are mighty fine; Two, four, six, eight, how do you know your grandma's straight; Unbutton; Warning: Sodomy can be habit forming; WE ARE ANGRY NOT GAY; We are everywhere; WE ARE YOUR BEST FANTASY, WE ARE YOUR WORST NIGHTMARE; We're here, we're gay and we're in the PTA; We're here, we're queer and we're not going shopping; We're here, we're queer, get used to it; We've been nice too long; When God made man she was only kidding; A woman without a man is like a fish without a bicycle. And thousands of others, to keep the spirit alive.

SM Abbreviation for SADOMASOCHISM which, perhaps apocryphally, has been attributed to the American sex researcher Alfred KINSEY. Apparently, he and his research team developed an extended series of abbreviations so that they could talk about their findings in public without offending any eavesdroppers. Those who are disaffected with the posing on the leather bar scene claim that SM actually means 'stand and model'. Not to be confused with M and S, the British chain store, which is more the preserve of the cardy-carrying gay man than the leather clad.

SM parties Where no bars for leather people exist, SM parties are crucial for people with leather interests. They are hosted in people's homes, and populated by means of informal networks of referral. The SM parties of the 1950s onwards in America created the contacts which led to the first leather bars there.

smash Name given to an infatuation by one woman for another in American colleges of the late nineteenth century. Thus a woman was said to be smashed when she attempted to gain the affection of another. A Yale newspaper of 1873 describes the tactics one woman might use when 'smashed', 'She straightaway enters upon a regular course of bouquet sendings, interspersed with tinted notes, mysterious

packets of "Ridley's Mixed Candies", locks of hair perhaps, and many other tender tokens.'

smash monogamy Slogan of the 1960s COUNTERCULTURE which argued against the restrictions of traditional morality. It was also taken up by gay activists who held that monogamy was a heterosexual paradigm used to restrict the free expression of sexuality. In effect, though, the insistence among radical communities on breaking heterosexual mores created new pressures on lesbians and gays who maybe didn't want to be swinging polygamists.

smeg(ma) Any bodily secretion, but used most often to describe the malodorous accumulation of seminal matter that can build up beneath an unwashed foreskin. Perversely derived from the Greek word for detergent. The cheesy aroma of smeg has given rise to a number of slang terms, such as cock cheese, duck butter, pecorino (Italian slang), roquefort or smetana after the Yiddish for soured cream. The female equivalent has been known as rag cheese.

Smith, Bessie (1894–1937) The legendary blues singer has become something of an icon, particularly for black women, since she was a great fighter and was reported to have once fought off a Ku Klux Klan gang singlehandedly. Smith occasionally accompanied the singer Ma RAINEY on tour, and was even thought to have bailed the latter out after being arrested at a party with a crowd of naked women. Never one to rein herself in, Smith was known for her temper, her periodic alcoholism, and her hedonistic life, which included sex with women as well as men. She died after a car crash, reportedly because the hospital where she went refused to accept her because she was black.

snap (1) In American gay circles, to click the fingers, also known as a royal command. Depending on the position of the arm it can give a variety of messages, to call someone over, to embellish a particularly enlivened monologue, or to dismiss something demeaning. To snap, or pluck, somebody off is to click the fingers derisively in someone's face to dismiss them or to respond to some act of effrontery on their part. (2) To tighten the sphincter muscles over a dick while being fucked.

snow queen US gay slang for a black gay man who is primarily attracted to white sexual partners. Black slang alternative to the racist term DINGE QUEEN.

so In the UK in the early twentieth century, the question 'Is s/he so?' functioned as a way of asking about someone else's sexuality without mentioning any more explicit words.

soap, to pick up the Slang term for getting fucked. Refers to those butter-fingered boys who keep dropping the soap in all-male showers and have to keep bending over to retrieve it. And then look what happens.

social constructionists Those who, within academic discourse on lesbian and gay history, assert that sexual categories are historically specific, and can only be seen as a result of a particular set of social circumstances. Thus they feel it would be erroneous to talk of lesbians and gays living in other centuries because the concepts of lesbian and gay as we know them can only be created with the specific aspects of twentieth-century lesbian and gay lifestyles. Although people in other times might have had same-sex erotic experiences and might have felt attraction to their own biological gender, they would not have identified with the social identity that we would feel nowadays.

Societies for the Reformation of Manners Organizations founded in Tower Hamlets, London in 1690, their aim being the suppression of unChristian conduct, particularly in the 'bawdy houses' where sex, both homosexual and heterosexual, was available. The societies created a network of guardians of public morality, with a system of stewards for each area of the city to report on sally deeds occurring in those areas. There was also a committee to record the particulars of miscreants. By 1720 there were almost twenty such societies in London. In their zeal to wipe out sodomitic practices, the societies were not averse to using entrapment, by putting up young men to give the come-on to men whom they believed to be homosexual. The societies did not always have the effect they wanted. Although they were responsible for the purges of the MOLLY HOUSES that occurred in the early eighteenth century, they also drove many men into the relative safety of the subculture and, through their own fanaticism and the literature they produced, they must in addition have alerted many gay men to the existence of a sizeable gay population. Thus in many ways they were responsible for the growth of the subculture in the period.

Society for Human Rights The first gay rights organization in America, established in Chicago in 1924, which published two issues of its journal FRIENDSHIP AND FREEDOM. It was founded by Henry Gerber who had spent some time in Germany and had witnessed the gay movement there. The group dissolved after less than a year when the wife of one of the members turned over some material she had found to the police and the officers of the society were arrested.

Society for Individual Rights American gay rights organization, founded in 1964 by members of a previous gay organization, the LEAGUE FOR CIVIL EDUCATION. The society produced its own newsletter, *Vector*.

Society for the Suppression of Virtue Society that Oscar WILDE and his mother Lady Speranza Francesca Wilde jokingly planned to set up in response to the Society for the Suppression of Vice which had been founded in the United States. Lady Wilde, poet, activist for women's rights and advocate of home rule for the Irish, was also a glamorous society hostess who scorned 'respectability' as being below her station. She was tremendously fond of her son Oscar, and projected, like him, an image of decadence.

Society of Janus SM organization which began in San Francisco in 1974. It was one of the first mixed sexuality groups of any kind, and quickly became a point of connection between straight, bi and queer sadomasochists in the San Francisco Bay area. Unfortunately, it became increasingly heterosexual, and its queer members tended to move off to exclusively lesbian or gay groups.

socraticism *See* SYMPOSIUM.

Sodom and Gomorrah Two biblical cities described in Chapter 19 of the Book of Genesis. They apparently met their end around 1900 BC when they were destroyed with fire and brimstone. The reason for this, as given by the translator Philo of Alexandria, was the fact that the residents wanted sexual intercourse with two angels who were lodging with Lot. Academic debate rages around the subject, with some scholars maintaining that homosexuality was only introduced by translators of the Hebrew, and it was inhospitality that was the actual crime of those unlucky citizens. *See also* À LA RECHERCHE DU TEMPS PERDU.

Sodom by the Sea Epithet first applied to San Francisco, but used nowadays to describe any coastal town with a sizeable lesbian and gay population.

Sodom, or the Quintessence of Debauchery Play by John Wilmot, Earl of Rochester (1647–80) which has the distinction of being the first British work to be suppressed by the government as indecent. It is the story of a monarch, the subtly named King Bolloxinion, who makes buggery compulsory in his kingdom, declaring that 'with my Prick, I'll govern all the land'. He is aided by his 'Buggermaster-General', the able Borastus, who advises the King to eschew Queen Cuntigratia for the delights of the back passages of either Prince Pockenello or Pine, a Pimp of Honour. Bolloxinion is so overcome that he announces, 'May as the Gods his name immortal be/That first received the gift of Buggery!' The play ends on a risible moral note – those members of the cast who are not afflicted with venereal disease are destroyed by fire and brimstone raining down on the kingdom. Wilmot, a libertine

who probably died of exhaustion, extolled the love of boys in other equally sophisticated writings, which demonstrate that for the right fee male servants were quite available: 'Then give me health, wealth, mirth and wine/And if busy love entrenches./There's a sweet, soft page of mine/Does the trick worth forty wenches.'

Sodoma Nickname for the Italian artist Giovanniantonio Bazzi (1477–1549), who was famed for his fondness for boys. According to the account by Italian art historian Giorgio Vasari, Sodoma's life was 'licentious and dishonourable', but he was unabashed about it all: 'He gloried in it, writing stanzas and verses on it, and singing them to the accompaniment of the lute.'

Sodomite's Walk Cruising area in the drained marshlands of Moorfields in eighteenth-century London. The area was so notorious that it became known to the police, who paid men to act as agents provocateurs in order to entrap men there. From the evidence given in such cases, it seems that the same methods of cruising were employed nearly three centuries ago as today. The area seems to have waned as a gay cruising area by the mid nineteenth century.

sodomy (1) Derived from the name of the biblical city of Sodom, sodomy has served historically as an umbrella term for any sexual practice to which sexual moralists took offence. Legally, it has encompassed a number of acts such as anal sex, lesbian sex, bestiality and even on occasion oral sex and masturbation. (2) Song from the musical *Hair*. It related the joys of sodomy, pederasty, fellatio and masturbation.

softball Queerly enough, the butch game of softball has often been associated in America with lesbians. In the period after the Second World War, when the military was seeking to weed out all serving lesbians, they especially targeted army softball teams as a potential breeding ground. Later in the 1950s and 1960s working-class American lesbians created their own teams, as a sort of social alternative to the bar scene.

Soho The London neighbourhood which has historically been the seedy underbelly of London life, as the locus for most of the outlets of its sex industry since the nineteenth century. Because it has had a reputation as the centre for outlawed sexuality, it is not surprising that it has become the gay subculture in late-twentieth-century London. It includes OLD COMPTON STREET.

Some of My Best Friends are... 1971 film directed by Mervyn Nelson. It deals with the clientele of a gay bar named the Blue Jay, which serves as a selection of various facets of the iconography of the queer ghetto. There is the scheming fag-hag, Lita Joyce, who outs one of the men to his mother who then appears and assaults her son on the dance floor; the hatcheck girl; the Jewish mother cook who protects her boys; and Karen, the drag queen who wants to be a real woman but who is beaten up in the lavs by a rent-boy who vehemently refutes that he is queer. At the time the film was a call for tolerance for an oppressed people, but failed to draw parallels between societal repression and self-hate.

Somerville, Jimmy (1961–) Diminutive Scottish pop performer who first shot to attention fronting the band BRONSKI BEAT in the mid-1980s. Always more than upfront about his sexuality, his later coupling The Communards also created some tunes that spoke to the gay experience. 'There's More to Love Than Boy Meets Girl' blew apart hetero-mythologizing on more than one level, while 'For A Friend' dealt with grief over a dead lover and still makes the little hairs on the back of the neck rise when Somerville does the song at London PRIDE. Its title indicated the difficulties lesbians and gay men find in having a bereavement acknowledged. In 1991, with a reference to US President George Bush's election pledge, Somerville released 'Read My Lips', a song influenced by the AIDS activist movement, which declared that 'money is what we need, not compla-

cency'. Almost a saint to many gay men, Somerville has always used his position to spread the gay and AIDS activist message, not only through his work but also through overt politicking. He has often supported activities by direct action groups ACT UP and OUTRAGE!. Fittingly, he appeared as a little angel in Sally Potter's film version of Virginia Woolf's *Orlando* (1992).

Somerville and Ross Edith Somerville (1858–1949) and Violet Martin (1862–1915) were Irish writers and cousins whose relationship, although we do not know if it was sexual, was of such a closeness that they described it as a marriage. They wrote together under the pen name of Somerville and Ross. Their first collaborative work was published in 1889; altogether they wrote fourteen. After Violet died in 1915, Edith carried on writing, and announced that the works were joint efforts, Violet providing her input from another 'plane'. The works were still published under both their names.

Somerville and Ross Edith Somerville (1858–1949) and Violet Martin (1862–1915) were Irish writers and cousins whose relationship, although we do not know if it was sexual, was of such a closeness that they described it as a marriage. They wrote together under the pen name of Somerville and Ross. Their first collaborative work was published in 1889; altogether they wrote fourteen. After Violet died in 1915, Edith carried on writing, and announced that the works were joint efforts, Violet providing her input from another 'plane'. The works were still published under both their names.

Something Unspoken 1953 one-act play by Tennessee Williams, which deals with the guarded relationship between a southern American lady and her private secretary.

A Song at Twilight Play by Noël Coward. In keeping somewhat with its author, the play argues the philosophy of the closet. Its protagonist Sir Hugo Latymer, renounces a gay relationship for a passionless marriage and professional acclaim.

When his former relationship rears its head in the form of news of letters from his long-dead ex-lover, Sir Hugo attempts to justify his desire to preserve his facade of heterosexuality.

Sonnet: To an Asshole Marvellously sumptuous evocation of a man's secret jewel by the tempestuous French poets Verlaine and Rimbaud. Describing the little bud in its post-coital state, they describe it as a 'Dark, puckered hole: a purple carnation/That trembles, nestled among the moss (still wet with love)'. As well as the sperm which is still clinging, the poets describe how in order not to let their cocks get all the action, they like to place their mouth to the orifice as well. One of the first literary celebrations of RIM-MING.

sotadic zone Theory of Sir Richard Burton expounded in the lengthy 'Terminal Essay' of his translation of THE THOUSAND AND ONE NIGHTS. The essay contained forty-two pages on pederasty, and identified the zone where it was 'popular and endemic', including the whole Muslim world as well as China, south-east Asia, Japan, and central Asia, though not Hindu areas of India. Burton's interest was engendered by his 'exposure' to pederasty while a British colonial official in Pakistan.

Spanish fly Substance made from the powdered bodies of a European species of beetle. It became commonly known in the nineteenth century for its supposed aphrodisiac qualities, since it has the effect of dilating the blood vessels around the genitals. However, its use can cause illness and death. The Marquis de Sade reportedly offered guests chocolates which were filled with the substance.

Spanner Case Legal case in the UK in December 1990 in which eleven gay men received prison sentences of up to four and a half years and another five were fined, for engaging in sadomasochistic sex acts. In some cases, the men were charged with antediluvian laws which dealt with assault on oneself. The prosecution was successful despite the fact that all the men had been entirely consenting to the behaviour, that it had taken place in private, and that none of the 'injuries' required medical treatment. The case followed a massive police operation (codenamed Spanner) between 1987 and 1990 after the police had raided one of the men's home and discovered videos of SM sex. SM communities were alarmed at the legal precedent that had been set by the decision.

Spare Rib British feminist magazine, founded in the 1970s and the longest running feminist publication in the country until it foundered in 1993. The magazine evolved during the course of its history from being run by mainly white middle-class women to a collective of black heterosexual women. Many lesbians, both white and black, made significant inputs on the way.

Sparta It seems that in ancient Sparta homosexual relations were used as the basis for a boy's, mainly military, education. At the age of twelve a Spartan boy would become eligible to be taken as a lover. An older youth of the same class would make a request for him, and if successful would become the 'inspirer' (*eisphelos*) to the boy's 'hearer' (*aîtes*). The lover would give the boy a suit of armour and would begin to teach him the use of arms. According to Plato, their relationship also involved anal sex. The practice was almost compulsory, and sanctions might be exerted over a youth or boy who did not take a lover. While their formal arrangement ended with marriage, even then men would live in sex-segregated accommodation, and would share wives and male lovers with other men of the same age.

Spartacus British gay magazine of the late 1960s which carried features on the growing gay scene, contact adverts, problem letters as well as the requisite ever-so-slightly-rude pictures of men. Along with JEREMY it was one of the first magazines in the UK to actually be out about the sexuality of its readership.

Spartacus 1960 film directed by Stanley Kubrick which gives the epic treatment to the Roman slave revolt led by the eponymous hero (played by Kirk Douglas). It includes one scene in which Crassus (Laurence Olivier), while being helped to bathe by his young slave Antoninus (Tony Curtis), establishes his attraction to both genders through an analogy to the eating of oysters and snails. The scene has often been censored.

Spartacus International Gay Guide The name of the most popular gay tourism guide, which includes listings for gay institutions, ghettos, cruising grounds, bars and clubs in cities worldwide.

speakeasies During the prohibition era in America (1920–34) when the manufacture and sale of alcoholic drinks were forbidden, a wealth of illegal and unadvertised bars proliferated throughout the country. These were often in areas of bohemian life, and as such attracted many lesbians and gay men. Such bars were found in Harlem and Greenwich Village in New York, in the French Quarter of New Orleans, and in the Barbary Coast area of San Francisco.

This Special Friendship 1964 film directed by Jean Delannoy as an adaptation of Roger Peyrefitte's novel *Les Amitiés Particulières*. It is a timely attack on the hypocrisy of the Catholic Church, and contrasts the healthy and affectionate love between two schoolboys and the self-hate of a closety gay priest who thinks their behaviour, like his own, sinful. The younger boy eventually kills himself by jumping from a moving train, not because of guilt, but because he has been told by the priest that his friend no longer loves him.

special k Recreational drug, a mixture of ecstasy and ketamine, produced in capsules or tablets which create an audio-visual mind-fuck for its users on the gay club scene. Named in reference to a well-known brand of cereal.

speed Recreational drug, amphetamine sulphate or dexamphetamine sulphate, which is found in powdered or tablet form and which is a staple on the gay club scene

because of the added sense of energy and well-being it gives. It causes an increase in the heart rate, but its most undesirable side-effect is perhaps the fact that, while not dampening the libido, it makes it almost impossible to come.

Spiritual Conference for Radical Fairies By 1979 the RADICAL FAIRY movement was attracting more and more interest from gay men seeking to develop new forms of gay lifestyle. In order to create the space for such men to come together to explore this gay consciousness, activist Harry HAY and his partner John Burnside convened a gathering of radical fairies on an ashram in a remote area of the Arizona desert in September 1979. The men, spending much of the time without clothes, anointed each other and engaged in dance, sex, conversation and ritual to invoke protective spirits. Since then, many similar gatherings of radical fairies have been held throughout America, Europe and Australia.

spook Middle-class lesbian slang of the 1930s to describe a woman who started by dabbling in lesbianism, but became a willing convert.

spoon Term for an infatuation felt by one woman for another in a late-nineteenth-century women's college in America.

Sporus The young Roman slave who was reportedly castrated at the order of the Roman Emperor NERO and wed to him in a public ceremony. Sporus has acted since then as a symbol of the effeminate and emasculated homosexual man. In 1735, the poet Alexander Pope (1688–1744) wrote a poem attacking the effeminacy of John, Lord Hervey. Entitled *Sporus*, it contained the lines 'Fop at the Toilet, Flatt'rer at the Board, Now trips a Lady, and now struts a Lord.' The poem served to perpetuate the notion of the effeminate homosexual for many years. Hervey himself was bisexual, and carried on affairs with men at the same time as fathering some eight children with the wife to whom he seemed genuinely devoted.

square Australian slang of the early twentieth century referring to straights.

The Squire Queen Nickname of Anne (1665–1714), Queen of Great Britain and Ireland. In 1683 Sarah Jennings (1660–1744), the wife of Lord Churchill, was appointed a lady of her bedchamber, and the two seem to have enjoyed a very close relationship. Sarah exerted great power over the Queen and Anne responded with generous gifts of land and annuities. When the Queen began to transfer her affections to Abigail Masham, who had been introduced into the royal household in 1704, and when political differences drove a wedge between Sarah and Anne, they had a number of public quarrels, which commentators had a hard time explaining away. Lesbian historians have asserted that their relationship makes most sense if seen as one of lovers.

Stein, Gertrude (1874–1946) US writer who studied psychology and medicine in America, but spent much of her life in Paris, with her lover of thirty-nine years, Alice B. Toklas, about whom she wrote in her work *the Autobiography of Alice B. Toklas* (1933). Her writing style sought to incorporate the theories of abstract painting, and her works used words for their sounds rather than their meanings and often repeated the same themes. She was also a patron of the arts, and held salons in her Paris residence where she gave support to up-and-coming artists such as Picasso, Matisse, Hemingway and Cocteau. Because of her open relationship, she has passed into lesbian and gay folklore. For example, she and Alice turned sleuths in Stephen Abbott's novel *Rhino Ritz: An American Mystery* (1979) and later in Samuel Steward's *Murder is Murder is Murder* (1985) (which echoed her famous line, 'Rose is a rose is a rose is a rose'), and *The Caravaggio Shawl* (1989).

stone butch Particularly popular within the lesbian bar scene of the 1950s and 1960s, a stone butch is a butch woman who will not allow herself to be touched during sex, and who gets her pleasure from servicing her partner. If a stone butch allows her partner to be sexually active, she is said to have been FLIPPED.

The Stone Wall Autobiography by Mary Casal (1864–?) published in 1930 which celebrates the sexual relationship she enjoyed with her lover Juno. Sex, she declares, was a revitalizing activity.

Stonewall Group British lesbian and gay lobbying organization, which was formed shortly after the passage of CLAUSE 28 through the British parliament. The group was able to achieve a high public profile due to the patronage of showbiz figures such as Sir Ian MCKELLEN, and Michael Cashman (who had played Colin RUSSELL in the soap opera *EastEnders*), which allowed it to run a professional campaign to reduce the British AGE OF CONSENT in 1993 and 1994. It represents the respectable side of British lesbian and gay politics, leaving the angry work to direct action organizations such as OUTRAGE!

Stonewall Riot Possibly the watershed moment in lesbian and gay history, perhaps something that occurred when the lesbian and gay communities were looking for a watershed, the Stonewall Riot over 27–29 June 1969 and intermittently for a few days thereafter is usually reckoned to be the inception of the modern lesbian and gay movement – the first time we fought back. Most histories start with the fact that 27 June was the day of Judy GARLAND's funeral, and certainly the end to this event cast a pall over a community that had lived her ordeal of a life along with her. Many gay men had queued the previous day to see her lying-in-state at the Frank E. Campbell funeral home, and some Greenwich Village bars were draped in black as a sign of respect. It was that night that what was probably a failure to pay off the police led to a raid on the Stonewall Inn, the divey Mafia-owned bar in Christopher Street in the heart of the Village. The police were not aware, and nor were the patrons probably, why this was to be different from other raids: the patrons of gay bars were used to police harassment and were not ones to put up a fight. Two barmen, three drag queens and a number of other patrons, including a Latino man and a lesbian, were arrested. The other patrons were allowed to leave, and congregated outside, where they were joined by curious onlookers. This was different enough in itself. Usually they scattered, and when the arrestees were brought out, the mood of the crowd changed suddenly. Many different reasons have been advanced as to why this should have happened. Gay activist Bruce Voeller advanced a common one: 'Several people who I've talked to who were there claim...the person who probably started the Stonewall Riot was a Puerto Rican, a very macho-looking Puerto Rican who may not even have been gay, who provoked people and who kept shouting, "Why do you let them get away with this, stop letting them beat you up."' When the arrested lesbian struggled with the police as they tried to get her into the patrol car, the crowd began to hurl beer bottles and coins. The police, hemmed in, went back into the bar, emerging only to grab a man from the crowd whom they beat up inside the bar, while the crowd threw cobblestones and bricks, and even used a parking meter to ram the door. Someone poured lighter fuel through the window, and ignited it. When Tactical Patrol Force reinforcements arrived, the activity intensified and the crowd would retreat from the police, only to race back round the block and pelt them from behind. On one occasion, the police turned to find themselves confronting a chorus line of dancing queens singing WE ARE THE STONEWALL GIRLS. By 3.30 a.m. the police had broken up the crowd, but the next day crowds gathered at the bar to see the debris, and the graffiti that read 'Legalize gay bars' and 'Support gay power'. When the police tried to scatter the onlookers, an even larger crowd did a reprise of their performance of the previous night. Although not everyone welcomed the events – many saw them as the antics of stoned bar queens rocking the boat – the riot sent shockwaves through the lesbian and gay

communities, releasing an energy that was to lead to the formation of groups such as the GAY LIBERATION FRONT and the GAY ACTIVISTS ALLIANCE to take the baton from the older HOMOPHILE MOVEMENT. The MATTACHINE newsletter described it as 'the hairpin drop heard round the world'. Moreover, the riots have rich symbolic importance, the coming out of the gay communities from a sleazy Mafia-run bar where their custom was abused, to angry defiance on the streets. It is for this reason that the image of the community of drag queens, Hispanics and BUTCH lesbians coming together to fight the police remains resonant today, and is celebrated in the annual PRIDE marches held in cities worldwide.

stop the clause *See* CLAUSE 28.

Stork Club Club in the Sylvania Waters area of Sydney, Australia which hosted drag performers in the 1950s. It suffered constant harassment from the police and the vice squad.

straight Within lesbian and gay slang, heterosexual. It is not a linguistic coincidence that the word is also widely used by young people as a slang term for conservative, with overtones of tediousness. Within drugs-taking subcultures, straight is also used to describe someone who is not under the influence of any mind-expanding substance, or who is opposed to the taking of such substances. In American camp slang, the phrase 'to the nearest dressmaker' might be added to the word if used to describe a man whose protestations of heterosexuality are not very persuasive.

straight-acting One term which this author believes should be struck for good from the queer lexicon. It is usually found in gay CONTACT ADVERTS to denote someone who would not be recognizable by others as gay, namely someone who is incapable of an effeminate mannerism (though it may also be used to describe unobvious lesbians). Whether straight-acting men go the whole hog by talking endlessly about football and lighting their own farts is not clear. Not usually the sign of a happily adjusted gay person.

straightening up Pastime practised by those lesbians and gay men who have parents, or other family members, coming to visit to whom they are not out. It involves frantically removing from view any Joan Crawford posters, signed photos of Cagney and Lacey, Peggy Lee albums, half the cosmetics cabinet, all the magazines on the floor, and any other incriminating evidence that might drop enough hairpins to give the game away. Not to mention the lover and/or the dildo. Also known as de-dyking or de-fagging the flat.

Stranded Disco in Sydney, Australia which was resurrected from the ashes of an old corset salon, and kept many of the camp fixtures from its previous incarnation. It was the venue for the Sydney 'Mr Leather' competition in 1981.

strap-on A dildo attached to a belt mechanism that can be worn by lesbians to enable them to fuck their partner using the movement of their hips, rather than manually wielding the toy. The exclusive preserve of PRO-SEX LESBIANS.

Stryker, Jeff American porn star, whose fame is such that he has become something of a minor celebrity who is assured of packing out gay clubs on his personal appearances, with crowds eager to catch an eyeful of his legendarily large dick. Stryker's porn movies are popular for having a bit of the spirit that seems to be lacking in other suck–fuck–cum porn, despite a dialogue that – consisting almost entirely of 'You like that, dont'cha' – soon fails to get a rise. Stryker has also given his name (and dimensions) to a popular make of dildo, with 'real feeling balls'.

Student Homophile League First on-campus lesbian and gay group at an American university, it was formed in 1967 at Columbia University in New York and it was founded by a student, Robert Martin.

Students for a Democratic Society One of several US organizations of the 1960s enlisted in the struggle for black empowerment. Many young lesbians and gays in the radical atmosphere of the late sixties elected to join the more confrontational SDS rather than the conservative 'homophile' groups such as the North American Conference of Homophile Organizations. Ironically, many also came to SDS because it was not a gay organization and their sexuality would not be obvious.

La Stupenda Name by which the great Australian soprano Dame Joan Sutherland (1926–) is known to her legions of fiercely loyal OPERA QUEEN fans. Sutherland, who became resident soprano at the Royal Opera House in London's Covent Garden after her debut there in 1952 in *The Magic Flute*, was more known for her technical precision than the virtuosity that was the hallmark of her rival for gay affections, Maria Callas (*see* LA DIVINA).

sub Slang term used within BONDAGE and SM communities. It is an abbreviation of submissive, and refers to the BOTTOM in an SM scene.

subject–subject vision Concept developed by American gay activist Harry HAY, which indicated the possibility for gay people to interact with each other in a new and nurturing way. He argued that straights see other people as objects, and with that objectification come the destructive phenomena of competition and self-advantage. Gay people, however, because they are erotically attracted to people of the same gender, are more able to empathize with others and see them as subjects. This subject–subject vision leads gay people to be more able to develop non-exploitative and respecting ways of interacting. He used the term 'analogue consciousness' to refer to the same notion.

suffragism The militant movement which agitated for the parliamentary vote for women in the UK in the early years of the twentieth century. Suffragism became a particularly potent force after 1903 when the members of the Women's Social and Political Union, under the leadership of Emmeline Pankhurst (1858–1928) and her daughter, Christabel Pankhurst (1880–1958), employed tactics such as chaining themselves to railings, attacking property, withholding taxes as well as calling large public meetings and demonstrations. The relation of suffragism to the growth of a lesbian movement is not direct. Clearly, any movement which stressed women's independence was important for women who wanted to organize their lives around other women. Anti-feminists of the time who were aware of the writings of the SEXOLOGISTS were not ignorant of this, and used the implication of unsexed suffragists as a stick to beat the feminist movement. Yet there was very little debate within the suffragist movement about lesbianism, other than the few articles in THE FREEWOMAN journal and the privately circulated *Urania*. It is possible that the suffragists did not want to detract from their political message by championing causes as unpopular as lesbianism. Nonetheless, suffragism remains an example of the possibility of a popular movement to attain its objectives through DIRECT ACTION, and as such give inspiration to the modern lesbian and gay liberation movement.

Sunday, Bloody Sunday 1971 film offering by John Schlesinger, which portrays a gay doctor, a straight woman and the bisexual artist with whom they are both in love. A film more about the differences between relationships as they are in reality and in our illusions. It successfully included a gay relationship which was functional, and not included just for the shock value of its same-sex quality. A scene of a passionate kiss between Peter Finch and Murray Head caused a stir among that open-minded phenomenon, the mass audience.

Sutherland, Joan *See* LA STUPENDA.

Swan of Lichfield Epithet for the English poet Anna Seward (1747–1809). Much of her work is devoted to Honora Sneyd, the woman with whom she had a passionate ROMANTIC FRIENDSHIP. Honora lived with Anna and her father for some fourteen years when young, until she returned to her own father and then got married. She died of consumption in 1780. Despite their separations, Anna remained devoted, and after the death of her friend kept her memory alive in verse, until her own death. Seward was close to Eleanor Butler and Sarah Ponsonby, THE LADIES OF LLANGOLLEN, and perhaps saw in their relationship the life which she did not have with Honora. Lichfield was the name of the family home where Anna and Honora lived during their youths.

sweetie darling The 1990s way for one gay man to address another, usually while exhaling a lung full of smoke, and often while playing the ingenu to get him to buy the next drink. It was the catchphrase of Jennifer Saunders in ABSOLUTELY FABULOUS when she was talking to her disappointment of an unfashionable and actively tedious daughter.

swish(y) Either gay, or effeminate; usually both. The word has been recorded as early as the 1940s in America.

switch-hitter American slang for bisexual person. It derives from the use of the term to describe a baseball batter who can use either hand to bat.

Switchboard *See* LONDON LESBIAN AND GAY SWITCHBOARD.

Sydney The Australian city, capital of New South Wales, has been home to nefarious sexual practices since its very founding. Indeed, concern was expressed over the sex between men on the ships carrying them over from Britain, and it was even suggested that the sex segregation on the ships should be ended to remove the temptation to same-sex acts. There was always a huge imbalance between the number of men and of women on the ships, and in 1821 there were seven men to every woman in New South Wales. You don't have to be Hercule Poirot to imagine how the men overcame this numerical problem. It is not surprising then that within a few years of colonization a gay subculture was developing within Sydney, with gay bars, drag shows and cruising grounds. The gay life in the city continues to this day, with the SYDNEY LESBIAN AND GAY MARDI GRAS drawing sightseers from over the world.

Sydney Lesbian and Gay Mardi Gras Annual parade through Sydney, Australia. The first, which was held in June 1978, when homosexuality was still illegal in New South Wales, ended in violent confrontations with the police, who in some cases had taken off their identification numbers and who waded in to intimidate and make arrests. In 1981 the Mardi Gras started being held in February, and began to be more of a party than a political march, which made some activists feel that it had lost its political edge. From February 1982 the parade was followed by a huge and glamorous party, which has drawn much media attention and many interested tourists. Sydney has long been a haven for those who didn't quite fit into mainstream Australian society. It has had its gay subculture since the 1920s, and has continually attracted homoerotically inclined men and women, who have developed a specifically gay social identity since the 1960s.

Sylvester (1948–88) The black, gay disco diva had his first gay sex at age seven when a local-church member deflowered him in God's own house. He first stepped on stage in 1970 with the drag troupe the Cockettes (*see* HIBISCUS), before going on to a best-selling pop career with the albums *Lights Out* (1972) and *Step II* (1977).

Sylvia Scarlett 1936 film with Katharine Hepburn masquerading as a young boy who is attractive to both Cary Grant and their female travelling companion. As well as Hepburn's attractive butchness, the film introduces the possibility of a queer subtext for a covert gay audience while providing laughs for the oblivious majority.

Symonds, John Addington (1840–93) Gay British poet, critic and writer on sex. Educated at Oxford, Symonds was a great historian of the Italian renaissance, and it was through much of his researches that

the world was presented with the original versions of some of Michelangelo's sonnets, with the male pronouns restored which had been excised by his nephew. Symonds was also fascinated by Greek culture and Greek tolerance of homosexual relations, and in 1883 published his *Problem in Greek Ethics*, which was perhaps the first dispassionate work on homosexuality published in Britain. It was his intention to show that when valued by society homosexual relations could be ennobling. Like many gay men of the affluent classes, Symonds was himself primarily attracted to young working-class men or labourers, whom he saw as embodying his ideal of masculine purity. He was greatly influenced by the works of Walt WHITMAN, which he saw as offering a glory in the manly male body. Symonds was eager to ascertain whether Whitman's ideas of ADHESIVENESS had any erotic component, but when he wrote to him about the matter received something of a rebuff. During the latter part of his life Symonds worked on his essay on homosexuality, A PROBLEM IN MODERN ETHICS, in which he argued against the theories of writers such as KRAFFT-EBING. Symonds wrote his memoirs, which he intended to be illustrative and edifying for any other individuals coming to terms with their inverted sexuality, and also worked on a joint venture with Havelock ELLIS, which eventually became the SEXUAL INVERSION volume of Ellis' *Studies in the Psychology of Sex*. Unfortunately, Symonds' writings on homosexuality were suppressed by his family after his death.

Symposium One of the philosophical dialogues of Greek philosopher Plato (*c.* 427–*c.* 348 BC), a banquet at which various speakers detail different aspects of the nobility of love, usually between males. Phaedrus concentrates on the way in which a worthy lover can assist the education of the boy and can inspire the lover to greater things, particularly giving them courage in battle. Pausanias, in his justification of pederasty, discusses the two kinds of love (Aphrodite), the heavenly (Urania) and the common (Pandemos).

The heavenly form is exclusively male and is superior because of the edifying effects it can have on both lover and beloved. While he does not say that there should not be any physical consummation of the match, he declares that the older lover should see the affair as a matter for the soul and that the boy should not be too eager but should at least play hard to get. Pausanias' division between two kinds of love was reclaimed by the writers on URANIANISM in the nineteenth century. Aristophanes tries to explain homosexual desire through the fantasy that originally humans had a double set of limbs, heads and genitalia. Some were double males, others double females or male-female twins. The gods split the couples up, and the range of human sexuality is explained by the search of the descendants of these twins for their 'other half'. While comic in presentation, the idea is interesting because it shows an underlying belief in sexual orientation as a defining characteristic. Plato's Socrates describes love as part of the human desire to transcend death through the creation of children to perpetuate the line. Here though, children need not be the flesh and blood, screaming sort, but can be children of the mind, ideas, which a youth can conceive through the patronage of an older lover and through the sublimation of sexual desire. Thus the ideal of socraticism, an uplifting non-sexual relationship, is at the root of the modern simplified and heterosexualized notion of platonic relationships. As if to give proof of Socrates' commitment to this ideal, Alcibiades then enters and tells the company how, in his youth he tried to garner Socrates' wisdom for himself by making love to him, but that Socrates resisted his attentions all night. The *Symposium* has given generations of (educated) gay people an endorsement of their feelings, or an explanation if one is needed. In E. M. Forster's novel MAURICE, our hero understands the nature of his feelings for his college friend Clive on reading it.

T

Tattooing

T-cells Also called T4-cells, CD4-cells or T-helper cells. A type of white blood cell which has a primary role in the body's defence mechanism. It mobilizes the other elements of the immune system which attack and destroy foreign bodies. It is the T-cells which are particularly targeted by the HIV virus, and a T-cell count is often used as a means of ascertaining the extent of HIV infection.

taking the veil In both British and American gay slang, the phrase was used of gay men who came clean about their sexuality in order to avoid serving in the armed forces.

Tales of the City The title of the first book in the series of novels by Armistead Maupin, it is also used as a generic title for the series. The series includes *Tales of the City* (1978), *More Tales of the City* (1980), *Further Tales of the City* (1982), *Babycakes* (1984), *Significant Others* (1987), and *Sure of You* (1989). Based initially on Maupin's column in the *San Francisco Chronicle*, the series details the ups and downs of the little every-household located at 28 Barbary Lane, San Francisco. All human life is there: transsexual, joint-taping land-lady with a heart of gold; loveable gay man always on the hunt for 'Mr. Goodbar'; bisexual QUAALUDE-munching ex-advertis-ing executive (until she exploded in the face of a client); ex-radical lawyer turned philandering straight barman; deceptively naive career-minded bitch from hell; sinis-ter private dick; lesbian model turned black lesbian model after a course of pigment pills; frustrated daughter of com-pany director turned radical lesbian-femi-nist; English aristocrat turned leatherman; religious cult leader escaped from mass Guyanan suicide. Produced with soap-operatic vision, this family is so pretend it verges on science fiction. And yet the books are a joyous and human celebration of 1970s hedonism and a dignified por-trayal of life going on in the 1980s, even under the affliction of AIDS. They have introduced a host of characters into gay folklore, including MADRIGAL, ANNA; MOUSE; HAMPTON-GIDDES. The first novel was made into a TV film in 1993 after years of negotiations with movie companies that had complained there were too many gays, or that the gays were too nice.

Tante Magnesia The nickname given to the German activist Magnus HIRSCHFIELD by his detractors.

Tante Urlurette Nickname that was given to Jean-Jacques Régis de CAMBACÉRÈS.

Tapuya tribes Native Indian tribes of the Amazon River which developed a form of WOMAN MARRIAGE. Although the Tapuya were decimated by colonial Europeans, we have an account from 1576 of a Spanish voyage down the Amazon where the indigenous women were described as determined to remain chaste and as having no contact with men outside hunting trips. Each woman had 'a woman to serve her, to whom she says she is married, and they treat each other and speak with each other as man and wife'.

A Taste of Honey 1961 film adaptation of Shelagh Delaney's play, directed by Tony Richardson. It portrays with poignant tenderness the friendship between Jo, a pregnant and deserted working-class woman, and Geoff, a lonely young gay man.

Tatchell, Peter (1952–) The doyenne of British gay politics, 'Peggy' Tatchell was thrust into the limelight when he stood as the Labour Party candidate in the 1983 BERMONDSEY by-election. He joined the GAY LIBERATION FRONT in London in 1971 and is now one of the UK's leading activists for AIDS awareness and lesbian and gay equality. In 1987 he founded the UK AIDS Vigil Organization, the first British movement to defend the civil liberties of people with HIV, and he drafted the world's first comprehensive charter on AIDS and human rights in order to challenge the escalating trend towards Government repression. The following year he coordinated a massive candlelit procession in London, which resulted in the World Health Ministers Summit on AIDS amending its final declaration to include a specific commitment to oppose AIDS-related discrimination. A founding member of ACT UP and OUTRAGE!, Tatchell was often interviewed in the aftermath of the failed age of consent campaign in February 1994, when his call for a 'suffragette-style' campaign of civil disobedience earned him the soubriquet 'Peggy Pankhurst'.

tattooing The etching of semi-permanent body decorations into the skin. In film, as in life, tattoos are usually associated with people who enjoy the wilder side of sexual expression, and although demure little ones are reasonably common, they are still something of a badge of transgression. NEW AGE LEATHERMEN and LEATHERWOMEN who regard the practice as a symbol of entry into the leather communities point to the anthropological studies of tattooing as part of the tribal rituals which confer a visible statement of a young person's entry into adulthood.

Tavern Guild San Francisco organization of the 1960s. It coordinated the funds and efforts of local gay businesses to counter the growing threat of state inspectors' and police harassment of gay bars. The guild was successful because it could mobilize more funding than other groups of the time.

Taxal Parish in the English county of Cheshire, which in its marriage registers from the early eighteenth century contains tantalizing information for a lesbian herstory. Two entries note the marriage of 'Hannah Wright and Anne Gaskill' (1707) and of 'Ane Norton and Alice Pickford' (1708). There is no other information, but all four names are unequivocally female, and raise the intriguing prospect of a progressive vicar who saw no fault in marrying women.

Taxi zum Klo 1980 film by Frank Ripploh, which explores different attitudes towards relationships within the lesbian and gay community. It depicts the real-life relationship between Ripploh and his lover Bernd Broaderup, who both play themselves.

Broaderup wants a peaceful life of domestic coupledom, while Ripploh, a teacher, wants the freedom to engage in casual sex. The title derives from a scene in which he leaves hospital one night to take a taxi to the local COTTAGE for a quick one.

TBH Australian and South African gay slang, an acronym for 'to be had', to describe a man who was sexually available. Its opposite was 'not to be had', or NTBH. TBHID stands for 'to be had in drink'. It is used to refer to men who would be sexually available once they have been loosened up with alcohol.

Tea and Sympathy Play by Robert Anderson which deals with an archetypal SISSY student in a boarding school who is subject to rumours of homosexuality. Suspicion is already high because he eschews manly sporting activities for acting, sewing and tennis, but when he is caught swimming nude with one of the masters they become unbearable. He is unable to learn to act butch, but is finally saved by Laura, the wife of the headmaster who initiates him sexually, arriving at his room and, while unbuttoning her blouse, delivering the classic line, 'Years from now...when you talk about this...and you will talk about it...you will be kind.' Made into a film in 1956, the play was more a plea for the unmanly heterosexual, than an exposé of the malice of rumour-mongering.

tearoom or **teahouse** American term for a public toilet where gay men go to cruise for sex, also known as a recruiting centre. When they are making a MILK RUN, gay men will either go inside a cubicle and wait for a man to come into the next one so they can have sex through the GLORY HOLE, or wait at the urinal or inside a cubicle with the door open so that they can inspect whatever comes in. The toilet on which they sit as they wait for action is known as a throne or an empress bench, and they are a lady-in-waiting while occupying it. The custom of alerting the attention of the man in the next cubicle using taps of the feet is called going foot-tapping. The practice has always been dangerous since the police are aware that they can easily make arrests by staking out toilets, and have even been known to send in plain-clothes officers to entrap other men, (see PRETTY POLICEMAN). Cruising gay men will often appoint one man to act as watch and warn against any police activity, or if they are having sex in a cubicle with another man one of them will sometimes put his feet into two shopping bags so that if anybody looks under the door it seems like someone having a rest on the way home from the sales. A man who is arrested in a tearoom is known as a dethroned queen in camp argot. See also COTTAGE.

tearoom trade Any man who is picked up in a TEAROOM. A tea engagement is a pre-arranged date to meet another man for sex in a tearoom.

teddy In the grand catalogue of different male physical types that was part of the gay scene in the UK and America in the 1970s, a teddy (or an uncle) was the kind of older man – possibly a little on the CHUBBY side – who was marked out by his body hair, on both chest and face. For his admirers his warm fuzz made him as cuddly to take to bed as the small stuffed toy from which he took his name.

teddy bear On the gay bar scene in the 1970s and 1980s some men took to carrying a small toy bear in a trouser pocket, or embroidering a teddy bear badge onto their clothes to indicate that they were looking for someone to cuddle or be cuddled by, rather than any rougher sexual activity.

Teleny, or the Reverse of the Medal A Physiological Romance. Published in 1893, the title of the book disguises its frenetically erotic content. Described in a prospectus by its publisher as 'a new departure in English amatory literature', it describes the love affair between the handsome Hungarian-born pianist René Teleny and his adoring fan, the well-to-do Camille des Grieux. The affair ends tragically with the suicide of Teleny after he prostitutes himself with des Grieux's mother. On the way, the book is unabashedly graphic in its depiction of gay sex of all types, taking in SM, oral and anal sex, as well as incest, orgies and transvestism. Because of this, it was published anonymously. The novel is often thought to have been the work of Oscar WILDE, but his full role in its writing is subject to much debate. According to Charles Hirsch, a French bookseller who ran a shop in London which was patronized by Wilde, the manuscript of the work was passed among several men, including Wilde, using the shop as a base, and was written in a number of different hands. When it was published in an edition of 200 copies, it was circulated privately among London's gay literati.

televangelists Since Billy Graham and Cardinal Fulton J. Sheen in the 1950s, the manic wing of Christianity has increasingly tried to co-opt the airwaves in pushing its usually homophobic message. In the 1980s, high-profile sexual and financial scandals involving Jim Bakker and Jimmy Swaggart led to much hilarity. American comedian Elayne Boosler expressed a forlorn wish when she said, 'Wouldn't it be great if you could only get AIDS from giving money to television preachers?'

ten per cent Most widely believed statistic for the number of lesbians and gay men within any population. It derives from Alfred KINSEY's influential study of 5,300 white American males, who were interviewed at some length about their sexual experiences.

Teresa of Avila, St (1515–82) Born in Spain, Teresa founded nearly twenty convents, which followed a strict religious regime, as well as reforming the Carmelite order, and writing several works on prayer and meditation. She was also reported to have had a loving relationship with a female cousin. She was canonized in 1622.

Terrence Higgins Trust The first and largest British AIDS SERVICE ORGANIZATION, criticized by some for being too monolithic and diverting attention from other community-based initiatives. It does however provide a huge range of services for PWAs, as well as a helpline to give information and support, and educational materials. The trust was named after Terrence Higgins who died of AIDS-related illnesses in 1982, one of the first people in the UK to do so. It was founded in the same year by his friends who were dismayed by the lack of professional support that existed for PWAs. Usually referred to as the THT.

testicles The word is derived from the latin word for witness because they gave testament to a man's masculinity.

The Fey Way Gallery Art gallery located in the South of Market district in San Francisco. It was the first gallery in the city devoted to 'leather' art, and featured the work of TOM OF FINLAND, Chuck ARNETT, Tom Hinde, Robert MAPPLETHORPE and others. Its founder, Robert Opel, known also for his streak during the 1975 Academy Awards ceremony, was unfortunately shot at his gallery by robbers in 1979.

The Love that Dares to Speak Its Name Poem by Professor James Kirkup which decribed the sexual fantasies of a Roman centurion on witnessing the body of Christ on the Cross. The publication of the poem in GAY NEWS led to the LEMON CASE in 1977, when the newspaper was successfully prosecuted for blasphemy. As a result, the (ironically titled) poem is still not available to the British public.

Theater des Eros Berlin theatre founded in 1921 and dedicated to putting on productions of plays with gay themes.

theatre The arts in general, and the theatre in particular have long been considered a gay haunt, even before the modern days of opera queens. The Elizabethan and Jacobean theatre were associated with all aspects of the sexual subcultures, and contemporary commentators described the sodomite 'who is at every play, and every night sups with his INGLES'.

Theatre of Black Women Theatre collective which was created by British black women in 1982 in order to allow the voice of black women to be fairly represented on the stage. Several of the performances were the work of black lesbian writers. It folded in the late 1980s.

Thelma and Louise 1991 film, directed by Ridley Scott, with Geena Davis and Susan Sarandon. The two women set off for a holiday which becomes an odyssey away from their past lives as waitress and housewife. An act of transgressive violence, when Louise shoots the man trying to rape Thelma, marks the point of no return, and in fleeing from the law the women find out what it is to be fully awake. When their attempt to get to Mexico is foiled, they take a leap into the unknown (in this case a precipice over the grand canyon), with an unerotic kiss and a triumphant hand clasp. The film became a symbol of female bonding and, while not explicitly lesbian, the lesbian reading was there for the taking.

Theosophist Society Religious grouping in Australia in the early twentieth century which was known for a very welcoming attitude towards queers. So welcoming in fact that its leader, Bishop Leadbeater, was often seen in the company of a group of attractive novices.

a thing of beauty is a boy forever The phrase, echoing the line from Keats' *Endymion* (where it is a 'joy' forever), was described as being imprinted on the stationery of the lustful Duke in the homo-themed novel *The Blind Bow Boy*, by Carl Van Vechten, who was central to the artistic outpourings of the HARLEM RENAISSANCE.

third sex Outdated term for homosexuals which sought to place them as an alternative gender midway between the male and female. The expression was particularly popular in the nineteenth century, although we may look back to Aristophanes' speech in Plato's SYMPOSIUM for a similar idea. The term appears in *Splendeur et Misère des Courtisanes* (1847) by the French writer Balzac referring to the male homosexual, but it was not until the writings of Karl ULRICHS that it gained much currency, eventually being co-opted

by the activist Magnus HIRSCHFIELD. It was intended to present a 'neutral' idea of homosexuality that did not construct it as a disease, but as a form of the CONGENITAL INVERSION argument, it fell into the same traps of creating gender stereotypes.

Third World Lesbians 1970s term for black lesbian communities.

The Thousand and One Nights A collection of ancient tales from Persia, India and Arabia. First written in Arabic, it appeared in the form known today around 1450. Although the work contained many homosexual references it tended to be bowdlerized. The first translation that included the homoerotic passages was that of the nineteenth-century traveller Sir Richard Burton in 1885–6, who declared that he wanted to describe pederasty 'in decent nudity not in suggestive fig-leaf or feuille de vigne'. Among tales of ABU NUWAS and debates on the relative merits of homosexual and heterosexual relations, the translation also included the marvellous verse, 'The penis smooth and round was made/With anus best to match it; Had it been made for cunnus' sake/It had been formed like a hatchet.'

thrush (oral candida) Fungal infection of the mouth which is commonly suffered by people with AIDS. It usually appears as a thick, curd-like coating on the tongue, gums and palate, and often occurs after a course of antibiotics. It can be treated with lozenges, mouthwashes or tablets.

THT *See* TERRENCE HIGGINS TRUST.

Tilden,   William (1893–1953) American tennis player who dominated the sport throughout the 1920s. After being arrested for sex with a minor in 1946, his life was ruined.

Tipton, Billy (1914–89) American jazz musician and one of the most famous PASSING WOMEN of all time. Tipton was only discovered after 'his' death from a bleeding ulcer to have been a woman. According to his 'wife', he adopted a male persona in order to have the opportunity to practise as a musician, in a time when women were confined to singing. Gaining fame as a sax-ophonist and a piano player, and founding the Billy Tipton Trio, Billy also adopted three sons, who knew nothing about the real gender of their father.

tit king American lesbian slang for a lesbian who is erotically attracted to women with big breasts.

tits Breasts, both female and (when pumped up on the nautilus) male. Unlike the heterosexual colloquial usages of the word, tits in gay male argot have positive connotations. To have tits is to have courage in the face of it all. Inexplicably enough, if something is as CAMP as tits, it is a supreme version of the style, usually said approvingly.

to the three of us Dedication in the novel *The Well of Loneliness* by Radclyffe HALL. The three were Hall, her lover Lady Una Troubridge, and Veronica Batten, the cousin of Troubridge and the former lover of Hall who had died several years before publication of the novel. Hall and Troubridge asserted that they remained in contact with Batten through seances.

Toklas, Alice B. (1877–1967) Best known as the lover of American writer Gertrude STEIN, Alice also wrote the autobiographical works, *What Is Remembered* (1963) and *Staying On Alone* (1973). She first met Stein in 1907, and stayed with her until she died from cancer in 1946. Brought up as a Jew, Alice later converted to Catholicism, because it offered the possibility of an afterlife where she and Gertrude could be together. Alice's importance to Gertrude is often effaced by hetero literary histories, which call her a 'secretary'. She gave her name to the ALICE B. TOKLAS DEMOCRATIC CLUB.

Tom of Finland (Touko, 1920–81) Finnish artist, who was singlehandedly responsible for creating the characteristic butch aesthetic of gay male art. Touko studied in Helsinki, and his first drawing was published on the cover of an American magazine in 1957. Thereafter he made regular trips to the United States where he met photographer Robert MAPPLETHORPE and artist Andy WARHOL. His drawings are populated solely by a cast of clone-type gay men, who all have improbable musculature and even more unfeasibly large dicks and who live in a seemingly perpetual state of arousal. They represent the range of clone iconography, with the uniforms of police, army, cowboy, trucker as well as leatherman commonly displayed. The SM themes in his works have led to them being criticized as politically incorrect, but their longlasting erotic appeal indicates that gay male communities have not quite laid their fascination with masculine stereotypes to rest.

tomboy Any woman, big or small, who doesn't quite live up to the feminine role expected of her. The sort of girl who is more interested in performing brain surgery on her Barbie doll than dressing her in her slinky après-ski ensemble, and who prefers oil stained to pink and frilly. The female counterpart of the male SISSY, although a tomboy is often looked on more favourably than her effeminate brother, possibly because she is seen to be mimicking the superior male. Many lesbians remember first feeling different from the others in their tomboy activities, rather than in any explicit lesbian feeling. The tomboy is a stock character in film and television. Doris Day made most of a career out of playing them. Although film tomboys are conveniently tamed into relationships with men in film, the lesbian audience would read them as they wished. Historical tomboys include CHRISTINA, QUEEN OF SWEDEN and CALAMITY JANE.

Tongues Untied 1989 film by Marlon T. Riggs which unfolded the black gay experience in America through interviews, poetry recital, performance documentary footage and obituaries of black gay men lost to AIDS.

Tool Box The first successful leather bar opened in San Francisco, founded in the early 1960s, somewhat later than those in cities such as Chicago, Los Angeles and New York. It began the trend of locating leather bars in the South of Market area of the city. It was featured in a *Life* magazine article in 1964, which brought the leatherman to the attention of the American public. *See* ARNETT, CHUCK.

tootsie American lesbian slang for a BUTCH lesbian.

tootsie trade From the British meaning in the Second World War of tootsie to refer to the queenly gay men who bravely formed the subculture at that time, the phrase referred to one tootsie having sex with another. It was the usual practice then for gay 'sisters' to save their sexual urges for butch TRADE, and use each other for emotional support (*see* SEXUAL EXOGAMY). During the war, when the 'real men' were thin on the ground, tootsie trade became the only sexual option a lot of the time, despite the fact that it was not quite the done thing.

top Although the term can be used for the active partner in any sexual activity, it is most often used in talking about more radical sex. Thus it refers to the sadist in an SM scene, to the fister in fistfucking, or to the one who binds in bondage. Among SM and leather communities of the 1950s the roles of top and BOTTOM were more clearly defined, and less transferable than at present. Since then the relative popularity of mild and infrequent SM play has resulted in the dilution of the rules of the 1950s scene. Thus it is now common to find people who enjoy both roles. In addition, in the 1950s there were more tops than bottoms on the scene, and tops had to practise to reach a high standard in their chosen art to attract partners. Some would become famous for their ability, and would be sought out as teachers by students of the discipline. Now there are far more bottoms than tops, and they can get by with far less expertise. Skills are today more likely to be communicated through workshops and SM open days than through the personal networks of the past.

top sergeant American prison and working-class lesbian slang of the 1930s which described the BUTCH partner in a lesbian BUTCH/FEMME relationship.

Torch Song Trilogy Harvey Fierstein's three-act exploration of the search by one Jewish drag queen, Arnold Beckoff/ Virginia Hamm, for a gay version of happy family life, through the QUEERBASHING of one lover and his ultimate adoption of the son that calls him 'Ma'. It opened off-OFF-BROADWAY at La Mama in 1979, and graduated to Broadway in 1982, winning two Tony awards. In 1988 it became an acclaimed film version starring Fierstein as the wisecracking queen, and Anne Bancroft as his 'Jewish mother' of a Jewish mother. It was praised by some for presenting a gay life without modifying its language and message, and handling with sensitivity the issue of queerbashing, and the pipedream of officially sanctioned child adoption. Others decried its implicit message that gay men were searching for a recreation of hetero-happy families. Arnold is a bit of a pipedream in himself, a sagging queen who has only his wit and style to hang on to and who still manages to inspire the devotion of two men who, according to Fierstein's notes are both above-average attractive. Nonetheless, he has dignity, and that is perhaps most important.

tortillera In Spanish, Latin American and Hispanic American slang, a term for a lesbian. It literally means a tortilla maker, although why lesbians should be associated with a cornmeal pancake is unclear.

tourists Straight people who wander unknowingly into gay establishments or districts. Usually quite impervious to their surroundings, they sit and wonder why everyone is dressed the same, why everyone is so attractive, and why everyone is having so much fun. Then they wander off. Unfortunately, they sometimes come back. To shock tourists by effeminately making them aware of just what they've wandered into is known as dazzling the audience.

Towards a Quaker View of Sex Pamphlet published by the Society of Friends in 1963. In a first for a religious organization, the work declared that society 'should no more deplore homosexuality than left-handedness...Homosexual affection can be as selfless as heterosexual affection and therefore we cannot see that it is in some way morally worse.' The Society of Friends has always been the exception that proves the rule among religions.

Townsend, Prescott (1894–1973) American gay activist who was prominent in the gay rights movement in his home town of Boston. When he was arrested on a public indecency charge in 1944, he reportedly said to the judge in court, 'So, what's wrong with a little cocksucking on the Hill?' He founded the Boston chapter of the gay rights organization, the MATTA-CHINE SOCIETY, in the 1950s, and another organization, the Boston Demophile Society, in the early 1960s.

toxoplasmosis An infection which causes abscesses in the brain and which is sometimes associated with HIV infection. Symptoms produced by the abscesses include headaches, fits, numbness and confusion. Cats represent the main host for the infection, and people with AIDS are encouraged to be careful around cats, especially if cleaning out their litter.

trade Gay slang term derived from POLARI which refers to the kind of casual pick-up who would call himself straight but would allow another man to go down on him, or who would agree to fuck another man, so long as he doesn't have his own orifices defiled. *See also* ROUGH TRADE. Gay trade is another gay man who does not reciprocate during sex.

trannie In camp gay slang, either a TRANS-VESTITE or a TRANSSEXUAL, although usually the former. With the same devastating humour that they apply to the TV, gay men often refer to the (transistor) radio as the 'transvestite'.

transgendered Trendy term used to describe a transsesxual who has had essential surgery. *See* TRANSSEXUALISM.

transsexualism The feeling that one has been born into the body of the 'wrong' biological gender, a feeling that has only really come to public attention in the 1950s, with the availability of GENDER REAS-SIGNMENT SURGERY. Transsexuals respond to this feeling in different ways, from simply incorporating it into the gender roles they act out in their lives in their original gender, through TRANSVESTISM (the two are not the same thing) which allows them to act in society as the gender with which they really identify, to the lengths of having surgery. Transsexuals and the lesbian and gay communities have traditionally not got on terribly well. On the one hand, many transsexuals have denied the connection between their feelings and homosexuality with an eagerness that indicates they are not wanting to question negative societal values of lesbian and gay sexuality. On the other hand, lesbians and gay men, particularly lesbian feminist critics such as British writer Sheila Jeffreys, who since the 1970s have been developing sophisticated theories of gender as an entirely socially created phenomenon, have criticized transsexuals for buying in to theories that gender is an inherent part of the identity, and that biological sex and the social roles that that entails are necessarily linked. Moreover, they see transsexuals as pandering to nineteenth-century theories that the gender that one feels must necessarily be attracted to the opposite sex; thus if one is attracted sexually to women one must necessarily be a man. The last point is somewhat erroneous; it is common that a transsexual will, for example, 'feel' like a man yet will be erotically attracted to men – they do not always 'become' heterosexual. Perhaps transsexuals are the antidote to any overarching theories that lesbians and gay men might develop regarding gender, and are proof-positive of the argument that we all experience our sex and sexuality in different ways; the trick is to accept that others might feel differently. The press have always been fascinated with the phenomenon and have shown great prurience in their coverage of famous transsexuals such as Christine Jorgensen (*see* AMSTERDAM), American celeb and Andy WARHOL protégé Holly Woodlawn, and British explorer Jan Morris. Female-to-male transsexuals are less well-covered, although there have been some television documentaries (such as a *World in Action* documentary on British television in 1978), despite the fact that, according to Christine Jorgensen, equal numbers of men and women seek gender reassignment. The law in most countries has been slow to recognize transsexuals. For example, in the UK it is impossible to change one's gender in the eyes of the law; thus if a male-to-female transsexual is raped she cannot prosecute the crime under rape, since in British law rape can only be perpetrated on a woman, and the transsexual is legally a man. In addition, transsexuals find it difficult to marry (since homosexual partnerships are of course not legal), although in 1994 a transsexual couple (one each way) was pushing their union as a test case.

transvestism Indicates the wearing by an individual of clothes considered appropriate to the opposite gender. It is a complex phenomenon that is not necessarily related to transsexualism or same-sex erotic behaviour. Anthropologists have documented numerous cases of transvestism connected to religious and shamanistic practices in different cultures. There are various explanations for this. In some cases transvestism evolved from a sex-based division of labour under which the shamanistic role was associated with that of womanhood. Men performing the role therefore adapt to fit this division. In other cases religious cosmology represents a fusion of gender, and the fusing of gender within the religious figures will be appropriate. Finally, on occasion, transvestism will be seen as a way of deceiving malignant spirits. Historical transvestites include HENRY III (1551–89), King of France, who filled his court with men who shared his taste in sumptuous gowns and powdered wigs, and Lord Cornbury, the British colonial govenor of New York, New Jersey and North Carolina in the early eighteenth century, who rather weakly asserted that his appearances in gowns were a tribute to his cousin Queen Anne. *See* EON DE BEAUMONT, CHARLES D'.

trapeze artist American lesbian slang, first recorded in the 1930s. It described a woman who liked to 'go down' on other women.

trapped in the wrong body Or rather trapped in the wrong-gender body. In the early years of the twentieth century this was a convenient pop explanation of same-sex erotic desires which was used not only by heterosexual commentators, but also by lesbian and gay people themselves. It followed from the nineteenth-century sexologists, with their ideas of GENDER DYSPHORIA and CONGENITAL INVERSION. The most notorious exemplar of this theory was the lesbian protagonist of THE WELL OF LONELINESS by Raclyffe HALL. At the end of the twentieth century, rather like the concept of gender dysphoria itself, the phrase is used more often to describe the causes behind TRANSSEXUALISM.

travesti shows American Latino term for transvestite shows.

Trethowan report Report of the Trethowan Committee which had been established in 1958 in order to examine the question of 'causes' and 'cures' for homosexuality in New South Wales, Australia. Produced in 1963, the report never saw the light of day. Unfortunately, the committee had come to the astoundingly radical conclusion that it was social attitudes rather than homosexuality itself which was the problem. It was suppressed by Government.

tribadism Lesbian sex where two women rub their bodies together, especially the breasts and genitals. The word is taken from the Greek verb *tribein* meaning to rub. The word is also used as a general term for lesbian sexuality.

trick towel The towel one keeps by the bed to wipe the sperm from bodies, sheets, headboard and walls after a session with a pick-up.

tricking To enjoy, as we always do, casual sex. A trick was a casual encounter, or the man bedded in such an encounter. To turn a trick was to succeed in getting the man you were after.

Trikone South Asian lesbian and gay group formed in 1985 in the US. It brings together lesbian and gay people from India, Pakistan, Sri Lanka, the Maldives, Bhutan and Nepal. The name is taken from the Sanskrit word for triangle, referring to the PINK TRIANGLE as a symbol of the lesbian and gay movement.

troilism Technical term for three-way sex.

troll Slang term with two meanings. Derived from the mythical Scandinavian creature which hides in caves, it came to refer to a man with a monstrously ugly appearance. In the British gay slang POLARI, it is also used as a verb meaning to go CRUISING for casual sex. The derivation of this use is probably from the fourteenth-century French term meaning to run about, or from the British usage meaning to angle for fish.

Troubridge, Una (1887–1963) Remembered only because she was RADCLYFFE HALL's partner from 1915 until Hall's death in 1943. Née Taylor, like Hall she came from an upper-middle-class family; at 28 years old she left her husband, Admiral Sir Ernest 'Zyp' Troubridge, for Hall. While femme to Hall's butch in their early years together, at that time the commonplace role-play, soon they both wore jackets and ties, and after 1943 Troubridge always wore men's clothing. She deliberately subdued her own abilities in order to give her darling 'Johnny' the limelight, but Troubridge did have influence, for example she was instrumental in getting COLETTE published in England. She wrote a very disappointing life of Hall (1961) and is buried with her in Highgate Cemetery, London. There is a detailed portrait of their relationship in Lovat Dickson's *Radclyffe Hall and the Well of Loneliness* (1975).

TS In CONTACT ADVERTS and phone-sex, an abbreviation for TRANSSEXUAL.

Tsecats Madagascan society described in Edward CARPENTER's *Intermediate Types among Primitive Folk* (1914). The society had a social class of dancers who dress as women, wearing gold earrings and assiduously removing facial hair, and imitate their mannerisms. They also live apart and never marry.

Tuke, Henry Scott (1858–1929) British painter whose stock-in-trade was his paintings of nude boys, who were usually depicted on the beach, on boats or in the water. Despite the fact that his chosen subject matter was not considered appropriate for a respectable artist, Tuke was admitted to the prestigious Royal Academy. Although he was not exactly open about his sexuality, his artistic works and the fact that he mainly associated with gay men indicate his sexual leanings.

Turing, Alan *See* BREAKING THE CODE.

turtle dove A pair of turtle doves was the emblem of the (possibly fictional) lesbian organization, the ANANDRYNES, in late-eighteenth-century Paris.

tuxedo As the stiletto heel is to the drag queen, so the tuxedo is to the drag king – the essential item of male-identified clothing. Particularly associated with the cross-dressing female BLUES singers of 1920s Harlem, it also contained transgressive implications of breaking apart the social world from which black women in particular were barred. Radclyffe HALL was also associated with male evening dress, although interestingly she usually did not go the whole hog, but wore a skirt underneath her jacket.

TV Abbreviation for transvestite. Predictably, gay people have called the television the transvestite after this abbreviation. *See* TRANSVESTISM.

twank Nineteenth-century term used by young men in the English armed forces to describe the older men who would cruise them and solicit them for sex.

Twickenham set The group of women who centred around the English sculptor Anne Seymour Damer (1749–1828) and Mary Berry (1763–1852), who were subject to a whispering campaign about their sexuality. Mary Berry was the literary executor of Horace Walpole, and Anne Damer, who was a great friend of his, sometimes appeared in a man's hat and jacket. After Walpole's death, Damer inherited his home at Strawberry Hill in Twickenham where she would put on amateur theatrical performances in which Mary would act. The two women also travelled together, and Damer's journals demonstrate the physical nature of their relationship. Whereas English pamphleteers and satirists of the eighteenth century had a wealth of gay male scandals to draw upon which present us with accounts of gay male life, in the case of lesbianism only the Twickenham set are referred to. An anonymous pamphlet of 1781 notes, 'Strawberry Hill at once doth prove/Taste, elegance and Sapphic love.' Other women associated with Damer and Berry: Kitty Clive, who was an actress; Elizabeth Farren, whom satirists described as feeling 'exquisite delight' from the touch of the cheek of Damer; and Elizabeth Cavendish, whom Walpole described as 'in-cun-sole-able' at the death of a Lady Dysart.

twilight Beginning in the 1920s, this became a standard media adjective for anything to do with the lesbian and gay community. The twilight world of the homosexual was used to describe any place where we congregated, on the margins of what we all know to be the glorious sun-saturated habitat of the hetero. Commonly used in the blurb on the backs of lesbian pulp fiction novels in the mid twentieth century. Even in the 1990s the word was still going strong. When a serial killer, Colin Ireland, was found to be responsible for the murders of five gay men in 1992 in London, the tabloid press revelled in fictitious descriptions of the 'sordid twilight' bars where he picked up his victims.

twink(le) In American gay slang of the 1970s the word referred to a goodlooking hetero. Since then it has contrarily been used to mean a young gay man, particularly a vacuous disco doll.

253 Legendary gay bathhouse situated in the gay ghetto of Oxford Street, Sydney, Australia which opened in 1970. It had a TV room with a glass coffee table through which one could peek at the nude activities occurring in a pool below.

Two, four, six, eight, gay is just as good as straight Slogan for shouting on gay rights marches which began its life on demonstrations of the GAY LIBERATION FRONT in the early 1970s. It was usually followed by the rejoinder, 'Three, five, seven, nine, lesbians are mighty fine.' Oh, those creative days. The slogan's assertiveness marked the sea-change in gay attitudes that had taken place since the STONEWALL RIOT and gay liberation.

Two, four, six, eight, how do you know your grandma's straight? Slogan shouted by lesbian senior citizens on lesbian and gay marches since the 1970s.

two hearts in counsel Phrase used by Frances E. Willard (1839–98), a woman who had several close relationships with members of her sex and who was head of the Women's Christian Temperance Union, which was a strongly feminist organization for its day. Descriptive of women's ROMANTIC FRIENDSHIPS of the nineteenth century in America. Indicative of the emotional closeness of such friendships.

Two Loves See THE LOVE THAT DARE NOT SPEAK ITS NAME.

tyke Word which was presented by Lisa Ben, in the magazine VICE VERSA, as an alternative to dyke, and to describe women who didn't want to take on the common roles of BUTCH or FEMME, who is 'at ease with either a passive or aggressive partner'.

U, V

Ulrichs, Karl Heinrich (1825–95) Prussian-German lawyer and early advocate of gay rights, Ulrichs was the main force behind the development of the theories and vocabulary of URANIANISM, which were so attractive to others of his time who were concerned with lesbian and gay issues. His public coming out to a convention of German jurists, when he announced to them that he was an Urning, was one of the first in modern history. He went on to write a number of pamphlets and articles about Uranianism. Predictably, he encountered opposition from members of the establishment, and he eventually settled in Italy.

uncle/aunt who never married Euphemism employed by heterosexuals to describe and dismiss their queer relatives. The mythical figure in heterosexual families who is referred to in hushed tones by parents, and to whom young lesbians and gay men feel a strange affinity. Also known as the relative who 'lives alone in London' or some other appropriate urban area.

uncut Uncircumcised. In American gay slang an uncircumcised dick is known as blind meat, so named because the foreskin closes over the opening or eye. Thus to cure the blind means to go down on an uncut dick and pushing back the foreskin in the process. *See also* CUT.

uniform One of the developments on the gay male scene of the 1970s was the adoption of BUTCH dress codes. Usually this was simply the CLONE look, which really did function as a uniform because it made bars full of men look exactly the same. Many were related to macho occupations such as construction worker, docker, policeman or soldier, and represented either a fetishistic obsession with traditional images of masculinity or a self-conscious and ironic drag, depending on who you were listening to.

The most visible uniform-wearers were the VILLAGE PEOPLE.

universal bisexuality Theory which is in some ways related to the POLYMORPHOUS PERVERSE of Sigmund FREUD. It holds that the 'natural' sexuality is capable of being attracted to either gender, and that exclusive heterosexuality, as well as exclusive homosexuality, is merely a product of repressing some urges. Since the 1960s it has been a staple of liberal thinking which announces itself as progressive by claiming that there can be no basis for vaunting heterosexuality as normal, but it also refuses to recognize that the lesbian and gay communities have a real difference which marks them off as a real minority. Thus it has been criticized as ASSIMILATIONIST by radical lesbian and gay activists who wish to demonstrate that they are inherently different from the heterosexual society to which they are opposed. Liberals also have the infuriating habit of proclaiming everyone to be bisexual without any intention of sleeping with anyone of the same sex themselves. There are elements of universal bisexuality in some strands of QUEER thinking.

The Unlit Lamp Radclyffe HALL's first novel, and preferred by some women who dislike the more famous *Well of Loneliness* because of its depressing tone and the fact that the hero, Stephen Gordon, is described as a 'man in a woman's body'. *The Unlit Lamp* was published in 1924 and depicts a possessive mother who guilt trips her daughter out of her autonomy. The daughter, Joan, is encouraged by her tutor Elizabeth to go and study in Cambridge, but her mother refuses to let her go. Elizabeth gives up and marries a man she does not love while Joan becomes a shadow of her former self.

Uranian school Name sometimes applied to the late-nineteenth-century writers, poets and artists who extolled the joys of the love of young men. Usually included in the category are Oscar WILDE, Lord Alfred DOUGLAS, John Addington SYMONDS, and Aubrey Beardsley. The name of the school derives from the terminology of URANIANISM that found expression in the works of Karl ULRICHS, rather than any coherent philosophical system between the writers concerned.

Uranianism or **Uranism** The theories and vocabulary associated with the writings of the gay lawyer Karl Heinrich ULRICHS. The theories are based on the section of Plato's SYMPOSIUM which describes the two different kinds of human love that are possible, and were initially introduced in a pamphlet *Vindex*, published in 1864. The first is that felt by those who worship Aphrodite URANIA, or heavenly love, and who 'are attracted towards the male sex, and value it as being naturally the stronger and more intelligent...their intention is to form a lasting attachment and partnership for life'. It is described as stronger and more intelligent than the second, Aphrodite Pandeumia, or common love, which is the love that finds expression in heterosexual relations. Thus Ulrichs called male homosexuals 'Urnings', after Urania, and heterosexuals 'Dionings' after Dione, the goddess who was said to be mother of the common Aphrodite. In his later works he also developed the vocabulary of 'Urninde/Dioninde' for lesbians and heterosexual women respectively, and even 'Uranodioning' for bisexuals. Ulrichs believed that same-sex desire was congenital, and thus that Uranians should not be forced into a form of sexuality that was beneath them. The symbolism of the superior Aphrodite Urania was extremely attractive to many of the writers of the day, since she was associated with the most sublime poetry (in Milton's *Paradise Lost*, for example), and the vocabulary caught on to the extent that homosexual writers at the turn of the century were termed the URANIAN SCHOOL.

Uranians of the world, unite! Slogan of some German gay activists in the early twentieth century, which echoed Marx's famous statement on the toiling classes. The activists' wishes were partially answered by the founding of the WORLD LEAGUE FOR SEXUAL REFORM.

Uranism *See* URANIANISM.

urning Term for gay men used in the theories of URANIANISM used by Karl ULRICHS.

urolagnia Technical term for water sports.

uterine society Women's society.

Valhalla Hall New York venue for transvestite balls which were already taking place as early as the 1890s, attended by gay men in evening gowns and some women in full evening dress, prototype BUTCHes, who would dance with the FEMME women who went along.

Vanguard Name given to organization of San Francisco hustlers in 1966. It sought to provide support for male sex-workers against police harassment and to prevent suicides among the hustler population.

vanilla Term used by people who practise RADICAL SEX to describe conventional sexual activities which do not involve the sharing of pain or the exercise of power. It alludes to the flavour vanilla as a standard one that is good to fall back on but which does not really challenge or excite the taste buds, and implies that there are more exciting sexual possibilities. This view is challenged by many within the LESBIAN FEMINIST movement, who see in the sexual acts dismissed by LEATHERMEN and LEATHERWOMEN the possibility of sex which is based on equality and mutual concern between partners (*see* POLITICALLY CORRECT SEX). A vanilla bar, or fluff parlour, is a bar which is not frequented by lesbians or gay men into radical sex.

vanilla vacation Term current among SM communities to describe any temporary periods of engaging in conventional, or VANILLA, sex. Such vacations are most likely to happen because of a lack of available sexual partners for more satisfying SM routines, but on occasion the physical and mental exertions of SM are such that people need periods of recuperation.

variant A term for homosexual which was current in the 1940s and 1950s as a seemingly neutral word.

vaseline Petroleum jelly, made by refining light petroleum. It was first developed in the United States in the 1860s. Among the many uses of this versatile substance was that of lubricant for anal sex. However, it was eclipsed in the 1980s since, being oil based, it had a damaging effect on condoms, and was of no use to those practising safer sex to avoid the transmission of the HIV virus.

Venus in Furs Novel by Leopold von SACHER-MASOCH which resulted in his name being used as the root for the term MASOCHISM to refer to the sexual appreciation of pain on oneself. The novel portrays the submissive Severin who is on a quest to find a dominant woman.

Venus Rising The largest dyke disco in Europe, which takes place at the Fridge club in Brixton, London.

Venus symbol The symbol (♀) of the Roman goddess of love or the planet Venus has become the most common symbol used to represent women. The symbol is supposed to represent a mirror, hardly a radical beginning. The symbol was passed from astrology to biology and psychology from where it entered popular use, and was taken up by the FEMINIST MOVEMENT in the 1960s. By the 1980s, however, its use within the feminist movement was so longstanding that it had gained progressive implications in the popular imagination. A variant form, which appeared in England in 1969, combined the symbol with a clenched fist, which demonstrates the links that existed between feminism and the black CIVIL RIGHTS MOVEMENT. Two Venus symbols interlocking have also been used within the LESBIAN FEMINIST movement to symbolize lesbianism, although there has been some confusion about this, and some British feminists have used three to indicate lesbianism, while two symbolize the sisterhood of women. A form which combined the Venus symbol with the corresponding MARS SYMBOL for men was used among groups of the GAY LIBERATION FRONT in America in the early 1970s to indicate the lesbian and gay movement.

Vere Street coterle *See* WHITE SWAN.

A Very Natural Thing 1973 film which promised to be a gay liberation love story that explored the variety of options within the community, but that alienated many by its romanticism. After the break-up of his relationship with Mark, David explores the alternatives, including BATHHOUSES and FIRE ISLAND orgies, which all proves unsatisfying. Finally, he embarks on another relationship with Jason, which this time involves only a commitment to explore one another with no strings attached.

Vesta Roman goddess of the hearth, counterpart to the Greek goddess Hestia. Vesta's hallmark was her chastity (from heterosexual relations), and her followers, the Vestal Virgins, who tended the flame brought by Aeneas from Troy preserved in a sanctuary at the forum in Rome, were similarly not allowed to consummate any heterosexual match. For this reason they have sometimes been co-opted into lesbian mythology.

vibewatcher With us since the 1970s, a vibewatcher (or facilitator in some American groups such as QUEER NATION) is someone appointed at large meetings of political groups, whose task it is to make sure that the discussion doesn't veer off towards personal attack, and to alert the meeting should that be the case. They serve to diffuse the sometimes tense atmosphere that can build up.

Vice Versa The first US periodical by and for lesbians, which was first produced in 1947 on the typewriter of Edythe Eyde, who went by the nom de plume of Lisa Ben (an anagram of lesbian). The periodical, which ran to nine issues, included short stories, reviews, editorials and bibliographies, and was subtitled 'America's gayest magazine'. It was circulated secretly from one reader to another.

Victim 1961 film directed by Basil Dearden, starring Dirk Bogarde, that called for legal acceptance of same-sex love. It dealt with the blackmail of a gay man. Bogarde sets out to bring to justice the blackmailers who precipitated the death of the young man with whom he had had a brief (but platonic) relationship. The film portrays the first gay figure to eschew anonymity and therefore challenge the status quo. The film drew an explicit link between the persecution of queer people and their legal repression. Screened during the debate following the publication of the WOLFENDEN REPORT in the UK, the film had a large influence over public feeling towards gay law reform, and can be seen to have had some part in leading to the passage of the 1967 SEXUAL OFFENCES ACT. It was also the first mainstream film to use that shocking word, 'homosexual'.

Victor, Emma Dyke detective who appears in Mary Wing's novels *She Came Too Late* and *She Came in a Flash*. Victor works on Boston's Women's Helpline.

Victoria, Queen (1819–1901) British monarch, notorious among lesbians and gay men not only for presiding over a little missed period of British prudery during which sexual acts between men were subject to even greater legal stricture (*see* LABOUCHERE AMENDMENT), but also (perhaps apocryphally) for refusing to believe that such a thing as a lesbian could exist when it was suggested that lesbian sex acts should be brought within the law. It was partly because of this that lesbians have remained unrecognized in law throughout the twentieth century.

Victorious Amour Painting by Caravaggio, painted in 1600, which portrays Cupid vanquishing diverse symbols of worldly achievement and success. Cupid is shown as a naked and attractive young boy. Contemporaries of the Roman artist were conscious of the homoerotic nature of his works and berated him for using male sex-workers as models for his religious images.

Vietnam war The expensive war which America fought from 1965 to 1973 in support of South Vietnam against the Vietcong communist guerrilla movement was to create a watershed period for the modern lesbian and gay movement. The huge cost in human as well as financial terms sparked off a massive protest against the war in the United States that ushered in a climate of dissent in which the establishment of government, churches and military supporting the war were discredited, and protest became commonplace. DIRECT ACTION demonstrations took place in numerous colleges and cities across America, many of which included lesbian or gay activists who later took that experience, and their faith in the power of protest, to demonstrate for lesbian and gay rights. Their ire was raised still further as many realized that the left-wing groups in which they participated were no more willing to explicitly support lesbian and gay rights than the government against which they fought. It is no great coincidence that the STONEWALL RIOT and the appearance of the GAY LIBERATION FRONT should take place during the Vietnam war period.

vigil The silent, usually candle-lit, vigil has often been employed within the lesbian and gay movement as a dignified form of protest. When the news broke in San Francisco in 1978 of the murder of supervisor Harvey MILK, thousands responded with a spontaneous vigil. WORLD AIDS DAY is also marked worldwide by vigils in memory of those we have lost to the epidemic. Sometimes, however, they become angry. In February 1994 a crowd of some 5,000 people gathered outside the British Parliament when the House of Commons was voting on bringing the AGE OF CONSENT for gay men down from 21 to 16. When it was only reduced to 18, the crowd surged forward to barrack the door, before moving off to blockade Downing Street and stop traffic around Central London.

The Village People American 1970s disco group, created by Jacques Morali, which presented audiences worldwide with the panoply of butch gay iconography. The lovely line-up included Alexander the soldier, David the construction worker, Felipe the Native American, Glenn the leather-man, Randy the cowboy and Ray the policeman, muscles rippling in formation. Initially, at least, they were completely upfront about their sexuality, and their songs provided a rundown of the possibilities for gay sex, 'In The Navy', at the 'YMCA' and in the bushes on 'Fire Island', that wasn't difficult to decipher. They appeared in a 1980 film, *Can't Stop the Music*, which presented the startling storyline of a group of men who become disco stars. The film bombed, and the group split soon after. Subsequent come-backs haven't set the world alight.

Vindex Pamphlet published in 1864 by the German sexologist Karl ULRICHS which aimed at setting forth a dispassionate discussion of homosexuality.

A Vindication of the Rights of Woman 1792 feminist tract by the British writer Mary Wollstonecraft that put the case for women's equality. It was inspired to some extent by the turmoil taking place in revolutionary France, and served as the initial salvo of the incipient British feminist movement. Wollstonecraft herself lived in a ROMANTIC FRIENDSHIP, a fictionalized account of which was published in her novel MARY.

violets As a flower which signifies homosexuality, the violet appears time and again throughout lesbian and gay history. In a poem, Sappho describes herself and a lover as wearing garlands of the flower, and violets have been worn in England to signify the homosexuality of their wearer. *See also* LA PRISONNIÈRE.

Violetta *See* CAMILLE.

viragint A masculine woman. The term appears to have been introduced from Richard von KRAFFT-EBING's *Psychopathia Sexualis* in which it denotes an extremely 'inverted' woman who bears many 'masculine' characteristics. Viragint was used in nineteenth-century American sexological discourse to mean both a lesbian and a feminist, and was indicative of the linkages drawn between the two. It was reclaimed by the lesbian and feminist movements to denote a strong woman.

virago (1) Derived from VIRAGINT, the word also originally meant a masculine woman, but again has been reclaimed by the feminist movement. (2) Name of a British feminist publishing house founded in 1978.

A virgin boy's jissom is incomparably delicious Line from *Pédérastie Active*, a French erotic novel published in 1906 by an author using the nom de plume of P.D. Rast. Tale of a chain of young men deflowered by a lucky older man.

virtue From their unique perspective on the margins, lesbian and gay people have always been able to see that 'virtue' is merely a defence of the ideological position of the dominant society. As Oscar WILDE wrote in a letter of 1897, 'Moral people, as they are termed, are simply beasts. I would sooner have fifty unnatural vices, than one unnatural virtue. It is unnatural virtue that makes the world, for those who suffer, such a premature Hell.'

Vissi d'Arte The aria from Puccini's tragic opera *La Tosca*, which begins 'I lived for art, I lived for love', is one of the best expressions of the high and theatrical passion which endears the art to its OPERA QUEEN fans.

Vivien, Renée Née Pauline Mary Tarn (1877–1909), Anglo-American poet who moved to Paris at the turn of the twentieth century. Vivien's lesbianism seems to have been intimately connected with her feminism. In her autobiographical novel *A Woman Appeared to Me*, San Giovanni, who represents Vivien, finds lesbianism and feminism at the same time; 'I was aroused on behalf of women, so misunderstood, so made use of by male tyranny.' Her poetry, which overtly describes the fiery passions of lesbian love, remains controversial for lesbian critics. Some see it as freeing lesbian writers to create powerful and ardent lesbian characters. Others, such as historian Lillian FADERMAN, see her works as carrying the legacy of the male French aesthetic writers who had employed lesbian imagery to EPATER LE BOURGEOIS. According to Faderman, Vivien's women are associated with 'vice, artificiality, perfume and death'. Perfume and death seem to have fascinated Vivien: French writer COLETTE describes Vivien's rooms as dark and heavily perfumed, with a funereal atmosphere. She eventually died, partly as a result of the unfortunate habit of drinking eau-de-cologne.

vogueing Black gay social style which evolved in the 1980s and 1990s in the Harlem and Bronx communities in New York. Vogueing is essentially the creation of social facades, and the adoption of different personae ranging from the unreal images of TV soap operas and glossy fashion magazines (from which the phenomenon derives its name) to those of the business executive and the heterosexual. A successful attempt is one in which the adopted persona appears most 'real'. The style was adapted by the American pop diva MADONNA in her 1990 record *Vogue* which advocated escapism into the world of Hollywood iconography.

VWE *See* WE.

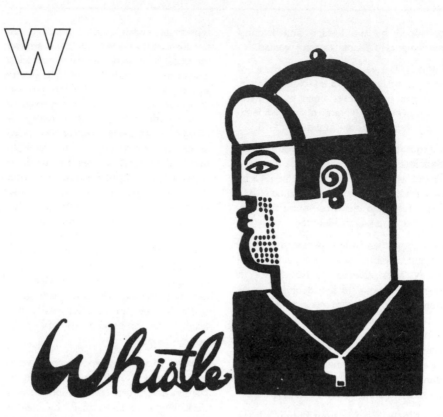

W

Waddell, Tom (1937–87) Physician and athlete in the 1968 American decathlon team at the Mexico City Olympic Games, where he was placed sixth. In 1976 he came out in the pages of the American *People* magazine. In 1980 he began to work towards founding the GAY GAMES, and participated in them, winning a gold medal in 1986. He died of AIDS-related illnesses.

Wadham College of Oxford University which became associated with male homosexuality in the eighteenth century after Warden Robert Thistlethwayte was charged and found guilty of having committed a 'Sodomitical Attempt' on William French, a student at the college in 1739. Thistlethwayte fled the country for France. As if to compound the ignominy, a college tutor, John Swinton, was accused of similar misdemeanours shortly afterwards, although he managed to bribe his way out of the charges. Wadham had the rare distinction of rhyming perfectly with

'Sodom', and thus became subject to a number of popular poems referring to the affair. One such ran, 'There once was a Warden of Wadham/Who approved of the folways of Sodom/For a man might, he said/Have a very poor head/But be a fine fellow at bottom.' The association of Wadham with a tolerant attitude towards sexual expression continues to this day, partly because it is regarded as one of the more left-wing of Oxford's colleges, and partly because of the other celebrated warden of the college, Maurice Bowra.

Wages Due Lesbians British political organization which was set up by black and white lesbians in 1975. It exists to show the links between gender, race and poverty, and demands compensation for the work that is performed by all women, but which is unpaid. In a 1991 statement the group explained, 'The fact is that greater economic possibilities for women definitely help to overcome the barriers of being lesbian, promoting lesbian visibility and discouraging sexism.' It has been one of the most successful examples of black and white women organizing together, and serves as a reminder that different liberation campaigns have a lot of points in common. The organization campaigned against CLAUSE 28, and in the early 1990s took a leading role in the campaign against the Child Support Act 1990, which was a piece of legislation aimed at forcing absent fathers to pay maintenance for their children, but which also sought to penalize women who were unwilling to reveal the name of the biological father of their child or children.

The Wanderground Sally Gearhart's 1979 novel which presented her vision of a lesbian utopia. It portrayed a community of hill-women who had escaped the male energy of the city, to live in a harmonious relationship within their natural surroundings. More of a vision than a manifesto, it demonstrates the ways women can bond emotionally and harmoniously, without going into the questions of how the hill-women survive and reproduce.

Ward 5B Ward of San Francisco General Hospital which was one of the first wards specifically for the treatment of people with AIDS in America. Actually called the Medical Care Special Unit, it was set up in July 1983 by hospital administrator Cliff Morrison. Previously, the hospital had resisted what might seem to be the quarantining of PWAs, but soon it was realized that special services might help to stem the lack of care that they were getting in other wards. Apart from medical experts, the ward also had counsellors on hand. It later became Ward 5A.

Warhol, Andy (Andrew Warhola, 1930–87) American artist and filmmaker, epitome of the anarchic, drugs-taking arts scene of downtown Manhattan of the 1960s and 1970s, and leading figure of the pop art movement known for his images of the mass-produced detritus of capitalism, including the repeated Campbell Soup cans and Brillo boxes. He ploughed the

profits from the sale of his artistic works into the series of films that he produced. These films, such as *Blow Job* (1963), were often crudely produced but sexually adventurous. *My Hustler* (1965) was more coherent, set on FIRE ISLAND and revolving around two gay men, a female friend and the man after whom they all lust. Other films, which featured the beautiful actor Joe Dallesandro, more successfully questioned male mythology and stereotypes: *Flesh* (1968) was one of the first films to deal with male prostitution, while *Lonesome Cowboys* (1968) suggested the erotic connections which probably existed between the men out west. Warhol survived a shooting attack by Valerie Solanas (who was behind the SCUM manifesto) in 1968.

warm brothers/sisters (warmer bruder/ schwester) German slang for gay men and lesbians. The term was recorded as early as the eighteenth century in Berlin.

warning: sodomy can be habit forming Gay rights slogan of the 1960s.

Washoga Name given to transgenderal people among the Muslims of Mombasa, Kenya.

watersports (WS) Sexual acts that involve one partner pissing over or into (*see* GOLDEN SCREW) the other and which usually take place in a bath or on a bed furnished with plastic sheets. From the 1960s the practice has been known as golden champagne, GOLDEN SHOWERS or, among the SM community, warm beer. A gay man who particularly enjoys watersports is known as a golden shower queen, a piss queen or a tinklerbelle. *See also* AUTUMN COLOURS.

WE Contact advert abbreviation for well-endowed, or in possession of a big dick. VWE stands for very well-endowed, for the more fortunate or more fanciful among us.

we are angry, not gay Slogan of the 1970s lesbian feminist movement. Not only did it point to the inadequacy of the term gay within a backdrop of oppression, but it also hinted at the fact that lesbian feminists chose to put their energies into the feminist movement rather than into an unsatisfying alliance with gay men, whose concerns they saw as entirely different from their own.

we are everywhere Slogan which has been worn on badges by lesbians and gay men since the mid-1970s and especially in the 1980s. It not only recognized the fact that lesbians and gays represented a significant proportion of the population, something which had been demonstrated in the 1940s and 1950s with the publication of the reports by Alfred KINSEY, but also acknowledged that this significance was being increasingly represented in the size and the diversity of the lesbian and gay scene. It spelt a warning to heterosexual society not to underestimate the power of the lesbian and gay movement.

We are the Stonewall girls One of the most memorable chants of the STONEWALL RIOT, sung by a chorus line of drag queens as they kicked their heels tauntingly, can-can style, in the face of an irate row of riot police. The full lyric sheet ran 'We are the Stonewall girls, We wear our hair in curls, We wear no underwear, We show our pubic hair, We wear our dungarees, Above our nelly knees!' The drag queens were so important a part of the riots that, as Derek JARMAN wrote, 'The best fighters were the trannies – a dress was a badge of courage.' In fact, some accounts say it was a drag queen who started it all by kicking back at a police officer trying to arrest her. Yet drag queens were not always welcomed into the groups that were founded as a response to the riot. A New York group to look after transvestite hustlers, Street Transvestite Action Revolutionaries (STAR) was not given the support it needed from the GAY LIBERATION FRONT and GAY ACTIVISTS ALLIANCE, despite the fact that it had been founded by two queens who had been part of the riots. Twenty-five years later, some of the PRIDE marches that commemorate the riot seem to want to forget that it was the drag queens who got us where we are.

we are your worst fear; we are your best fantasy Early gay liberation slogan which drew attention to the paradoxical fascination which the heterosexual world, and its media, hold for lesbian and gay sexuality while professing to disapprove. We represented the personal and sexual liberty which their 'respectability' would not allow them.

We Too Are Drifting 1935 novel by Gale Wilhelm, seen by many lesbians to be far better than the lesbian novel which eclipsed it, THE WELL OF LONELINESS, although it shares the rather gloomy prognosis of its more famous shelf-mate. It tells the tale of a lesbian artist, Jan Morale, who has a sexual relationship both with an older married woman and with a younger woman. The latter relationship ends, however, since the younger lover, Victoria, succumbs to familial expectation to marry, and Jan is willing to allow her to go, aware of the difficulties of living a lesbian life. Wilhelm wrote another novel, *Torchlight to Valhalla*, which is more optimistic.

we're here because we're queer because... Popular chant, sung to the tune of 'Auld Lang Syne' which features on lesbian and gay marches. It has the downside of not having an obvious place to end, and tends to carry on until it dies a pitiful death. The chant 'We're here because we're here' sung to the same tune has been recorded as being used by British soldiers in the First World War.

we're here, we're queer, get used to it! Slogan used on demonstrations by the new QUEER-oriented groups that appeared on both sides of the Atlantic around the turn of the 1990s. It indicated the new, 'in your face', 'it's your problem and not our responsibility' feel to lesbian and gay politics that was occurring at the time.

wearing the mask In the 1930s in America, a slang term to describe another homosexual, as in 'Is s/he wearing the mask?'. The phrase is descriptive of the subterfuge with which lesbians and gay men of the time had to run their lives in order to avoid detection.

weasel Animal which had an association with homosexuality in the middle ages. *See* THE EPISTLE OF BARNABUS.

The Well of Loneliness 1928 novel by Radclyffe HALL. Referred to by some women as the lesbian Bible, it is the most famous lesbian novel of all time. Its plot is, however, hardly radical, since it was intended to make a plea for tolerance by demonstrating the difficulty of practising lesbian love, rather than to show the positive choices that might lead a woman to a lesbian affair. The protagonist Stephen GORDON, a well-off, horse-riding TOMBOY, is sexually enlightened by Angela Crossby, who uses and abuses her. She embarks on a literary career before beginning the affair with Mary which forms the heart of the book. Their relationship is depicted in terms of role differentiation between Stephen's butch and Mary's femme and, while sex between them was not explicitly described, the line 'and that night they were not divided' indicates that they, at least, left nothing out. Stephen is, however, beset by pessimism and self-pity about her sexuality and ultimately renounces Mary to a male partner so that she can lead a 'normal' life without the miseries of INVERSION. Despite its pleading, the book caused something of a negative sensation when it was published. The editor of the *Sunday Express* described it as worse than prussic acid for the nation's morals, and it was withdrawn at the behest of the Home Secretary. Copies came to England from France, but they were seized under the Obscene Publications Act. This furore turned it into a succès de scandale, and few lesbians have not picked it up at some point. Many are, however, turned off by Stephen's gloomy prognosis of the possibility for lesbian love and what they see as the anachronistic characterization of its protagonist, who is presented as a man trapped in a woman's body (Hall was influenced by the works of Havelock ELLIS). Moreover, the work has been blamed for perpetuating theories of CONGENITAL INVERSION throughout the century – with all the connotations of sickness that

that entails. Yet many choose to focus rather on the visibility it gave to lesbianism, and see it as the ovarian lesbian novel.

well-hung *See* HUNG.

West, Mae (1892–1980) American actress, and gay ICON, though not one who has stood the test of time quite as well as GARBO and DIETRICH. Much of West's fascination for a gay audience lay in the way she projected gender. In appearance she fulfilled the male stereotype of female desirability to the point of parody, but she had a pre-emptive wit and a clear scorn for all sexual hypocrisy and repressiveness. Like gay people, she was aware of the shocking power that control of her sexuality could give, and she so affronted public decency that not only is she claimed to be one of the reasons that Hollywood's self-censoring Hays Office was established, but also rumours persisted that she was a transvestite or a hermaphrodite. She also wrote, and was prosecuted for, one of the first plays about homosexuality to appear on Broadway, THE DRAG.

West Hollywood Small municipality located between Beverly Hills and Old Hollywood which contains an eye-opening array of gay venues, shops and services. West Hollywood has pioneered pro-gay legislation, and has a large number of openly gay officials.

Westphal, Carl von (1833–90) Nineteenth-century German physician whose work, while not sympathetic to homosexuality, helped to introduce it as a subject for scientific research. In 1869 he published a case-study of a young woman who had from childhood preferred to dress as a boy and play boys' games and who had erotic attractions to women. Thus he conflated sexuality and gender, the lesbianism of the woman in his case-study being recognized by an unwillingness to conform to traditional gender role. Other writers contributed similar case-studies to medical journals, agreeing with Westphal's diagnosis. While these ideas accorded with already popular stereotypes, such writings gave them the respectability of medical science. Their effect in the short term was negative. Many conservatives chose to use his theories of gender as a stick to beat the movement for women's emancipation, saying that if it gave employment and education to women, society would spawn a brood of unsexed inverts. It also made things more difficult for people who had lived in same-sex relationships which had been free of any suspicion of untoward sexuality. However, in the long term, it gradually created a belief in a homosexual identity, a belief which was arguably essential to the identity-based politics of the lesbian and gay liberation movement in the twentieth century. *See* THE MEDICALIZATION OF HOMOSEXUALITY.

When God Was a Woman Book published in 1978, written by Merlin Stone, which asserted that goddess worship was the dominant form of religious activity up until 8000 BC according to the Christian calendar. Moreover, at this time women held much secular power within their societies. The book was very appealing to lesbian feminists who were trying to elaborate a women-centred spirituality.

where's the man could ease a heart like a satin gown Dorothy PARKER in 'The Satin Dress' from the 1937 collection *Not So Deep as a Well*.

whistle The whistle, usually on a cerise bootlace and strung round the neck, has become the most useful tool, and most recognizable attribute, of the 1980s and 1990s lesbian, gay, AIDS and QUEER political activist. Blown en masse on a demonstration, whistles create the kind of noise even heterosexuals can't ignore; on a ZAP they disrupt the work of the office which has been targeted. They are also distributed by lesbian and gay groups to be carried at all times to alert others in the event of a queerbashing incident (though remember always to use a slip knot so no one can garrot you with it).

White Horse Public house in the English town of Poplar, which in 1766 became the epicentre of a lesbian scandal. It was in that year that the landlord of the pub,

James How, revealed that he was actually Mary East, who had taken to male clothing in the 1730s and had married. East, who was usually seen in 'an old man's coat, woollen cap, blue apron, etc.', had become a respected member of the community, sitting on a number of parish committees. She finally went public about her sex in order to prosecute a blackmailer who had rumbled her secret and who had been extorting ever larger amounts of money. The prosecution was a success, and the two women even seem to have convinced the other townsfolk that Mary had begun to dress as a man after both women had lost their husbands who had been hanged for highway robbery. Although they had to give up ownership of the White Horse, they continued to live together.

White Night Riot Also known as the 'Twinkie Riot' or the 'Night of Rage'. The violent night of riot that occurred in San Francisco after the acquittal of Dan White for murder, and his conviction instead for manslaughter, despite the fact that he had had to reload his gun between the killings of Mayor George Moscone and supervisor Harvey MILK. The city's gay community had resented the trial all along as unfair – no gay people had been allowed to sit on the jury – and regarded the verdict as a travesty. A crowd of well over 5,000 of them came out from the bars on the CASTRO and made their way to the City Hall where, chanting 'All straight jury/No surprise/Dan White lives/and Harvey Milk dies', they pelted the windows of the place with rocks, attacked the entrance and overturned and set fire to police cars, despite the pleas of some gay community leaders. When police reinforcements arrived, the crowd beat them back with branches ripped from trees, chrome taken from buses, and slabs of asphalt taken from the street. After the situation had quietened down, the police made a retaliatory attack on gay men in bars on the Castro. In all, sixty-one police officers and some hundred gays were hospitalized that night. The riots were heavily covered in the media, and shocked America with the strength of feeling in a community which had hitherto been regarded as timid.

The White Paper 1928 novel usually attributed to Jean COCTEAU, although he did not publicly acknowledge authorship. It describes an adolescent from the French city of Toulon and his attractions to members of the 'stronger sex', whether they are fellow classmates, young sailors or working-class lads, whom he watches masturbating at the public baths from behind a two-way mirror. However, unable to find his sexuality accepted, the narrator eventually renounces society.

White Swan Public house in Vere Street, which also served as a male brothel and which was at the centre of one of the most notorious, and disgraceful, purges of gay men in early-nineteenth-century London. It started trade in early 1810, and laid on a range of services for its clientele, including a large room with four beds for sex, a powder room, and a 'Chapel' where the male patrons could 'marry' one another. The inn served as a place where male lovers could have sex, as well as a procurement service with male sex-workers on hand. It seems that the class divisions in male homosexual relations that were so characteristic of the nineteenth century were already coming about, and the White Swan had a number of upper-class patrons who would procure the services of men from the lower classes. Less than six months after its opening, the White Swan was raided by police who arrested over twenty men, and nine were convicted of sodomy or attempted sodomy. Six were made to stand in the pillory in September. Their treatment at the hands of the huge and hostile crowd displayed the worst excesses of mob frenzy. By the end of the day the men had been subject to a barrage of vegetables, eggs, fish, offal, blood, mud and rocks. Two additional men were hanged in March the following year. The high-profile punishments were instrumental in making the gay subculture far more clandestine, and in persuading gay men that it was a better idea to flee to Europe (with the more liberal CODE NAPOLÉON)

than to brave things out at home. The affair was recorded in a 1813 pamphlet by a lawyer Robert Holloway, 'The Phoenix of Sodom, or the Vere Street Coterie', which provides fascinating documentation of early-eighteenth-century gay life.

white T-shirt Worn with erotic tightness by Marlon Brando in *A Streetcar Named Desire*, and a staple of gay male fashion since. On the gay scene the tight variety has always been a favourite to show off the muscles that have been built up by weeks of iron-pumping (or steroid-injection). More recently the singlet has been favoured, as it gives a hint of macho armpit hair as well.

Whiteoaks Play produced in London in 1936 and adapted by Mazo de la Roche from her own novel. The protagonist, Finch, is endowed with a wealth of homosexual signifiers. He is a 'sensitive and nervy' youth, who possesses musical talent. In the play, his homosexuality is revealed to his grandmother when a letter from another man falls from his pocket. Contrary to convention of the time, this serves to forge a closer relationship with his grandmother, and she declares, revealingly, 'You're a queer boy, but I like you, yes, I like you very much.' Despite an (un)fair measure of self-loathing, the play closes with Finch being revealed as the beneficiary to the old woman's will, a denouement which, one imagines, rather stuck in the throat of a 1930s audience.

Whitman, Walt (1819–92) American poet, author of the collection LEAVES OF GRASS and propagator of ADHESIVENESS. In his day Whitman was an icon for those who were coming to terms with their own homosexuality. He served as an inspiration for many of the people who were to be extremely influential, at least among liberal and left-wing circles, in setting the terms under which homosexuality was discussed, such as John Addington SYMONDS, Havelock ELLIS and Edward CARPENTER.

Whoever you are – I have always depended on the kindness of strangers Words spoken by Blanche in Tennessee

Williams' play *A Streetcar Named Desire*, 1947. The quotation has become a staple of camp gay talk, usually in arch reference to a casual sexual encounter.

wicce Women's wisdom.

wide-on State of female sexual excitement, which results in the relaxation of vaginal muscles. A counterpart of a male hard-on.

wife American prison and working-class lesbian slang, first recorded in the 1930s. It referred to the FEMME woman within a BUTCH/FEMME lesbian relationship.

Wilde, Oscar Fingall O'Flahertie Wills (1854–1900) Poet, wit, dramatist, martyr and saint, Wilde takes centre stage in gay mythology and iconography because his whole life incorporating his wit, writings, aesthetic ideals, suffering, imprisonment, style, public persona and, of course, sexuality is so resonant for gay people. Even his marriage in 1884 can be seen as representative of the pressures that act on gay people to conform. If, as he said, he put his 'genius into [his] life', his genius is one that can be claimed by gay people as part of their heritage. Born in Dublin and educated at Oxford, he became editor of the magazine *The Woman's World* in 1889, and in 1891 published his polished but sinister novel *The Picture of Dorian Gray* (*see* GRAY, DORIAN). In the same year he met and began an affair with Lord Alfred DOUGLAS. Douglas' father, the Marquess of Queensberry, demanded that the two discontinue their relationship, and the refusal led to several public incidents which culminated in the Marquess leaving a note 'To Oscar Wilde, posing Somdomite [sic]' at Wilde's club. It was this note which led to the ill-fated WILDE TRIALS, and Wilde's imprisonment for two years under the LABOUCHERE AMENDMENT.

Wilde trials The series of court cases that ultimately led to Oscar WILDE being sentenced to two years' imprisonment under the LABOUCHERE AMENDMENT. Wilde said that 'all trials are trials for one's life', and his ill-fated move to prosecute the Marquess of Queensberry was to lead to his own destruction. When Wilde received a card addressed 'To Oscar Wilde, posing Somdomite' from the Marquess at the Albemarle Club, on 28 February 1895, he took legal advice, and on 1 March the Marquess was arrested for libel. However, even before the first trial started in April, the defence had done its detective work and had uncovered several of Wilde's former contacts who were persuaded to testify against him. The libel trial went badly. Wilde made witty flourishes on being cross-examined about the 'corrupting' nature of *The Picture of Dorian GRAY* but failed to impress, and the judge instructed the jury to rule that the Marquess was justified in calling Wilde a sodomite in the public interest, making it certain that Wilde himself would be prosecuted for sodomy. Wilde was advised to flee to France, but vacillated and eventually decided to 'stay and do my sentence whatever it is'. Others were not so brave and panic broke out among London's homosexual circles. It was reported that 600 men had crossed from Dover to Calais the night the first trial ended, when only sixty would normally have done so. Meanwhile, Wilde's name was taken down from the London theatres where his *Importance of Being Earnest* and *An Ideal Husband* were playing to full houses. At the second trial, which opened on 26 April, Wilde was asked about Douglas' poem THE LOVE THAT DARE NOT SPEAK ITS NAME, and what it meant. In his reply he said, 'It is that deep spiritual affection that is as pure as it is perfect. It is beautiful, it is fine, it is the noblest form of affection. There is nothing unnatural about it.' His speech, according to Max Beerbohm, 'carried the court away'. When the jury could not decide, a third trial was ordered, which started on 22 May. Again he was implored to leave for France, and a Jewish businessman put a yacht at his disposal for the purpose. Again he stayed, and this time the jury found him guilty. The judge, Mr Justice Wills, had been hostile from the start and declared it 'the worst case I have ever tried'. Wilde was sentenced to two years' imprisonment with hard labour. The trials had caused such a furore that they had a profound effect not only on Wilde's life, but also on the public image of homosexuality. Thereafter Wilde's face was the public face of male gayness, just as Radclyffe HALL's would be for lesbians a generation later. And the public saw in its face what they chose to. Effeminacy and decadence, to whatever extent they were present in Wilde, became the recognizable features of the male homosexual for generations to come. The forces of reaction set in, and artistic AESTHETICISM was frowned on, the YELLOW NINETIES were over. But in his downfall Wilde carved a resonant martyr figure for the modern gay movement. His decision to stay for trial, his passionate defence of the love that dare not speak its name, and the prison sentence which broke him have so appeared to gay people as representative of the oppression they face that decades later they were still swearing to AVENGE OSCAR WILDE.

William and John Australia's first commercial gay magazine, published in Sydney.

Wimmin See WOMYN.

wine A great releaser of sexual inhibitions. As Larry comments on straight men in Mart Crowley's THE BOYS IN THE BAND, 'With the right wine and the right music, there're damn few that aren't curious.'

Wings, Mary (1949–) American writer of highly successful lesbian comic books and feminist LESBIAN THRILLERS, particularly the adventures of Emma Victor in SHE CAME TOO LATE and SHE CAME IN A FLASH which have been translated into many languages. She won the Lambda award for best crime writing in 1994.

Wishing Well Lesbian contact ads magazine produced in America in the 1970s. Advertised as an 'alternative to the Well of Loneliness', the ads tended to concentrate on romance rather than sex.

witches Became an emblem of women's resistance to men for the lesbian feminists of the 1970s. Witches represented a tradition of women's wisdom and women's spiritual values, which the feminist move-

ment was trying to reconstruct in an attempt to build alternative social structures to the patriarchal ones currently in the ascendant. See WICCE.

The Wizard of Oz The 1939 film adaptation of L. Frank Baum's Oz stories, directed by Victor Fleming, has entered gay cinematic iconography, not only because of the beginghamed starring role by the queen of gay icons, Judy GARLAND, but also because of the fabulous escapism of the whole thing. It tells the story of Dorothy's (Garland) dream adventures in the land of Oz, her search for a way home, her trials at the hands of a marvellously camp wicked witch (Margaret Hamilton), and her discovery that home was right there all along. Among the friends she picks up on her odyssey was the sissy COWARDLY LION (Bert Lahr). As well as giving us the phrase FRIEND OF DOROTHY, the film also included the song which most epitomizes the gay desire to transcend the KANSAS in which we find ourselves so often, OVER THE RAINBOW.

Wolfenden report After the highly publicized MONTAGU–WILDEBLOOD trial, a great deal of pressure was placed on the British Home Secretary to set up a Royal Commission to investigate the laws on homosexuality, and he eventually responded by establishing the Wolfenden Committee under the guidance of Sir John Wolfenden, the Vice-Chancellor of Reading University. It also had the remit of examining British law as it affected sexwork and soliciting 'for immoral purposes'. When the committee reported in September 1957, it surprised many by indicating that, while the law should protect public 'decency', it should not attempt to impose private morality. It declared, 'There must be a realm of private morality and immorality which is, in brief and crude terms, not the law's business.' It recommended that consensual gay sex between adults should be decriminalized, that those under the age of twenty-one should not be prosecuted except with the express sanction of the Director of Public Prosecutions, and that penalties should be revised. Less happily, it also recommended that research into the 'causes' of homosexuality should be carried out, and that forms of 'treatment' should be monitored for their effectiveness and that prisoners who wanted hormone treatment should be allowed to do so. Despite the slightly progressive nature of the report, however, Government stalled, and the recommendations did not see the light of parliamentary debate until the sexual liberalism of the 1960s made the SEXUAL OFFENCES ACT of 1967 possible.

A Woman 1915 film in which Charlie Chaplin appears in full drag and, what is more, suits it very well indeed. In the film he flirts with a man. Chaplin also starred in an earlier film, *The Masquerader*, in which he plays an unemployed actor who drags up in order to get acting roles.

woman marriage Anthropological term for a marriage form in which women can take other women as wives in a socially formalized and sanctioned relationship. For example, it is said that in Dahomey (now Benin) a woman who was already married to a man could give bridal gifts and acquire wives. She would found a compound of her own by letting her wives become pregnant through sexual relationships with males who she designated. Woman marriage was also found in Nigeria, Sudan and the Transvaal, as well as among native tribes of North America and the Amazon basin (*see* TAPUYA TRIBES). (Male) anthropologists claim that these are not incidences of lesbianism, but that would seem rather presumptive.

a woman without a man is like a fish without a bicycle Radical feminist slogan of the 1970s which indicated the dispensability of men, including within the realm of the sexual.

womanist A woman who spends the majority of her energy, both sexual and nonsexual, on other women, or as Alice Walker explains, 'Womanist is to feminist as purple is to lavender.' Thus the term describes a woman who prefers to spend her time with other women and who surrounds herself with women's culture, as well as a woman who sleeps with other women. It is sometimes used within black communities to refer to a black feminist. *See also* LESBIAN CONTINUUM.

womben *See* WOMYN. Womben also stressed the female anatomy.

women-identified-women Term, used within the lesbian feminist movement, to describe women who organized their entire lives with women as a priority. It therefore created a definition of lesbianism which did not, of necessity, include genital expression. The term was propagated in a 1970 article by the New York group RADICALESBIANS.

women-only space A space in the public arena where men are barred. It may be a women's disco, a room in a bar, or a caucus at a conference. The idea that women-only space was important developed out of a feminist belief that women needed to have room to be with other women which was not encroached on by men. This has two aspects: that women want to be with other women to talk or socialize without male input, and that in mixed space men tend to monopolize what's going on by being louder and bigger or by sexual and verbal harassment. The fact that a need for women-only spaces still exists in the lesbian and gay community shows that gay men are not immune from this monopolization of public space. Women-only usually indicates lesbian-friendly (indeed, it often indicates lesbian-only).

women's festivals Large outdoor music festivals which became popular with the growth of the feminist movement in the 1960s and 1970s. Taking inspiration from hippie festivals and be-ins of the 1960s, they had lesbian feminist workshops and promoted strong politically correct values. The most enduring and popular of these festivals is the MICHIGAN WOMYN'S FESTIVAL, although others included the New England Womyn's Music Retreat, the East Coast Lesbian Festival, and the Midwest Women's Festival. During the 1980s these festivals served as the site for arguments between LESBIAN FEMINISTS and PRO-SEX DYKES.

women's land circuit An objective of the American lesbians who had moved into the country to set up their women's communes in the 1970s. Their ideal was to set up a network of such communes which women could wander between and live on for short periods.

women's music Term given by lesbian communities to music performed by women for women. It developed in America in the 1970s and was popularized through women's music festivals, although it also achieved much mainstream success. It tended to borrow from folk roots but had a strong political content. The first major and out lesbian feminist artist was Maxine Feldman whose ANGRY ATTHIS is considered by some as the first lesbian record, and others included Margie Adams, Alix Dobkin (whose LAVENDER JANE LOVES WOMEN was the first openly lesbian record to be distributed internationally), and Cris Williamson.

women's presses The growth of the feminist movement in the 1970s led to a blooming of women's publishing concerns, which produced periodicals and books written and edited by women, for a women's readership. Usually very politically conscious, many of the presses produced low-priced periodicals which all women could have access to. Some women's presses are: Cleis Press; Firebrand Books; Kitchentable, Women of Colour Press; Naiad Press; Onlywomen Press; Persephone Press; Seal Press; Sheba; Sinister Wisdom Inc.; The Women's Press.

women's symbol See VENUS SYMBOL. In the 1970s some lesbian feminists wore badges with three women's symbols to indicate their rejection of patriarchal standards of monogamy, rather than the two symbols of the lesbian couple. In some circles three symbols indicated lesbianism, whilst two symbols, mystifyingly, represented heterosexual feminists.

womyn Also wimmin, womben and wombyn. Alternative ways of spelling woman and women developed within the feminist movement of the 1970s which were seen as suitable because they removed the words man and men as the root of terms used by women to describe themselves.

World AIDS Day International day to raise awareness of the issues of HIV and AIDS, of the needs and rights of people living with them, and to commemorate the many lives we have lost to the syndrome. It was started in 1988 by the World Health Organization, who each year decide a different theme which the day should publicize. The day is often marked by candlelight vigils in remembrance.

the world is damned queer – it really is. But people won't recognise the immensity of its queerness. Written in a letter from Lytton STRACHEY to Duncan Grant, June 1908 (*see* BLOOMSBURY GROUP).

World League for Sexual Reform Organization founded in 1928 in Copenhagen, Denmark to push for legal and social progress on a range of sexual issues. This naturally included matters gay, and point 6 of its platform declared the aim of 'a rational attitude towards sexually abnormal persons, and especially towards homosexuals, both male and female. The league aimed at lobbying legislators using the weight of scientific opinion, in order that the law be removed substantially from the realm of private sexuality. Magnus HIRSCHFIELD and Havelock ELLIS were among its first honorary presidents. A British section was founded in 1928 and in 1929 a congress was held in London. The work of the organization was ruined by the rise to power of the Nazis in Germany.

WS *See* WATERSPORTS

X, Y, Z

xanith Name given to a group of transsexual men in Oman who wear clothing midway between the traditional clothing for men and women, and who are allowed to mix with women even where the sexes should be segregated. They work as servants or singers and often have sex with men for money. Their career as women may carry on until old age, but some marry and then revert to a traditional male role. They are very common.

yaar Hindi word which over history has variously meant lover or platonic best friend. The word is currently used by some South Asians to describe their lovers, as is yaarana, which means the same, and saheli, which refers to a woman's very close female friend.

A Year in Arcadia Book by Herzog August von Sachsen Gotha, published in 1805. The first homoerotic book that appeared in German.

yellow In the gay male HANKIE CODE and in CONTACT ADVERTS, yellow refers to the practice of WATERSPORTS. WS is also used as an abbreviation in contact ads.

Yellow Nineties Name given in England to the 1890s, also known as 'the naughty nineties', when the puritanism of Victorian culture seemed to be giving way within certain social circles and a cult of hedonism seemed to be taking hold. The age was that of AESTHETICISM as Oscar WILDE talked about ART FOR ART'S SAKE, and scorned the bourgeois morality. Linked to this was a belief that there was a growth in sexual 'impropriety' manifested in a more visible gay subculture in London. The 'yellow' is probably derived from the title of the journal that was required reading for the avant garde of the time, *The Yellow Book*. The journal was so called because it was bound in a yellow cover to suggest qualities of the 'yellow-backed' French novel, which in itself suggested the amorality of the DECADENTS and the writers who sought to EPATER LE BOURGEOIS. *The Yellow Book* included contributions from both WILDE and Aubrey Beardsley. The WILDE TRIALS meant the reimposition of a bourgeois moral code.

YMCA Abbreviation for Young Men's Christian Association, which founded hostels in cities worldwide. The first was started in Boston in 1851. The hostels often incorporated gyms and swimming pools, and soon became famous as meeting places for gay men, where sex was freely available. This notoriety was celebrated in the classic 1979 disco hit by the camp group VILLAGE PEOPLE, which remained in the American charts for some forty weeks and became a gay dancefloor classic. The song suggested that men went to the YMCA to 'hang out with all the boys'. And many did.

Young Man with a Horn 1950 film directed by Michael Curtiz in which Amy North (Lauren Bacall) finds herself unable to make a heterosexual relationship with Kirk Douglas work. She eventually leaves for Paris with a young woman artist whose patron she has become. In the 1938 novel by Dorothy Baker from which the film was adapted, Amy is described as having lesbian tendencies, but by the film she becomes 'a neurotic young girl who's tried everything'(!).**zami** Women who conduct sexual relationships with one another. The term comes from the Caribbean island of Carriacou, and was popularized by writer Audre LORDE in her book *Zami: A New Spelling of my Name*. It is used mainly within black lesbian communities in America and the UK. In the latter country two conferences of black lesbians have been named Zami 1 and 2. Zami 1 took place in London in October 1985, and was attended by some 200 lesbians of African and Asian descent. The conference discussed issues of COMING OUT as a black les-

bian, disability and prejudice, and was a great achievement for black lesbian visibility. Zami 2 was held in Birmingham at the turn of the decade, and was open to black lesbians with one or both parents from places other than Africa and Asia. It debated issues of sexuality, interracial relationships and motherhood. Since then there have been Zami days for black lesbians held in Birmingham.

zami Women who conduct sexual relationships with one another. The term comes from the Caribbean island of Carriacou, and was popularized by writer Audre LORDE in her book *Zami: A New Spelling of my Name*. It is used mainly within black lesbian communities in America and the UK. In the latter country two conferences of black lesbians have been named Zami 1 and 2. Zami 1 took place in London in October 1985, and was attended by some 200 lesbians of African and Asian descent. The conference discussed issues of COMING OUT as a black lesbian, disability and prejudice, and was a great achievement for black lesbian visibility. Zami 2 was held in Birmingham at the turn of the decade, and was open to black lesbians with one or both parents from places other than Africa and Asia. It debated issues of sexuality, interracial relationships and motherhood. Since then there have been Zami days for black lesbians held in Birmingham.

Zami: A New Spelling of My Name The 1982 'bio-mythography' of lesbian writer Audre LORDE, which introduced the term ZAMI for black lesbians to describe themselves. The book examined the tensions of Lorde's life in New York of the 1950s, between her life on the lesbian scene of Greenwich Village and as a student uptown: 'Downtown in the gay bars I was a closet student and an invisible black. Uptown at Hunter I was a closet dyke and a general intruder.' She also describes the difficulties of having an identity which meant that she didn't fully fit in with either the black or the gay subculture.

Zamimass Black lesbian organization which was founded in Britain in 1990 after the sixth international conference of International Lesbian and Gay People of Colour in London. It welcomes lesbians of African, Asian and Middle Eastern descent, as well as lesbians who are indigenous to North and South America, the Caribbean, Australia and Pacific nations, and seeks to work for the unity and liberation of black lesbians from all ethnic and cultural backgrounds.

zap Term dating from the gay liberation movement of the 1970s, and still current among radical lesbian and gay organizations such as OUTRAGE! and ACT UP to refer to the use of direct action techniques against a particular target. A zap can take many forms, depending on the organization which has merited action against it. Traditionally, picketing the front of buildings with placards or occupying buildings to disrupt proceedings and approach members of staff have been popular methods. Now, though, there is scope for more creativity. Banners can be smuggled in and hung from buildings, while with the advent of technology phones and faxes can be jammed. Although it is not used much at present, breaking into computer systems is an obvious next step.

zi shu nu Literally meaning 'women who comb their own hair'. This phrase refers to women in Southern China who joined the burgeoning marriage resistance movement. They were given their chance when the global demand for silk increased. Since it was mainly women who worked in the silk industry, and single women at that, they were able to earn an independent wage. Many vowed not to marry, and joined spinsters houses with other women, engaging in sworn sisterhood with them. After the Chinese Communist Party assumed power, such women were criticized as a vestige of feudalism. Many women left to go to Singapore or Hong Kong where they continued to live in women-only homes. *See also* GOLDEN ORCHID ASSOCIATIONS.